Toshiaki Iwashiro

The cover art of this volume combines with that of volume 10 to form a continuous picture.

I just felt like doing it that way, so I did.

So, um, I hope you'll buy volume 10 too.

Toshiaki Iwashiro was born December 11, 1977, in Tokyo and has the blood type of A. His debut manga was the popular *Mieru Hito*, which ran from 2005 to 2007 in Japan in *Weekly Shonen Jump*, where *Psyren* was also serialized.

PSYREN VOL. 9
SHONEN JUMP Manga Edition

STORY AND ART BY TOSHIAKI IWASHIRO

Translation/Camellia Nieh
Lettering/Annaliese Christman
Design/Matt Hinrichs
Editor/Joel Enos

PSYREN © 2007 by Toshiaki Iwashiro
All rights reserved.
First published in Japan in 2007 by SHUEISHA Inc., Tokyo.
English translation rights arranged by SHUEISHA Inc.

Printed in the U.S.A.

Published by VIZ Media, LLC
P.O. Box 77010
San Francisco, CA 94107

10 9 8 7 6 5 4 3 2 1
First printing, March 2013

www.viz.com

THE WORLD'S
MOST POPULAR MANGA

www.shonenjump.com

SHONEN JUMP MANGA EDITION

PSYREN

9

THE LIVING ISLAND

Story and Art by
Toshiaki Iwashiro

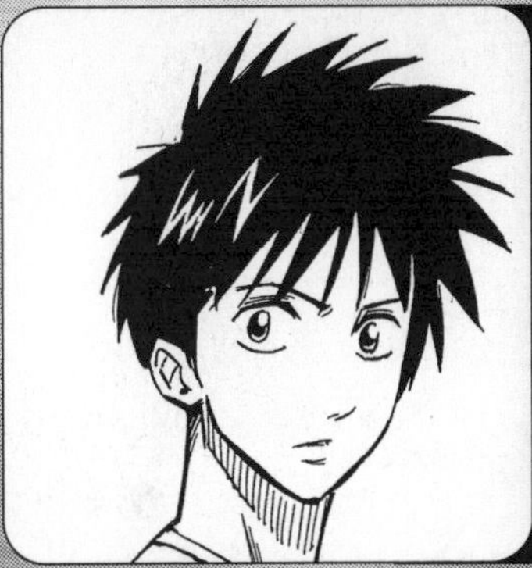

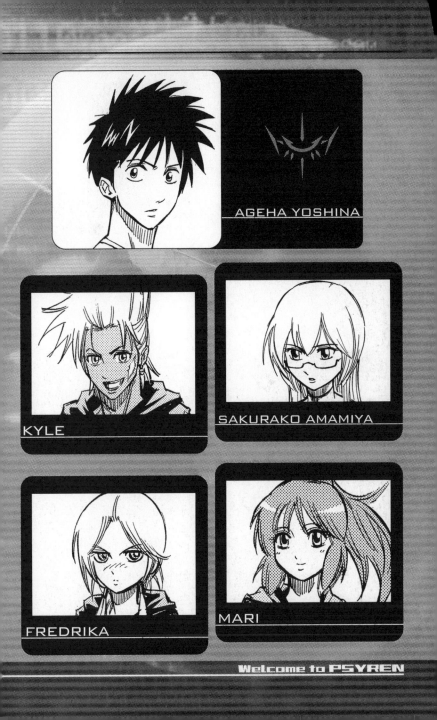

AGEHA YOSHINA

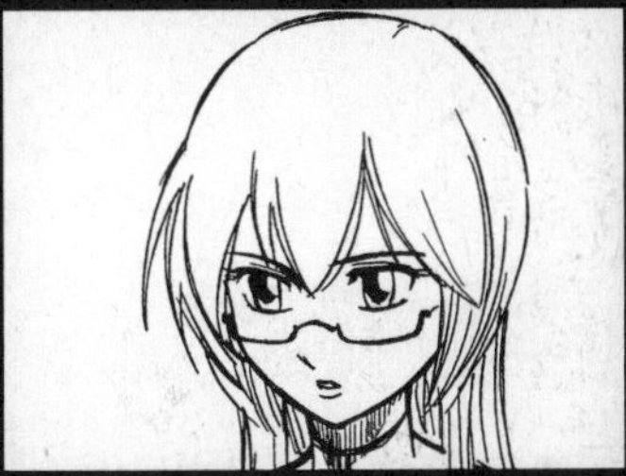

SAKURAKO AMAMIYA

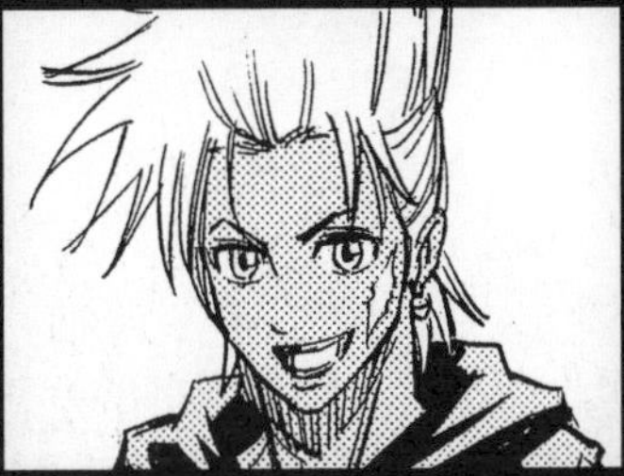

KYLE

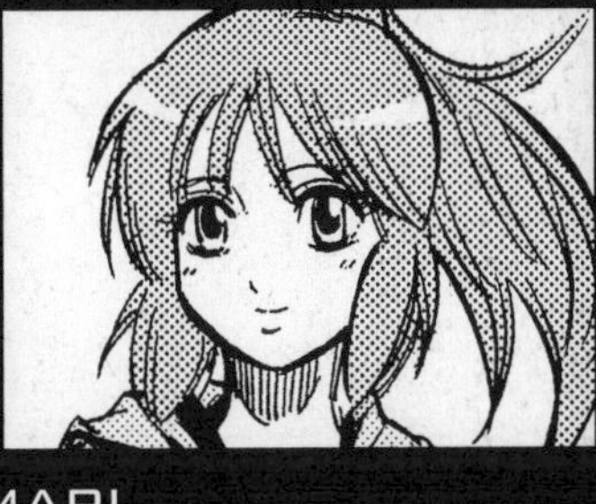

MARI

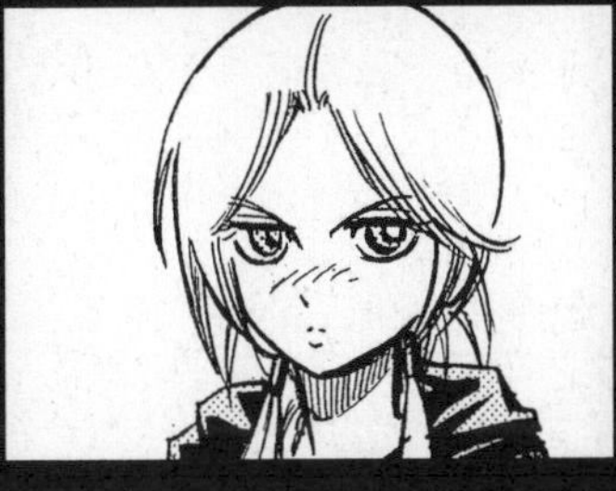

FREDRIKA

Characters

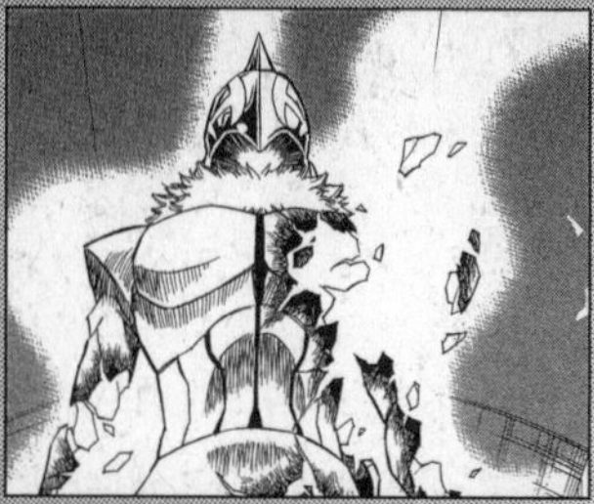

NEMESIS Q

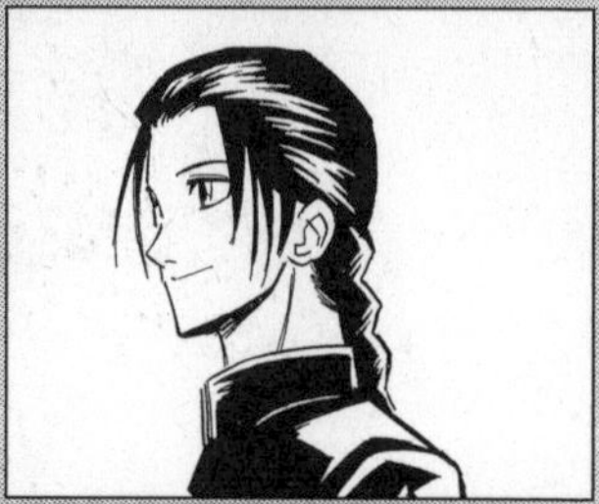

SHAO

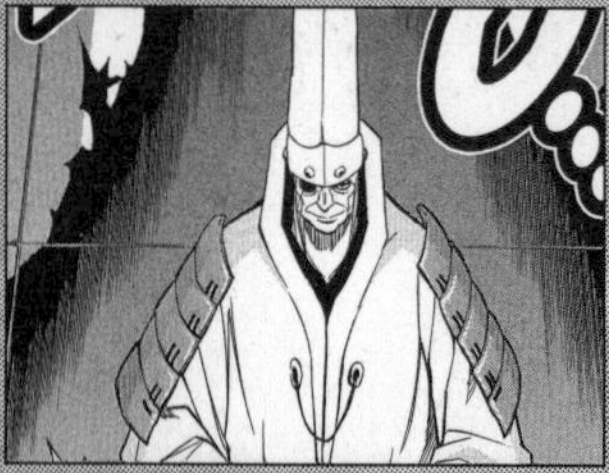

UNKNOWN

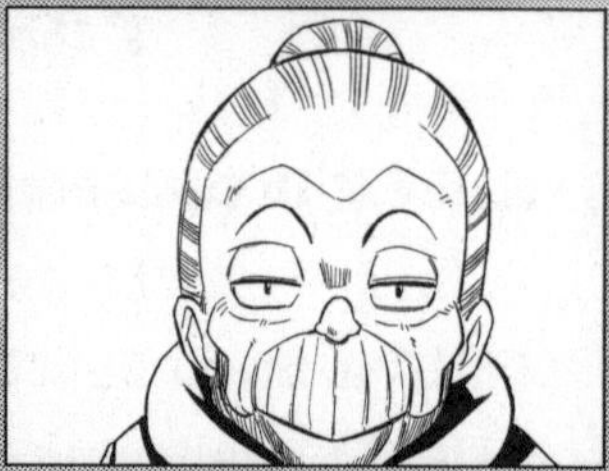

ELMORE TENJUIN

Story

HIGH-SCHOOLER AGEHA YOSHINA HAPPENS UPON A RED TELEPHONE CARD EMBLAZONED WITH THE WORD *PSYREN* WHILE SEARCHING FOR HIS MISSING FRIEND SAKURAKO AMAMIYA. HE SOON FINDS HIMSELF CAUGHT UP IN A LIFE-OR-DEATH GAME IN A BIZARRE WORLD CALLED PSYREN.

ON THEIR FOURTH TRIP TO PSYREN, THE FRIENDS SUFFER A BITTER DEFEAT AT THE HANDS OF THE STAR COMMANDERS. JUST WHEN IT SEEMS ALL IS LOST, THE CHILDREN OF ELMORE WOOD APPEAR ON THE SCENE. KYLE AND FRIENDS CRUSH DOLKEY WITH THEIR INCREDIBLE PSIONIC POWERS AND BRING AGEHA AND AMAMIYA BACK TO THE ROOT, FILLING THEM IN ON THE EVENTS SINCE THE GLOBAL REBIRTHDAY. AS AGEHA GRAPPLES WITH THE DECISION OF WHAT TO DO NEXT, NEMESIS Q SHOWS UP UNEXPECTEDLY WITH NEWS OF AN EMERGENCY.

VOL. 9

THE LIVING ISLAND
CONTENTS

Call.72: Dreameater Island 007

Call.73: False Emperor 027

Call.74: Brain Beast 047

Call.75: The Living Island 067

Call.76: Home 087

Call.77: Circle 107

Call.78: Cage 127

Call.79: Left Hand 149

Call.80: Smile 169

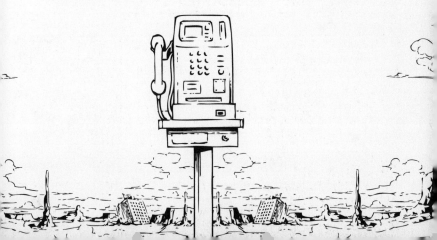

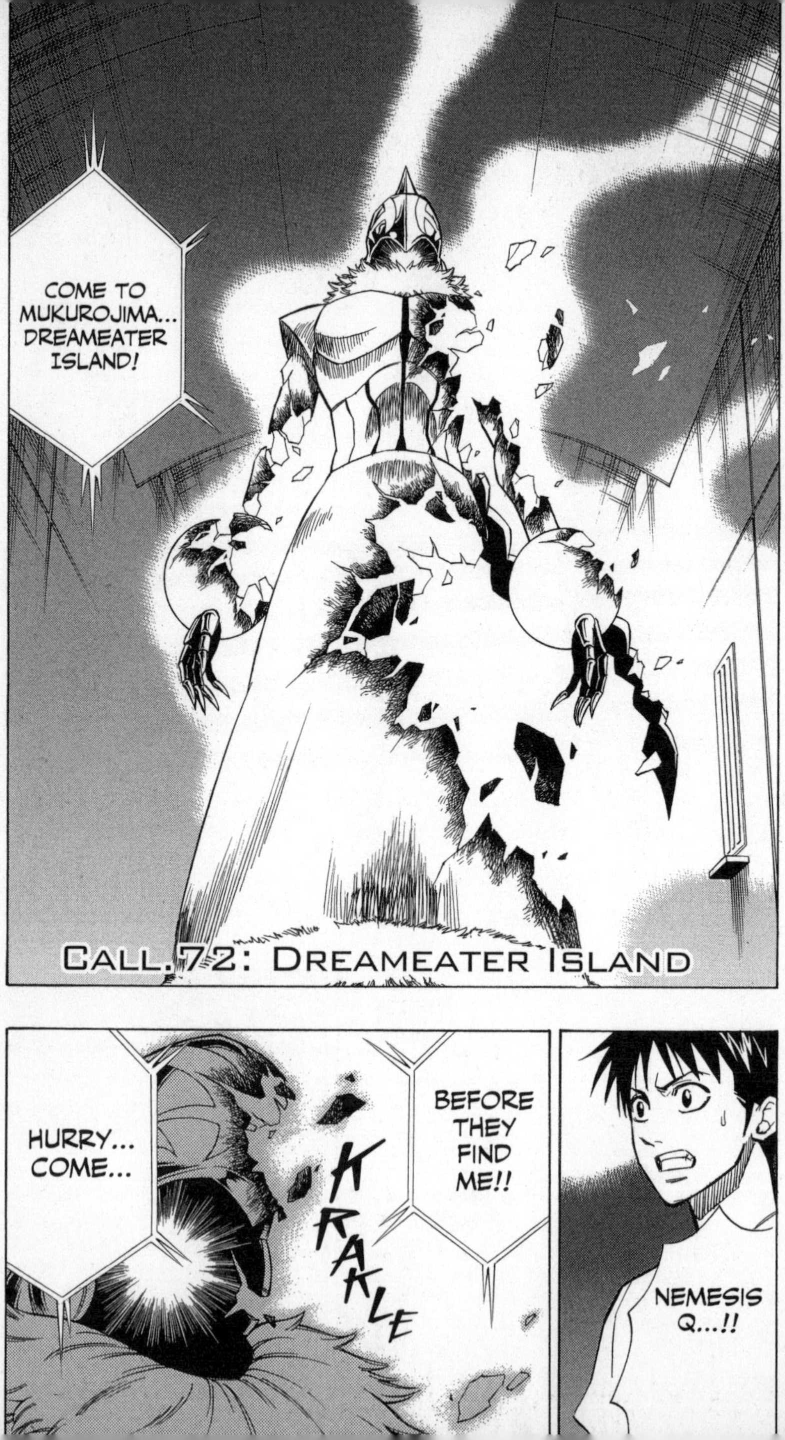
COME TO MUKUROJIMA... DREAMEATER ISLAND!
CALL. 72: DREAMEATER ISLAND
NEMESIS Q...!!
BEFORE THEY FIND ME!!
KRAKLE
HURRY... COME...

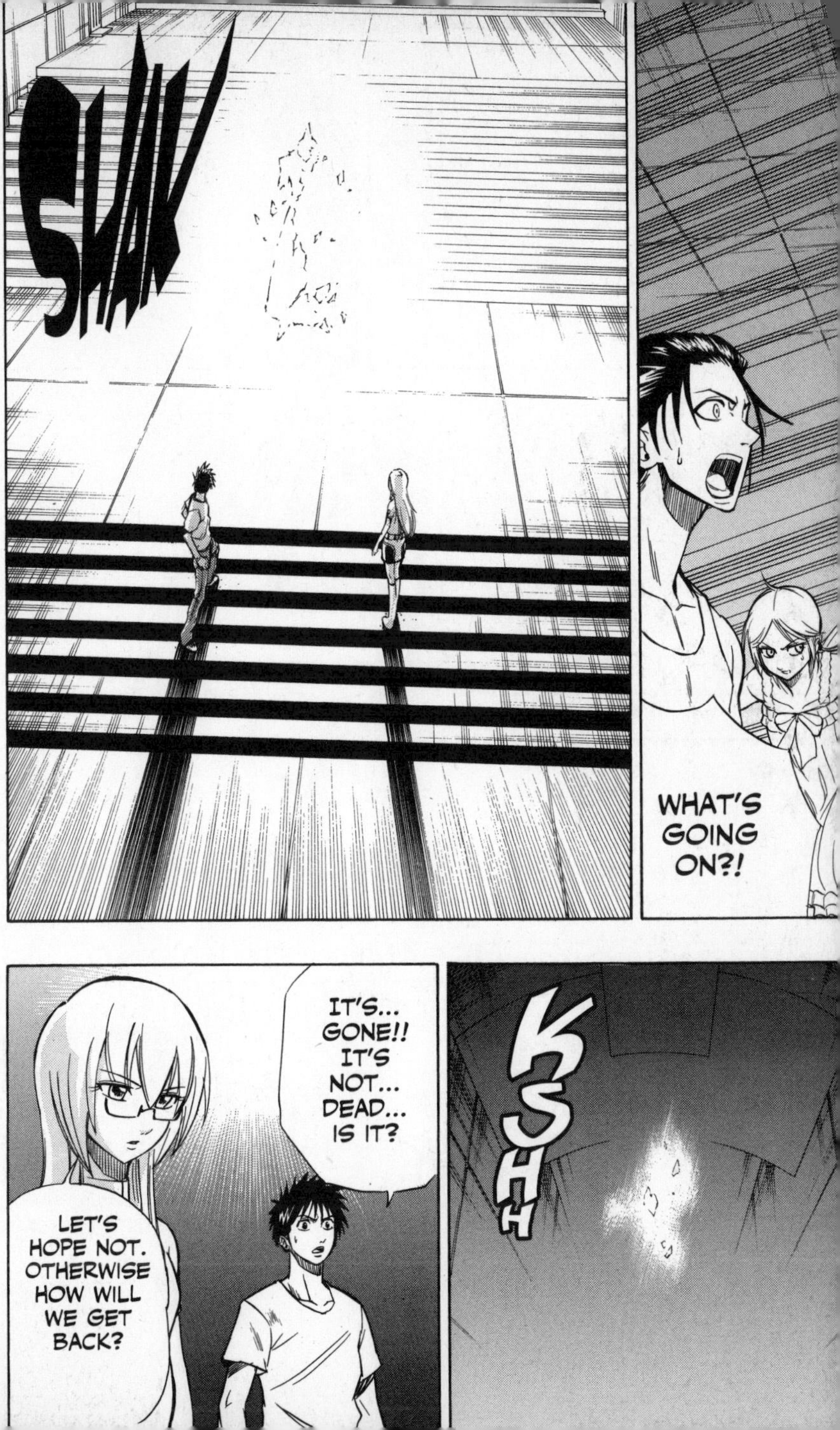
WHAT'S GOING ON?!
SHAK
KSHHH
IT'S... GONE!! IT'S NOT... DEAD... IS IT?
LET'S HOPE NOT. OTHERWISE HOW WILL WE GET BACK?

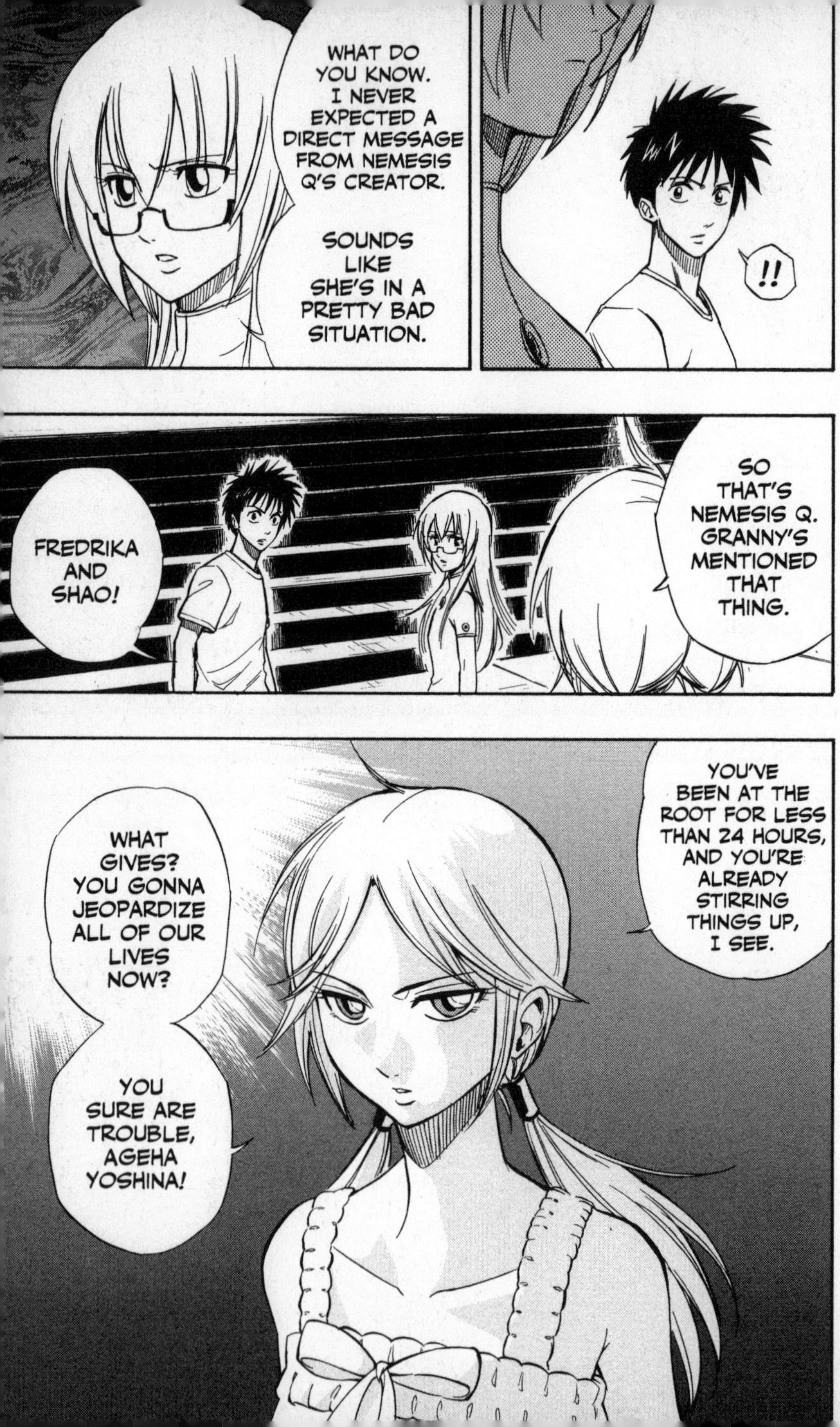
!!
WHAT DO YOU KNOW. I NEVER EXPECTED A DIRECT MESSAGE FROM NEMESIS Q'S CREATOR.
SOUNDS LIKE SHE'S IN A PRETTY BAD SITUATION.
SO THAT'S NEMESIS Q. GRANNY'S MENTIONED THAT THING.
FREDRIKA AND SHAO!
YOU'VE BEEN AT THE ROOT FOR LESS THAN 24 HOURS, AND YOU'RE ALREADY STIRRING THINGS UP, I SEE.
WHAT GIVES? YOU GONNA JEOPARDIZE ALL OF OUR LIVES NOW?
YOU SURE ARE TROUBLE, AGEHA YOSHINA!

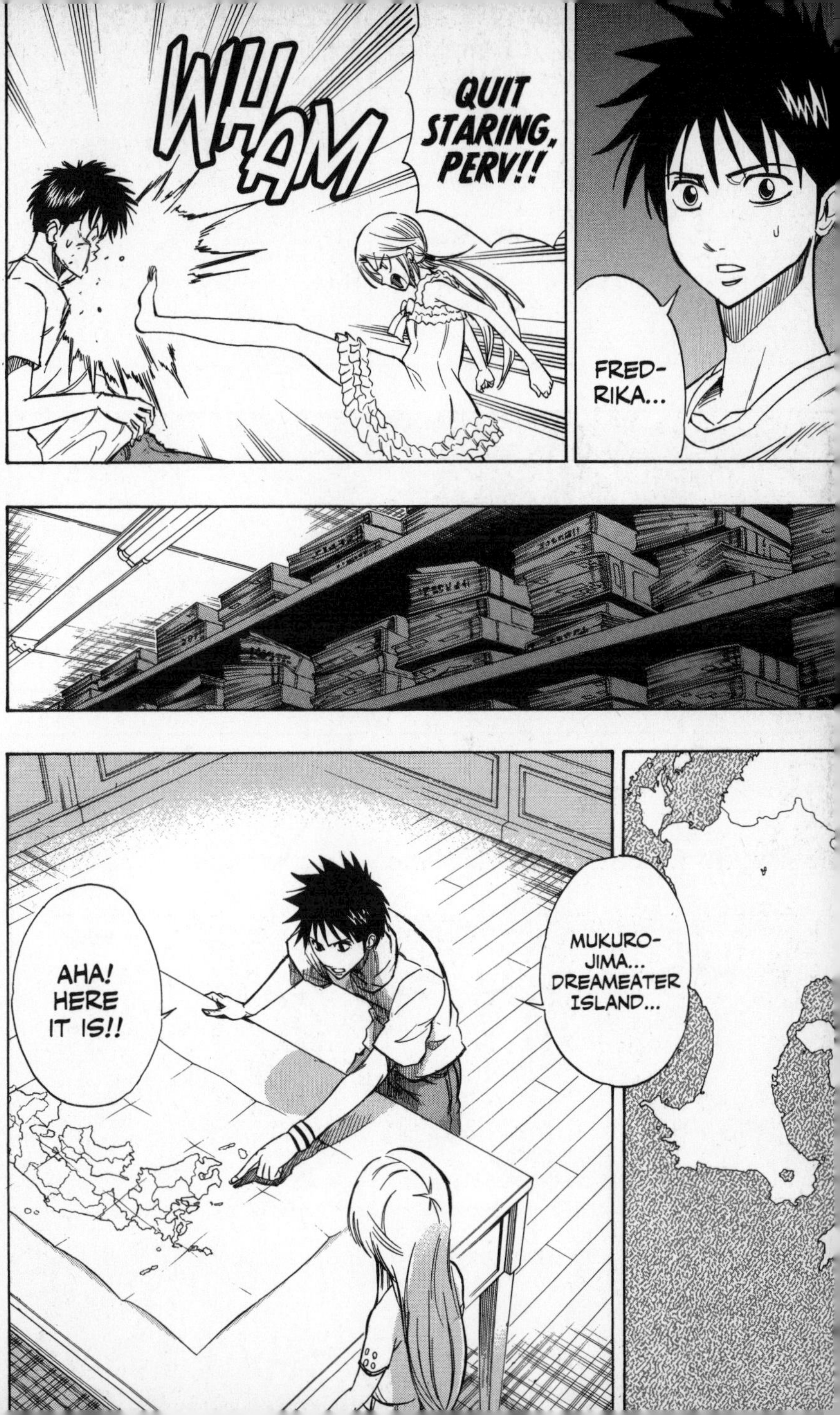
FRED-
RIKA...
WHAM
QUIT
STARING,
PERV!!
MUKURO-
JIMA...
DREAMEATER
ISLAND...
AHA!
HERE
IT IS!!

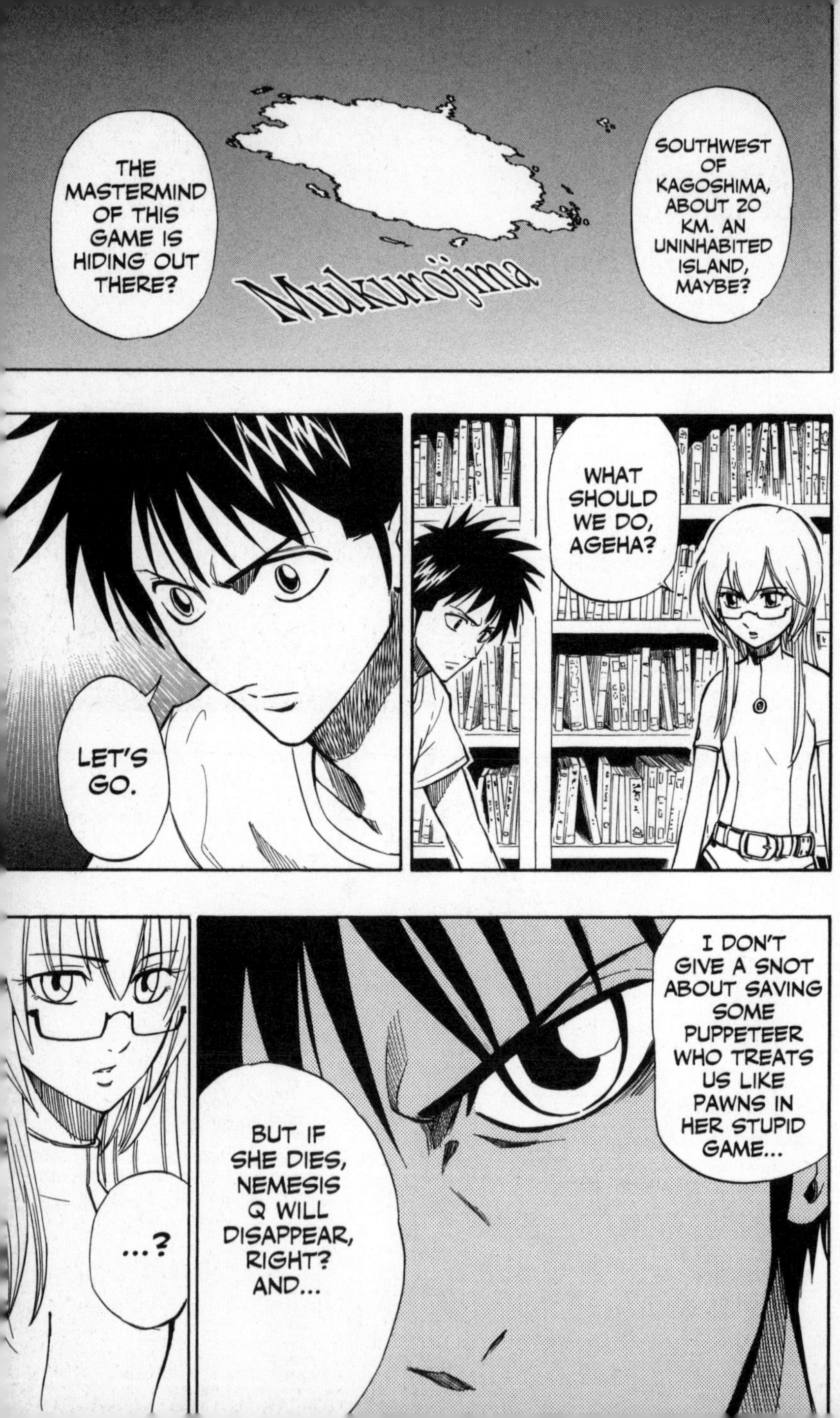
SOUTHWEST OF KAGOSHIMA, ABOUT 20 KM. AN UNINHABITED ISLAND, MAYBE?
Mukurojima
THE MASTERMIND OF THIS GAME IS HIDING OUT THERE?
WHAT SHOULD WE DO, AGEHA?
LET'S GO.
I DON'T GIVE A SNOT ABOUT SAVING SOME PUPPETEER WHO TREATS US LIKE PAWNS IN HER STUPID GAME...
BUT IF SHE DIES, NEMESIS Q WILL DISAPPEAR, RIGHT? AND...
...?

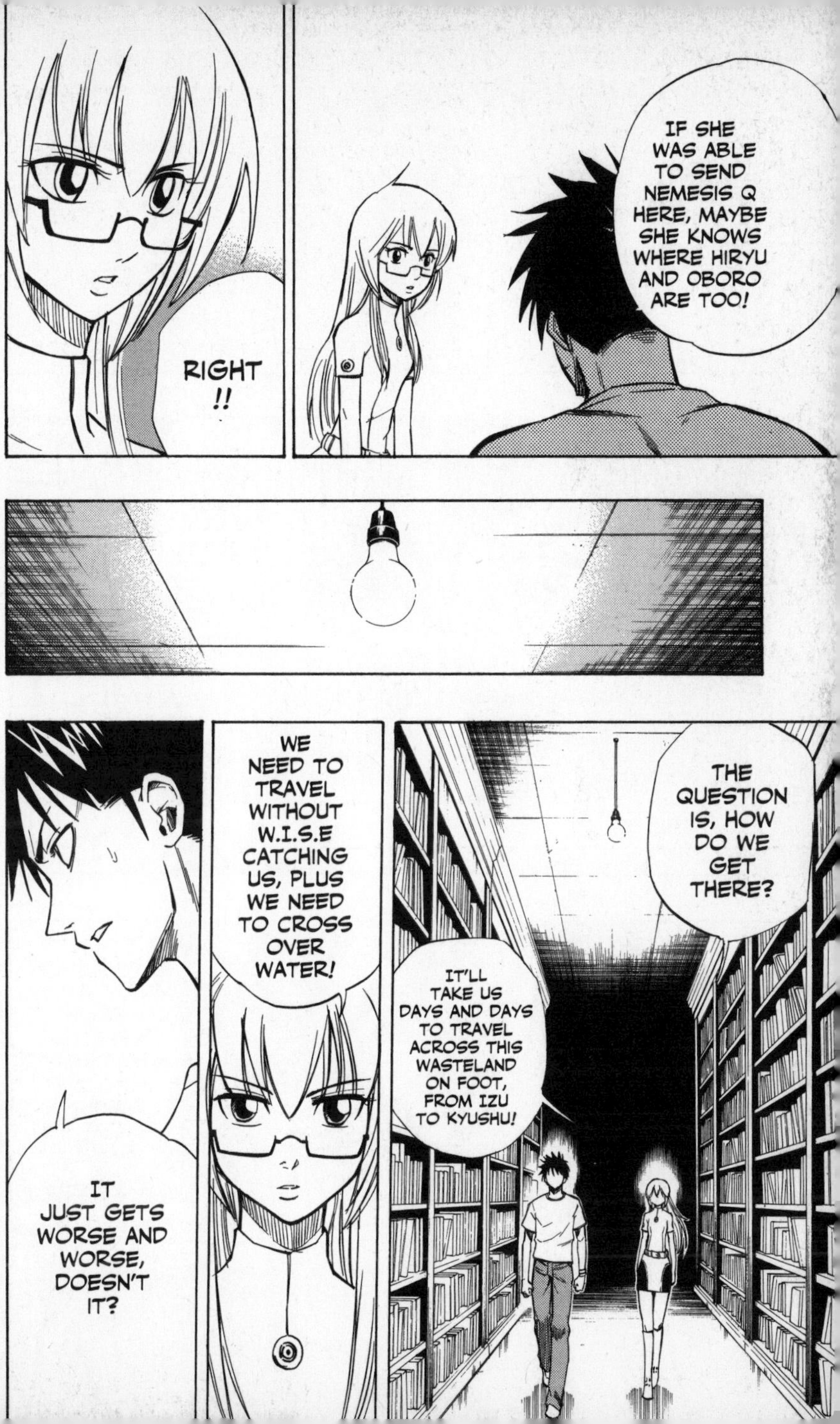
IF SHE WAS ABLE TO SEND NEMESIS Q HERE, MAYBE SHE KNOWS WHERE HIRYU AND OBORO ARE TOO!
RIGHT !!
THE QUESTION IS, HOW DO WE GET THERE?
IT'LL TAKE US DAYS AND DAYS TO TRAVEL ACROSS THIS WASTELAND ON FOOT, FROM IZU TO KYUSHU!
WE NEED TO TRAVEL WITHOUT W.I.S.E CATCHING US, PLUS WE NEED TO CROSS OVER WATER!
IT JUST GETS WORSE AND WORSE, DOESN'T IT?

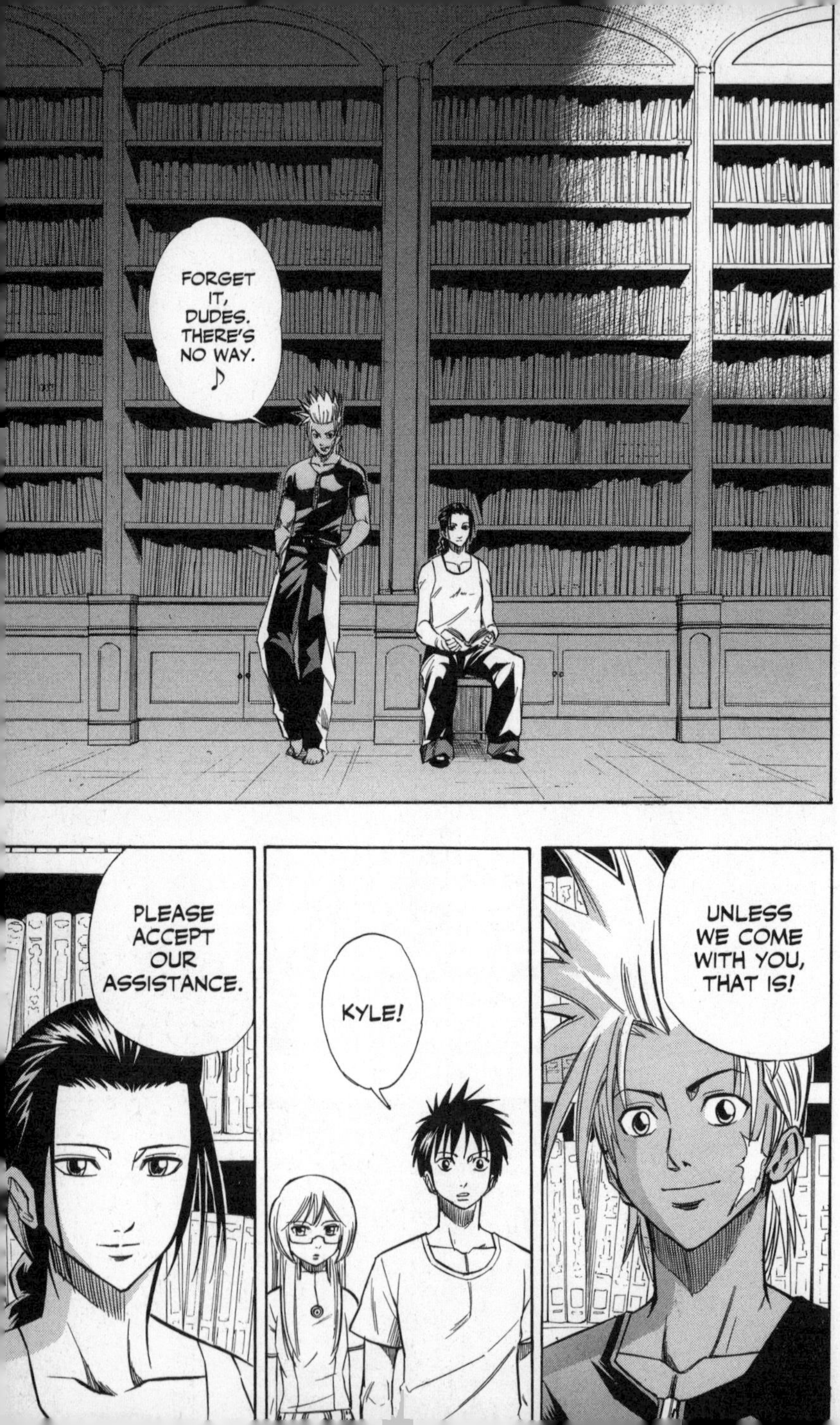
FORGET IT, DUDES. THERE'S NO WAY. ♪
UNLESS WE COME WITH YOU, THAT IS!
KYLE!
PLEASE ACCEPT OUR ASSISTANCE.

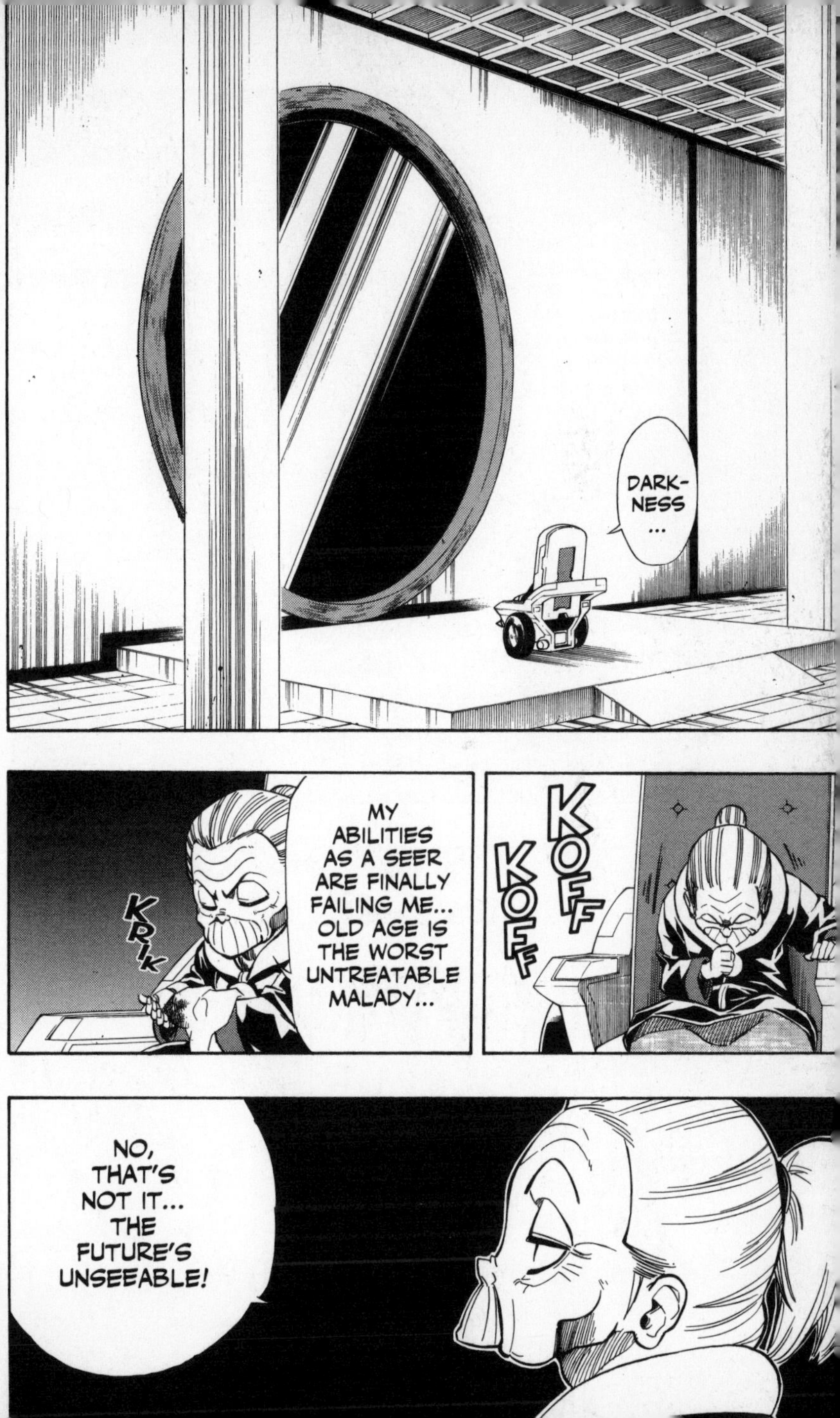
DARKNESS...
KOFF
KOFF
MY ABILITIES AS A SEER ARE FINALLY FAILING ME... OLD AGE IS THE WORST UNTREATABLE MALADY...
KRIK
NO, THAT'S NOT IT... THE FUTURE'S UNSEEABLE!

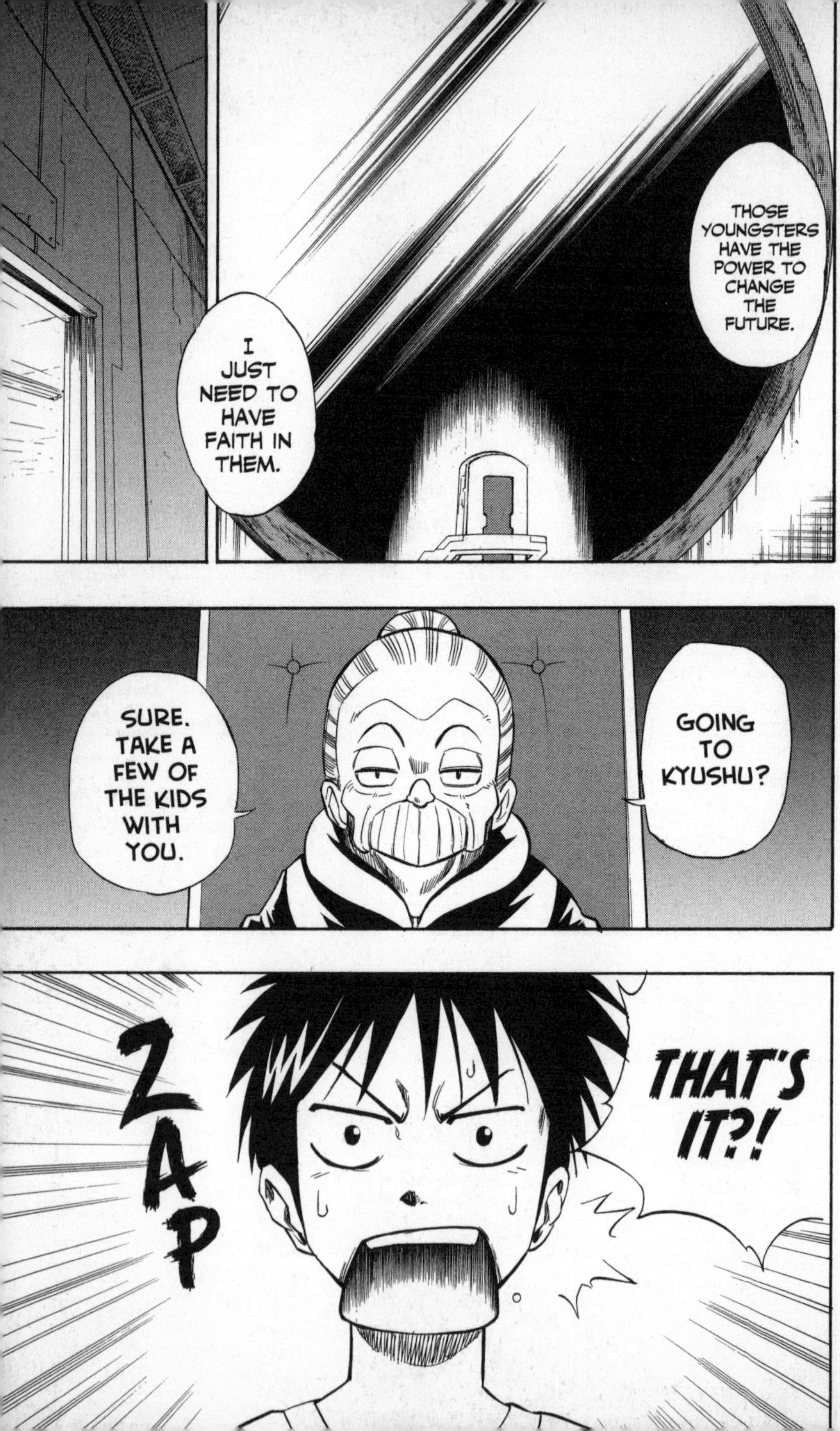
THOSE YOUNGSTERS HAVE THE POWER TO CHANGE THE FUTURE.
I JUST NEED TO HAVE FAITH IN THEM.
GOING TO KYUSHU?
SURE. TAKE A FEW OF THE KIDS WITH YOU.
THAT'S IT?!
ZAP

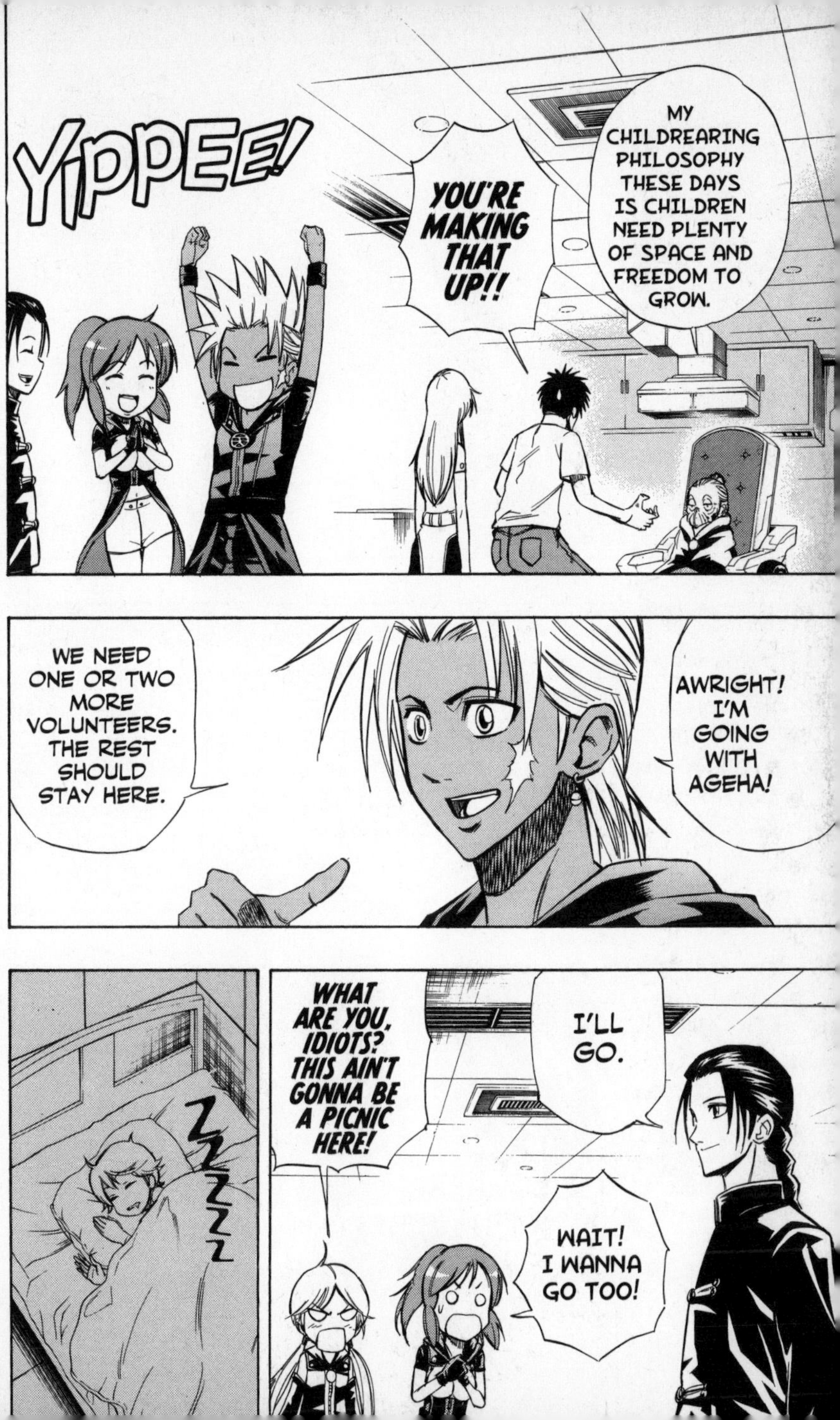
MY CHILDREARING PHILOSOPHY THESE DAYS IS CHILDREN NEED PLENTY OF SPACE AND FREEDOM TO GROW.
YOU'RE MAKING THAT UP!!
YIPPEE!
AWRIGHT! I'M GOING WITH AGEHA!
WE NEED ONE OR TWO MORE VOLUNTEERS. THE REST SHOULD STAY HERE.
I'LL GO.
WHAT ARE YOU, IDIOTS? THIS AIN'T GONNA BE A PICNIC HERE!
WAIT! I WANNA GO TOO!
ZZZZZ

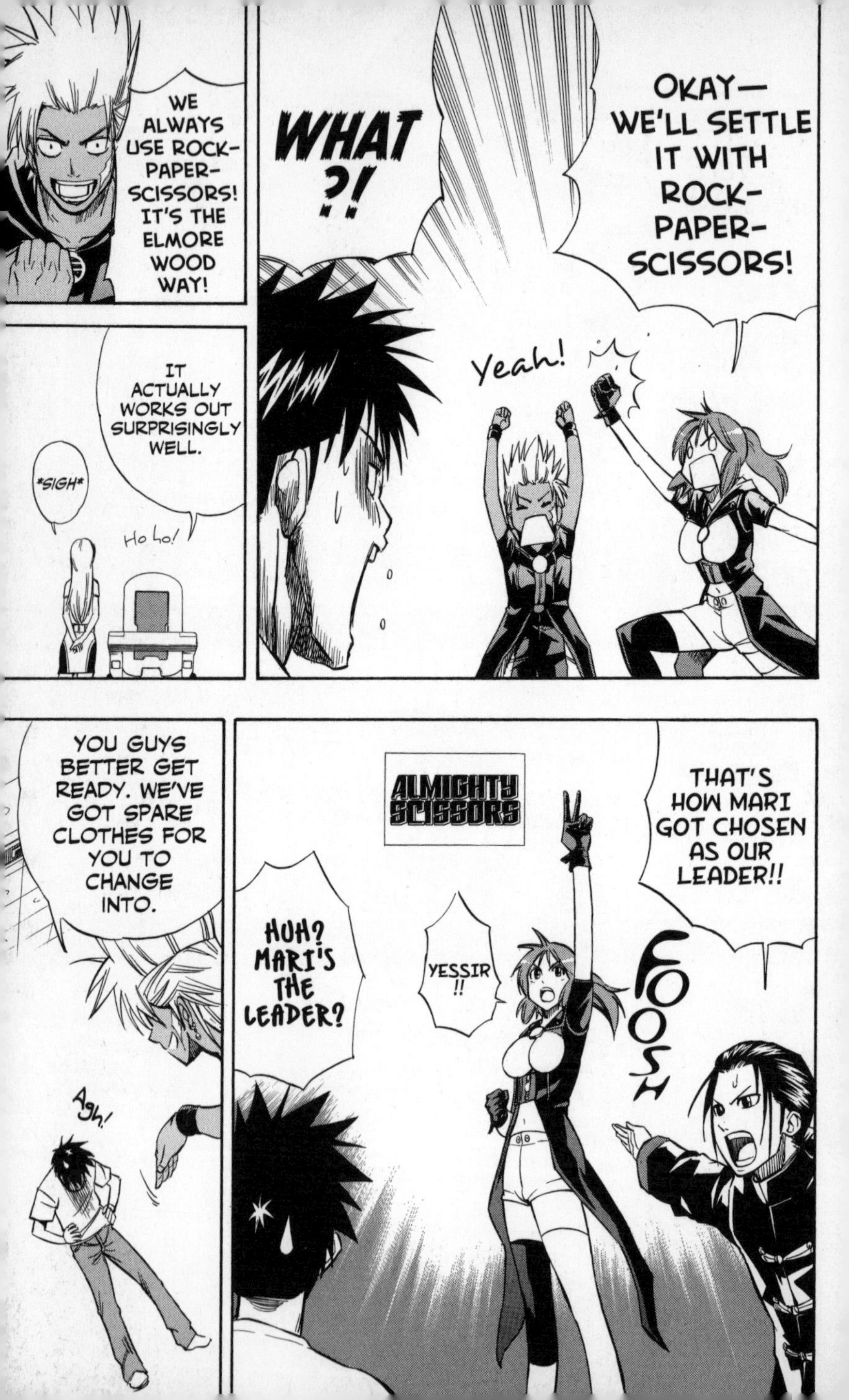
OKAY— WE'LL SETTLE IT WITH ROCK-PAPER-SCISSORS!
WHAT?!
Yeah!
WE ALWAYS USE ROCK-PAPER-SCISSORS! IT'S THE ELMORE WOOD WAY!
IT ACTUALLY WORKS OUT SURPRISINGLY WELL.
Ho ho!
SIGH
THAT'S HOW MARI GOT CHOSEN AS OUR LEADER!!
ALMIGHTY SCISSORS
WOOSH
YESSIR!!
HUH? MARI'S THE LEADER?
YOU GUYS BETTER GET READY. WE'VE GOT SPARE CLOTHES FOR YOU TO CHANGE INTO.
Agh!

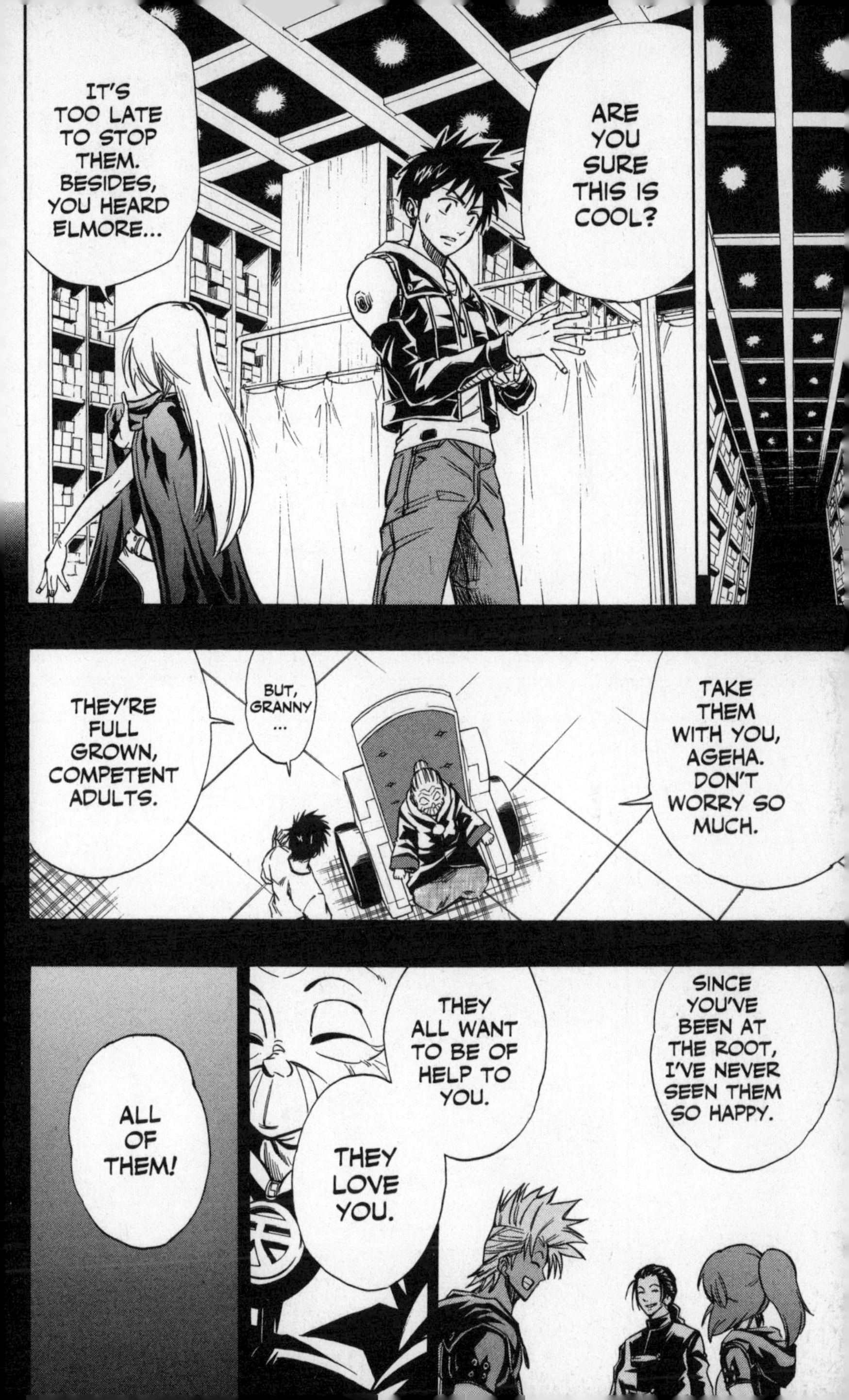
ARE YOU SURE THIS IS COOL?
IT'S TOO LATE TO STOP THEM. BESIDES, YOU HEARD ELMORE...
TAKE THEM WITH YOU, AGEHA. DON'T WORRY SO MUCH.
BUT, GRANNY ...
THEY'RE FULL GROWN, COMPETENT ADULTS.
SINCE YOU'VE BEEN AT THE ROOT, I'VE NEVER SEEN THEM SO HAPPY.
THEY ALL WANT TO BE OF HELP TO YOU.
THEY LOVE YOU.
ALL OF THEM!

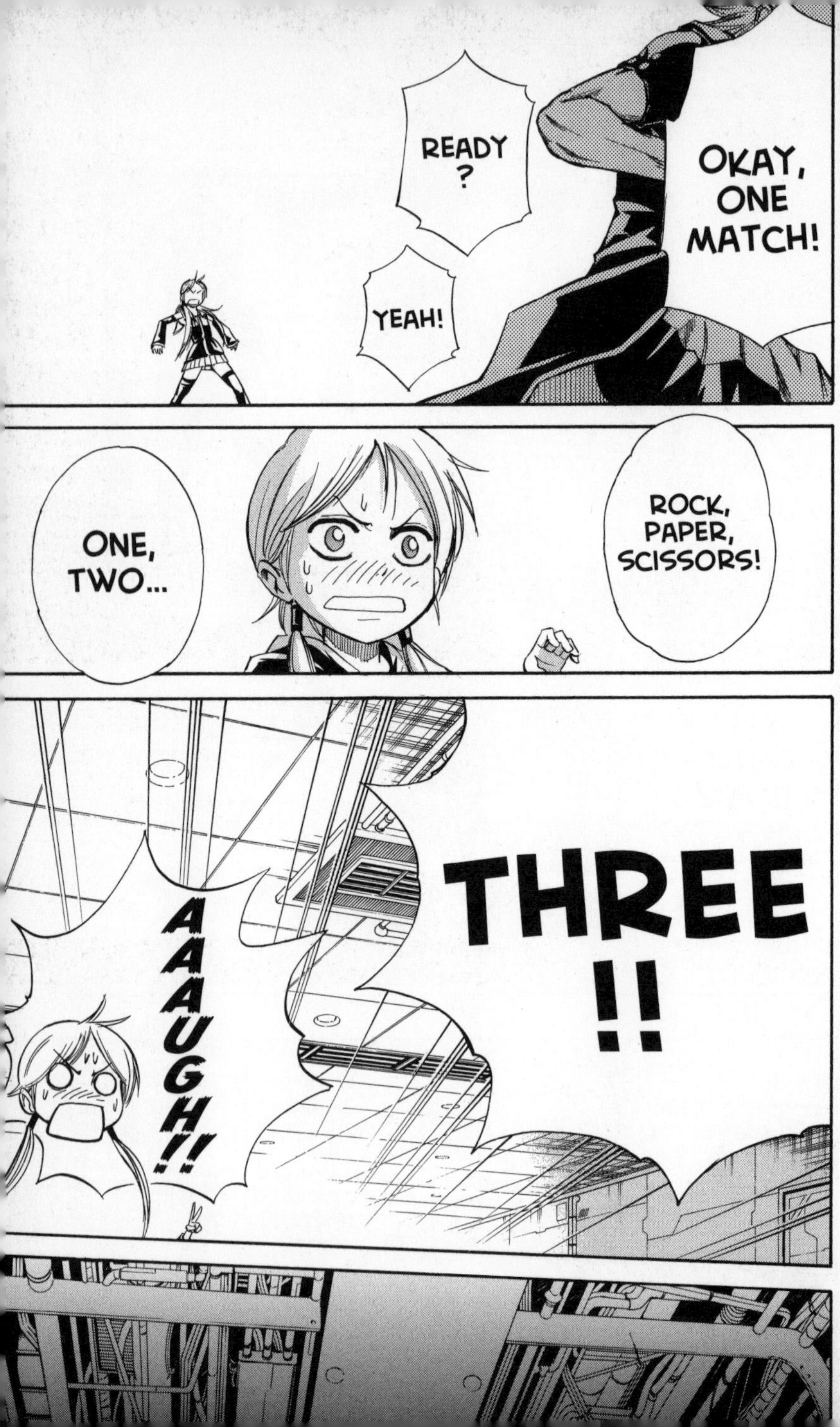
OKAY, ONE MATCH!
READY?
YEAH!
ROCK, PAPER, SCISSORS!
ONE, TWO...
THREE!!
AAAAUGH!!

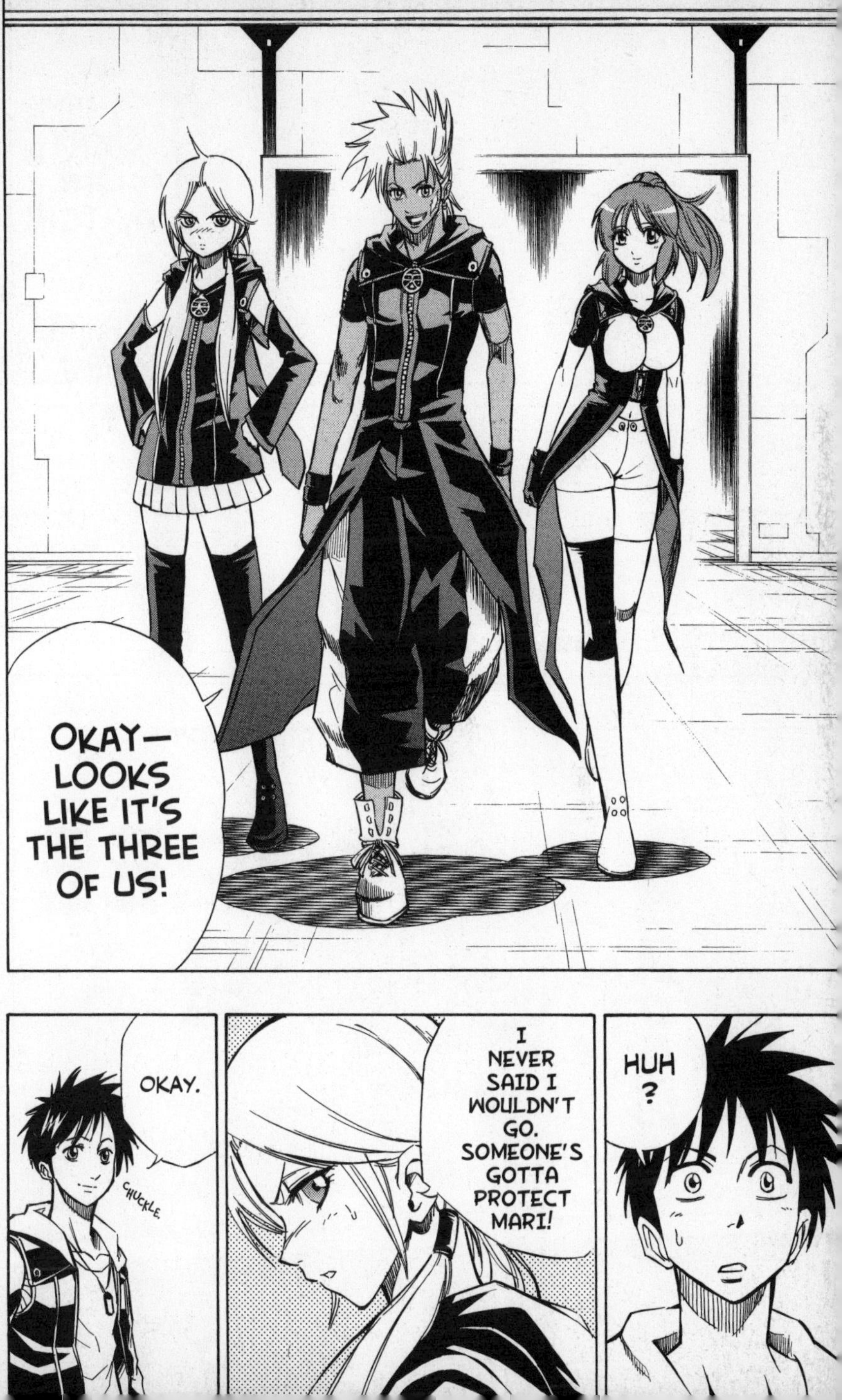
OKAY—LOOKS LIKE IT'S THE THREE OF US!
HUH?
I NEVER SAID I WOULDN'T GO. SOMEONE'S GOTTA PROTECT MARI!
OKAY.
CHUCKLE.

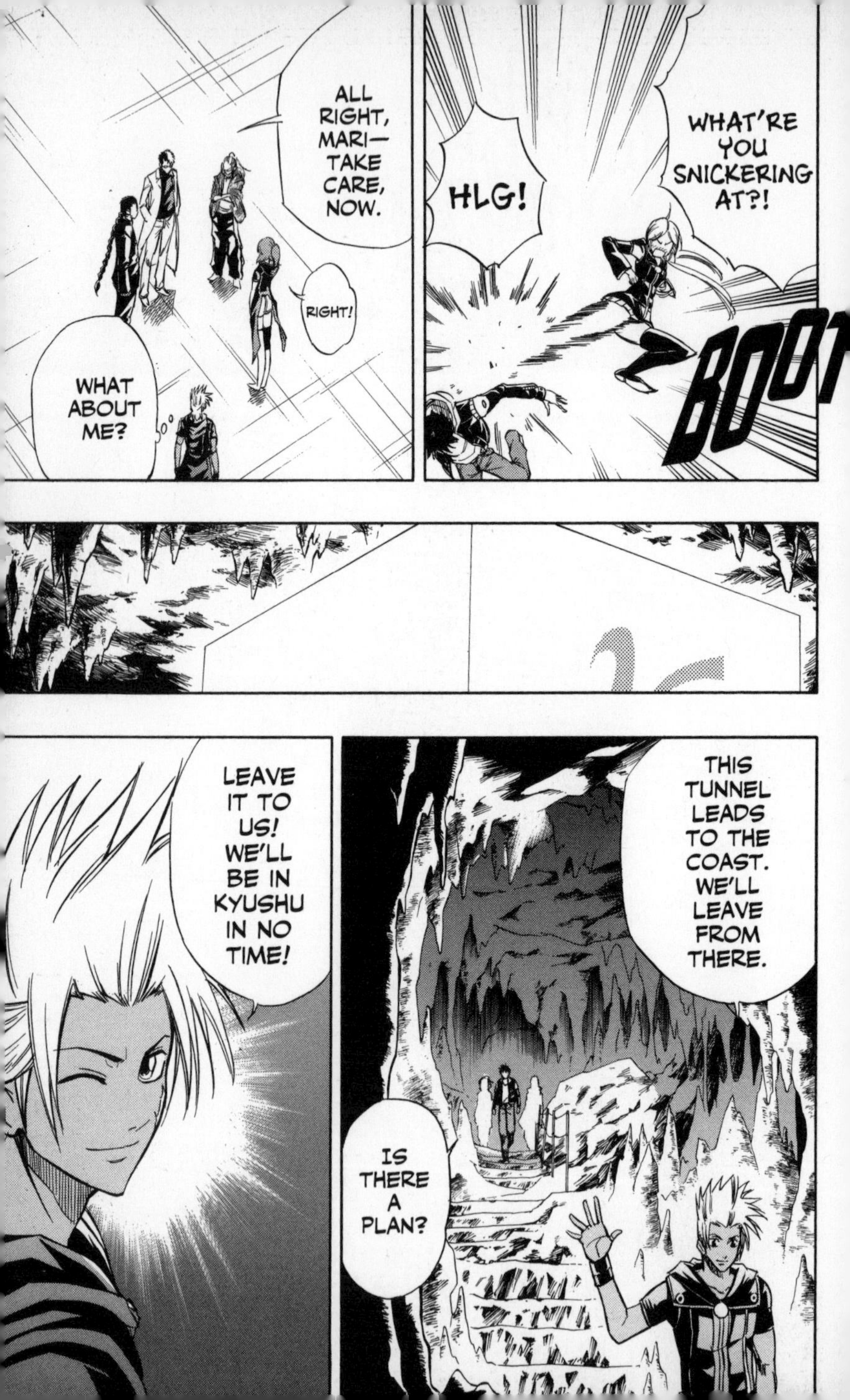
WHAT'RE YOU SNICKERING AT?!
HLG!
BOOT
ALL RIGHT, MARI— TAKE CARE, NOW.
RIGHT!
WHAT ABOUT ME?
THIS TUNNEL LEADS TO THE COAST. WE'LL LEAVE FROM THERE.
IS THERE A PLAN?
LEAVE IT TO US! WE'LL BE IN KYUSHU IN NO TIME!

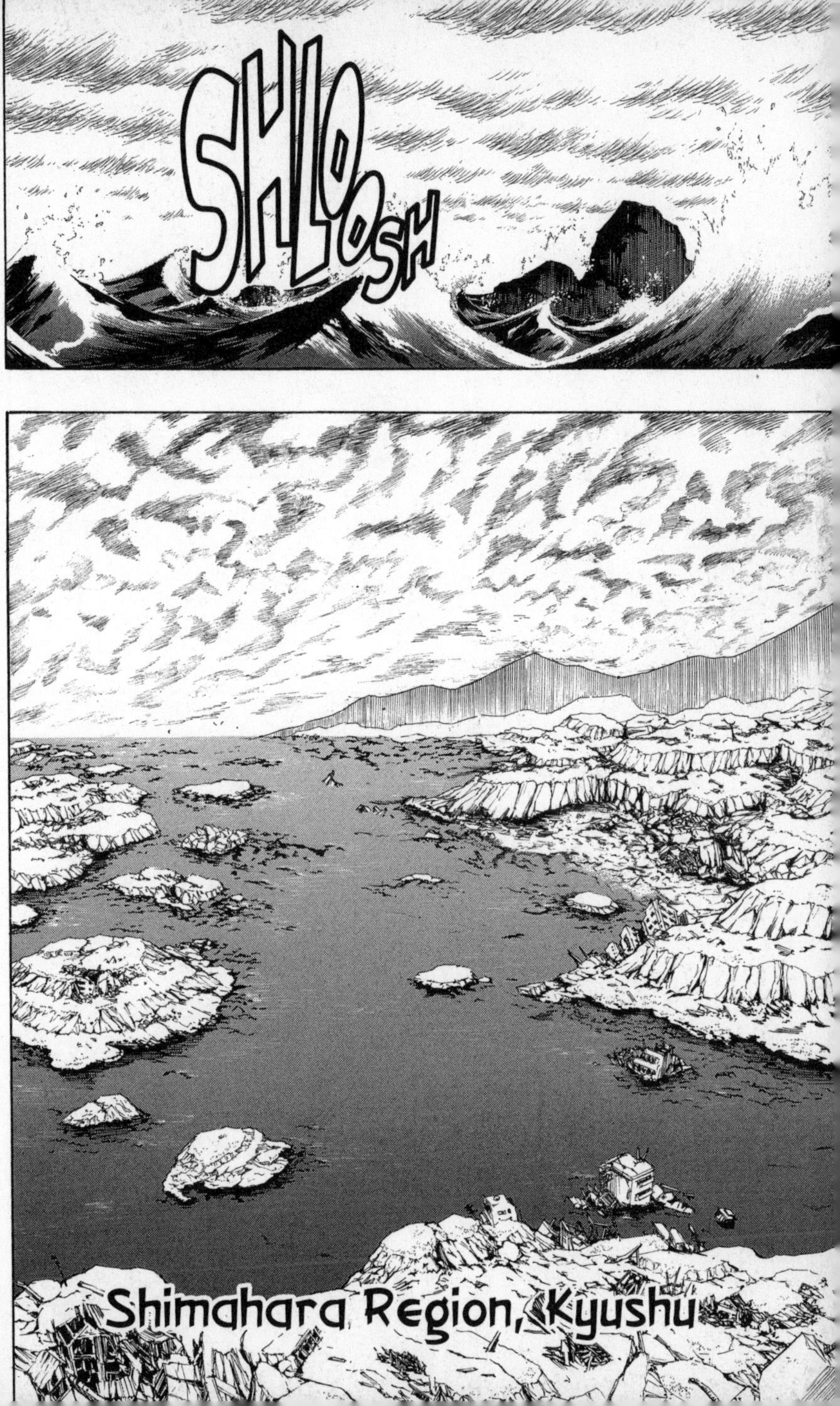
SHLOOSH
Shimahara Region, Kyushu

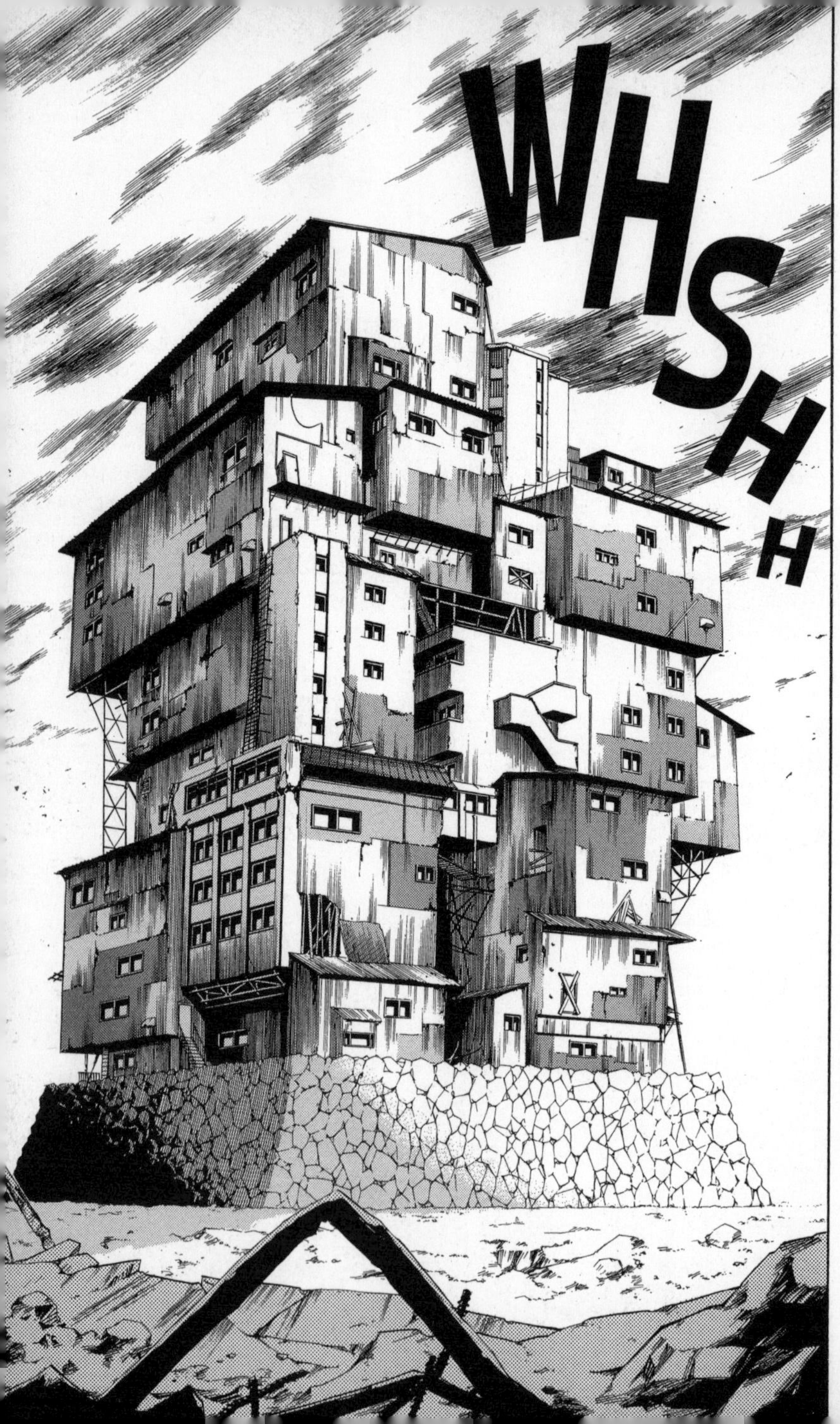
WHSHH

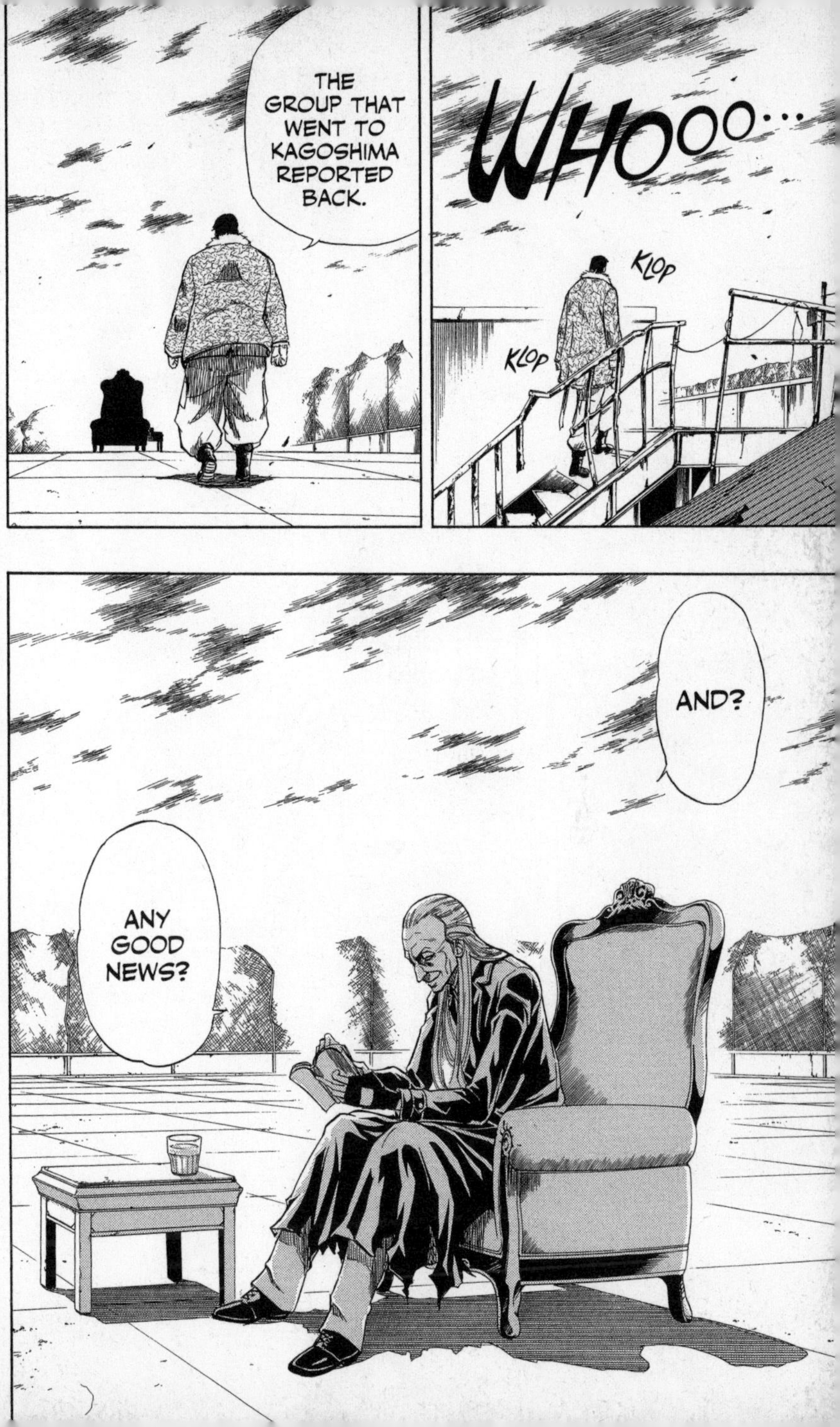
WHOOO...
KLOP
KLOP
THE GROUP THAT WENT TO KAGOSHIMA REPORTED BACK.
AND?
ANY GOOD NEWS?

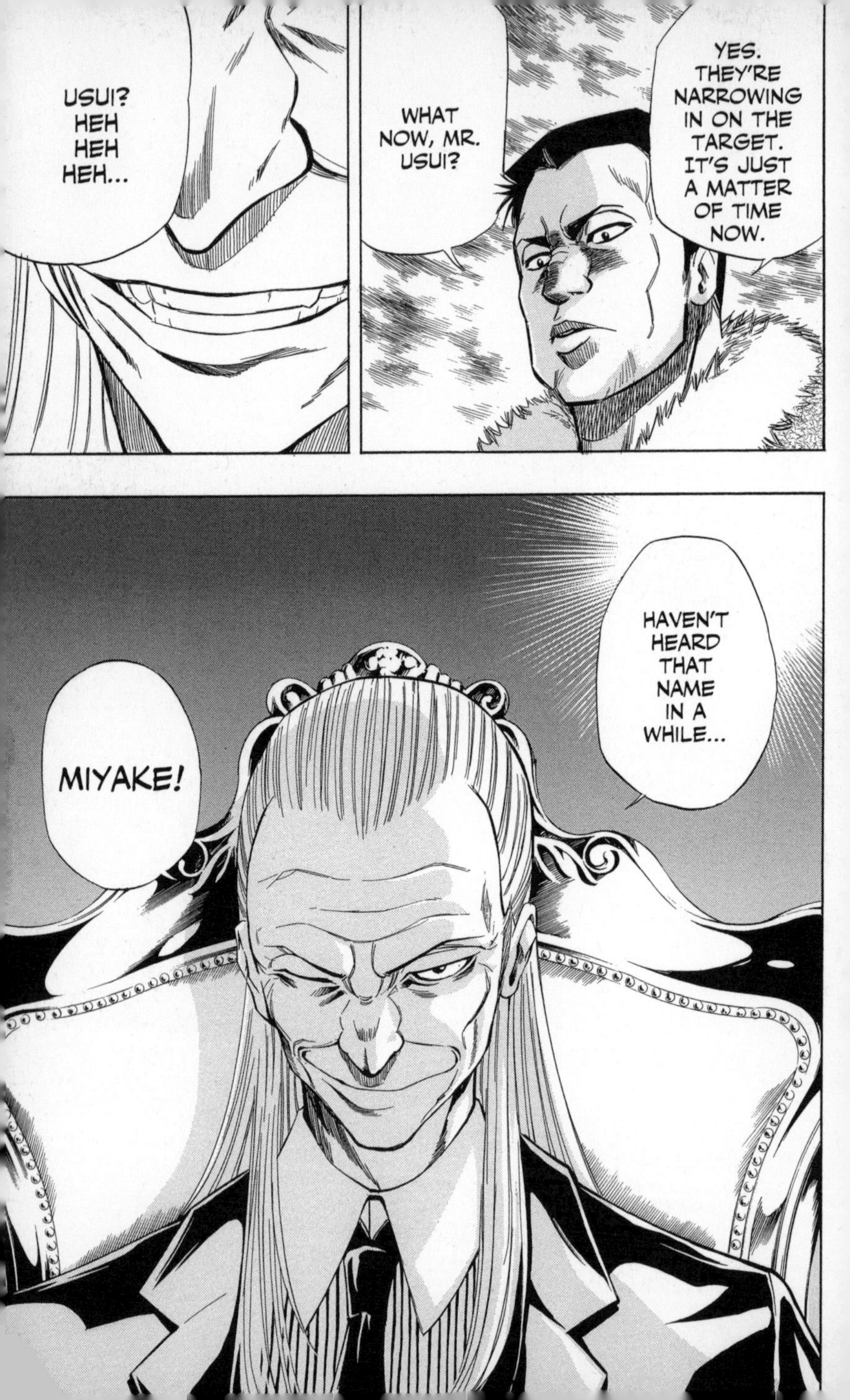
YES. THEY'RE NARROWING IN ON THE TARGET. IT'S JUST A MATTER OF TIME NOW.
WHAT NOW, MR. USUI?
USUI? HEH HEH HEH...
HAVEN'T HEARD THAT NAME IN A WHILE...
MIYAKE!

A DAY IN THE LIFE OF VAN

5:00 AM

ELMORE'S DAILY PHYSICAL

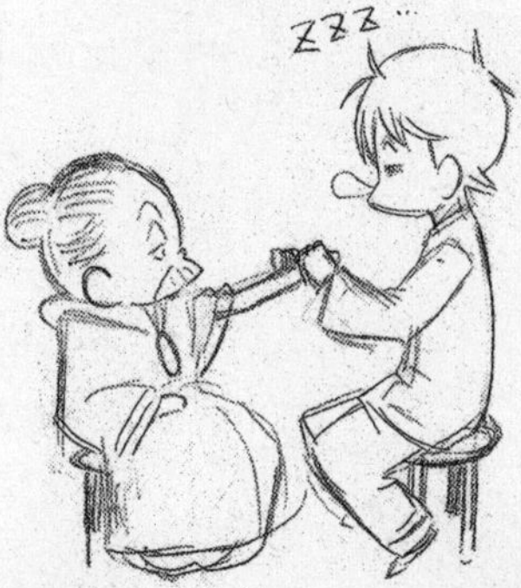
ZZZ...

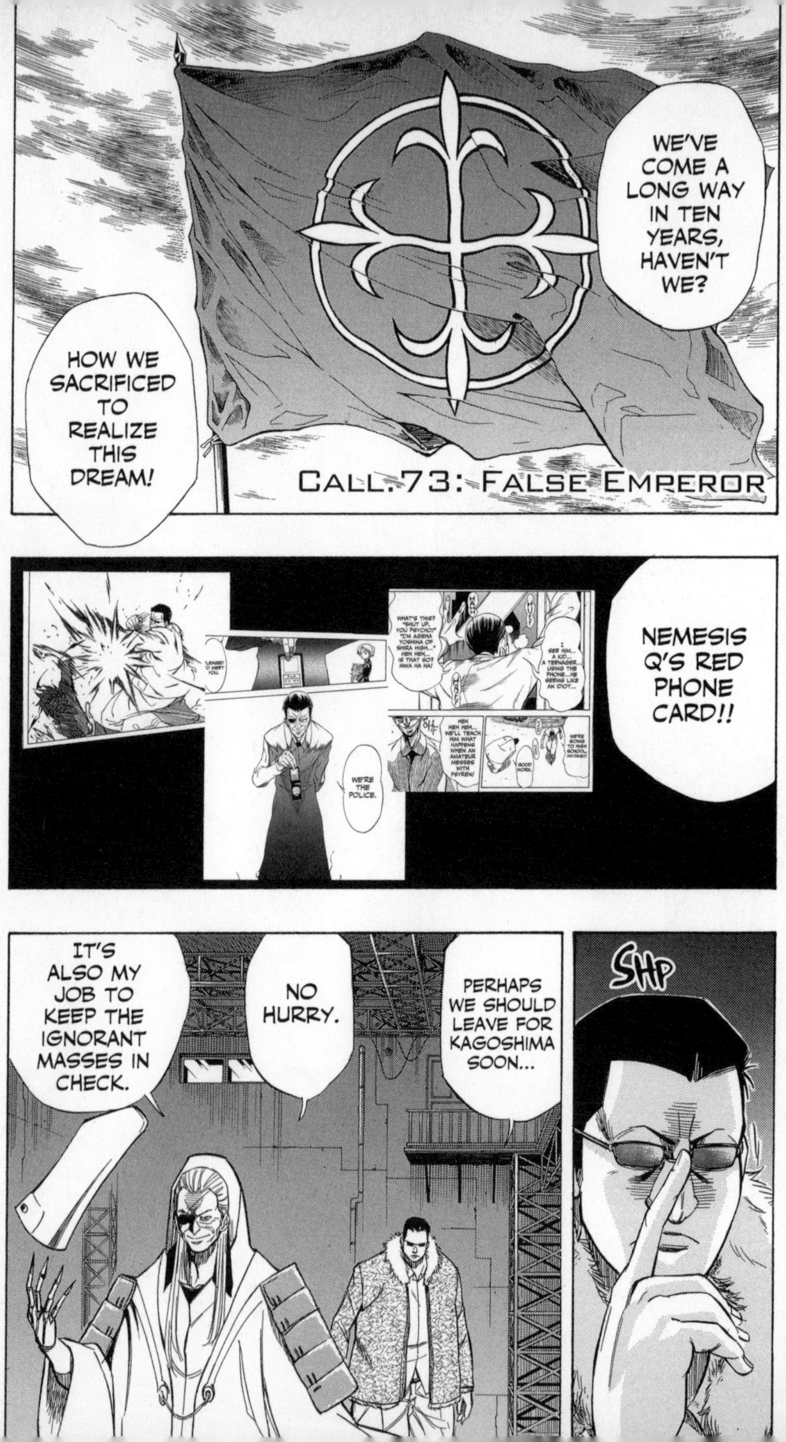
WE'VE COME A LONG WAY IN TEN YEARS, HAVEN'T WE?
HOW WE SACRIFICED TO REALIZE THIS DREAM!
CALL.73: FALSE EMPEROR
NEMESIS Q'S RED PHONE CARD!!
I SEE HIM... A KID... A TEENAGER... USING THE PHONE...HE SEEMS LIKE AN IDIOT...
WHAT'S THIS? "SHUT UP, YOU PSYCHO!" "I'M AGEHA YOSHINA OF SHIRA HIGH..." HEH HEH... IS THAT SO? MWA HA HA!
HEH HEH HEH... WE'LL TEACH HIM WHAT HAPPENS WHEN AN AMATEUR MESSES WITH PSYREN!
WE'RE GOING TO HIGH SCHOOL, MIYAKE!!
GOOD WORK.
WE'RE THE POLICE.
SHP
PERHAPS WE SHOULD LEAVE FOR KAGOSHIMA SOON...
NO HURRY.
IT'S ALSO MY JOB TO KEEP THE IGNORANT MASSES IN CHECK.

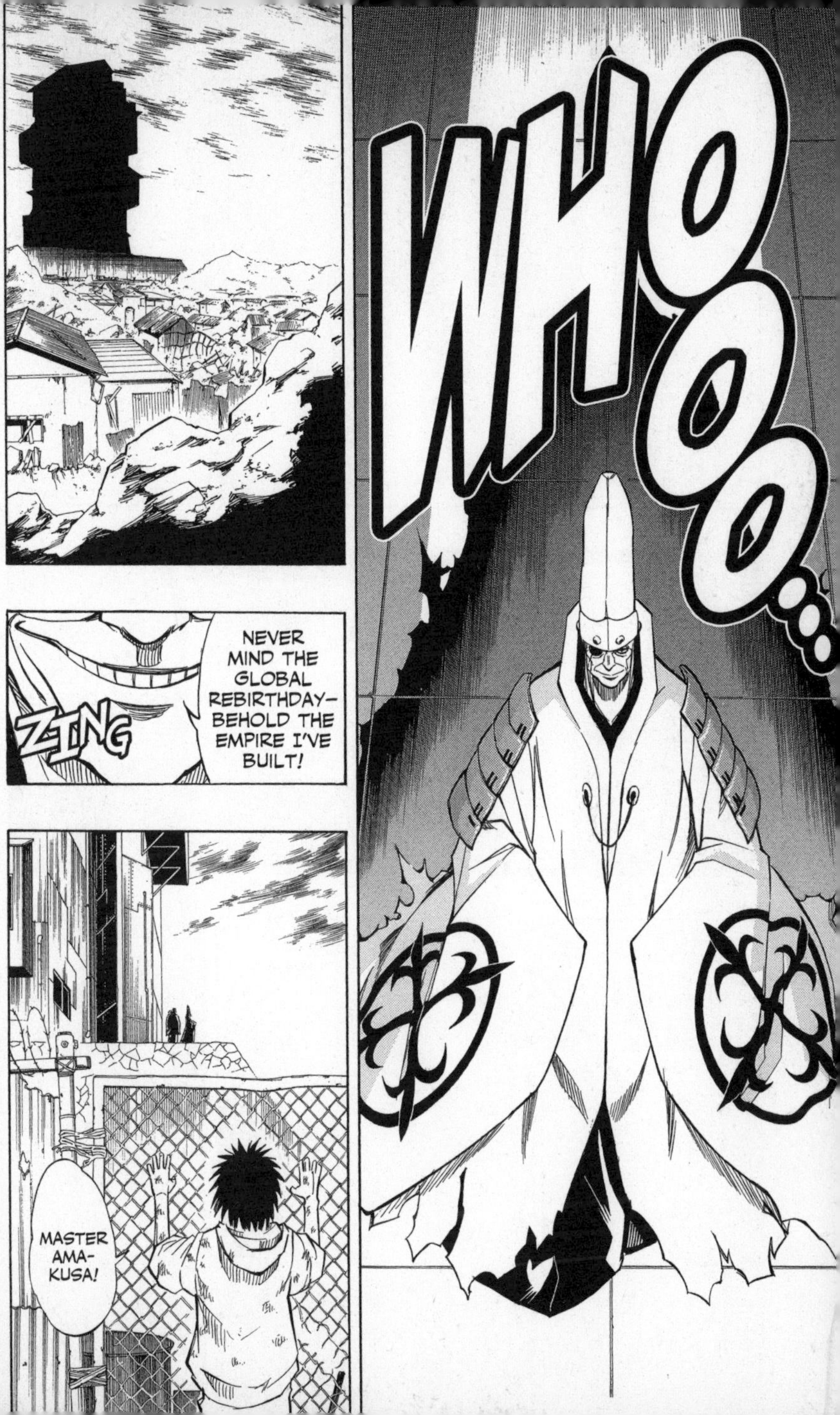
WHOOO...
NEVER MIND THE GLOBAL REBIRTHDAY— BEHOLD THE EMPIRE I'VE BUILT!
ZING
MASTER AMA-KUSA!

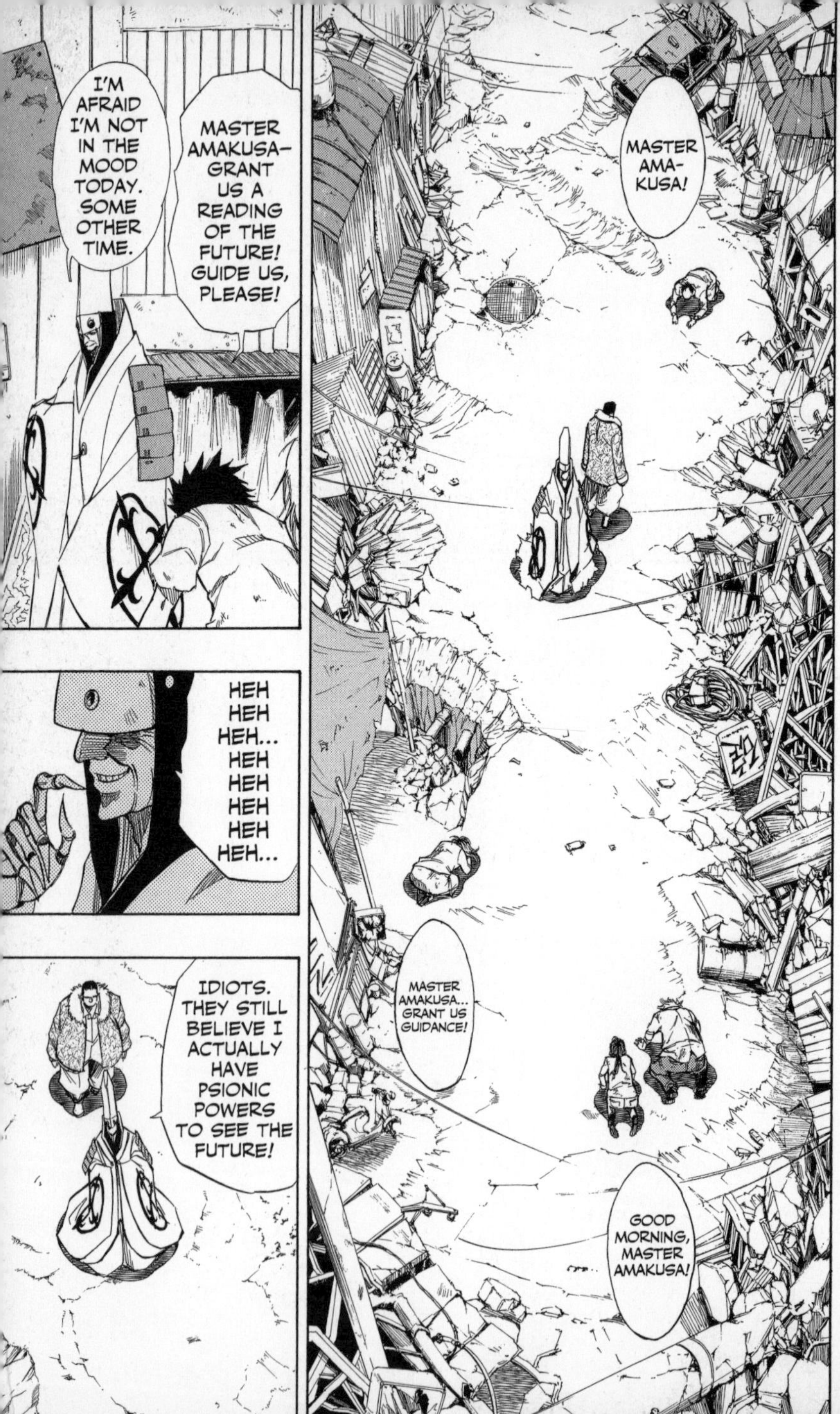
MASTER AMA-KUSA!
MASTER AMAKUSA... GRANT US GUIDANCE!
GOOD MORNING, MASTER AMAKUSA!
MASTER AMAKUSA-GRANT US A READING OF THE FUTURE! GUIDE US, PLEASE!
I'M AFRAID I'M NOT IN THE MOOD TODAY. SOME OTHER TIME.
HEH HEH HEH... HEH HEH HEH HEH HEH...
IDIOTS. THEY STILL BELIEVE I ACTUALLY HAVE PSIONIC POWERS TO SEE THE FUTURE!

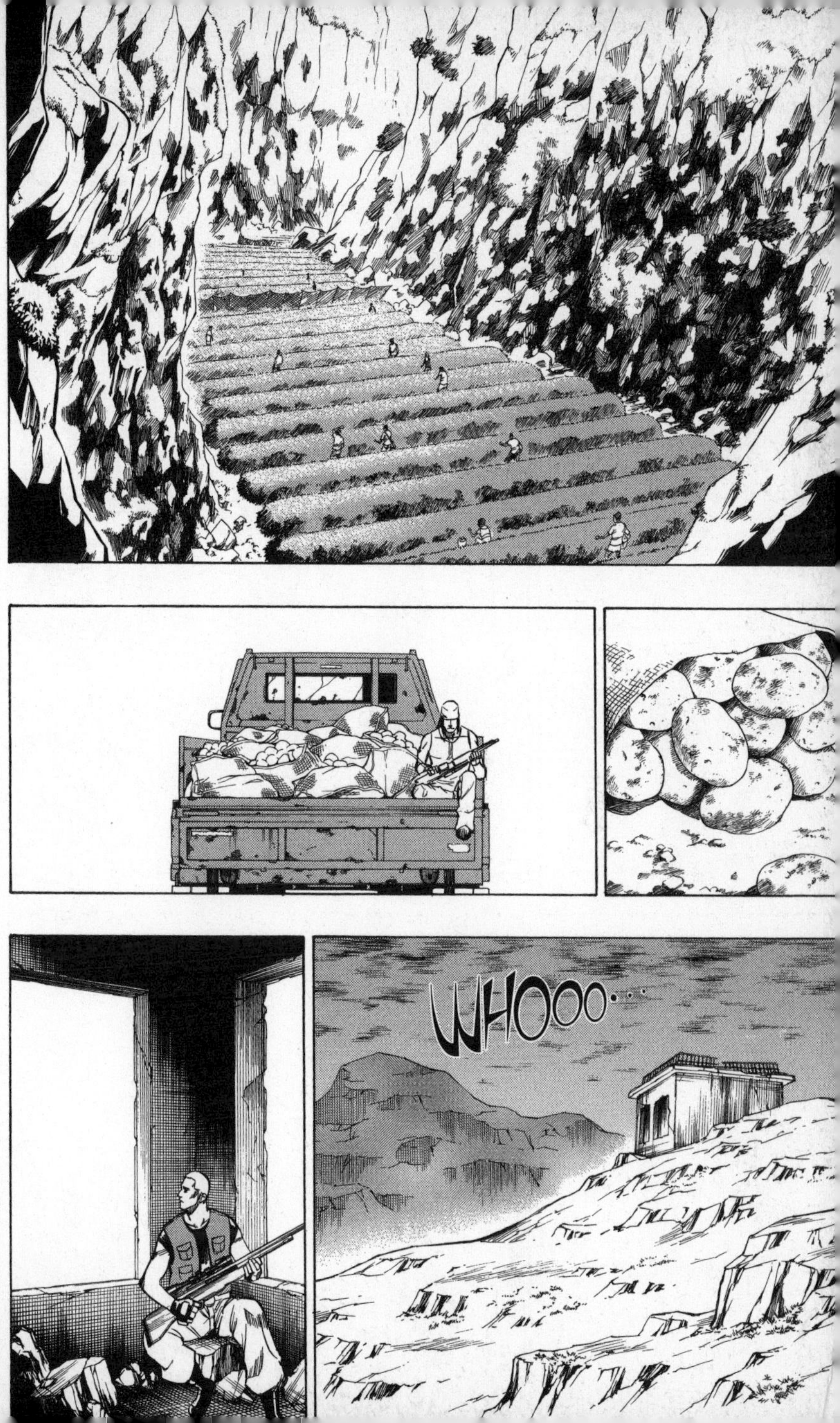
WHOOO...

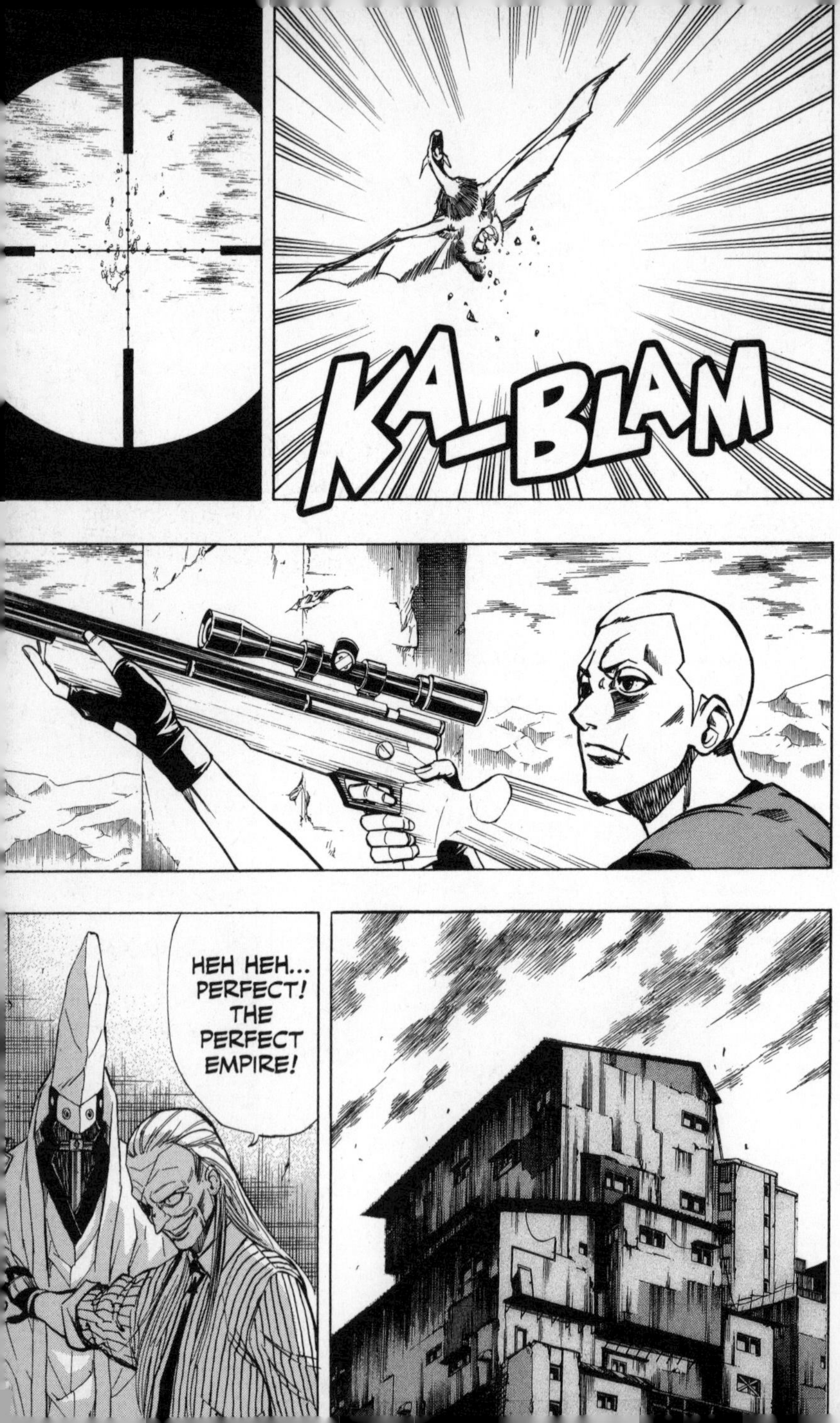
KA-BLAM
HEH HEH... PERFECT! THE PERFECT EMPIRE!

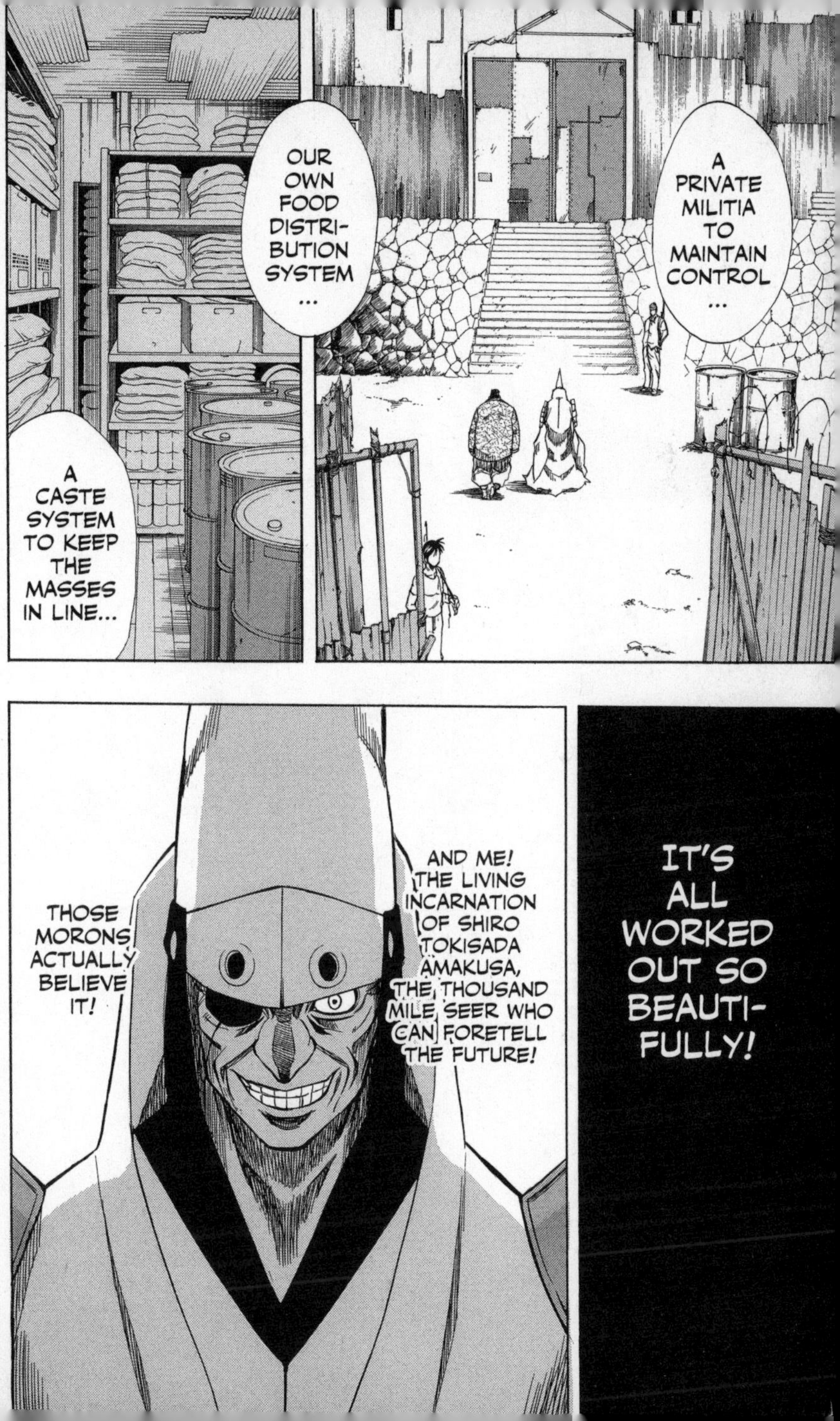
A PRIVATE MILITIA TO MAINTAIN CONTROL...
OUR OWN FOOD DISTRI-BUTION SYSTEM...
A CASTE SYSTEM TO KEEP THE MASSES IN LINE...
IT'S ALL WORKED OUT SO BEAUTI-FULLY!
AND ME! THE LIVING INCARNATION OF SHIRO TOKISADA AMAKUSA, THE THOUSAND MILE SEER WHO CAN FORETELL THE FUTURE!
THOSE MORONS ACTUALLY BELIEVE IT!

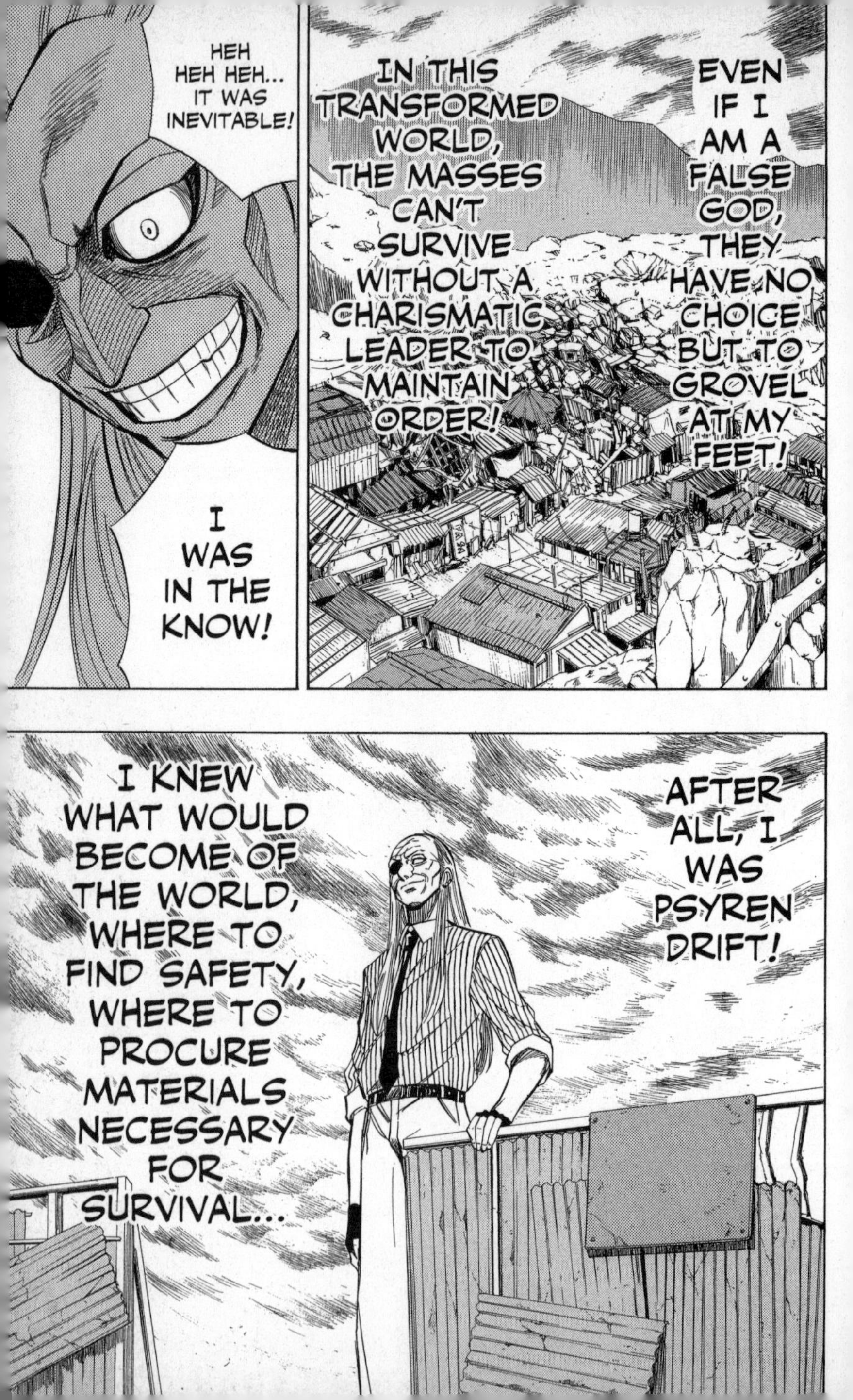
EVEN IF I AM A FALSE GOD, THEY HAVE NO CHOICE BUT TO GROVEL AT MY FEET!
IN THIS TRANSFORMED WORLD, THE MASSES CAN'T SURVIVE WITHOUT A CHARISMATIC LEADER TO MAINTAIN ORDER!
HEH HEH HEH... IT WAS INEVITABLE!
I WAS IN THE KNOW!
AFTER ALL, I WAS PSYREN DRIFT!
I KNEW WHAT WOULD BECOME OF THE WORLD, WHERE TO FIND SAFETY, WHERE TO PROCURE MATERIALS NECESSARY FOR SURVIVAL...

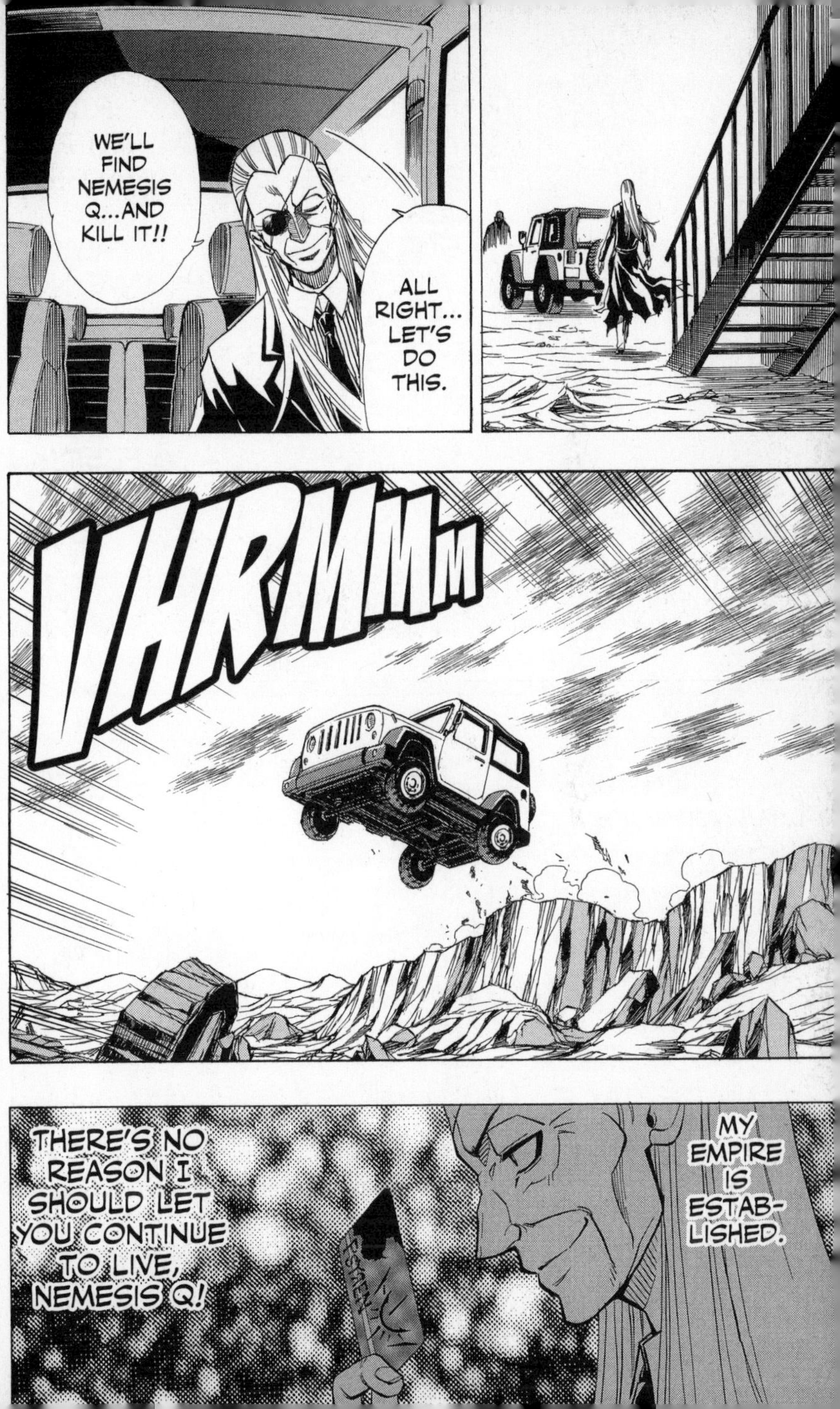
WE'LL FIND NEMESIS Q...AND KILL IT!!
ALL RIGHT... LET'S DO THIS.
VHRMMMM
MY EMPIRE IS ESTAB-LISHED.
THERE'S NO REASON I SHOULD LET YOU CONTINUE TO LIVE, NEMESIS Q!

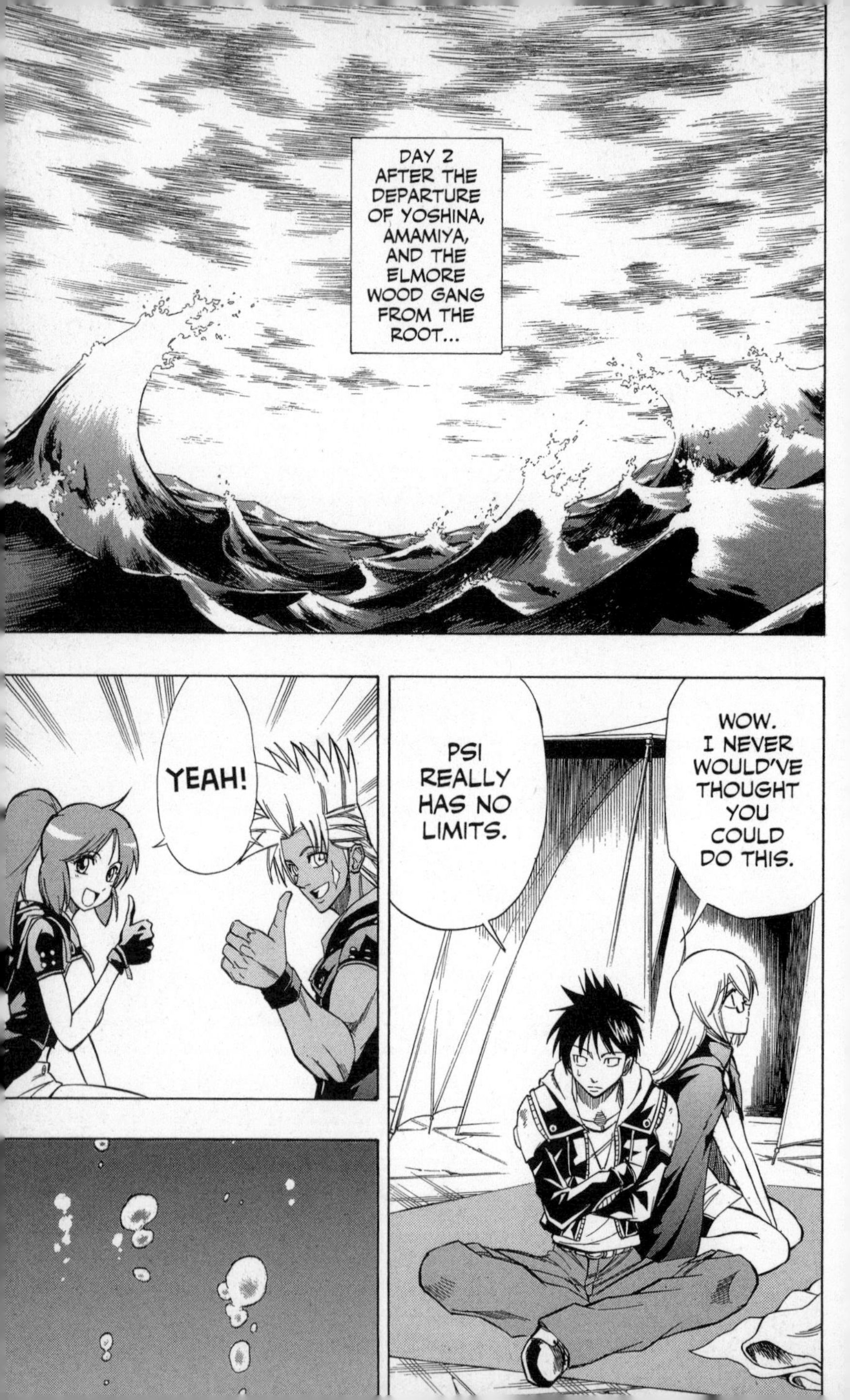
DAY 2 AFTER THE DEPARTURE OF YOSHINA, AMAMIYA, AND THE ELMORE WOOD GANG FROM THE ROOT...
WOW. I NEVER WOULD'VE THOUGHT YOU COULD DO THIS.
PSI REALLY HAS NO LIMITS.
YEAH!

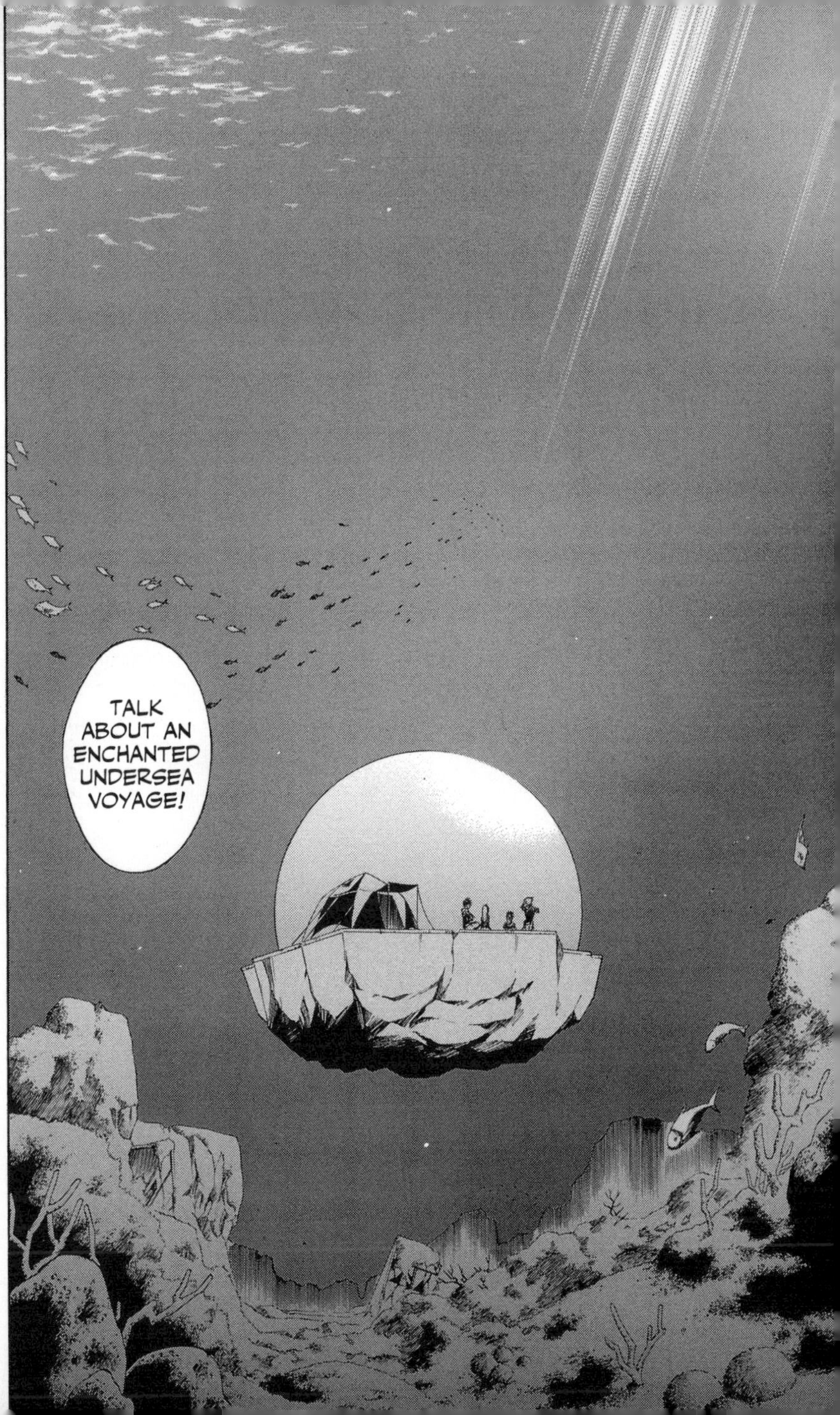
TALK ABOUT AN ENCHANTED UNDERSEA VOYAGE!

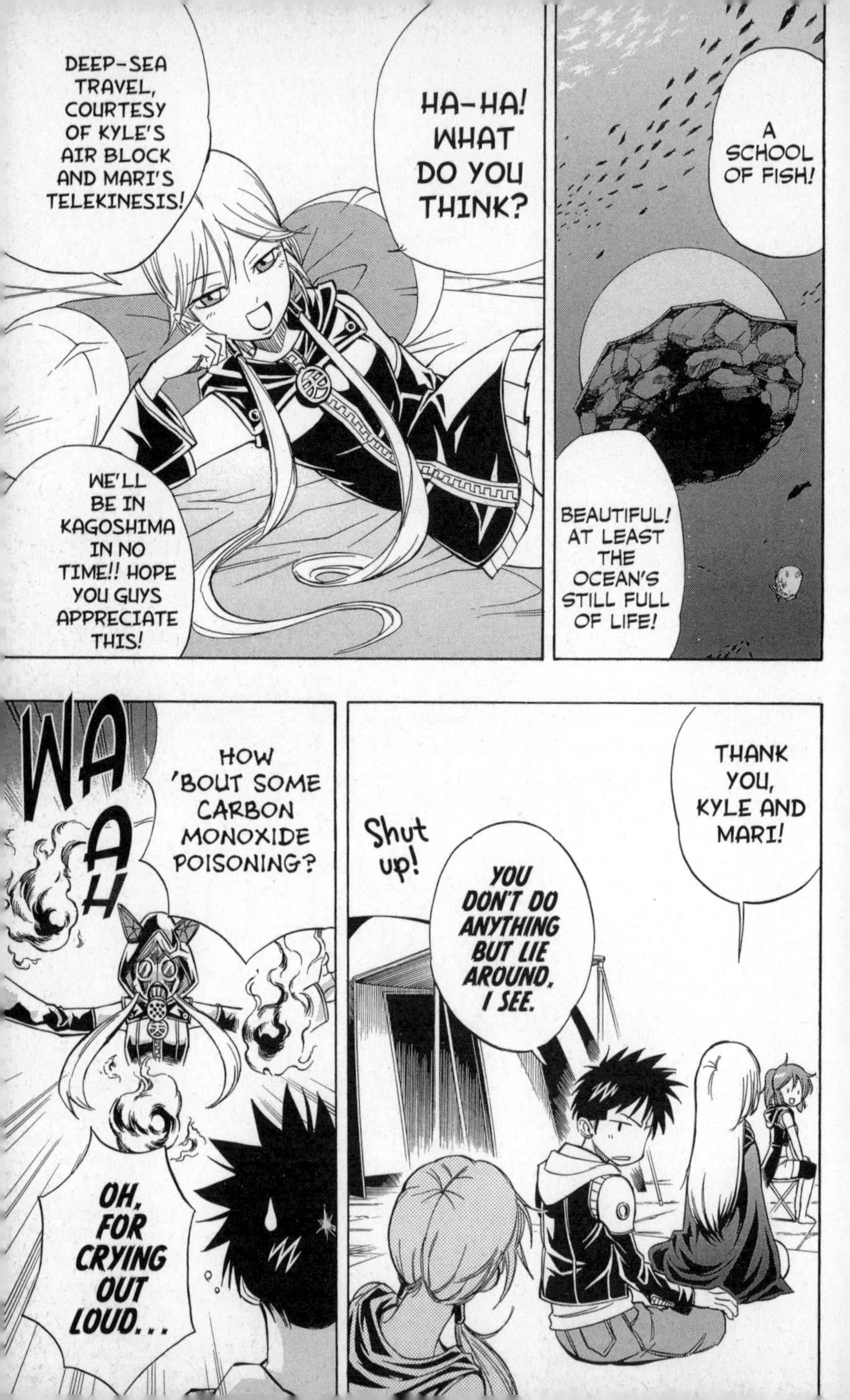
A SCHOOL OF FISH!
BEAUTIFUL! AT LEAST THE OCEAN'S STILL FULL OF LIFE!
HA-HA! WHAT DO YOU THINK?
DEEP-SEA TRAVEL, COURTESY OF KYLE'S AIR BLOCK AND MARI'S TELEKINESIS!
WE'LL BE IN KAGOSHIMA IN NO TIME!! HOPE YOU GUYS APPRECIATE THIS!
THANK YOU, KYLE AND MARI!
YOU DON'T DO ANYTHING BUT LIE AROUND, I SEE.
Shut up!
HOW 'BOUT SOME CARBON MONOXIDE POISONING?
WA A HA
OH, FOR CRYING OUT LOUD...

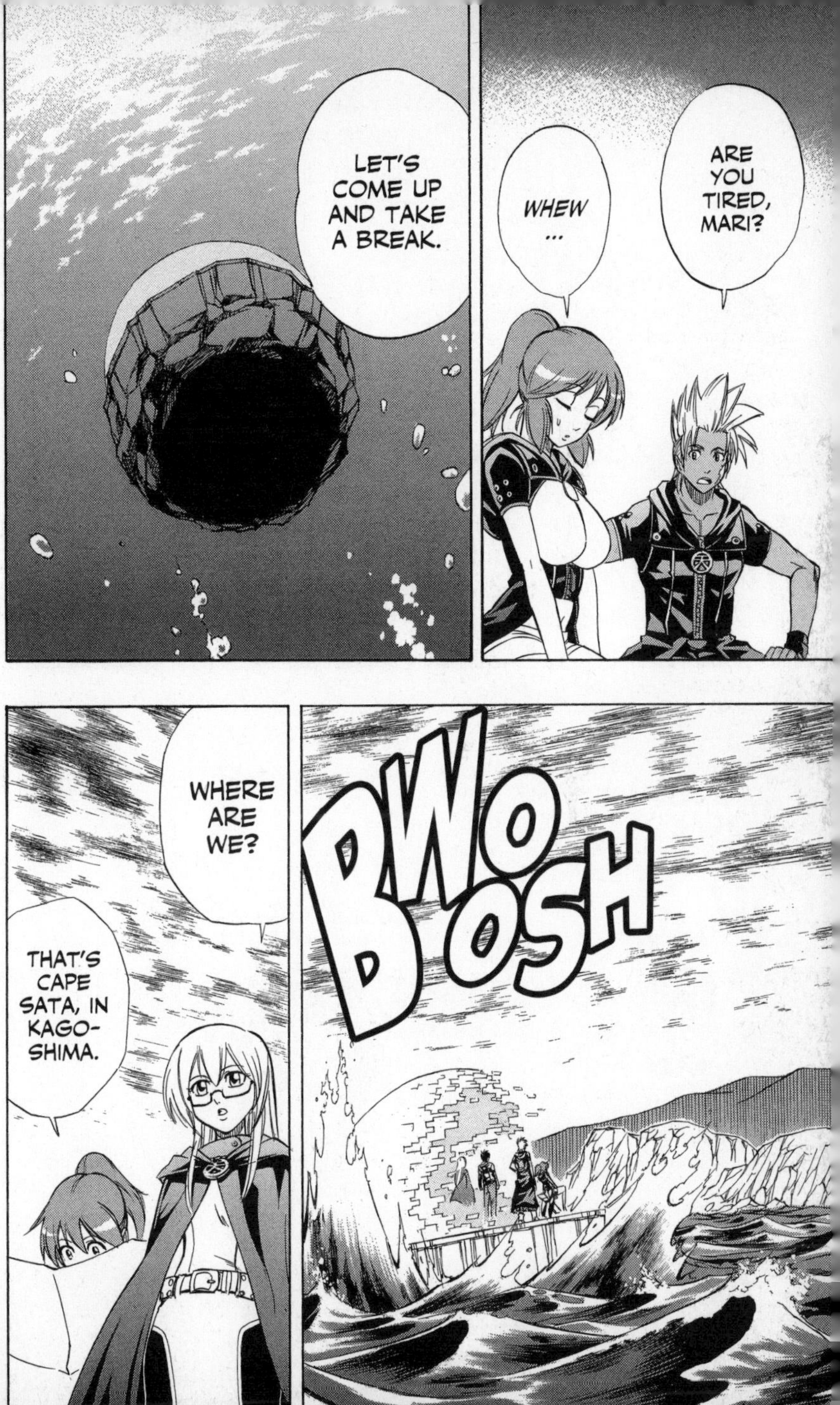
ARE YOU TIRED, MARI?
WHEW ...
LET'S COME UP AND TAKE A BREAK.
BWOOSH
WHERE ARE WE?
THAT'S CAPE SATA, IN KAGO-SHIMA.

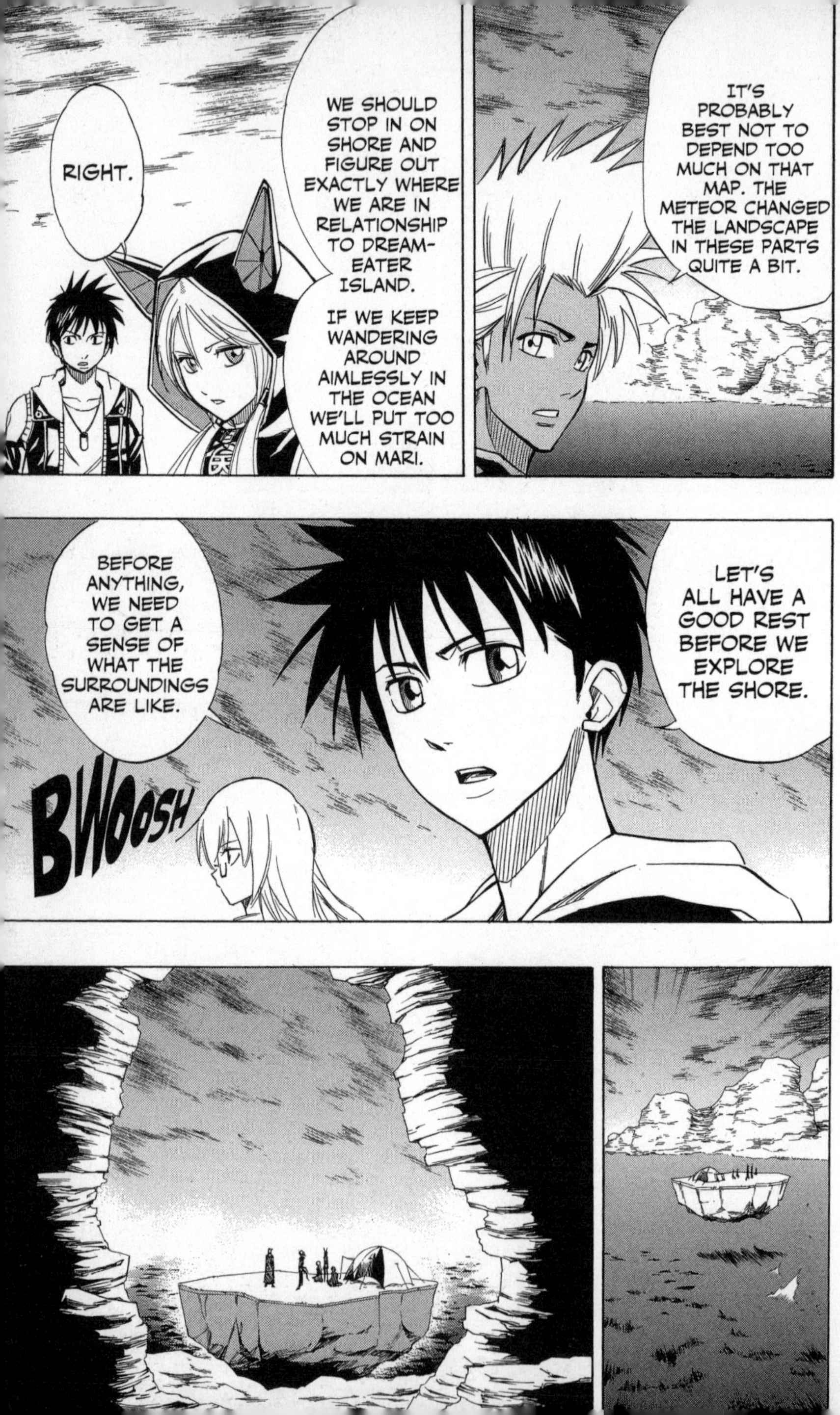
IT'S PROBABLY BEST NOT TO DEPEND TOO MUCH ON THAT MAP. THE METEOR CHANGED THE LANDSCAPE IN THESE PARTS QUITE A BIT.
WE SHOULD STOP IN ON SHORE AND FIGURE OUT EXACTLY WHERE WE ARE IN RELATIONSHIP TO DREAM-EATER ISLAND.
IF WE KEEP WANDERING AROUND AIMLESSLY IN THE OCEAN WE'LL PUT TOO MUCH STRAIN ON MARI.
RIGHT.
LET'S ALL HAVE A GOOD REST BEFORE WE EXPLORE THE SHORE.
BEFORE ANYTHING, WE NEED TO GET A SENSE OF WHAT THE SURROUNDINGS ARE LIKE.
BWOOSH

I'LL GO HAVE A LOOK AROUND.
ME TOO!
YOU WAIT HERE AND REST, MARI!
GOT IT!
WHOOSH
...
RIGHT. DREAM-EATER ISLAND IS THIS WAY.

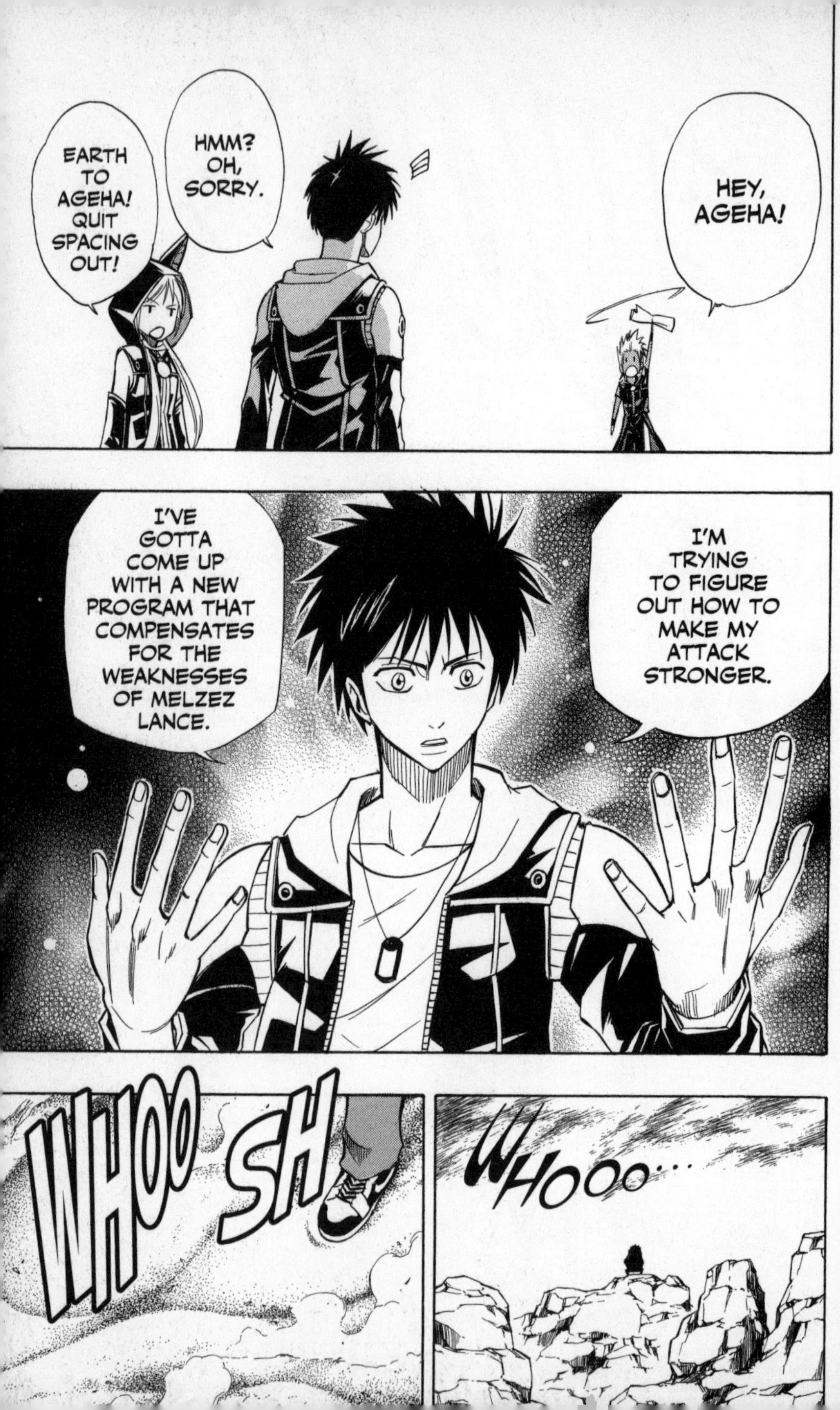
HEY, AGEHA!
HMM? OH, SORRY.
EARTH TO AGEHA! QUIT SPACING OUT!
I'M TRYING TO FIGURE OUT HOW TO MAKE MY ATTACK STRONGER.
I'VE GOTTA COME UP WITH A NEW PROGRAM THAT COMPENSATES FOR THE WEAKNESSES OF MELZEZ LANCE.
WHOOO...
WHOOSH

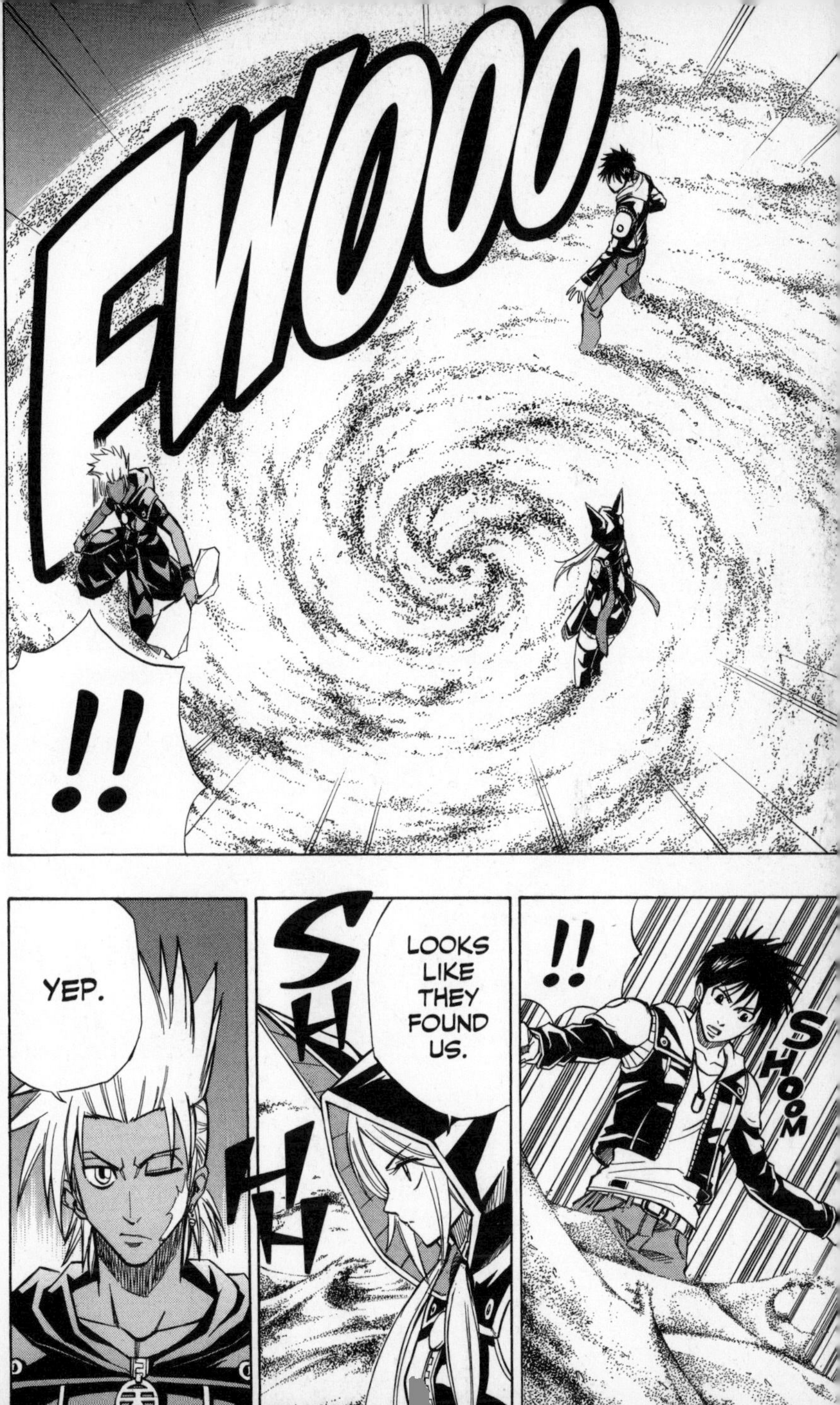
FWOOO
!!
!!
SHOOM
SHHH
LOOKS LIKE THEY FOUND US.
YEP.

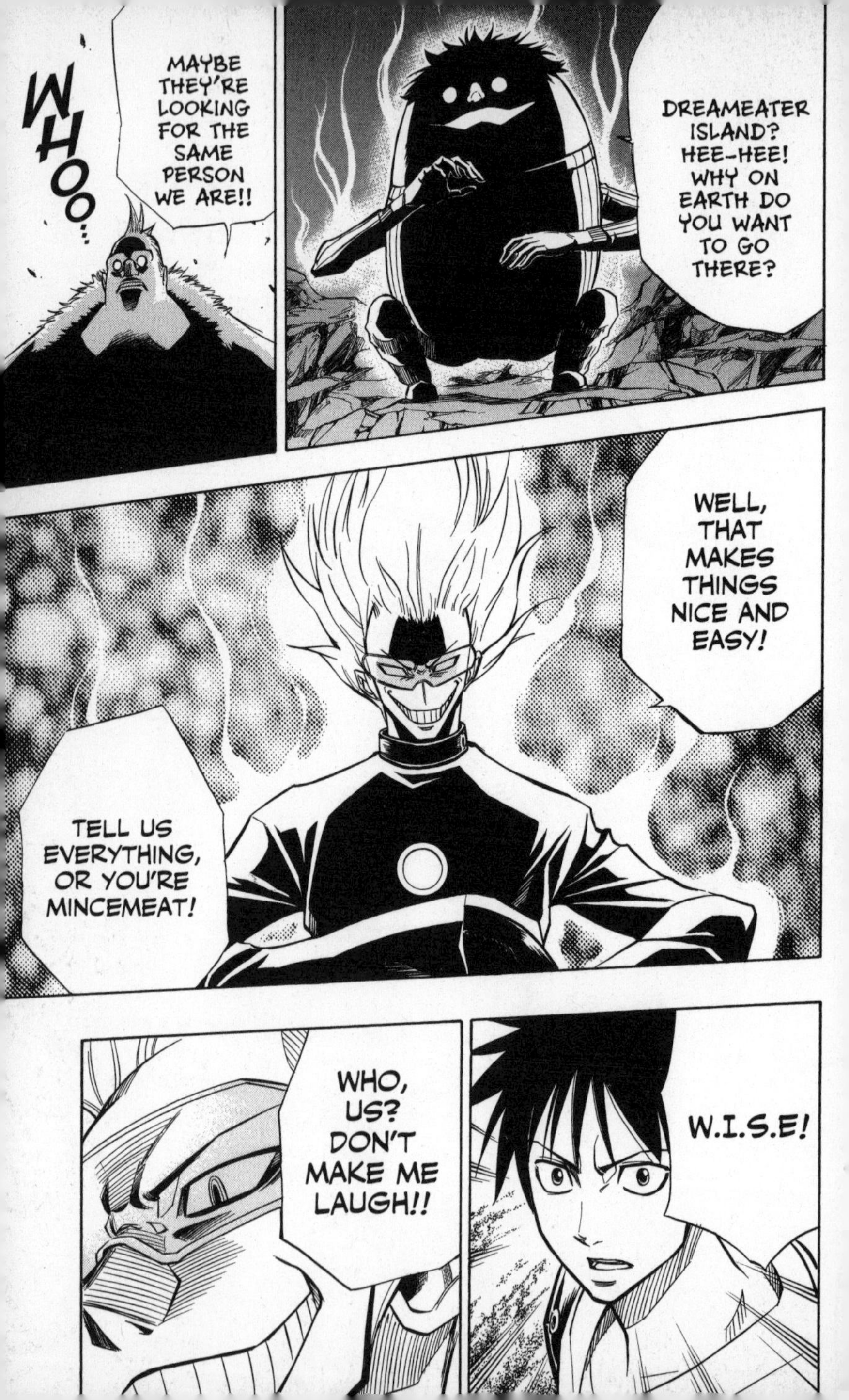
DREAMEATER ISLAND? HEE-HEE! WHY ON EARTH DO YOU WANT TO GO THERE?
MAYBE THEY'RE LOOKING FOR THE SAME PERSON WE ARE!!
WHOO...
WELL, THAT MAKES THINGS NICE AND EASY!
TELL US EVERYTHING, OR YOU'RE MINCEMEAT!
W.I.S.E!
WHO, US? DON'T MAKE ME LAUGH!!

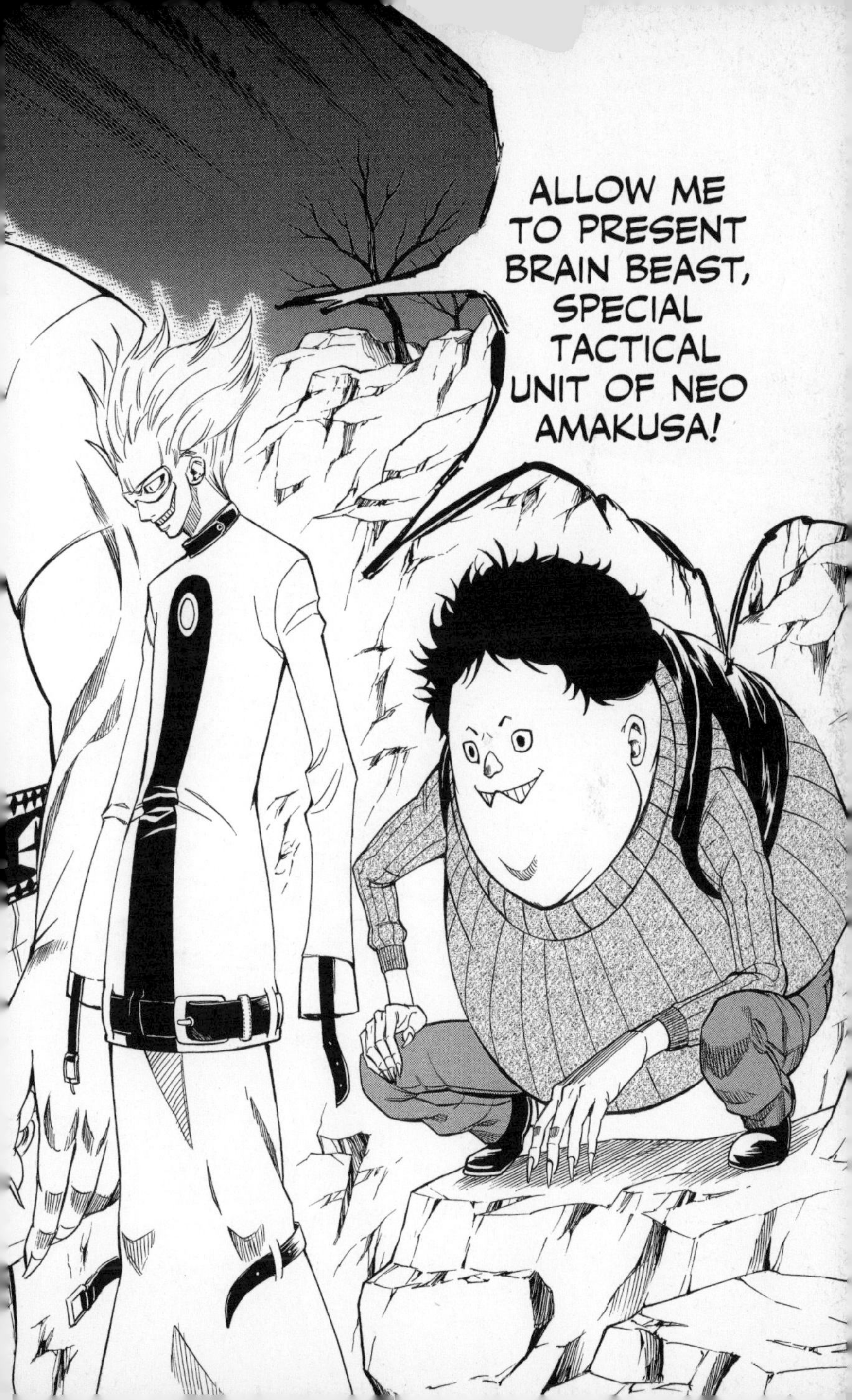
ALLOW ME TO PRESENT BRAIN BEAST, SPECIAL TACTICAL UNIT OF NEO AMAKUSA!

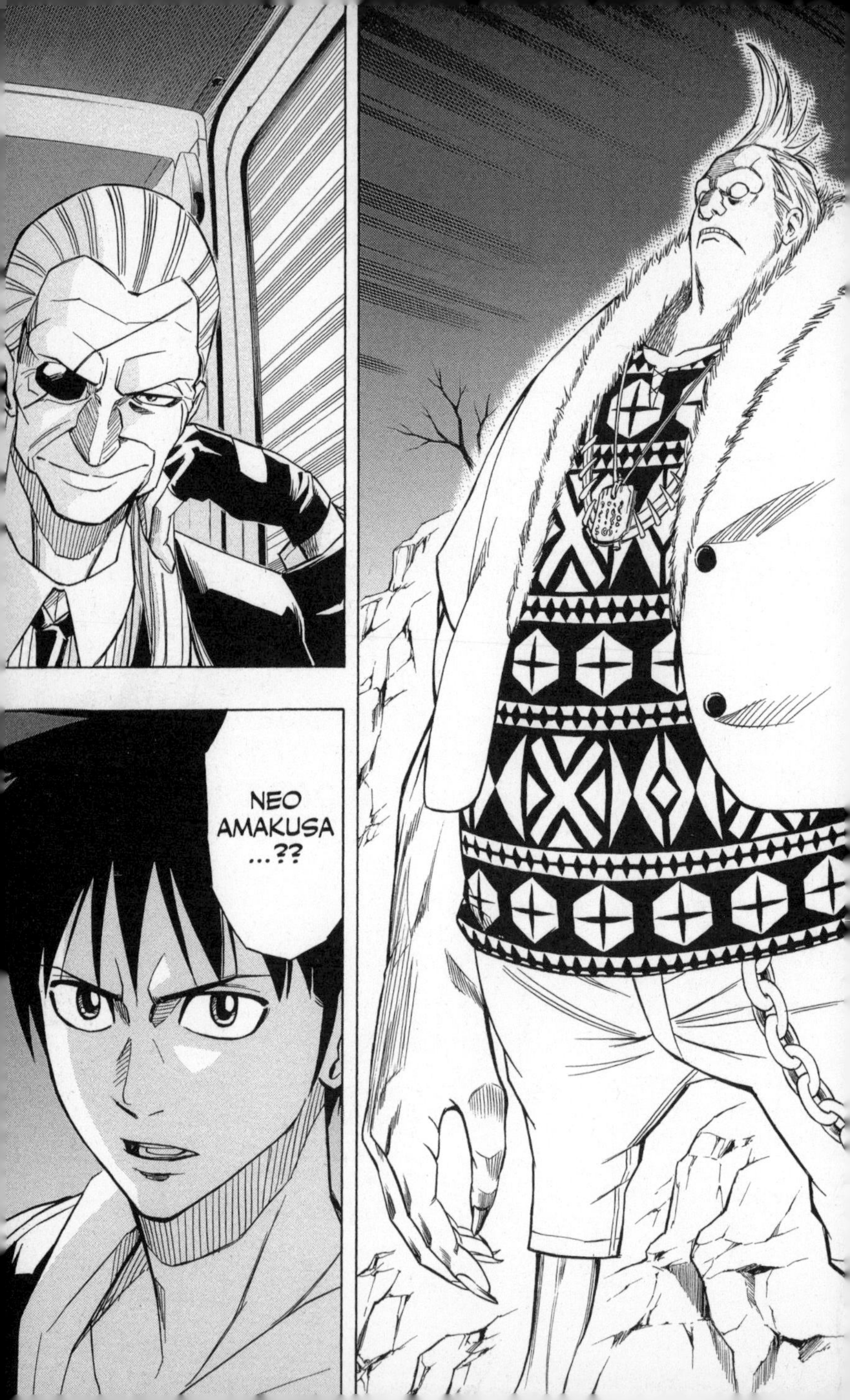
NEO AMAKUSA ...??

A DAY IN THE LIFE OF VAN

10:30 AM   VAN AWAKENS

8:30 AM   BREAKFAST

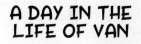

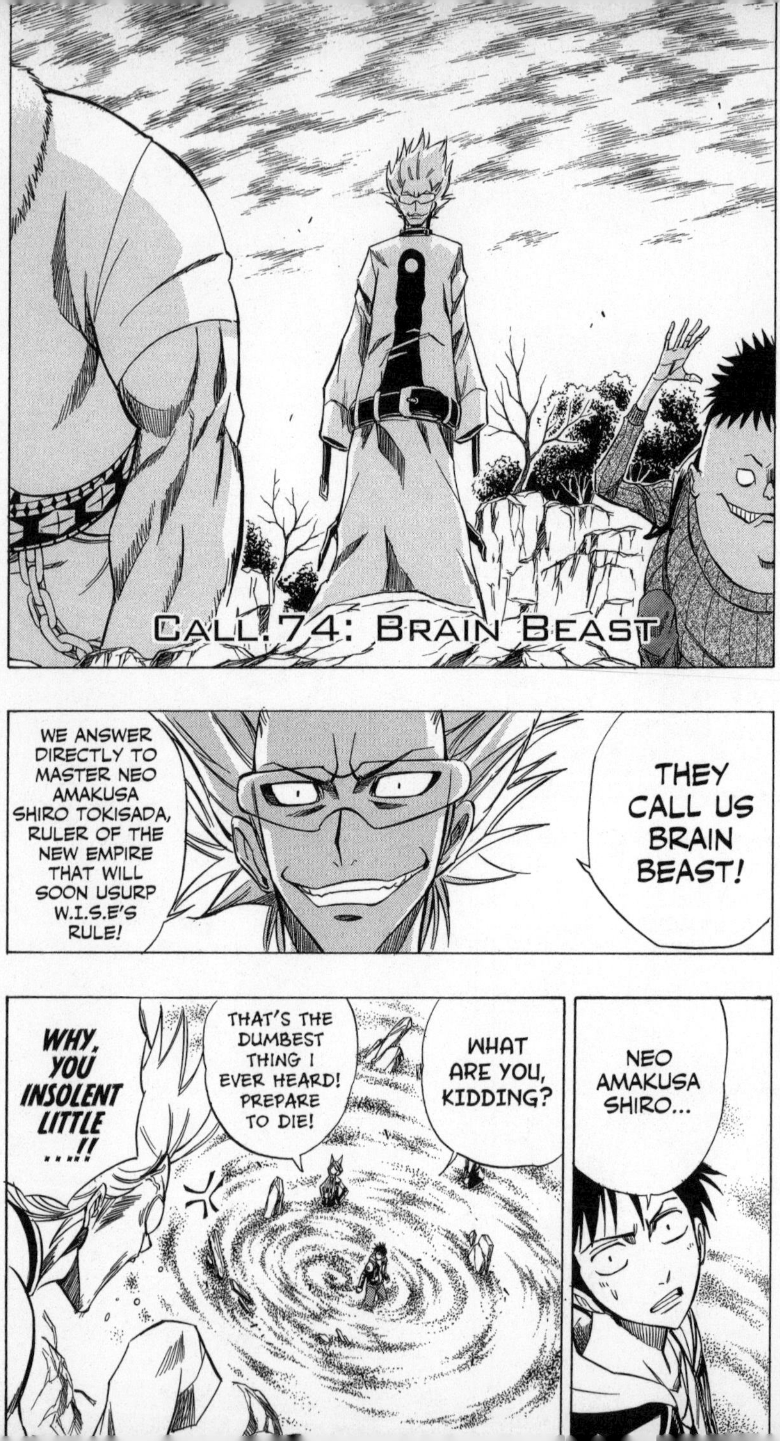
Call.74: Brain Beast
THEY CALL US BRAIN BEAST!
WE ANSWER DIRECTLY TO MASTER NEO AMAKUSA SHIRO TOKISADA, RULER OF THE NEW EMPIRE THAT WILL SOON USURP W.I.S.E'S RULE!
NEO AMAKUSA SHIRO...
WHAT ARE YOU, KIDDING?
THAT'S THE DUMBEST THING I EVER HEARD! PREPARE TO DIE!
WHY, YOU INSOLENT LITTLE ...!!

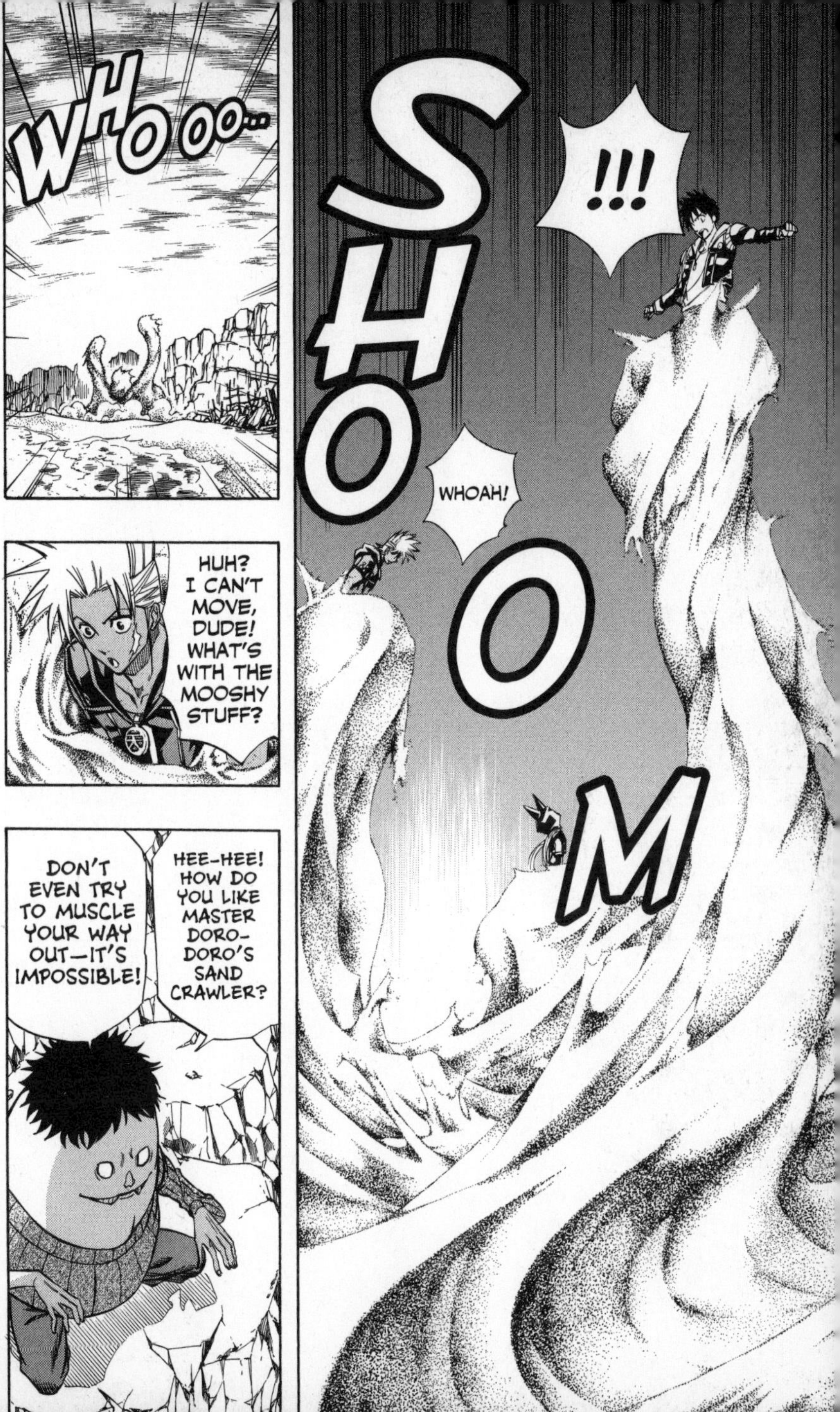
SHOOOM
!!!
WHOAH!
WHOOO...
HUH? I CAN'T MOVE, DUDE! WHAT'S WITH THE MOOSHY STUFF?
HEE-HEE! HOW DO YOU LIKE MASTER DORO-DORO'S SAND CRAWLER?
DON'T EVEN TRY TO MUSCLE YOUR WAY OUT—IT'S IMPOSSIBLE!

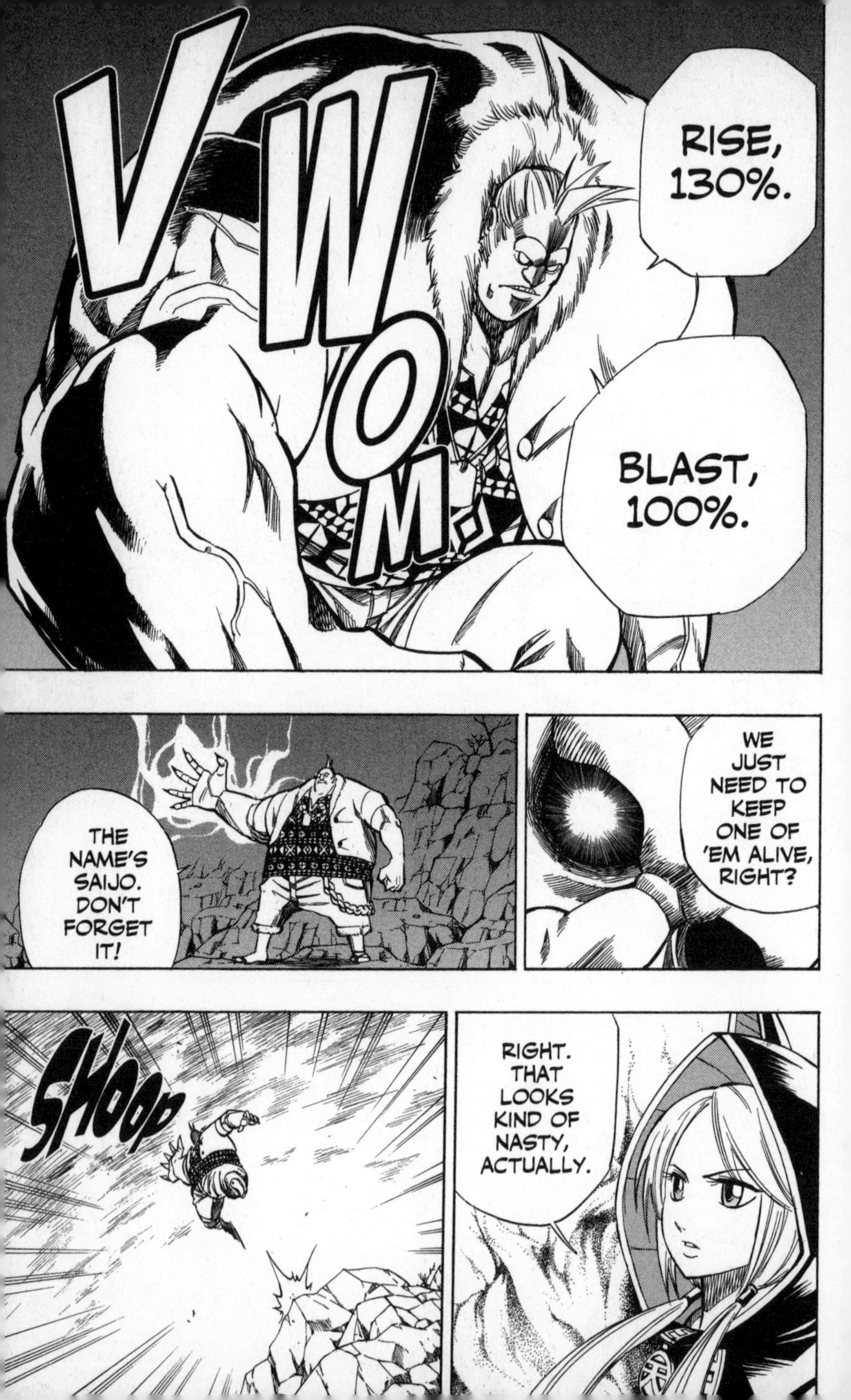
RISE, 130%.
VWOM.
BLAST, 100%.
WE JUST NEED TO KEEP ONE OF 'EM ALIVE, RIGHT?
THE NAME'S SAIJO. DON'T FORGET IT!
RIGHT. THAT LOOKS KIND OF NASTY, ACTUALLY.
SHOOP

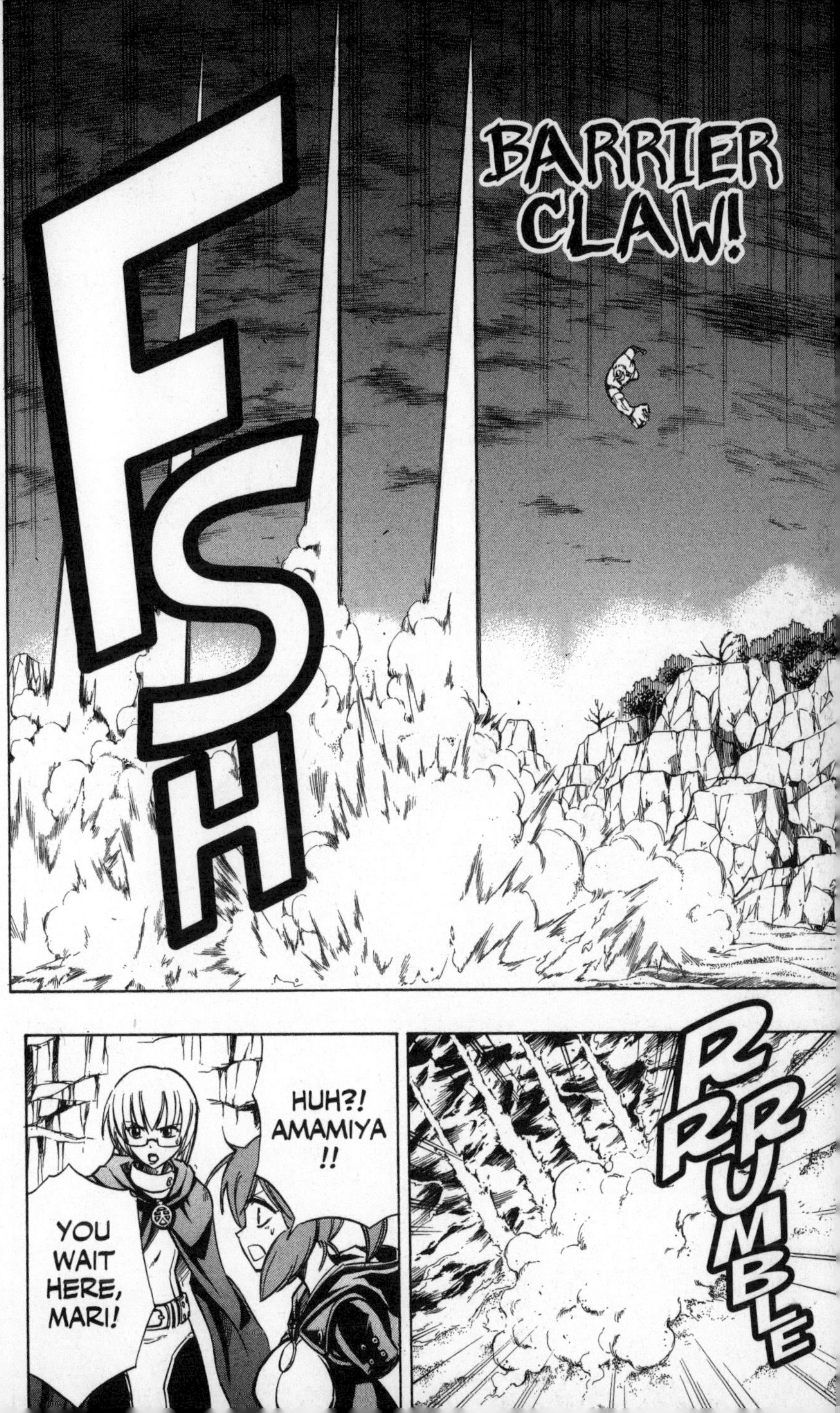
BARRIER CLAW!
FSH
RRRUMBLE
HUH?! AMAMIYA !!
YOU WAIT HERE, MARI!

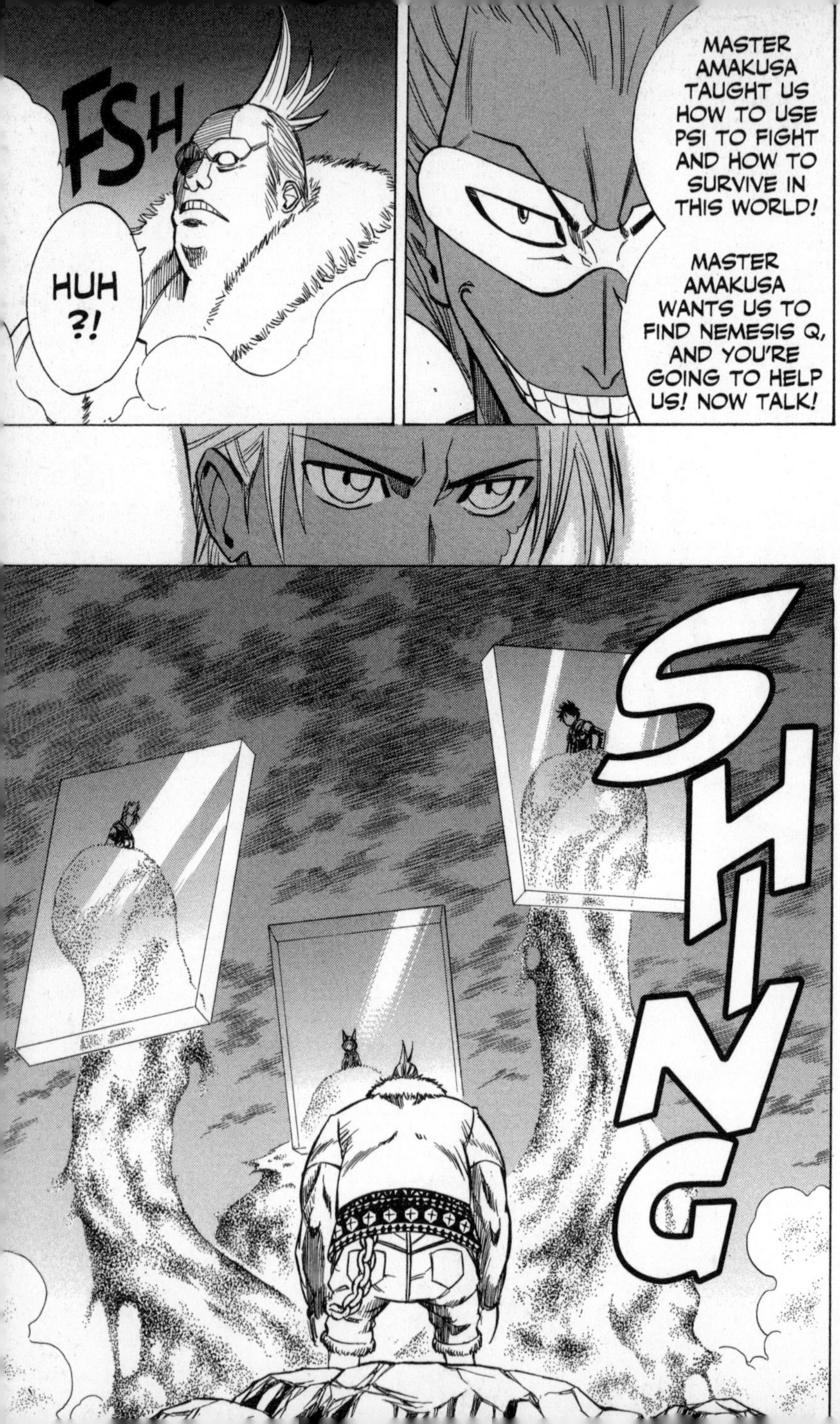
MASTER AMAKUSA TAUGHT US HOW TO USE PSI TO FIGHT AND HOW TO SURVIVE IN THIS WORLD!
MASTER AMAKUSA WANTS US TO FIND NEMESIS Q, AND YOU'RE GOING TO HELP US! NOW TALK!
FSH
HUH?!
SHING

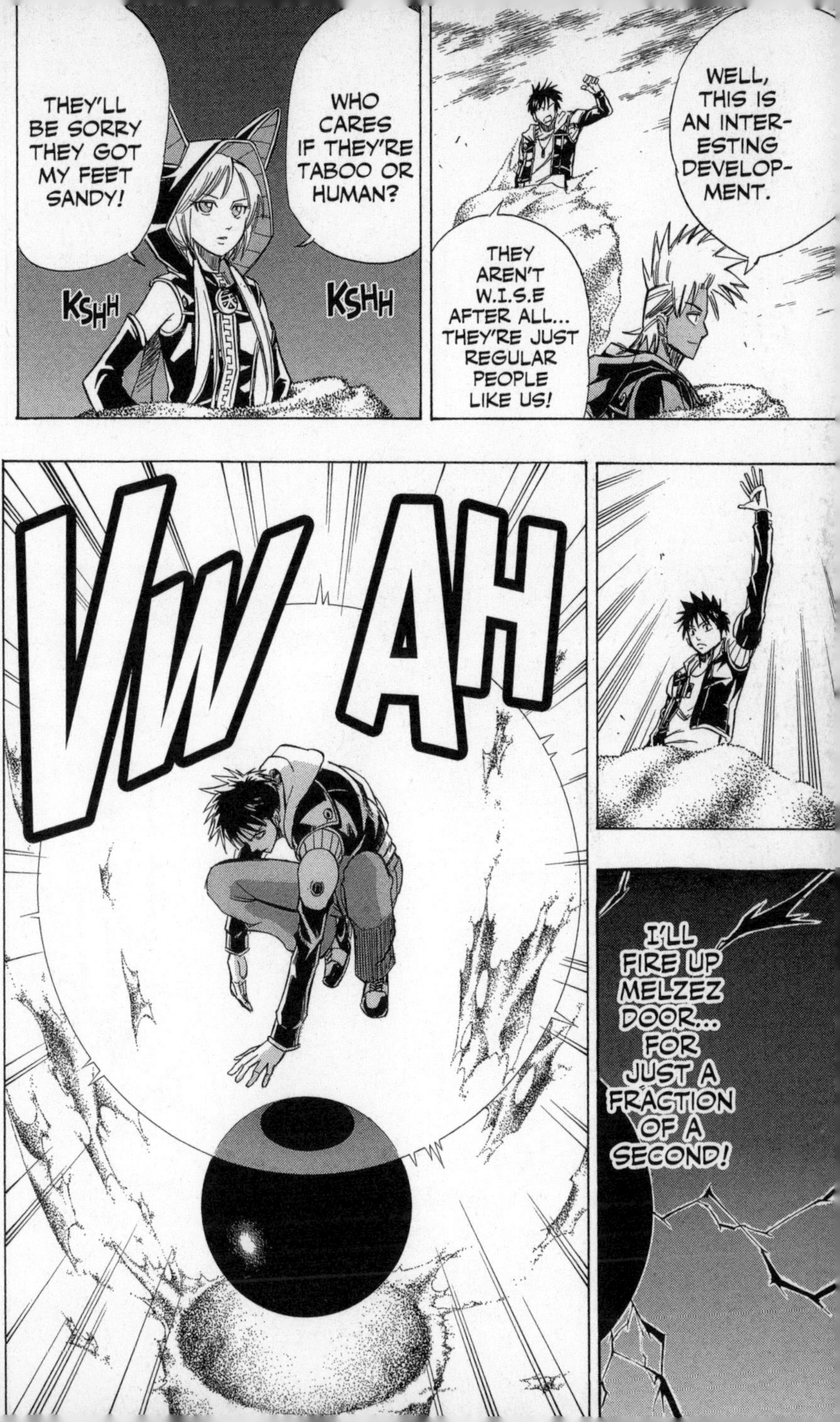
WELL, THIS IS AN INTER-ESTING DEVELOP-MENT.
THEY AREN'T W.I.S.E AFTER ALL... THEY'RE JUST REGULAR PEOPLE LIKE US!
WHO CARES IF THEY'RE TABOO OR HUMAN?
THEY'LL BE SORRY THEY GOT MY FEET SANDY!
KSHH
KSHH
I'LL FIRE UP MELZEZ DOOR... FOR JUST A FRACTION OF A SECOND!
VW AH

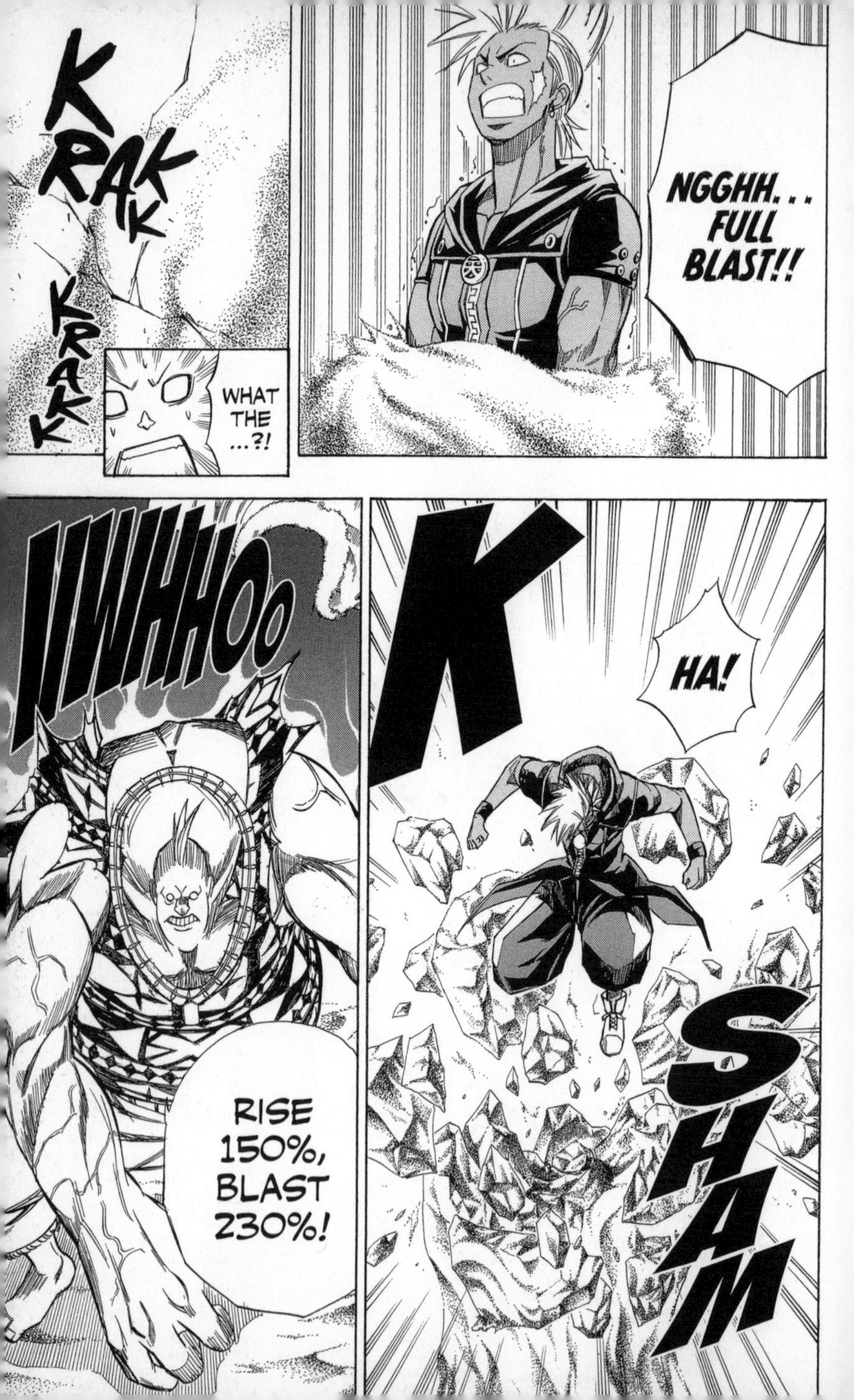
NGGHH... FULL BLAST!!
KRAKKK
KRAKK
WHAT THE ...?!
K
HA!
SHAM
WHHOO
RISE 150%, BLAST 230%!

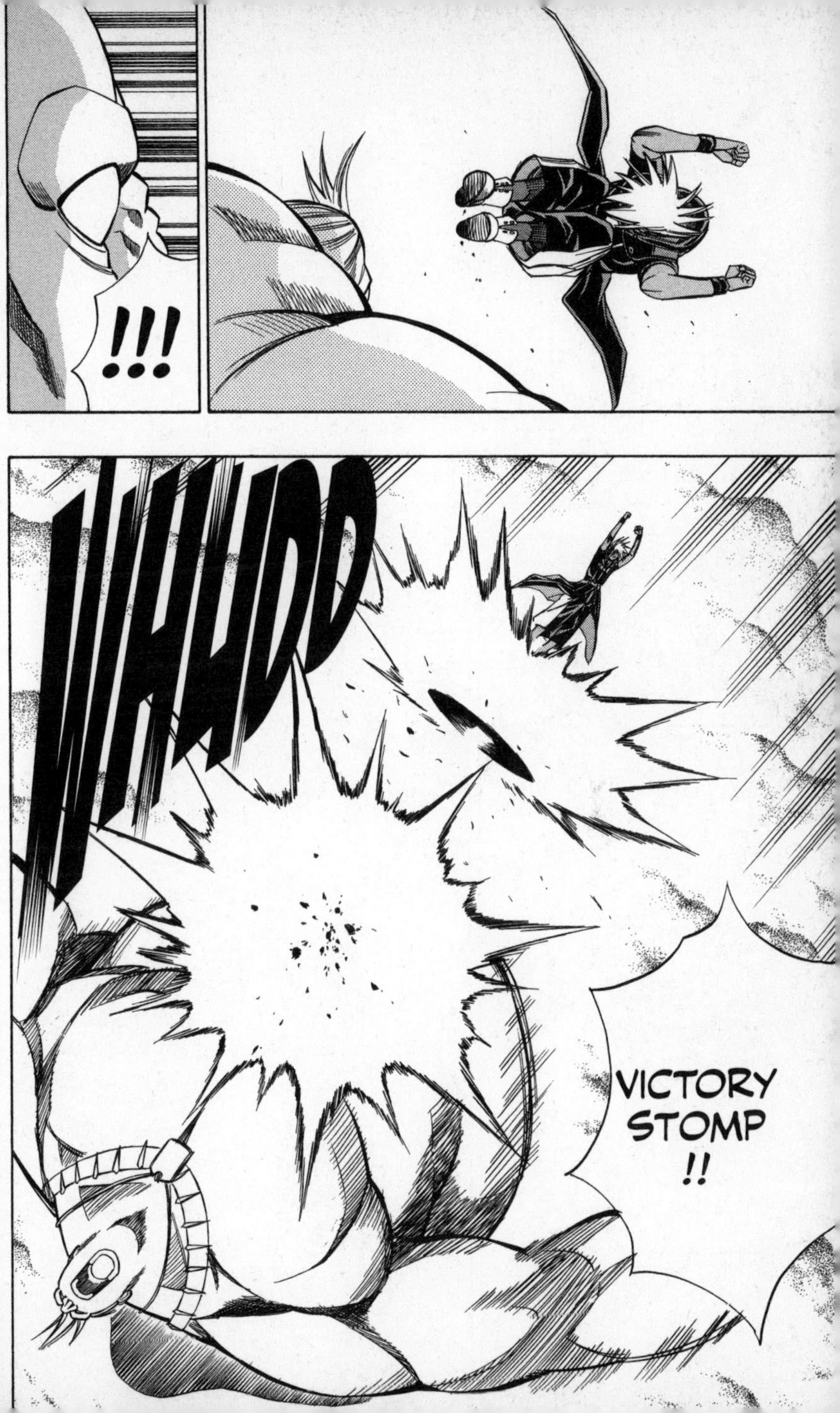
!!!
WHUDD
VICTORY STOMP !!

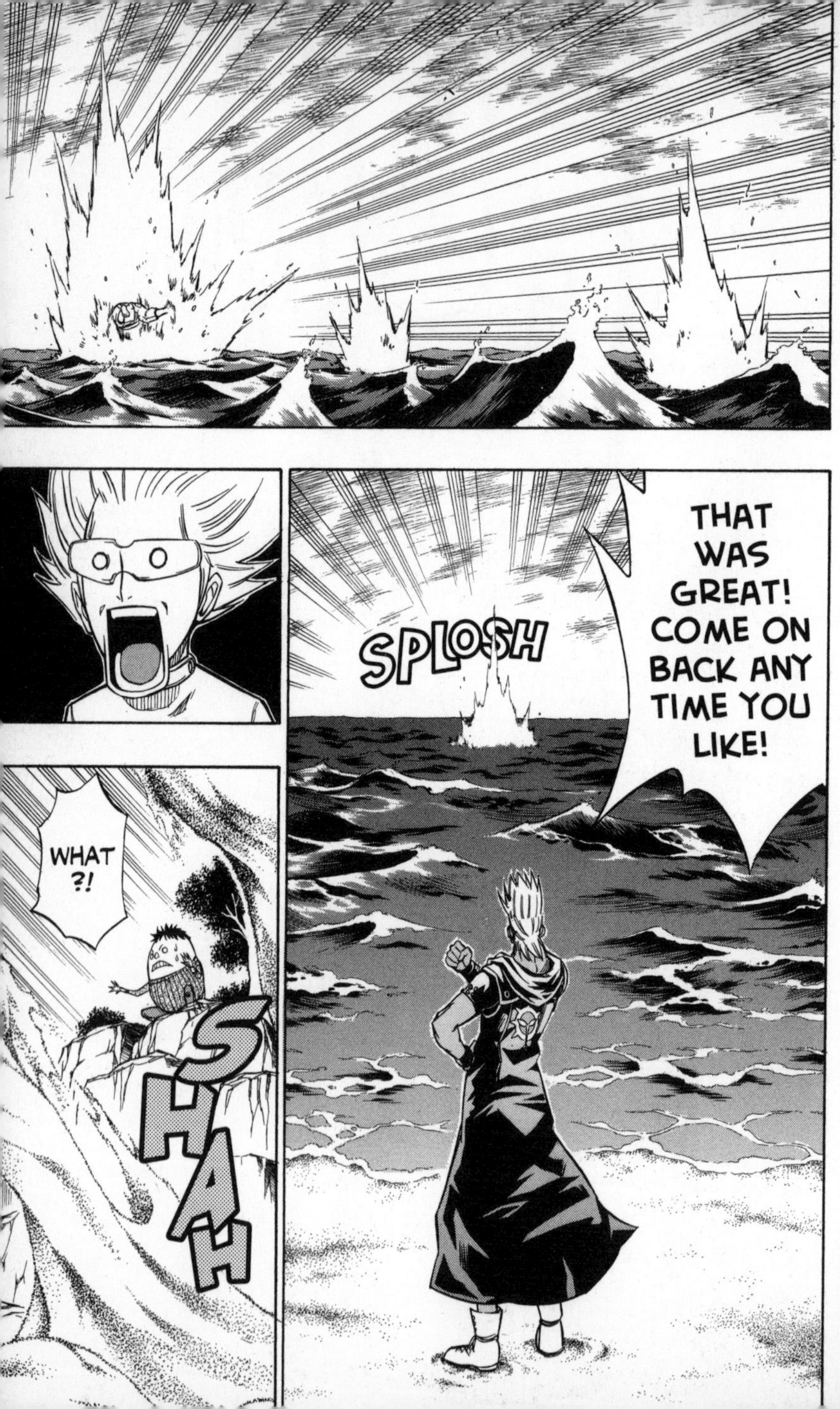
THAT WAS GREAT! COME ON BACK ANY TIME YOU LIKE!
SPLOSH
WHAT?!
SHAAH

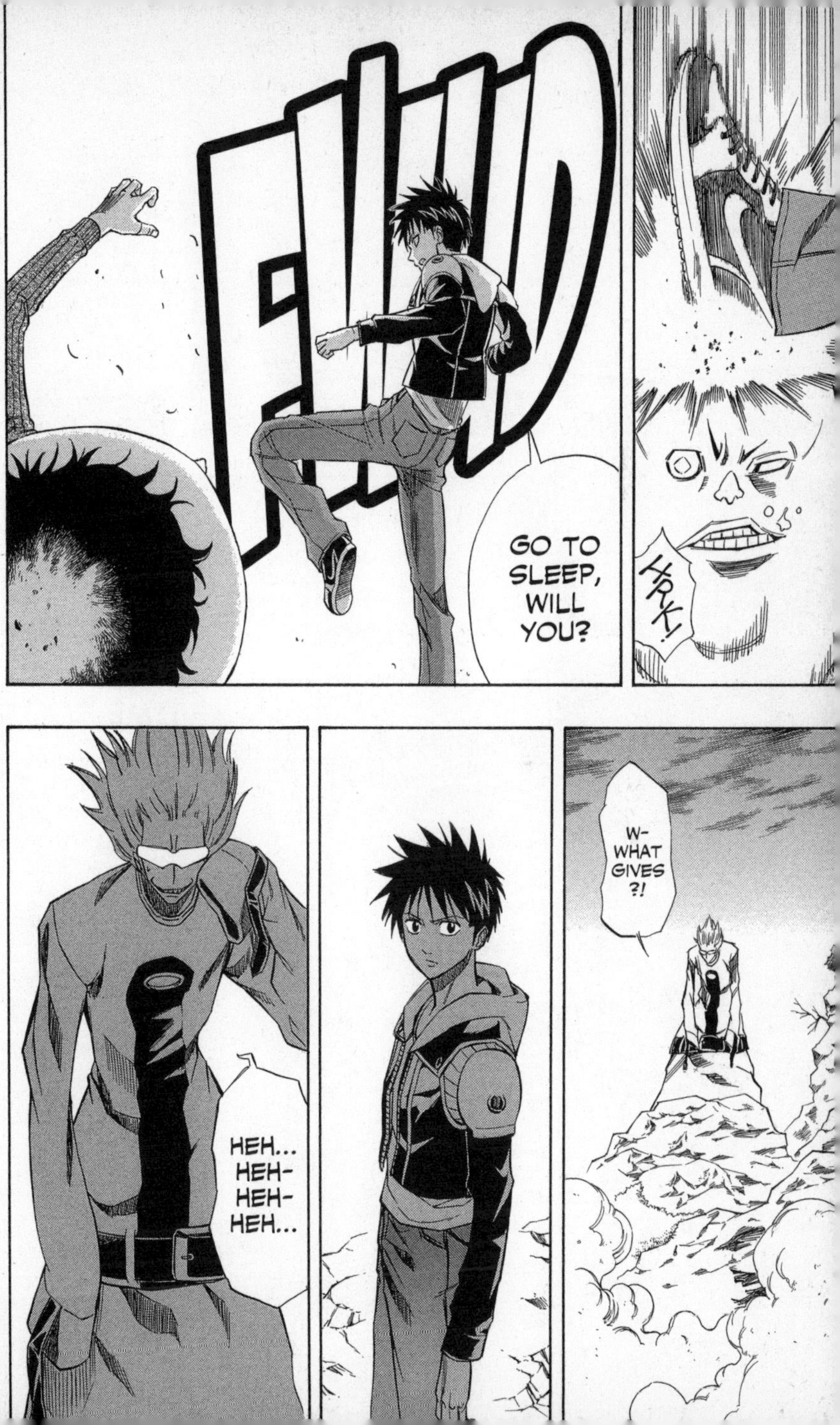
HRK!
GO TO SLEEP, WILL YOU?
W-WHAT GIVES?!
HEH... HEH-HEH-HEH...

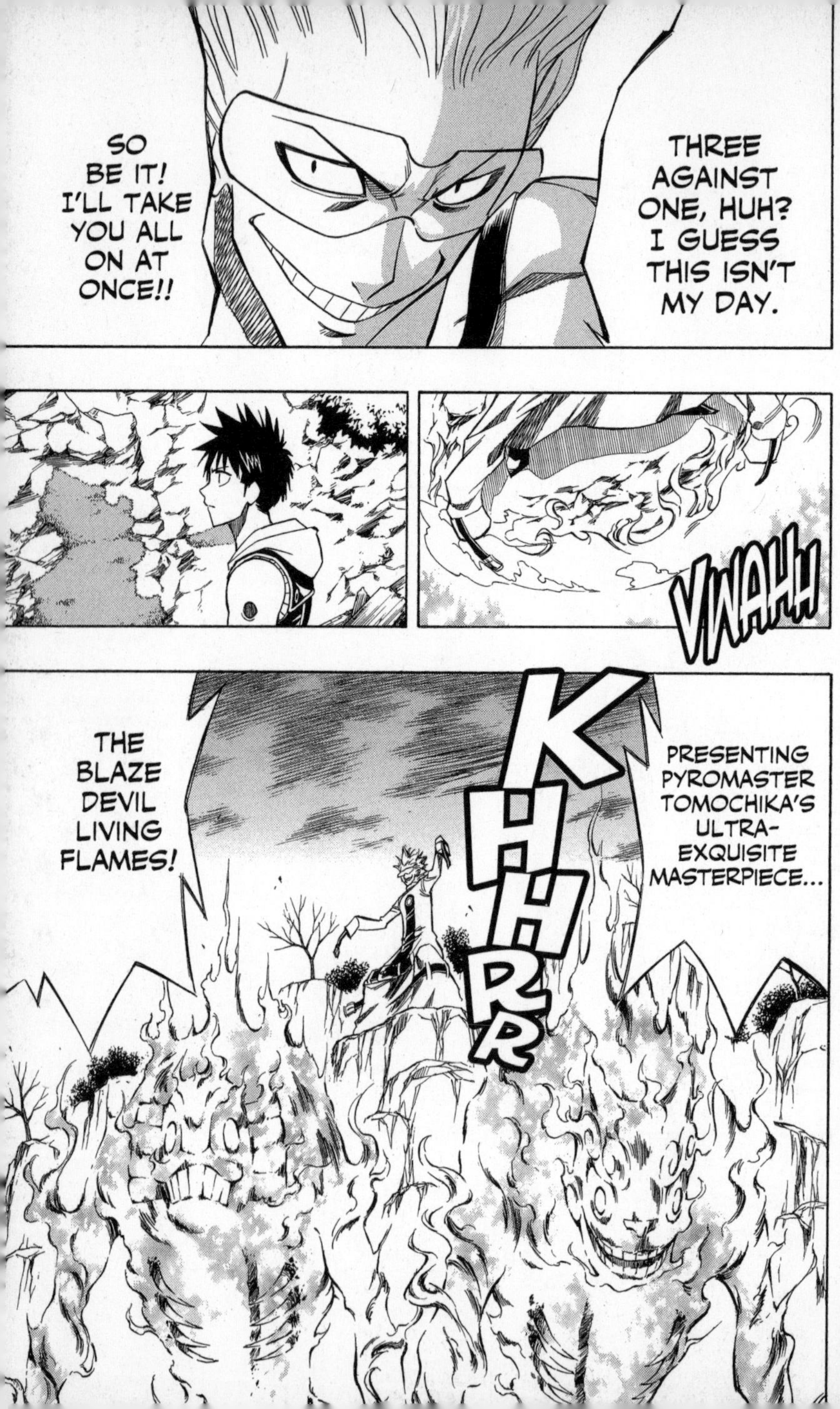
THREE AGAINST ONE, HUH? I GUESS THIS ISN'T MY DAY.
SO BE IT! I'LL TAKE YOU ALL ON AT ONCE!!
VWAHH
PRESENTING PYROMASTER TOMOCHIKA'S ULTRA-EXQUISITE MASTERPIECE...
KHHHRR
THE BLAZE DEVIL LIVING FLAMES!

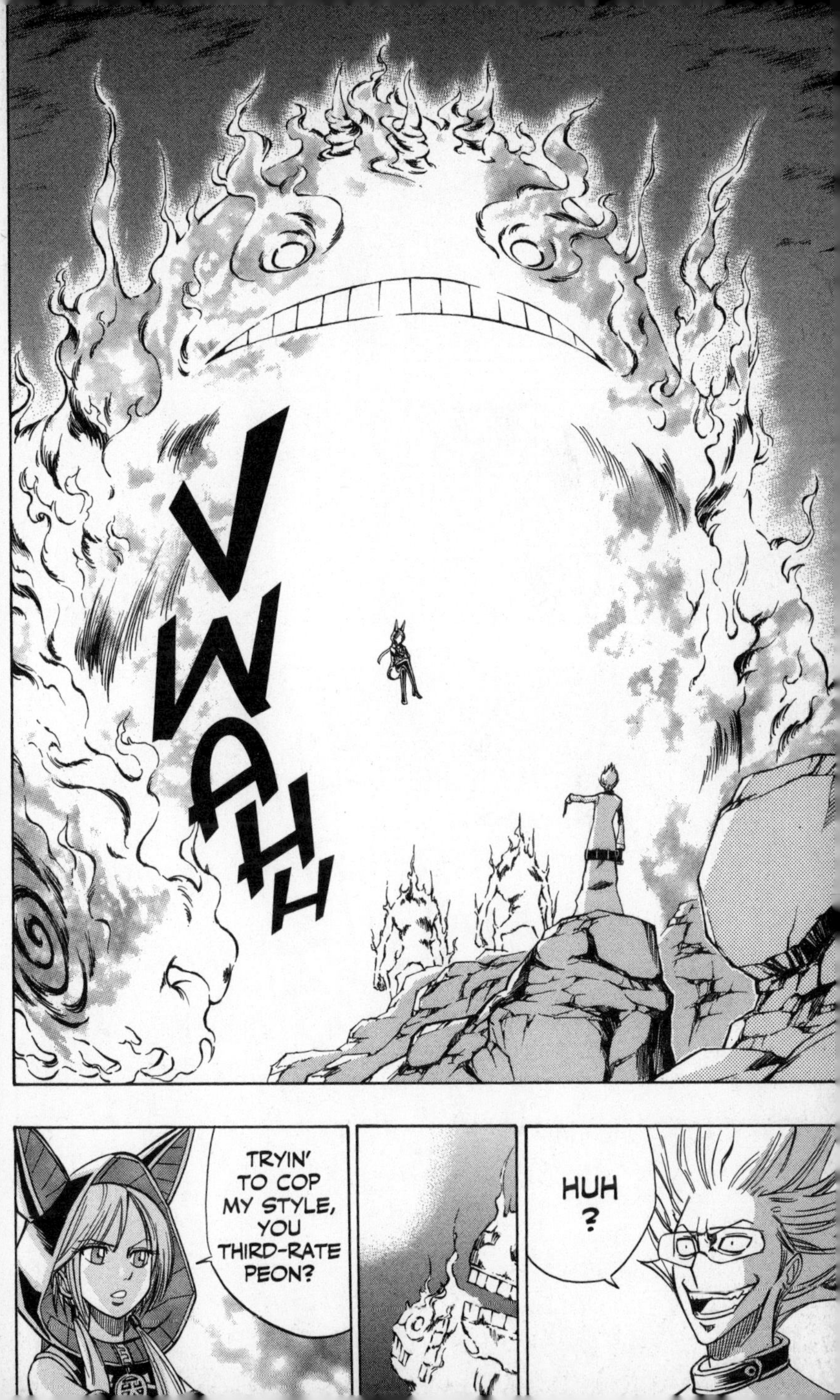
VWAHH
HUH ?
TRYIN' TO COP MY STYLE, YOU THIRD-RATE PEON?

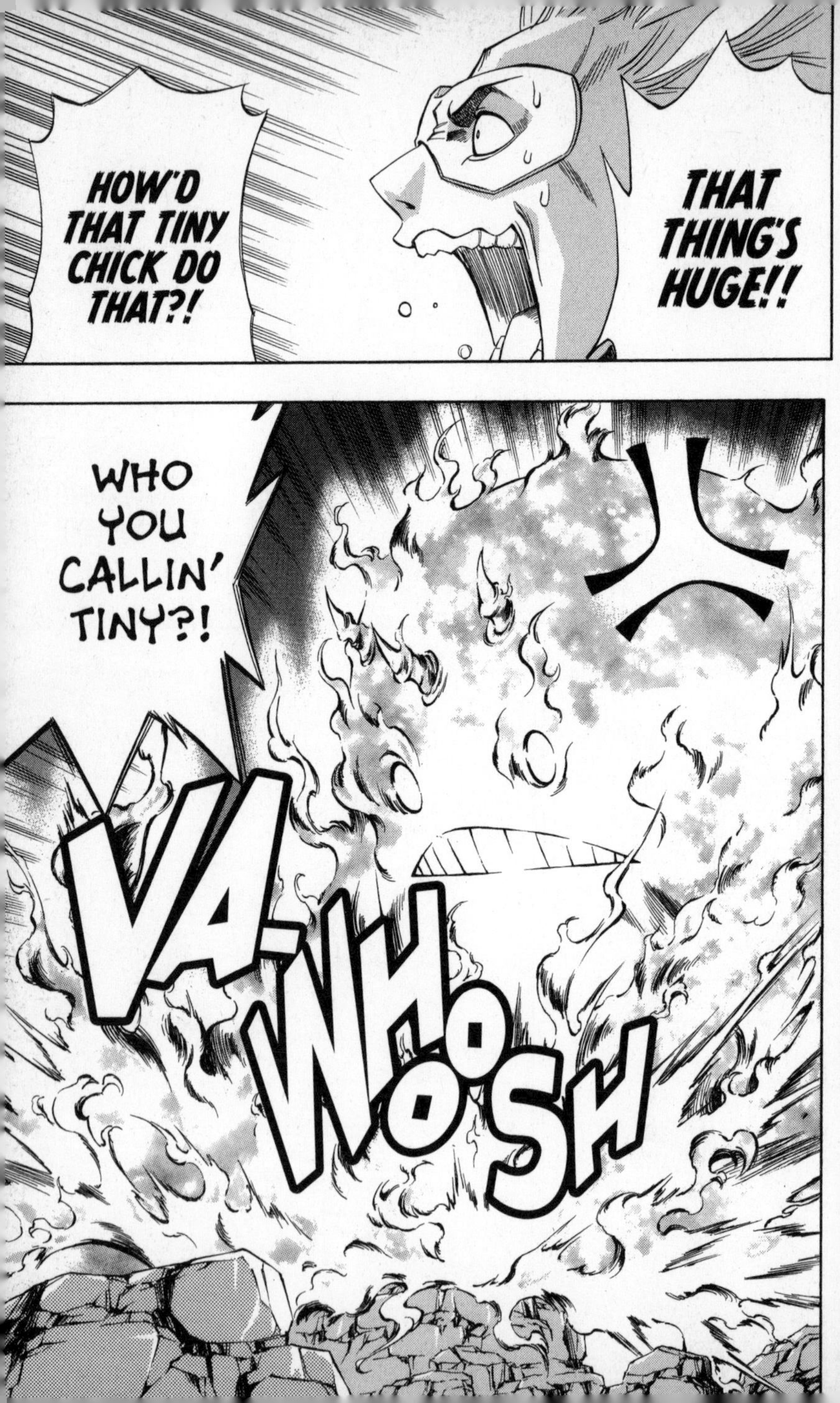
THAT THING'S HUGE!!
HOW'D THAT TINY CHICK DO THAT?!
WHO YOU CALLIN' TINY?!
VA-WHOOSH

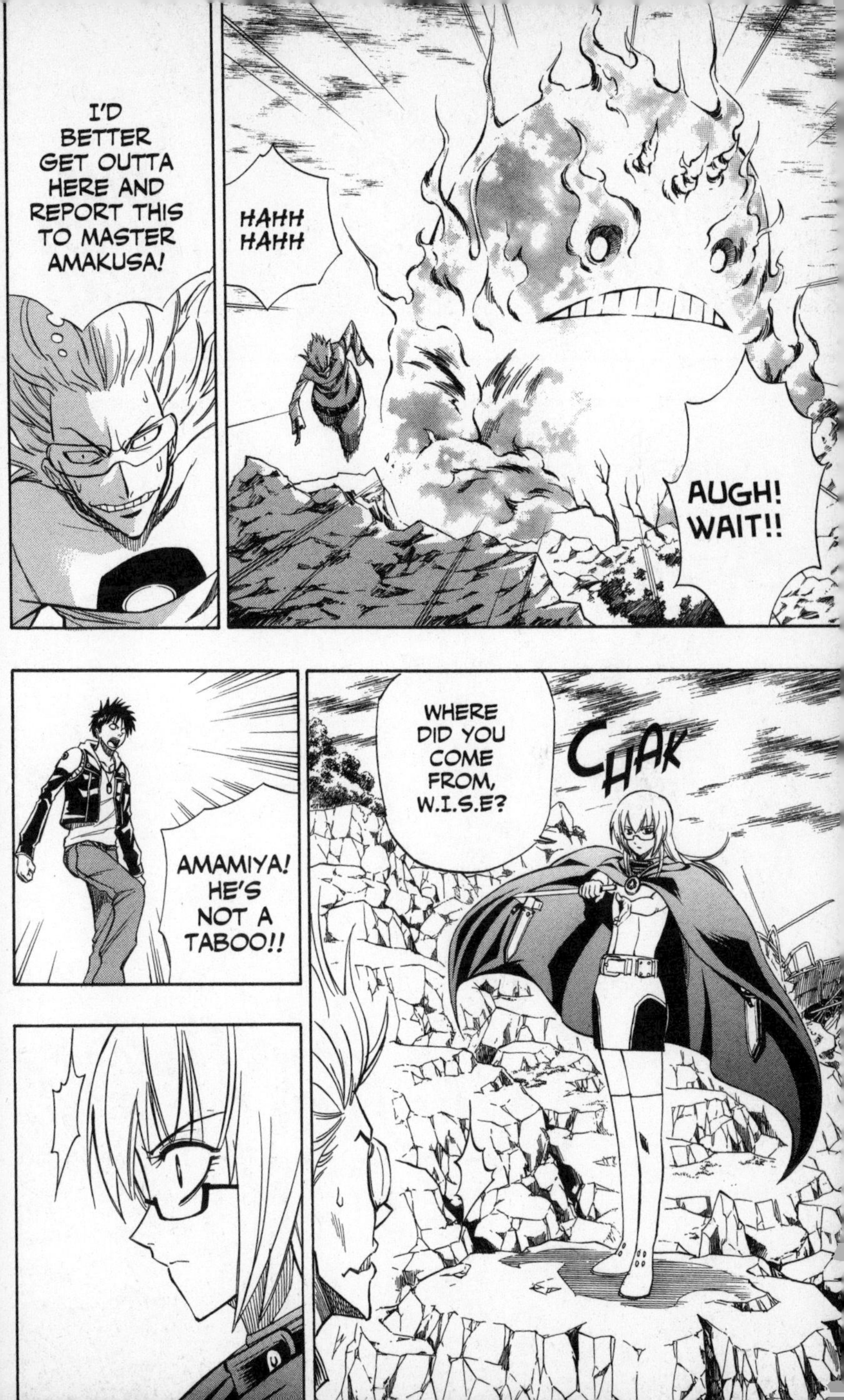
HAHH HAHH
AUGH! WAIT!!
I'D BETTER GET OUTTA HERE AND REPORT THIS TO MASTER AMAKUSA!
CHAK
WHERE DID YOU COME FROM, W.I.S.E?
AMAMIYA! HE'S NOT A TABOO!!

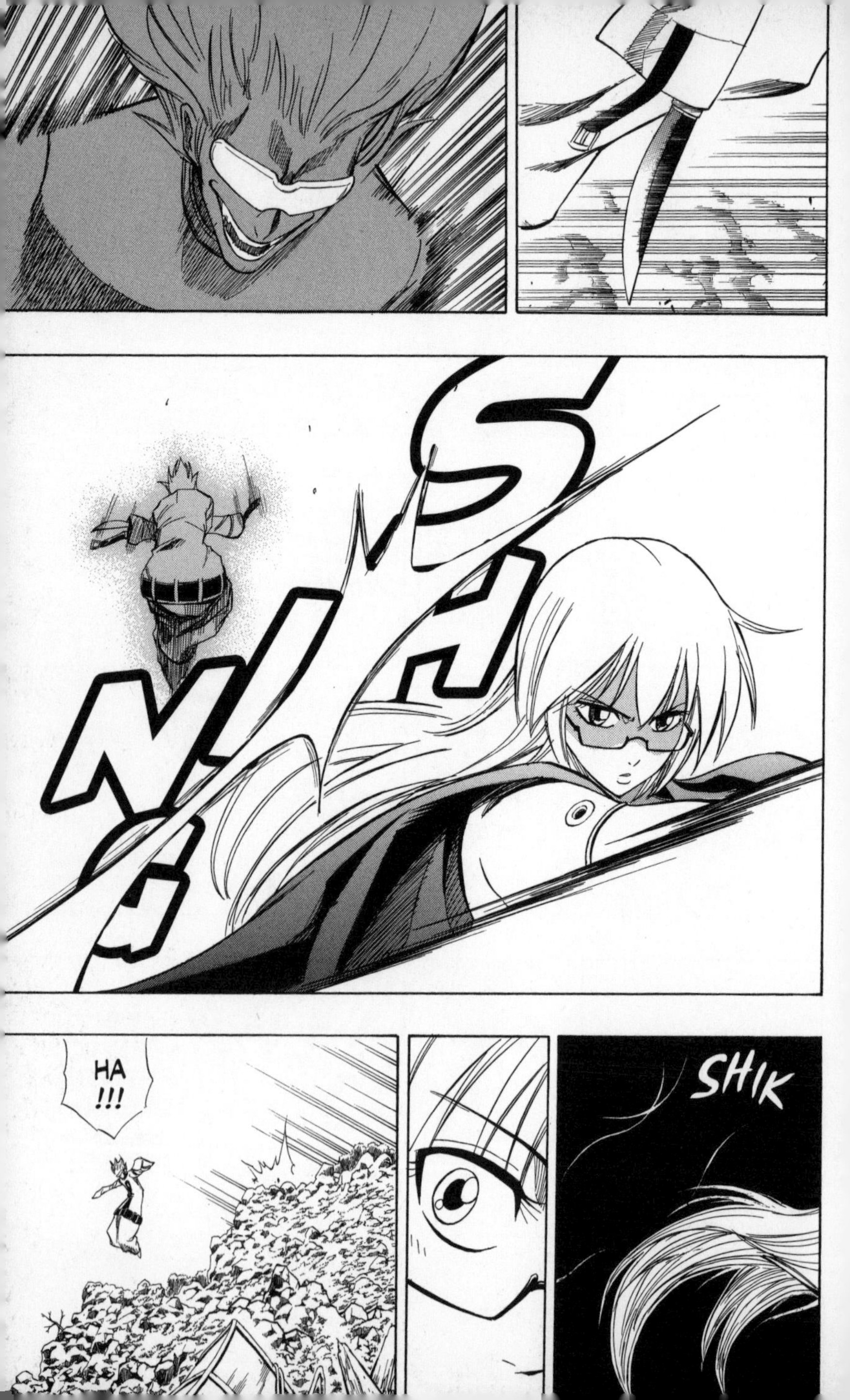
SHIK
HA !!!

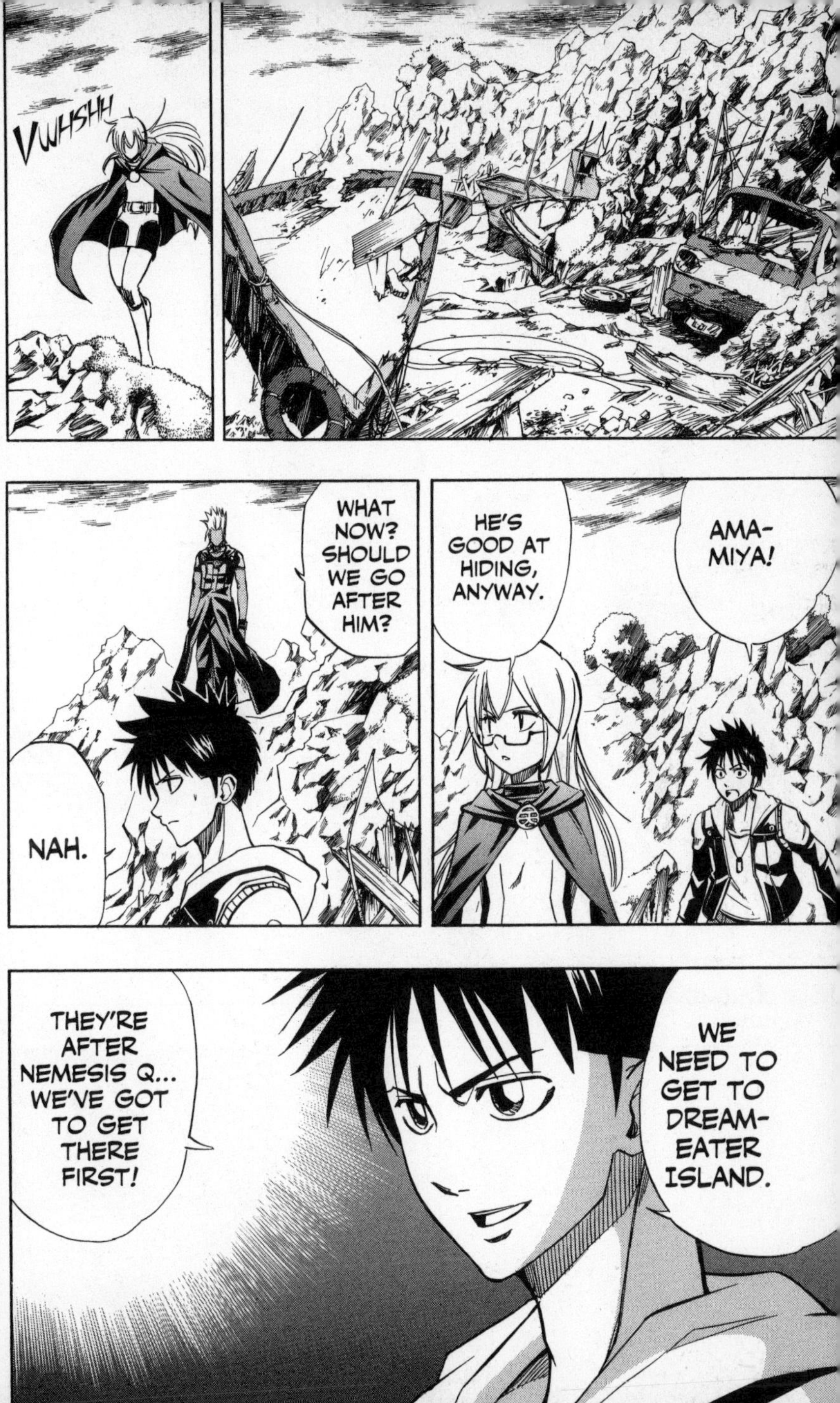
VWHSHH
AMA-MIYA!
HE'S GOOD AT HIDING, ANYWAY.
WHAT NOW? SHOULD WE GO AFTER HIM?
NAH.
WE NEED TO GET TO DREAM-EATER ISLAND.
THEY'RE AFTER NEMESIS Q... WE'VE GOT TO GET THERE FIRST!

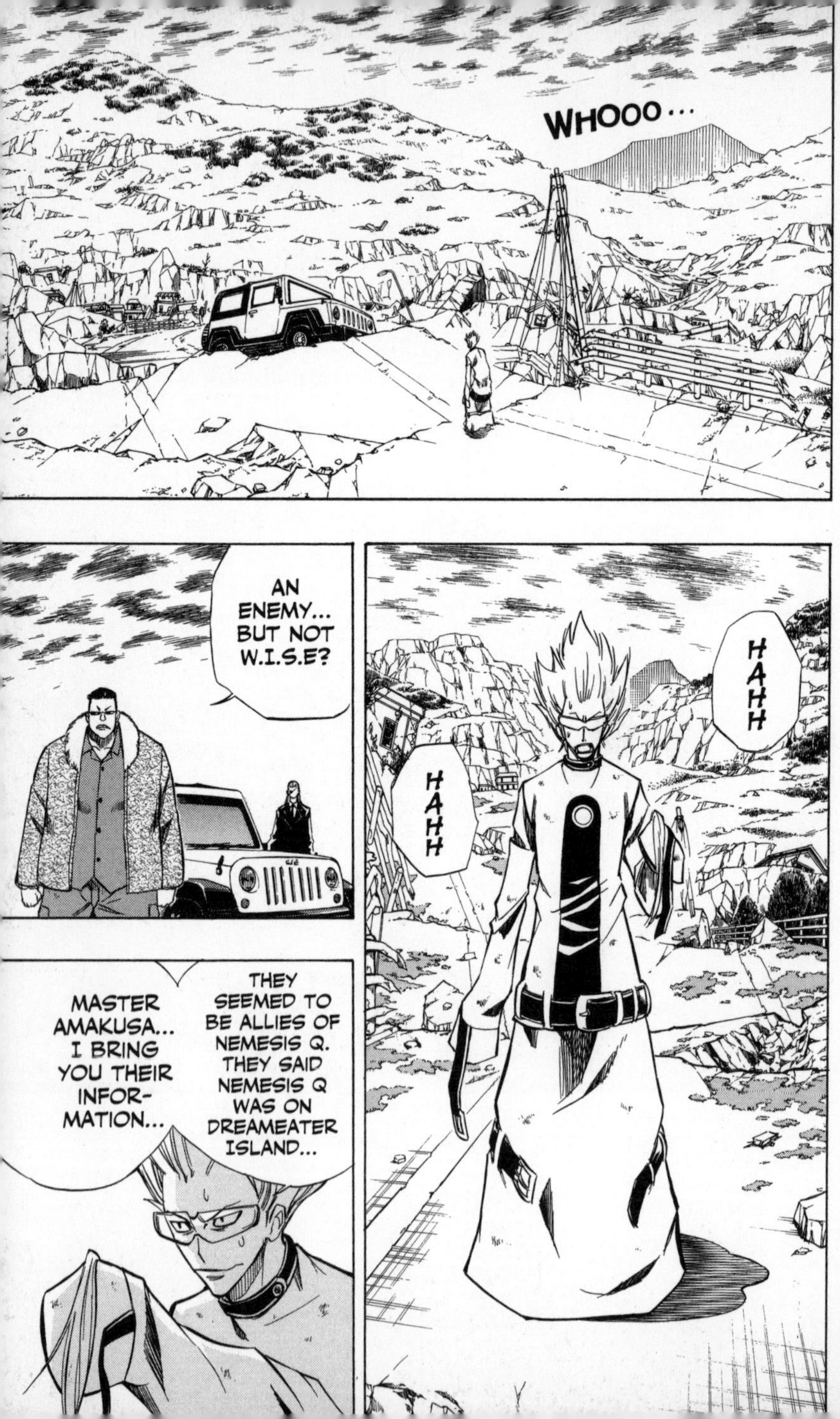
WHOOO...
HAHH
HAHH
AN ENEMY... BUT NOT W.I.S.E?
THEY SEEMED TO BE ALLIES OF NEMESIS Q. THEY SAID NEMESIS Q WAS ON DREAMEATER ISLAND...
MASTER AMAKUSA... I BRING YOU THEIR INFOR-MATION...

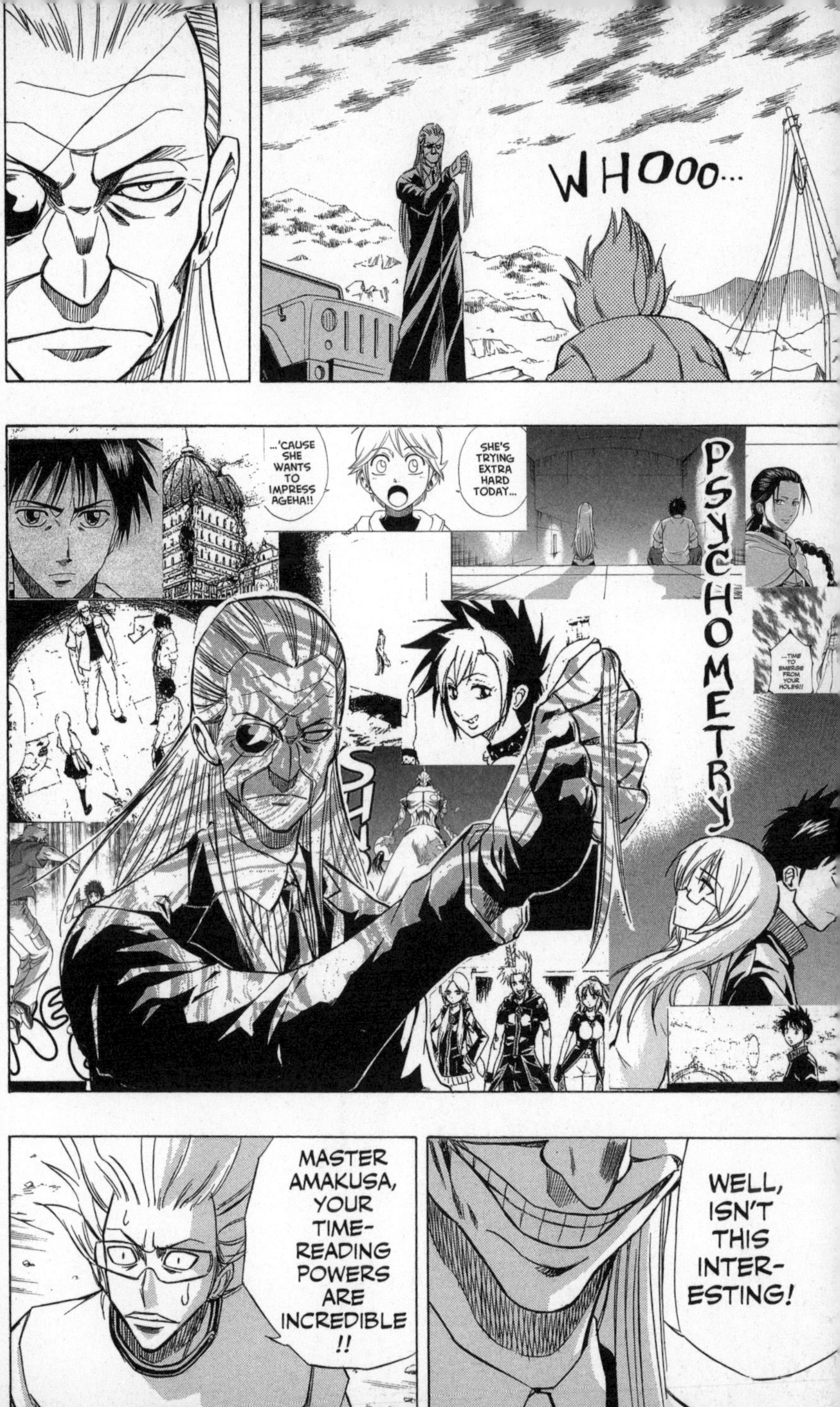
WHOOO...
PSYCHOMETRY
...TIME TO EMERGE FROM YOUR HOLES!!
SHE'S TRYING EXTRA HARD TODAY...
...'CAUSE SHE WANTS TO IMPRESS AGEHA!!
WELL, ISN'T THIS INTER-ESTING!
MASTER AMAKUSA, YOUR TIME-READING POWERS ARE INCREDIBLE!!

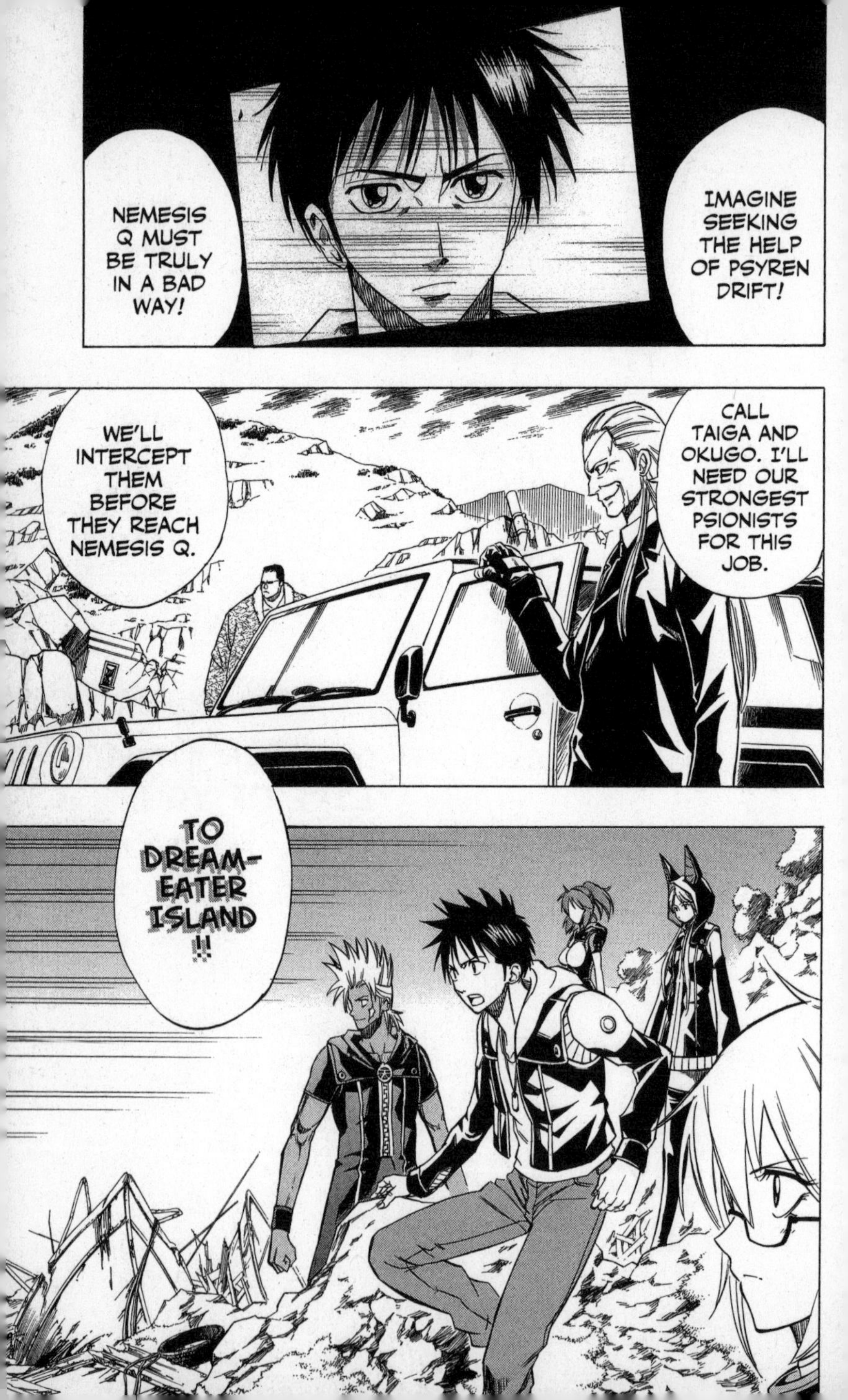
IMAGINE SEEKING THE HELP OF PSYREN DRIFT!
NEMESIS Q MUST BE TRULY IN A BAD WAY!
CALL TAIGA AND OKUGO. I'LL NEED OUR STRONGEST PSIONISTS FOR THIS JOB.
WE'LL INTERCEPT THEM BEFORE THEY REACH NEMESIS Q.
TO DREAM-EATER ISLAND!!

A DAY IN THE LIFE OF VAN

1:30 PM AFTERNOON STROLL

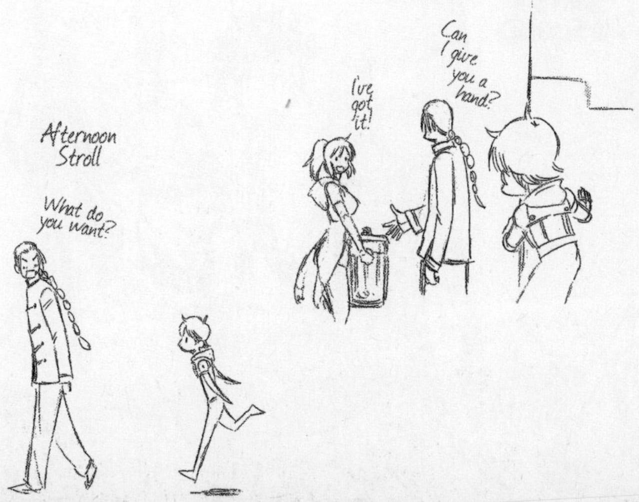
Can I give you a hand?
I've got it!
Afternoon Stroll
What do you want?

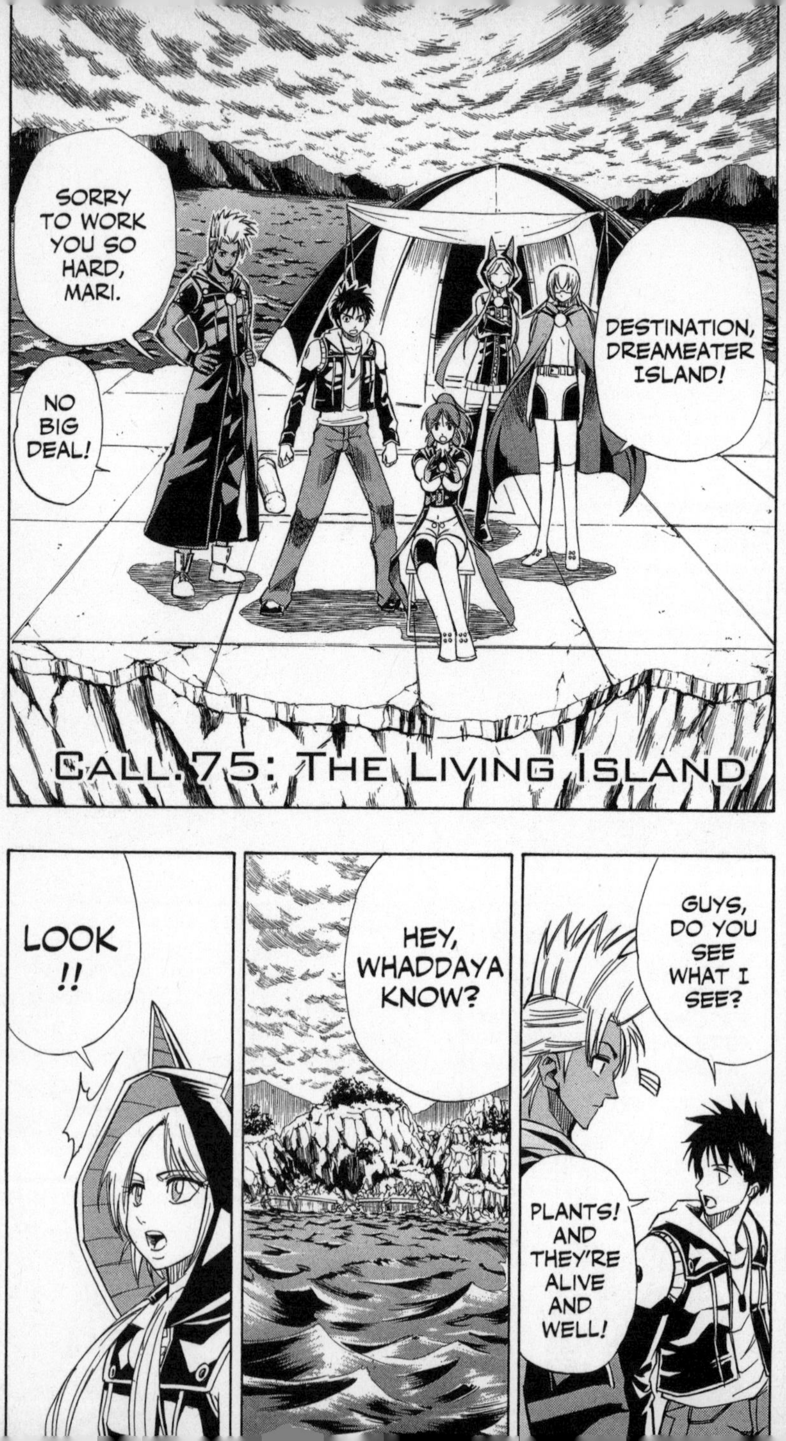
DESTINATION, DREAMEATER ISLAND!
SORRY TO WORK YOU SO HARD, MARI.
NO BIG DEAL!
CALL. 75: THE LIVING ISLAND
GUYS, DO YOU SEE WHAT I SEE?
PLANTS! AND THEY'RE ALIVE AND WELL!
HEY, WHADDAYA KNOW?
LOOK!!

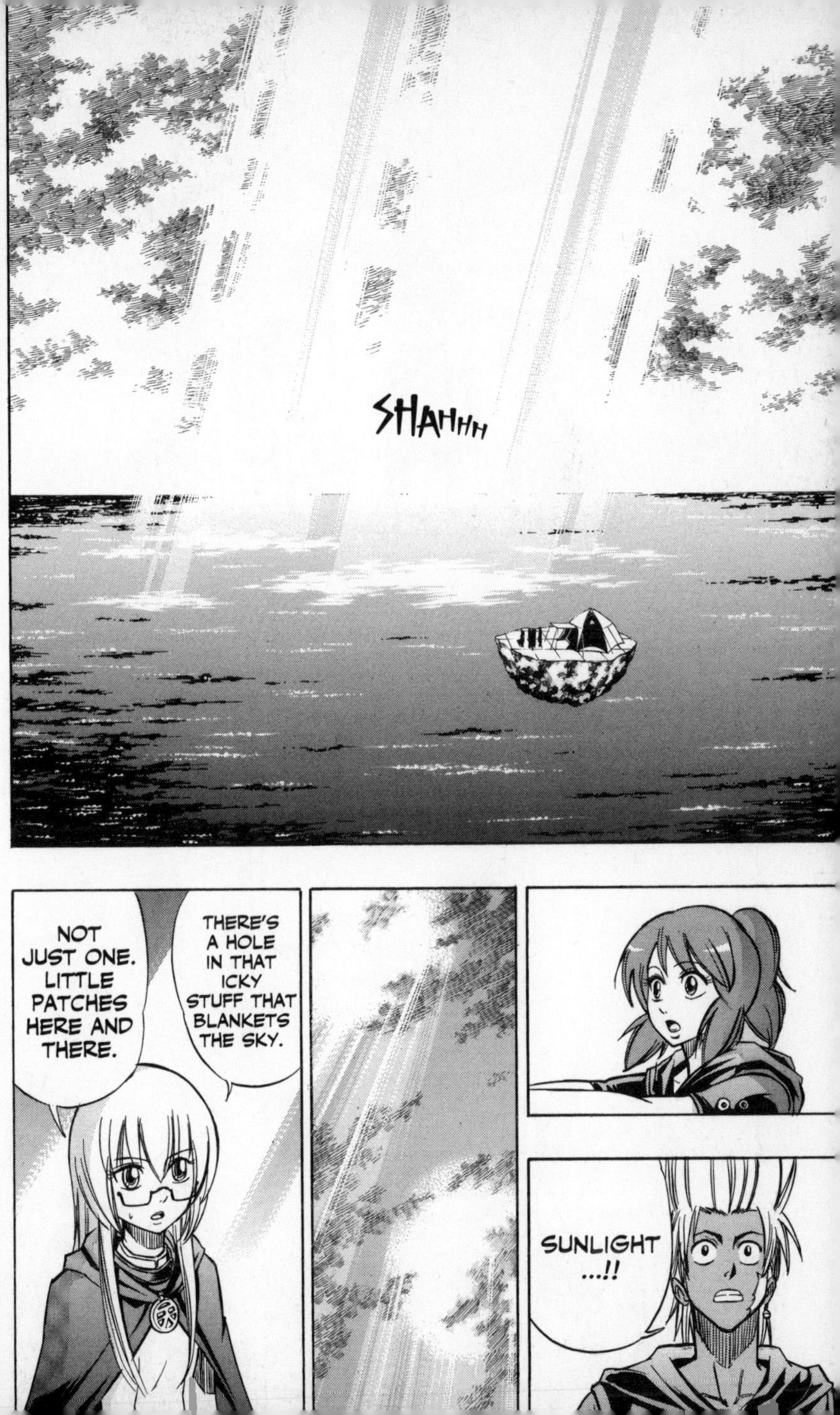
SHAHHH
SUNLIGHT ...!!
THERE'S A HOLE IN THAT ICKY STUFF THAT BLANKETS THE SKY.
NOT JUST ONE. LITTLE PATCHES HERE AND THERE.

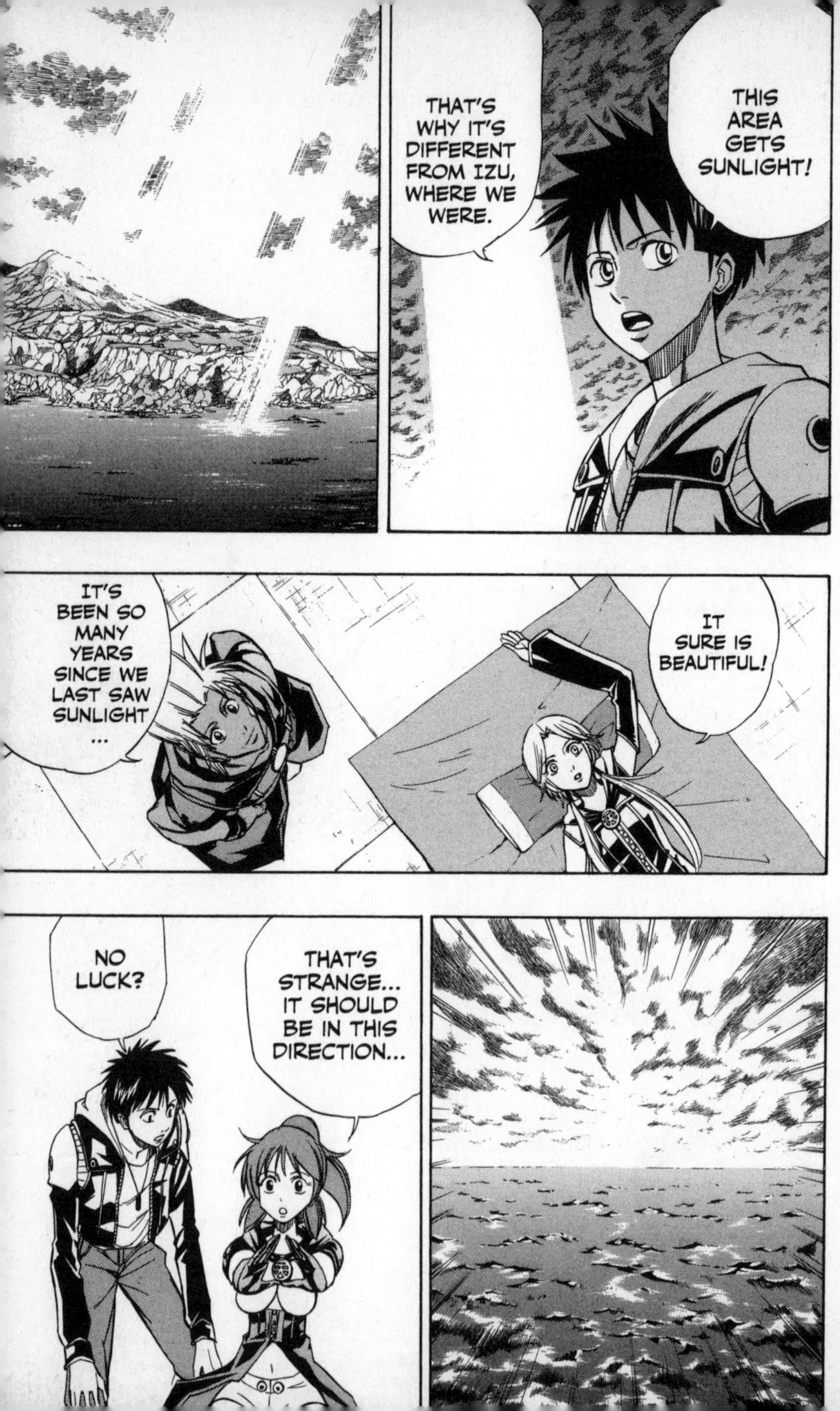
THIS AREA GETS SUNLIGHT!
THAT'S WHY IT'S DIFFERENT FROM IZU, WHERE WE WERE.
IT SURE IS BEAUTIFUL!
IT'S BEEN SO MANY YEARS SINCE WE LAST SAW SUNLIGHT ...
THAT'S STRANGE... IT SHOULD BE IN THIS DIRECTION...
NO LUCK?

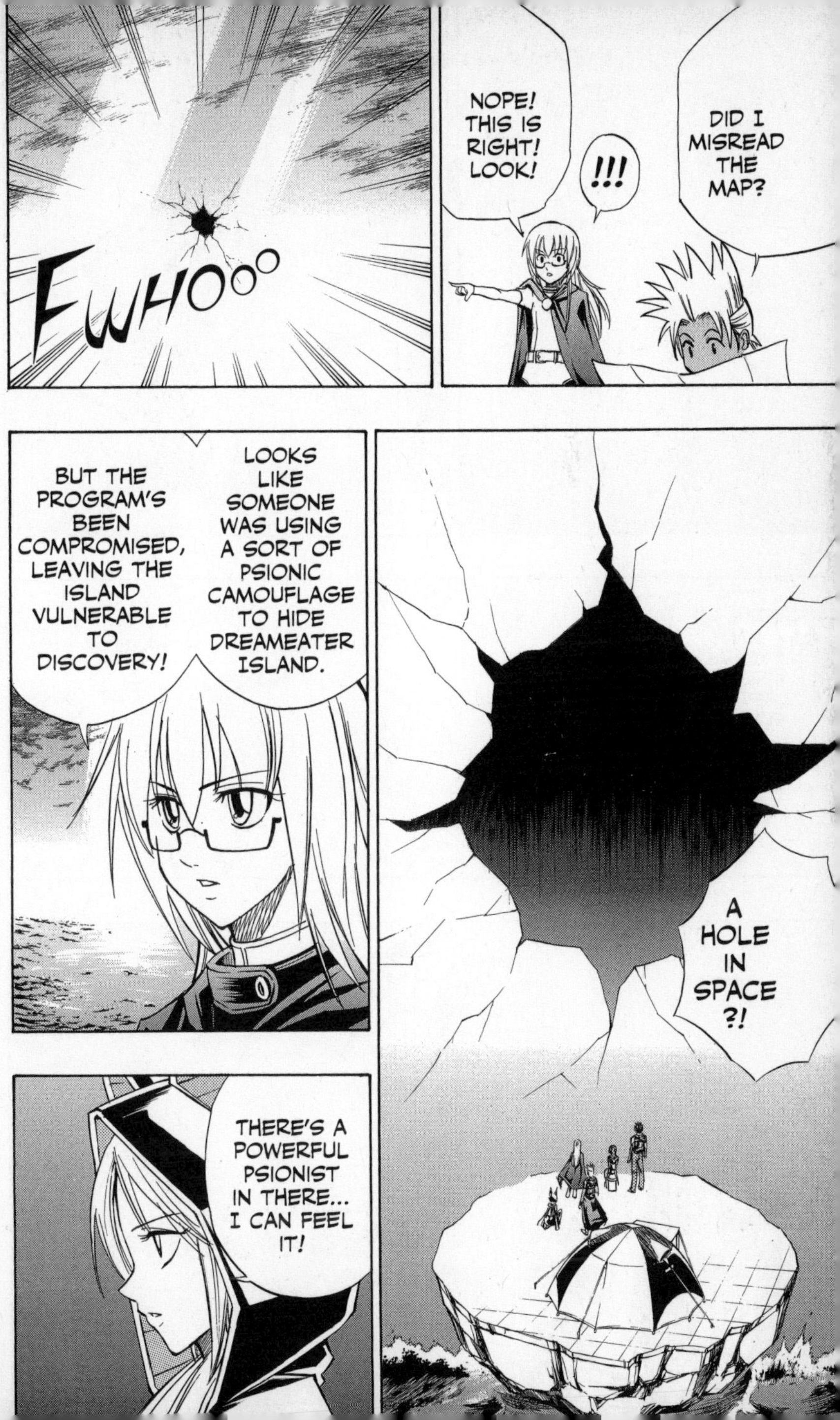
DID I MISREAD THE MAP?
!!!
NOPE! THIS IS RIGHT! LOOK!
FWHOOO
A HOLE IN SPACE?!
LOOKS LIKE SOMEONE WAS USING A SORT OF PSIONIC CAMOUFLAGE TO HIDE DREAMEATER ISLAND.
BUT THE PROGRAM'S BEEN COMPROMISED, LEAVING THE ISLAND VULNERABLE TO DISCOVERY!
THERE'S A POWERFUL PSIONIST IN THERE... I CAN FEEL IT!

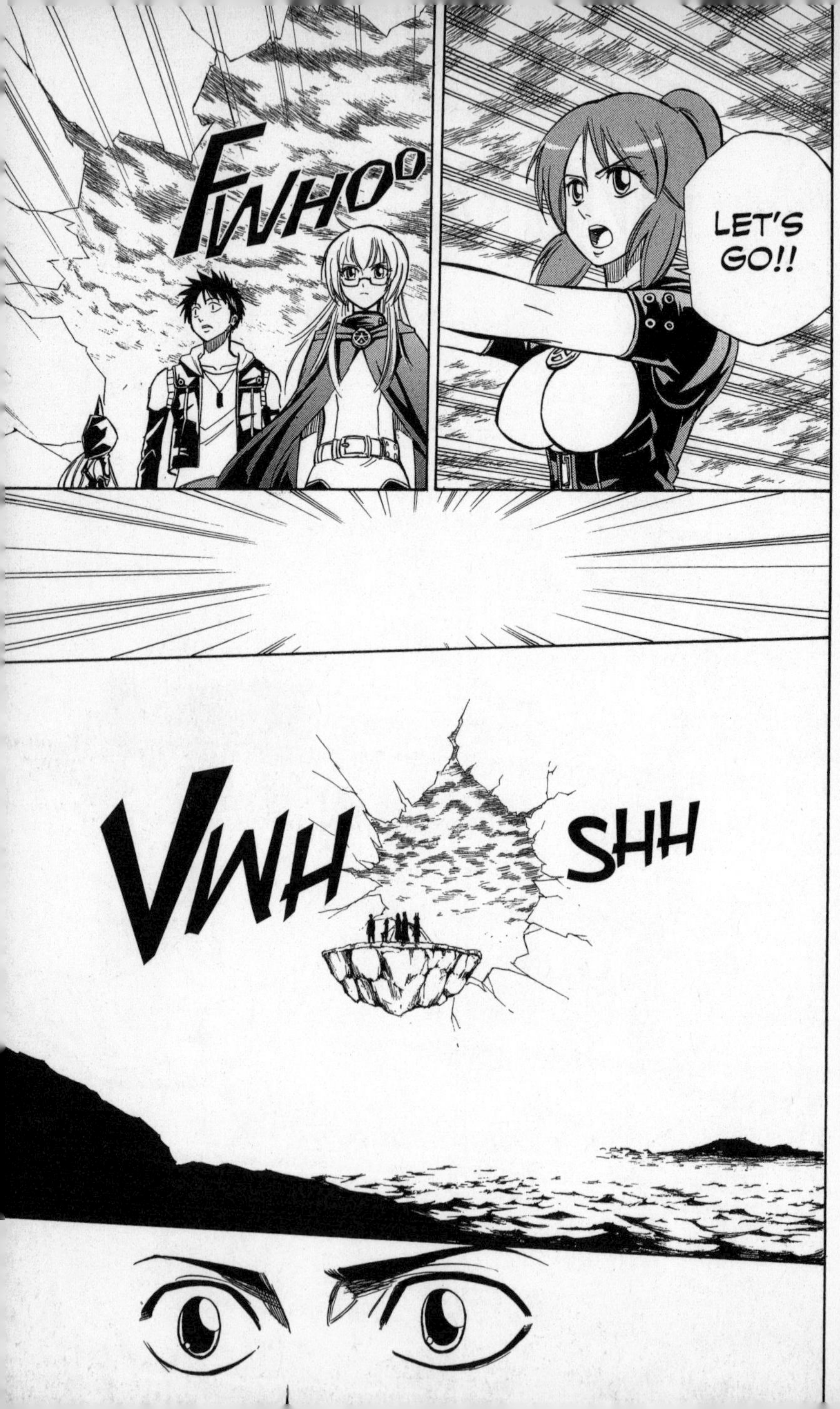
LET'S GO!!
FWHOO
VWHSHH

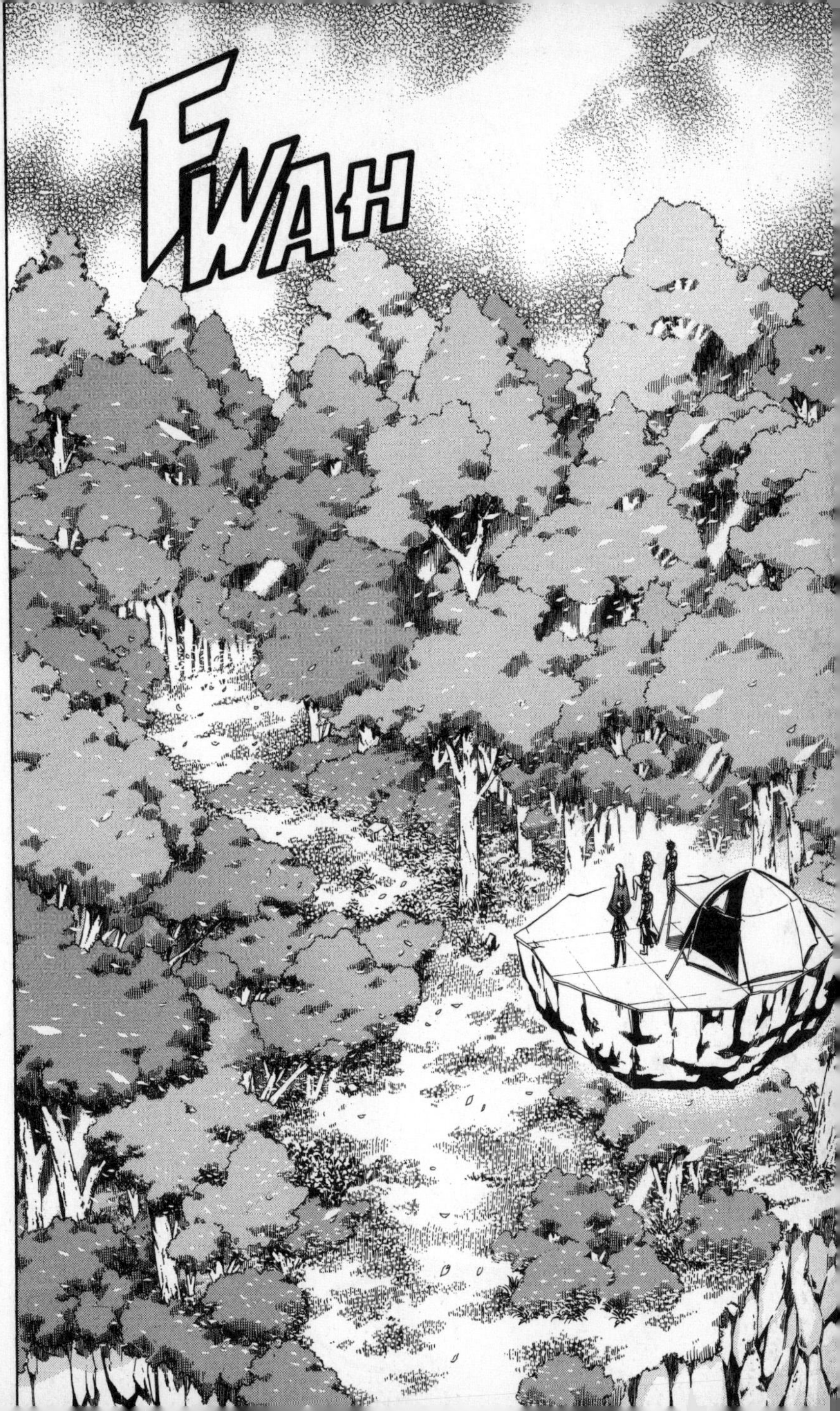
FWAH

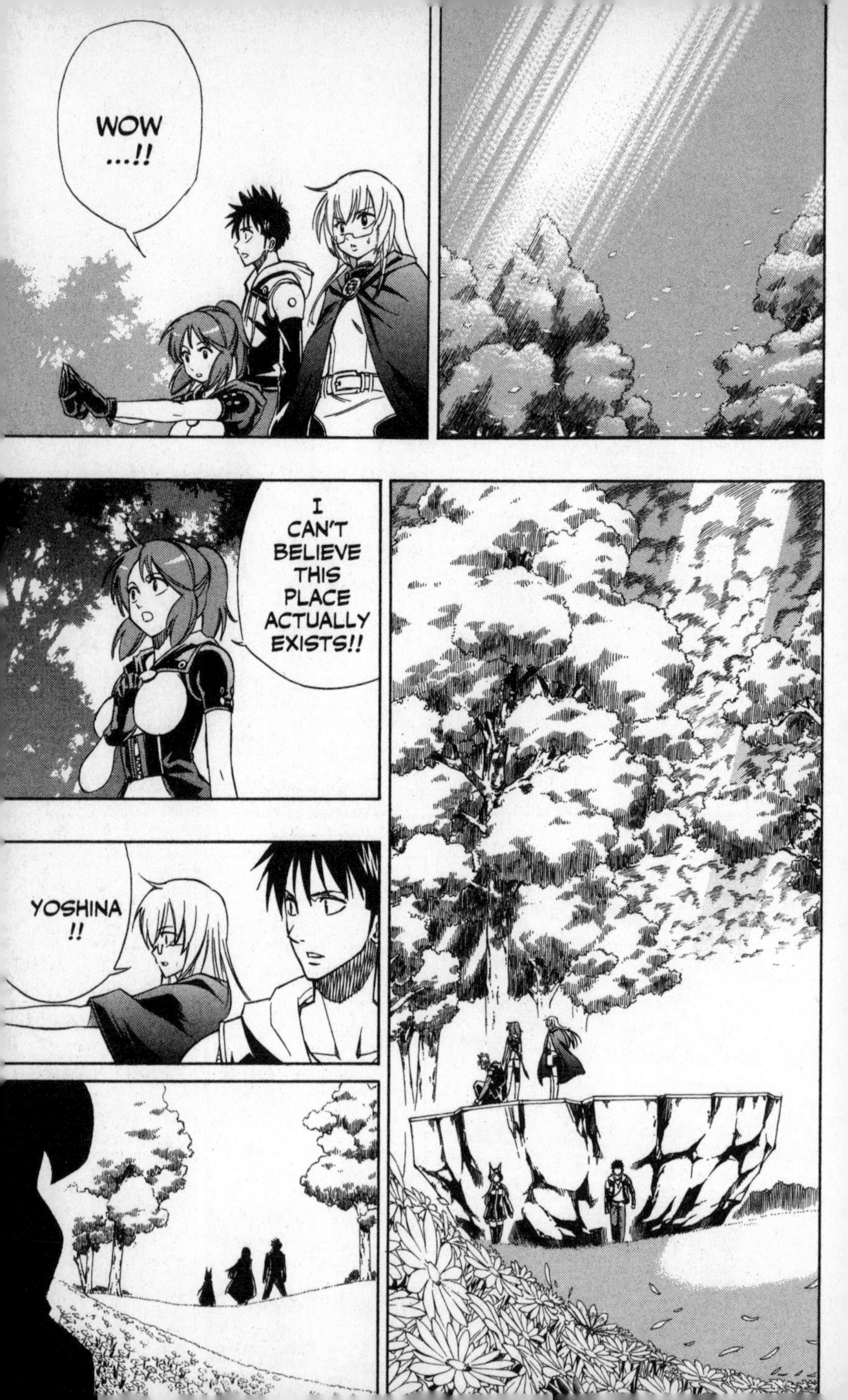
WOW ...!!
I CAN'T BELIEVE THIS PLACE ACTUALLY EXISTS!!
YOSHINA !!

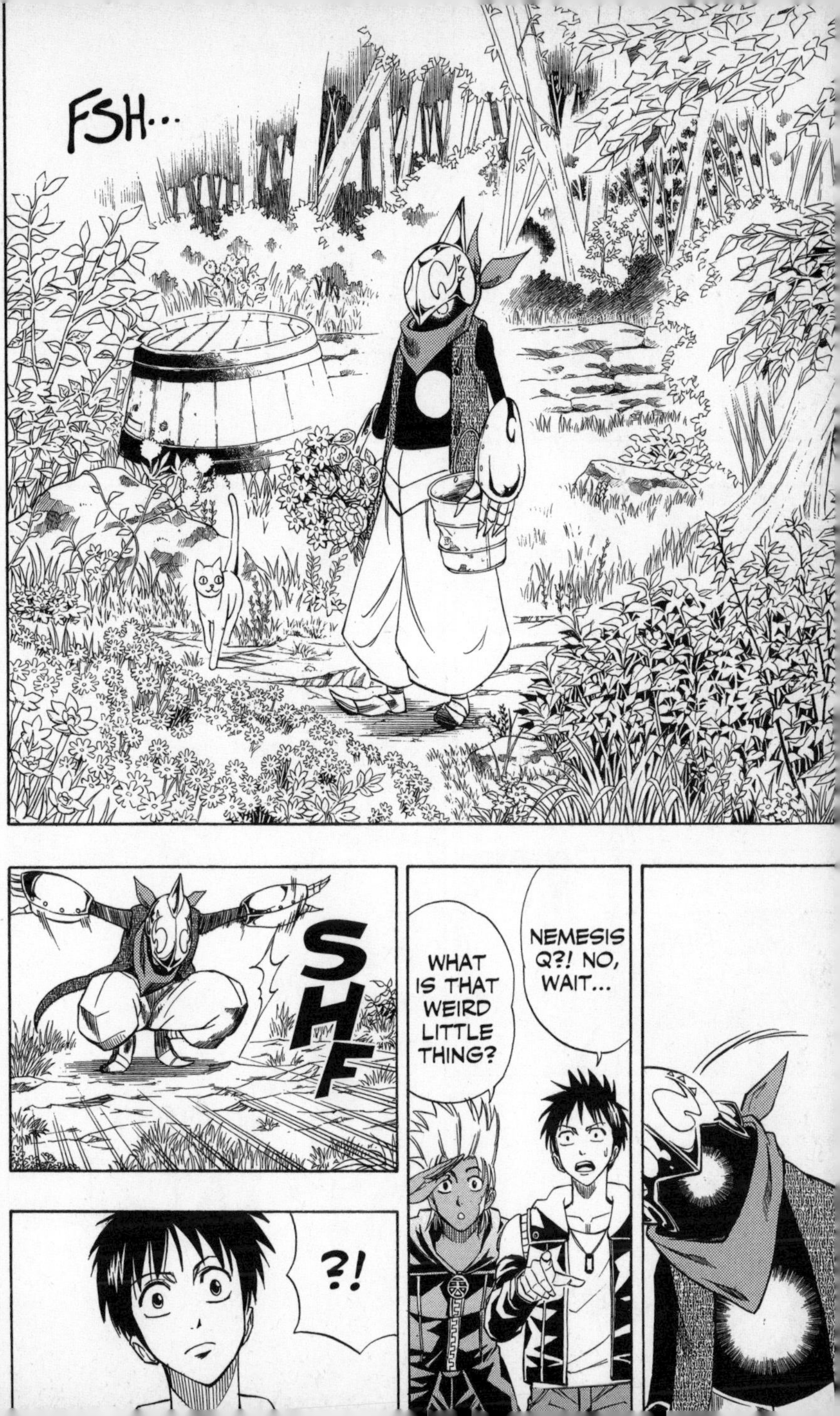
FSH...
NEMESIS Q?! NO, WAIT...
WHAT IS THAT WEIRD LITTLE THING?
SHF
?!

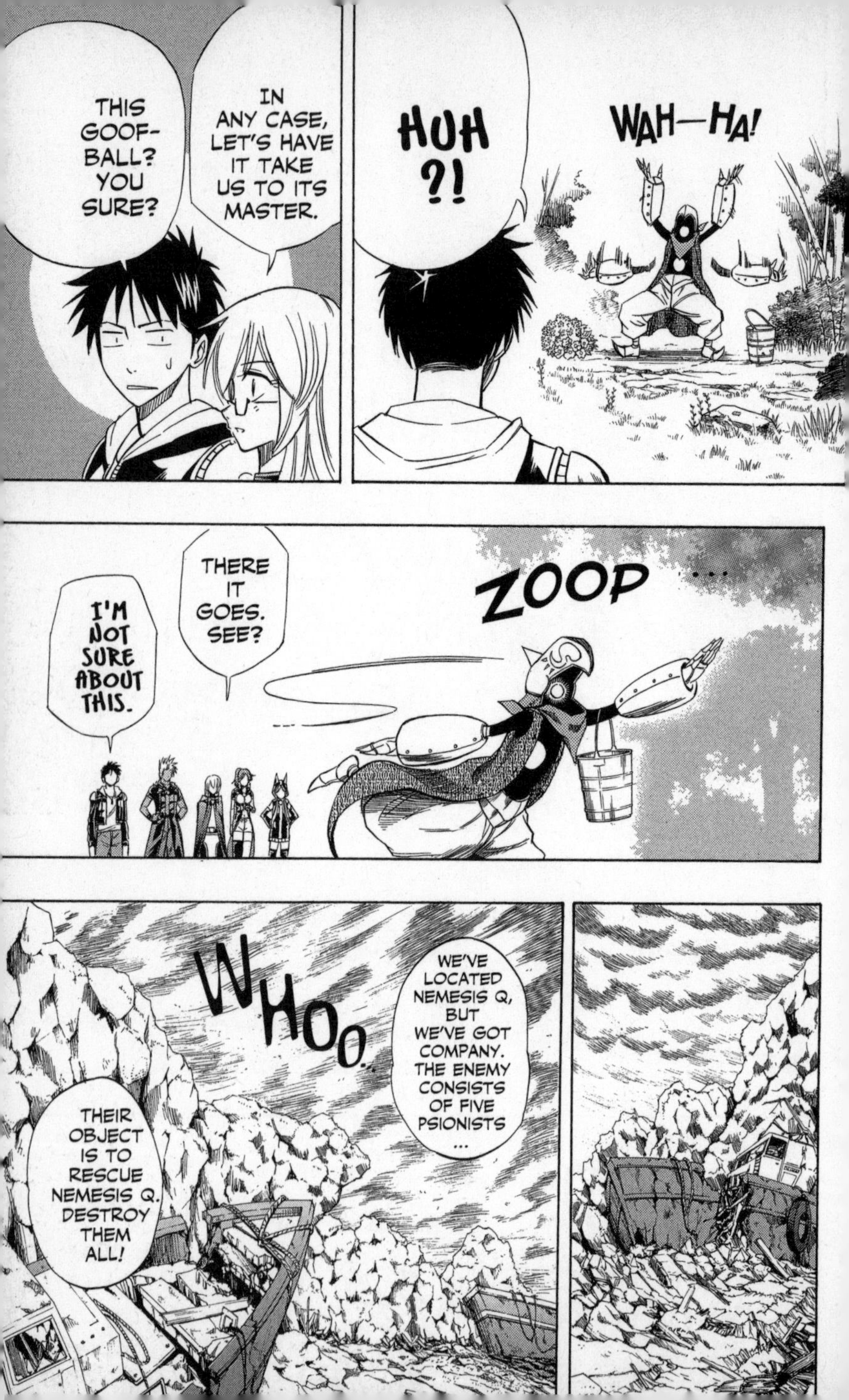
WAH—HA!
HUH ?!
IN ANY CASE, LET'S HAVE IT TAKE US TO ITS MASTER.
THIS GOOF-BALL? YOU SURE?
...
ZOOP
THERE IT GOES. SEE?
I'M NOT SURE ABOUT THIS.
WHOOO..
WE'VE LOCATED NEMESIS Q, BUT WE'VE GOT COMPANY. THE ENEMY CONSISTS OF FIVE PSIONISTS ...
THEIR OBJECT IS TO RESCUE NEMESIS Q. DESTROY THEM ALL!

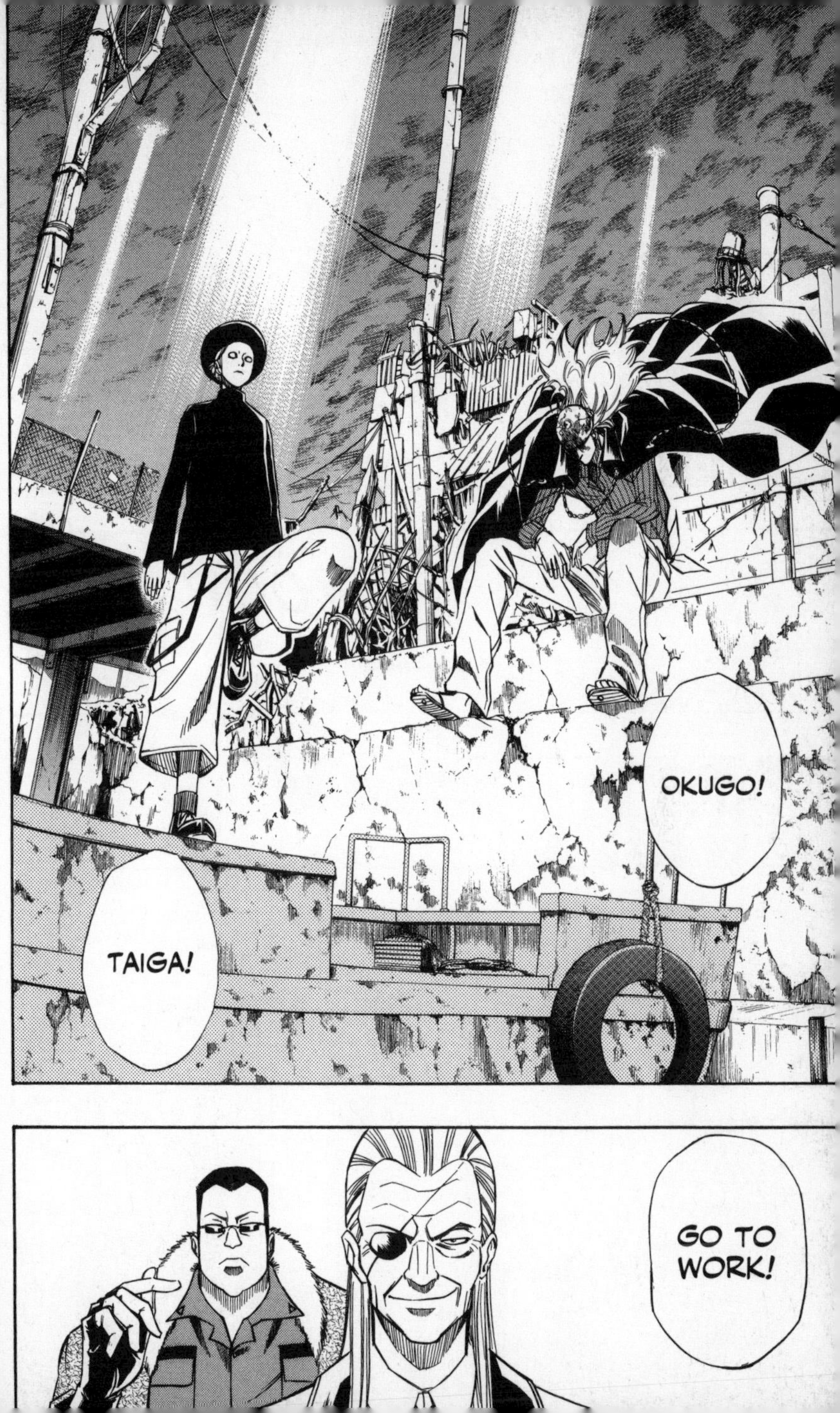
OKUGO!
TAIGA!
GO TO WORK!

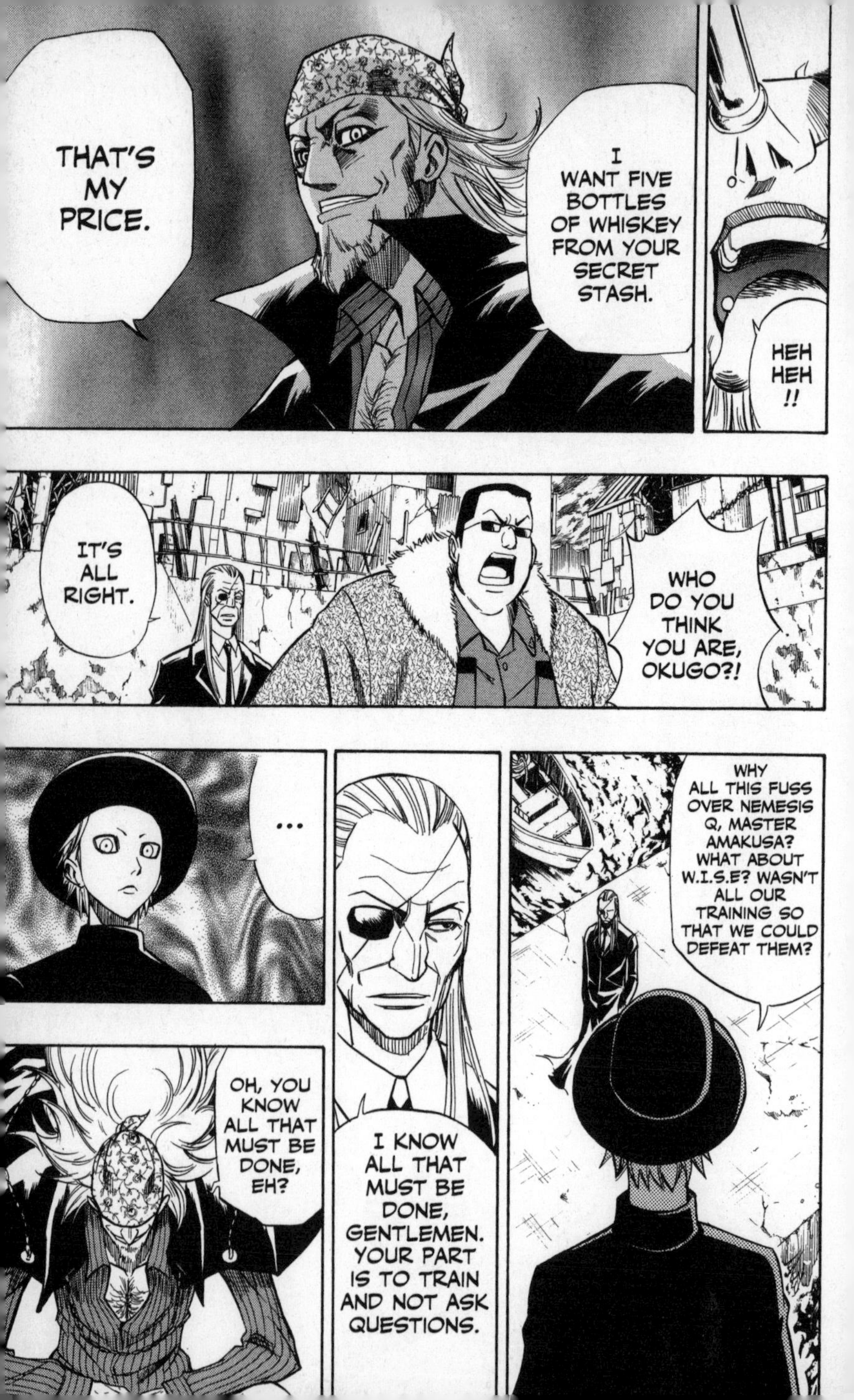
HEH HEH !!
I WANT FIVE BOTTLES OF WHISKEY FROM YOUR SECRET STASH.
THAT'S MY PRICE.
WHO DO YOU THINK YOU ARE, OKUGO?!
IT'S ALL RIGHT.
WHY ALL THIS FUSS OVER NEMESIS Q, MASTER AMAKUSA? WHAT ABOUT W.I.S.E? WASN'T ALL OUR TRAINING SO THAT WE COULD DEFEAT THEM?
...
OH, YOU KNOW ALL THAT MUST BE DONE, EH?
I KNOW ALL THAT MUST BE DONE, GENTLEMEN. YOUR PART IS TO TRAIN AND NOT ASK QUESTIONS.

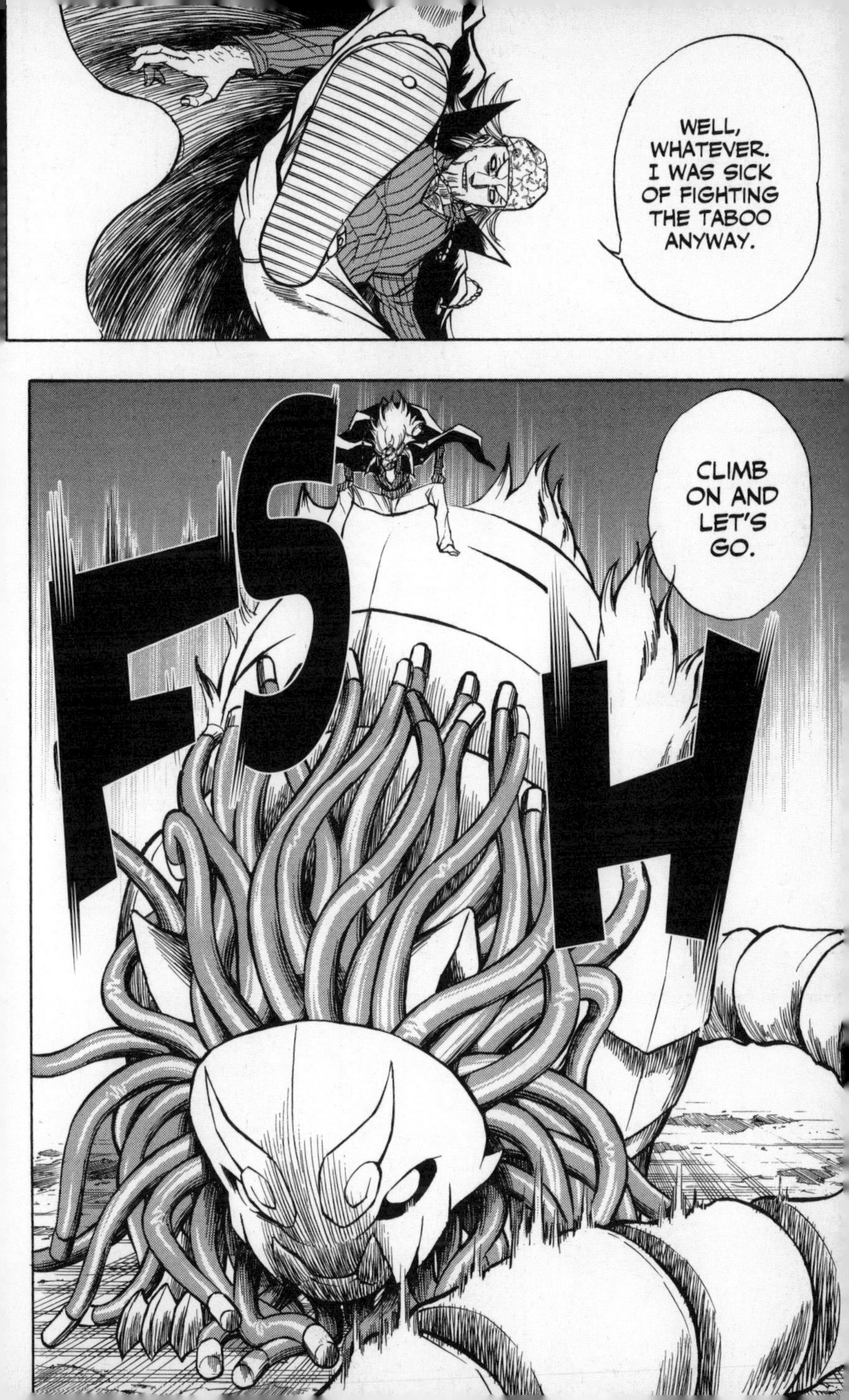
WELL, WHATEVER. I WAS SICK OF FIGHTING THE TABOO ANYWAY.
CLIMB ON AND LET'S GO.
FSSH

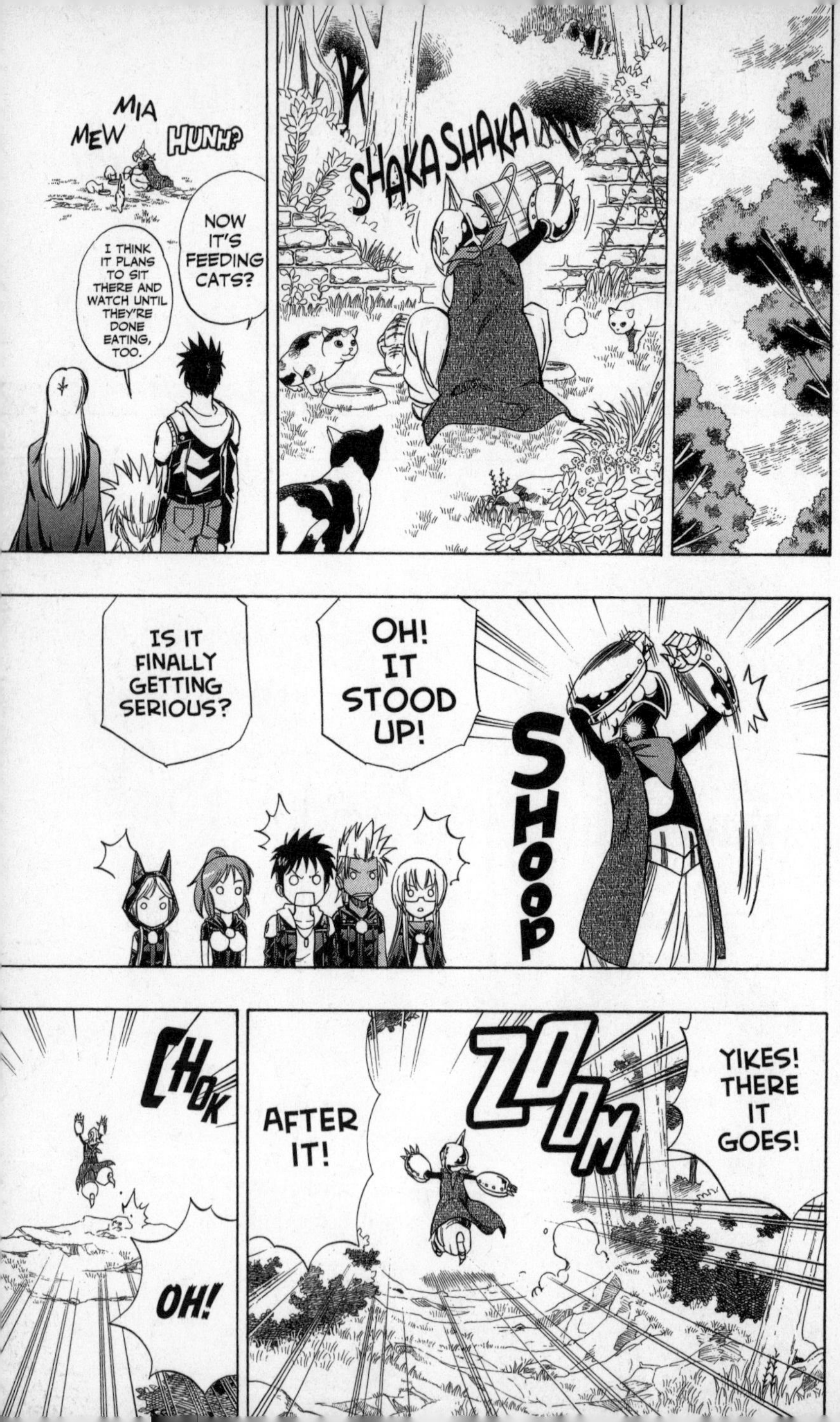
SHAKA SHAKA
MIA
MEW
HUNH?
NOW IT'S FEEDING CATS?
I THINK IT PLANS TO SIT THERE AND WATCH UNTIL THEY'RE DONE EATING, TOO.
SHOOP
OH! IT STOOD UP!
IS IT FINALLY GETTING SERIOUS?
YIKES! THERE IT GOES!
ZOOM
AFTER IT!
CHOK
OH!

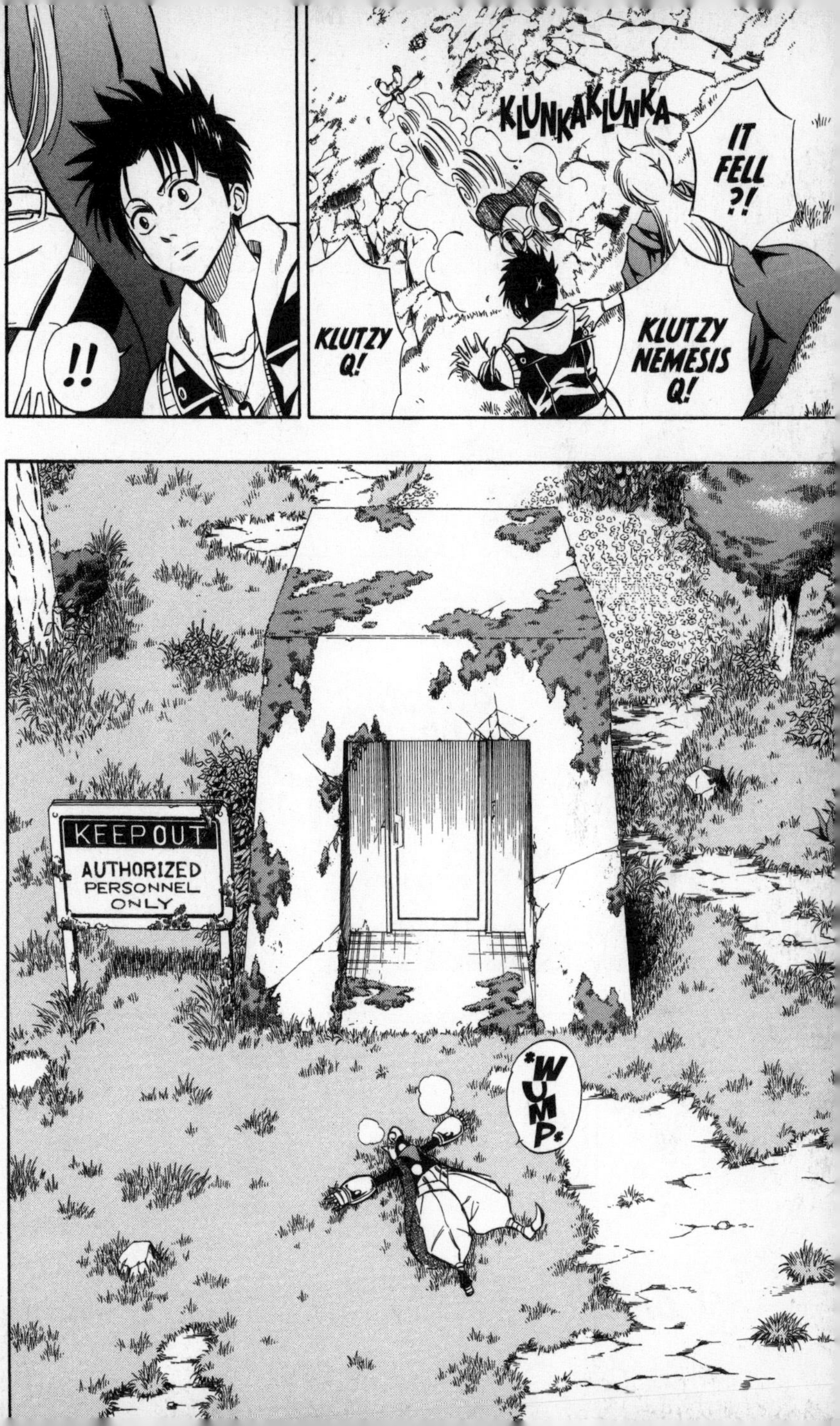
IT FELL?!
KLUNKAKLUNKA
KLUTZY NEMESIS Q!
KLUTZY Q!
!!
KEEP OUT
AUTHORIZED PERSONNEL ONLY
WUMP

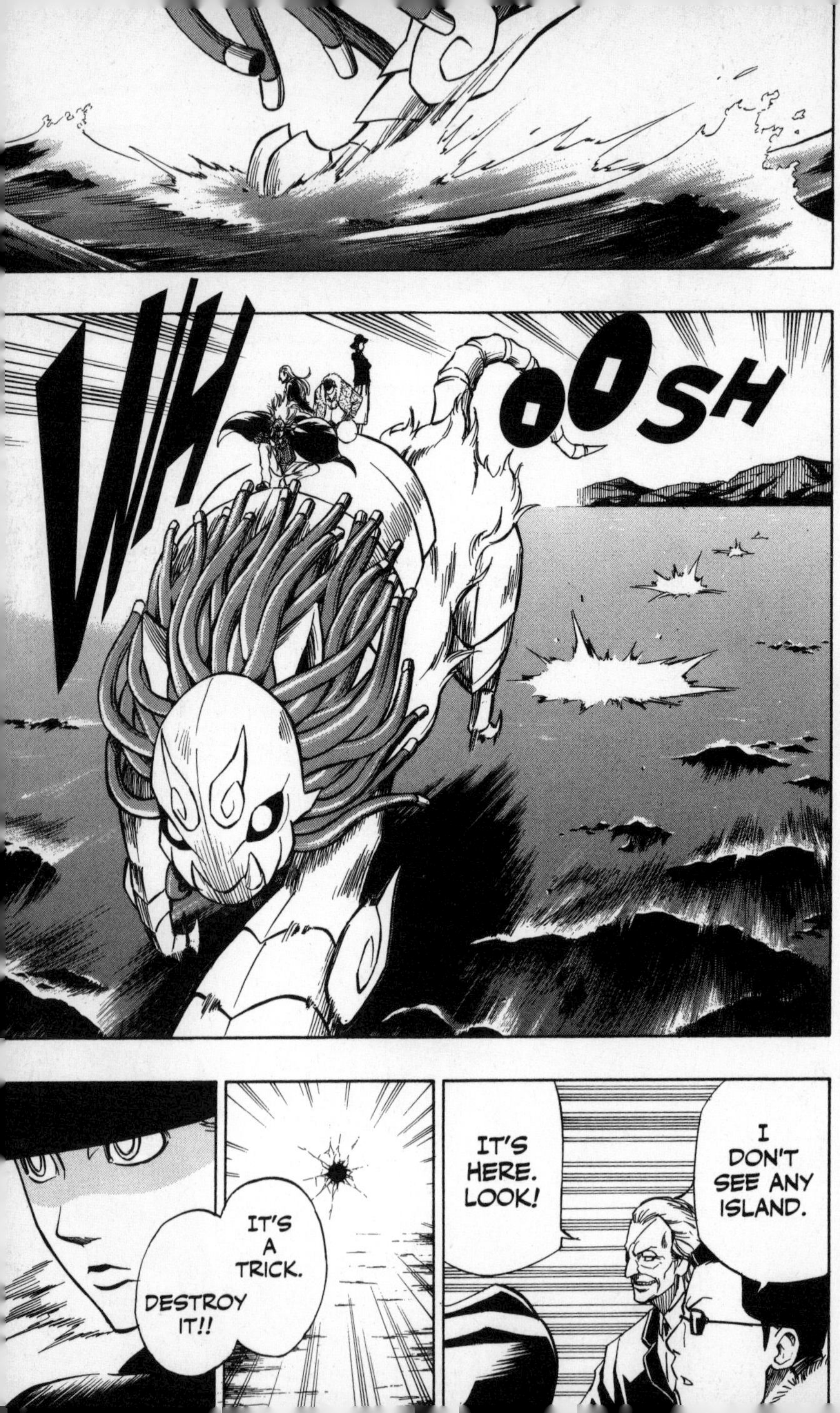
VWOOSH
I DON'T SEE ANY ISLAND.
IT'S HERE. LOOK!
IT'S A TRICK.
DESTROY IT!!

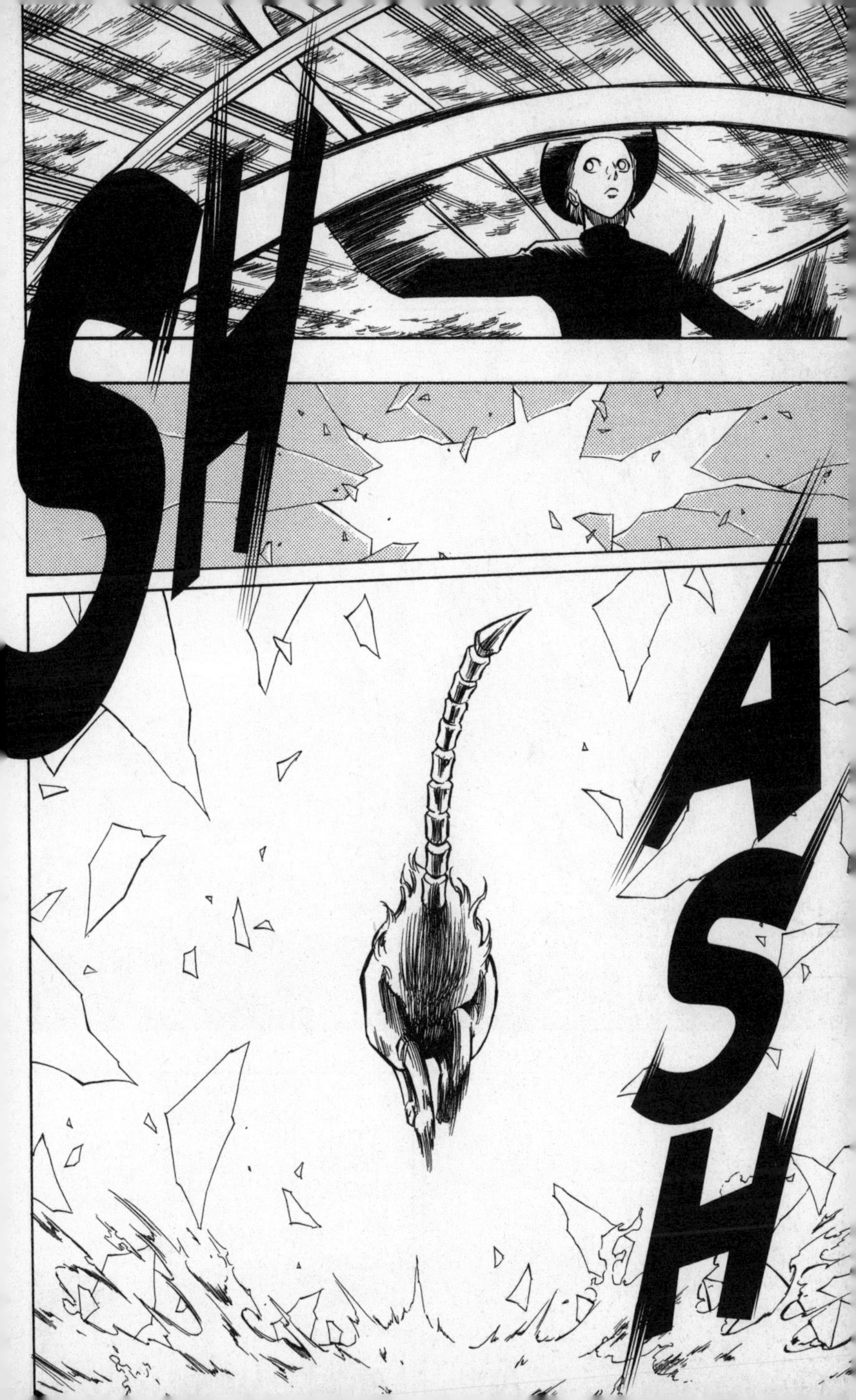
SHASH

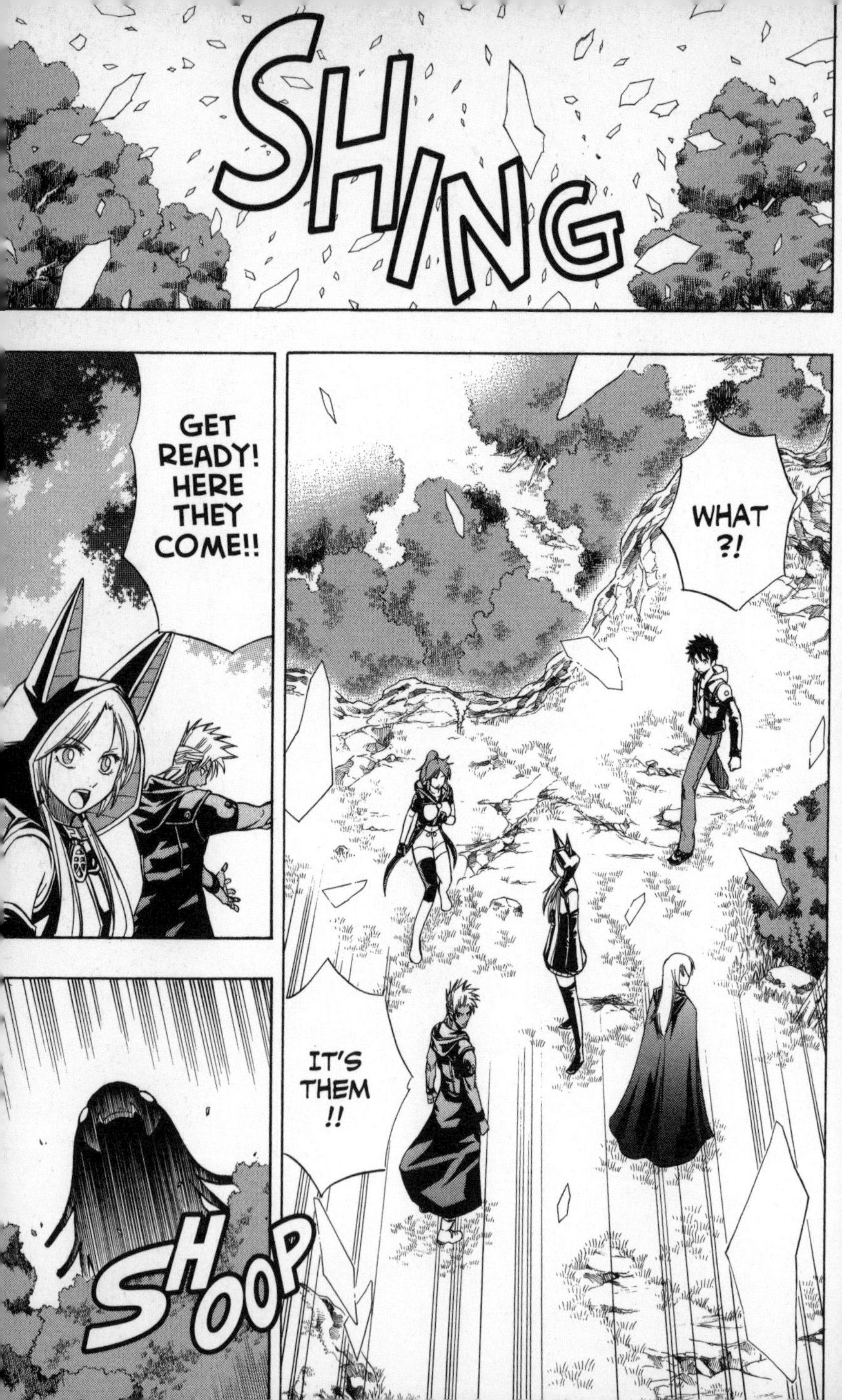
SHING
WHAT?!
IT'S THEM!!
GET READY! HERE THEY COME!!
SHOOP

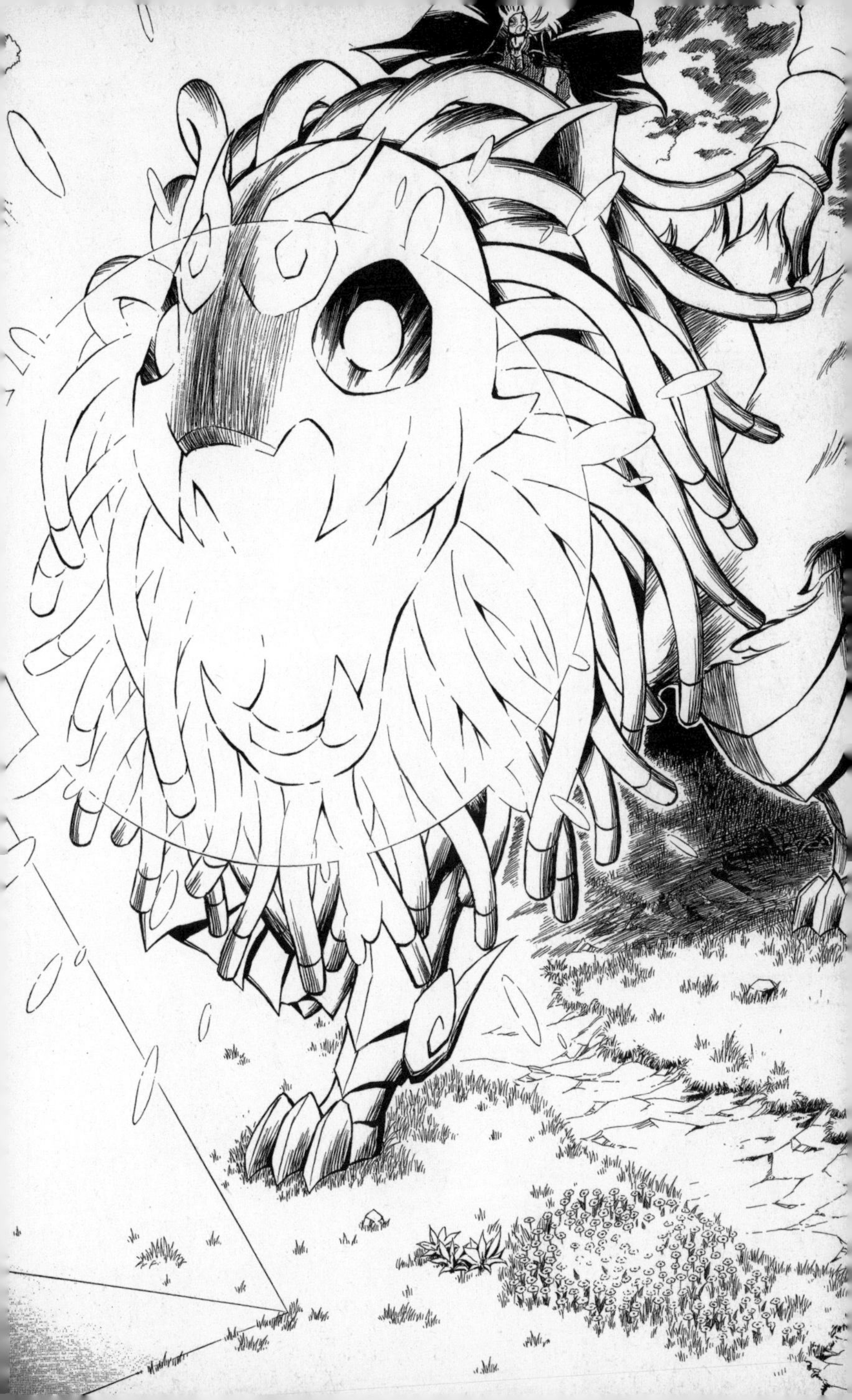

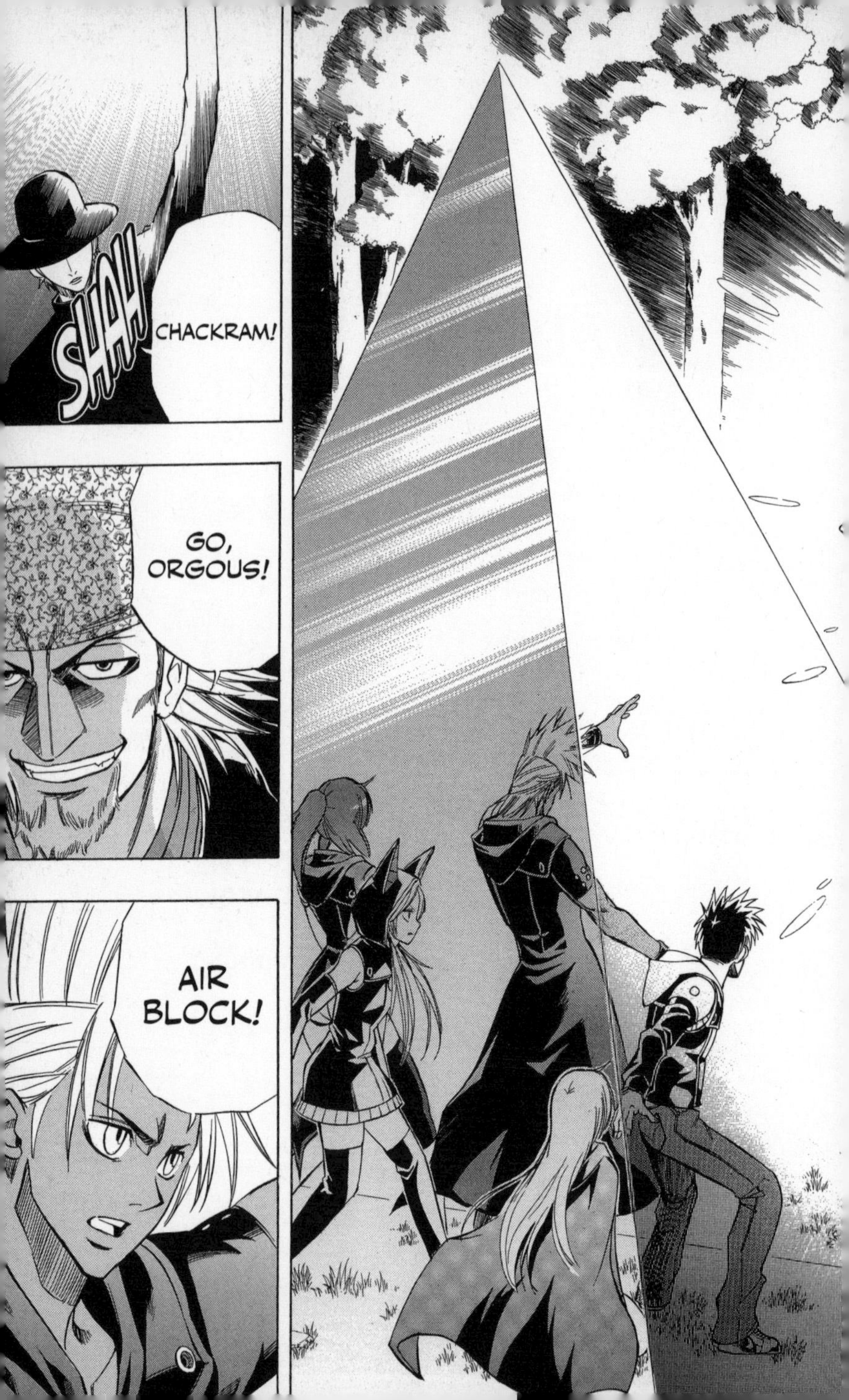
SHAH
CHACKRAM!
GO, ORGOUS!
AIR BLOCK!

A DAY IN THE LIFE OF VAN

EVENING TRAINING

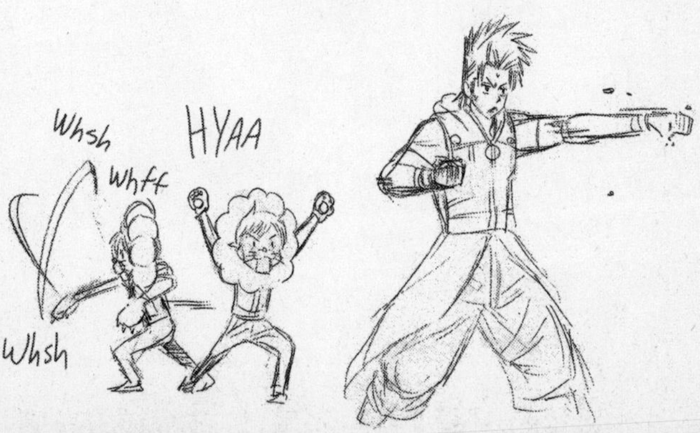
HYAA
Whsh
Whff
Whsh

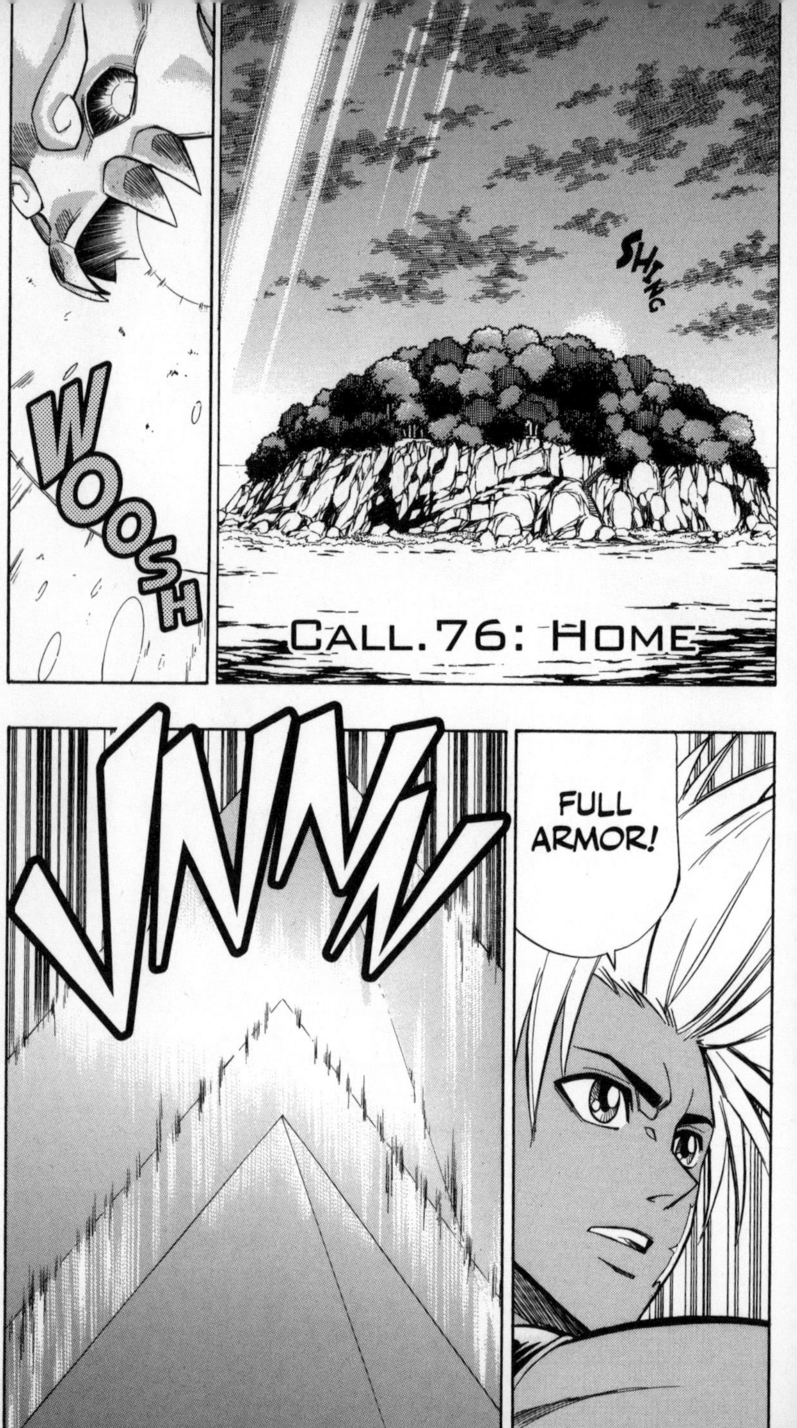
SHING
CALL. 76: HOME
WOOSH
FULL ARMOR!

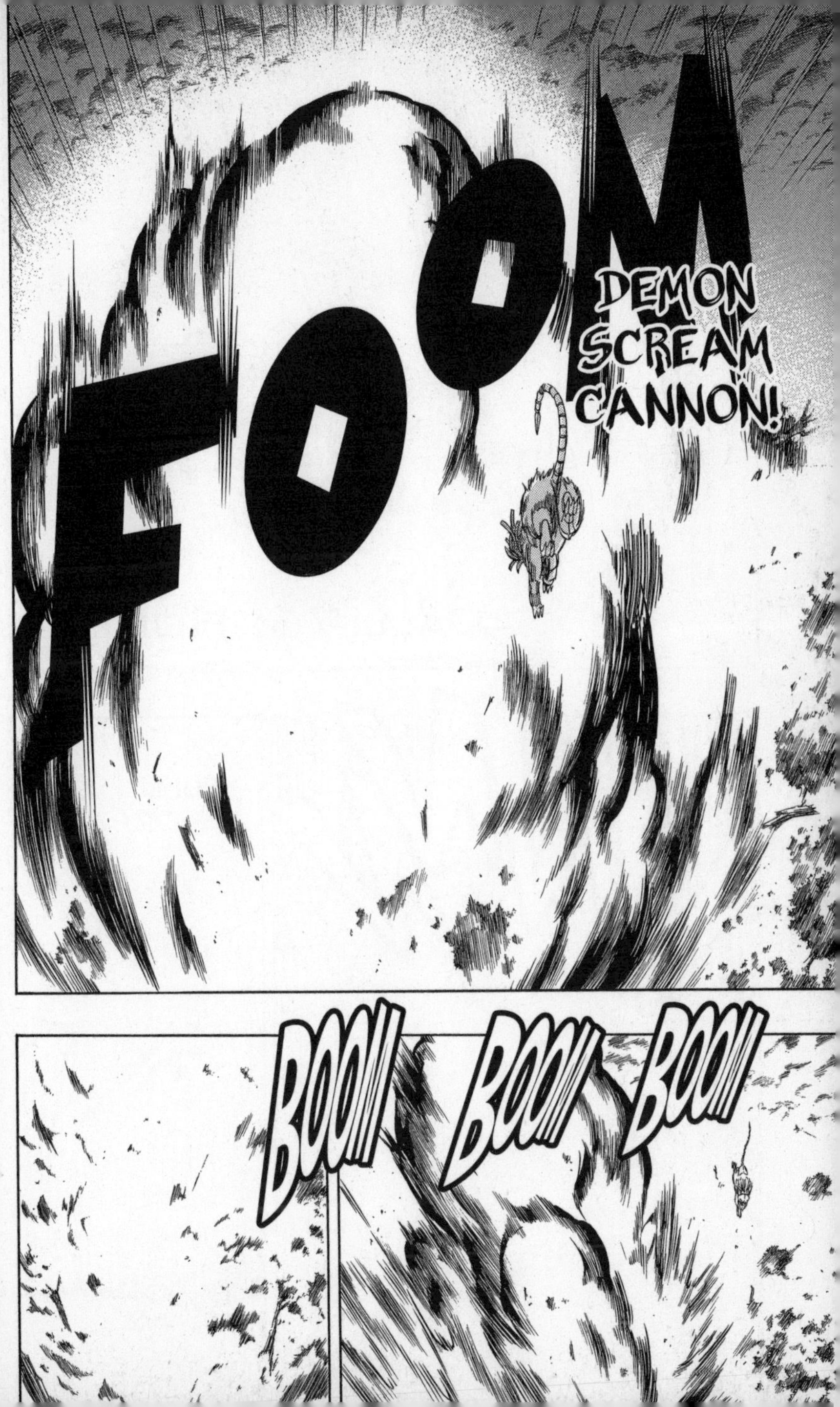
FOOM
DEMON SCREAM CANNON!
BOOM
BOOM
BOOM

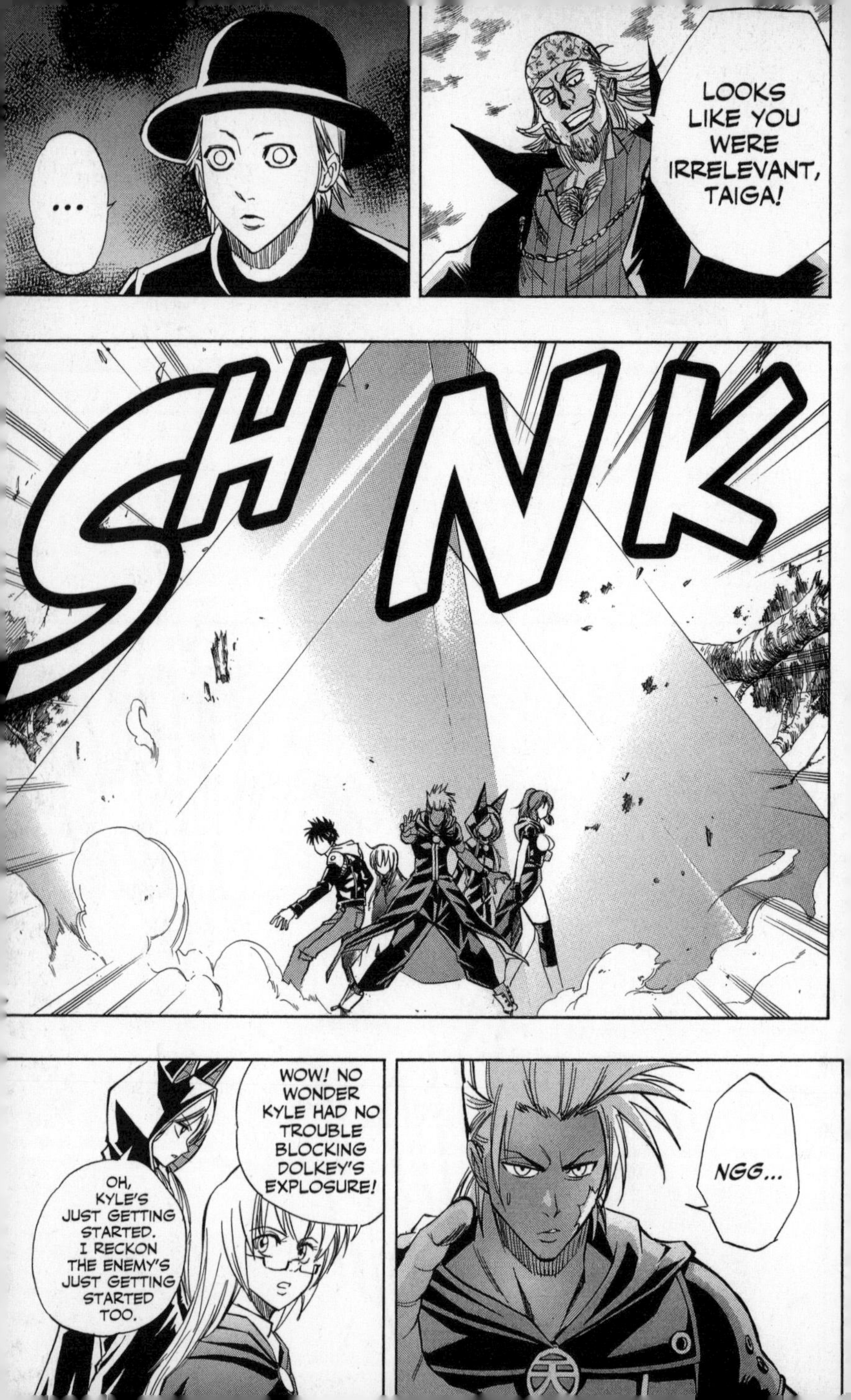
LOOKS LIKE YOU WERE IRRELEVANT, TAIGA!
...
SHNK
NGG...
WOW! NO WONDER KYLE HAD NO TROUBLE BLOCKING DOLKEY'S EXPLOSURE!
OH, KYLE'S JUST GETTING STARTED. I RECKON THE ENEMY'S JUST GETTING STARTED TOO.

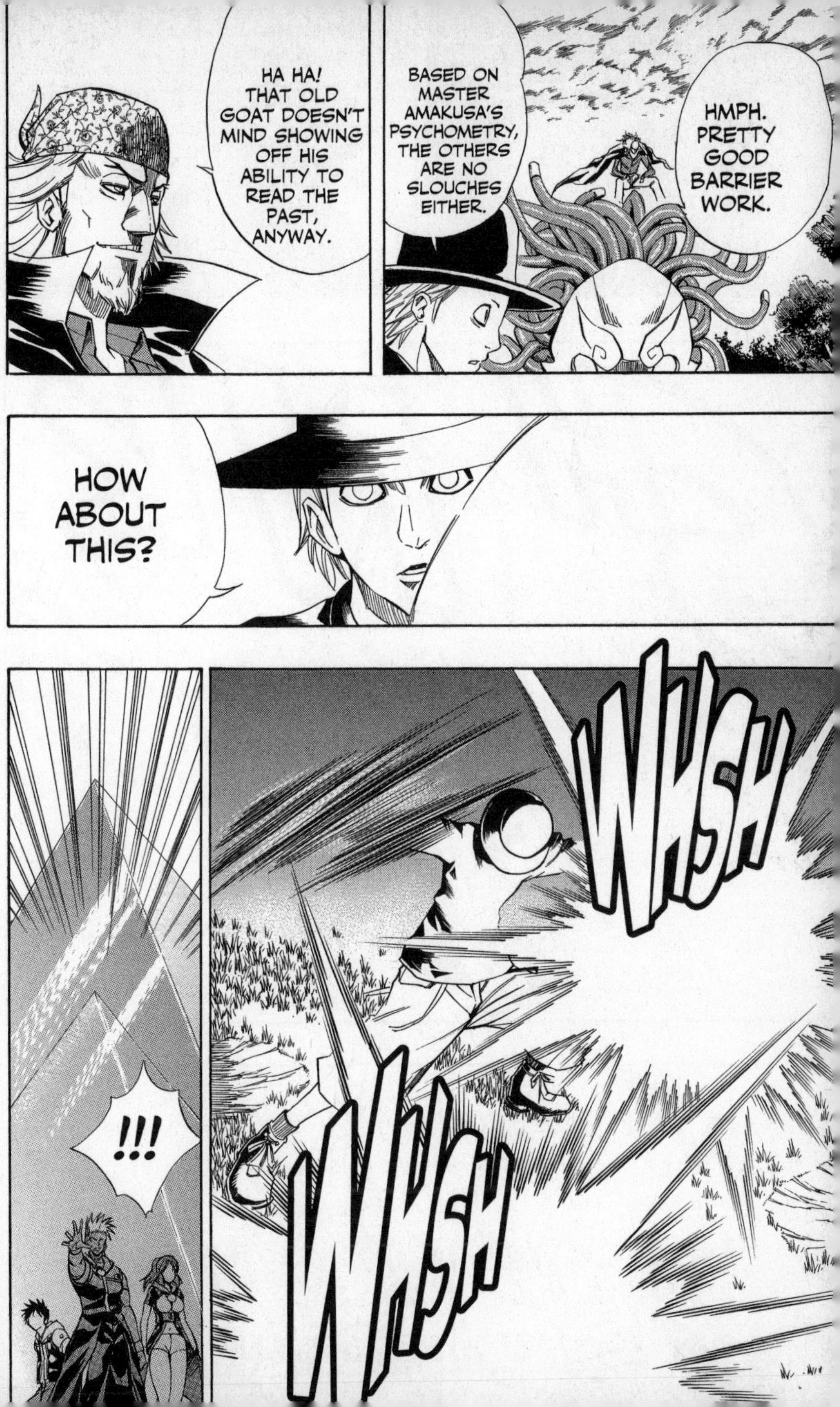
HMPH. PRETTY GOOD BARRIER WORK.
BASED ON MASTER AMAKUSA'S PSYCHOMETRY, THE OTHERS ARE NO SLOUCHES EITHER.
HA HA! THAT OLD GOAT DOESN'T MIND SHOWING OFF HIS ABILITY TO READ THE PAST, ANYWAY.
HOW ABOUT THIS?
WHSH
WHSH
!!!

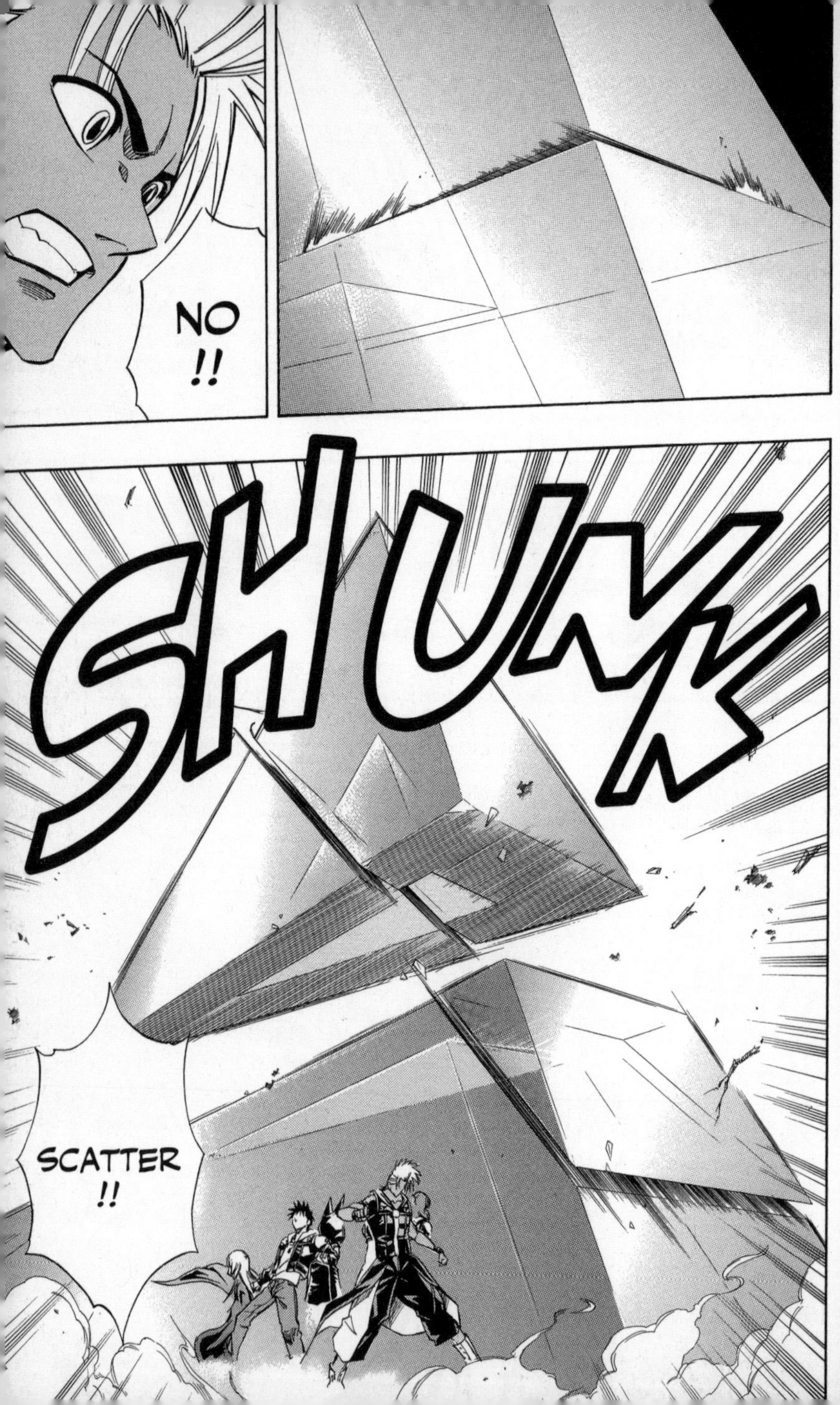
NO !!
SHUNK
SCATTER !!

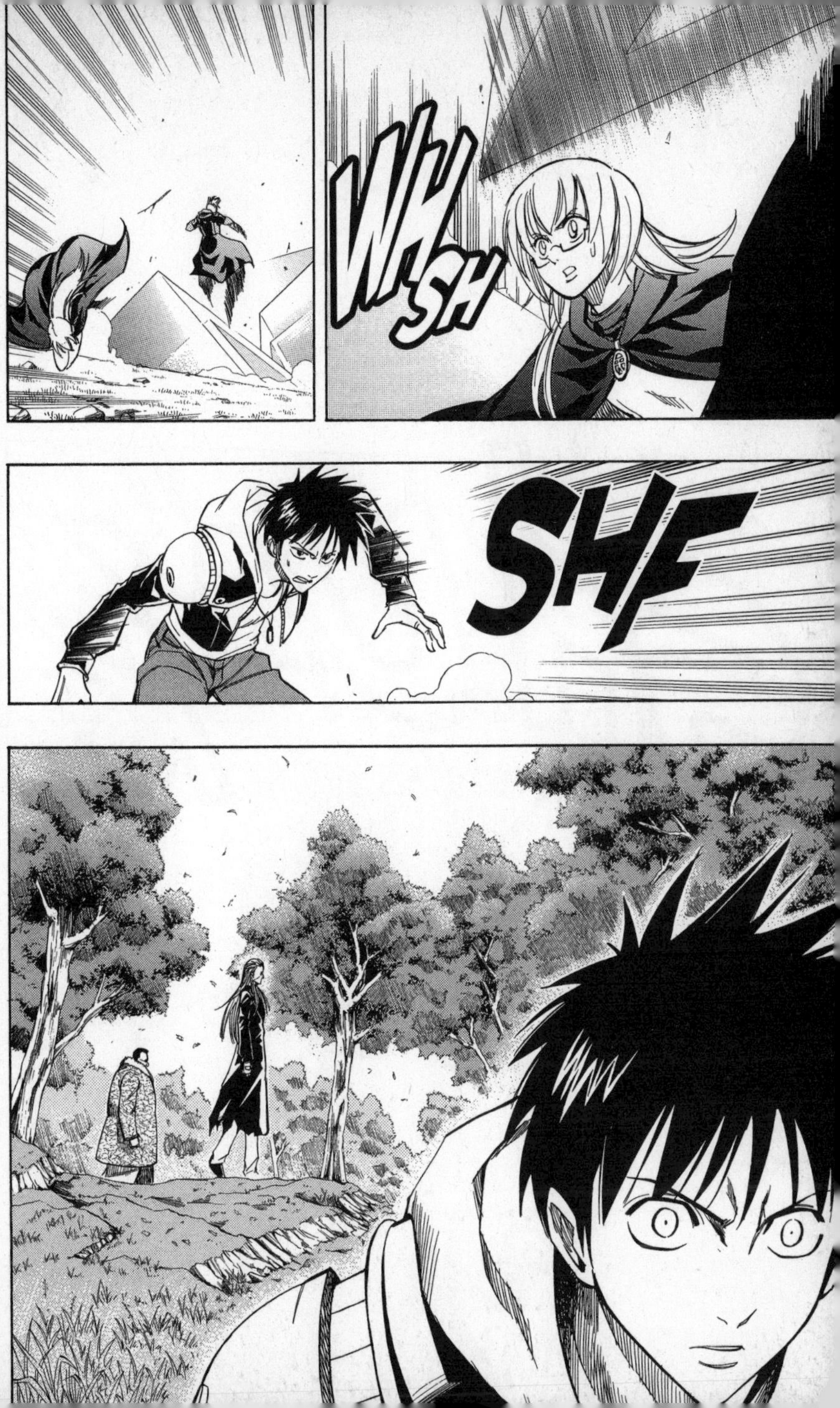
WHSH
SHF

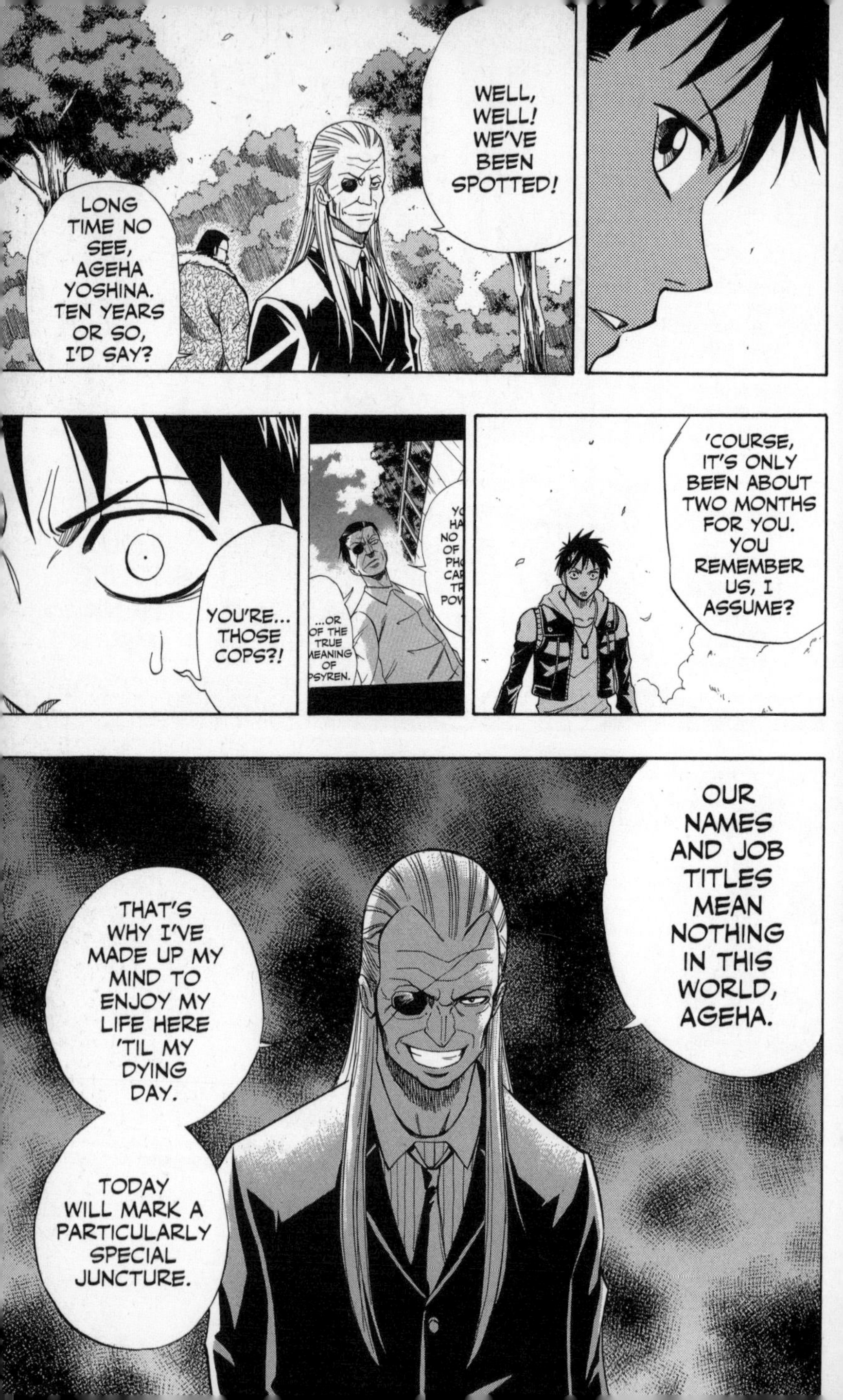
WELL, WELL! WE'VE BEEN SPOTTED!
LONG TIME NO SEE, AGEHA YOSHINA. TEN YEARS OR SO, I'D SAY?
'COURSE, IT'S ONLY BEEN ABOUT TWO MONTHS FOR YOU. YOU REMEMBER US, I ASSUME?
...OR OF THE TRUE MEANING OF PSYREN.
YOU'RE... THOSE COPS?!
OUR NAMES AND JOB TITLES MEAN NOTHING IN THIS WORLD, AGEHA.
THAT'S WHY I'VE MADE UP MY MIND TO ENJOY MY LIFE HERE 'TIL MY DYING DAY.
TODAY WILL MARK A PARTICULARLY SPECIAL JUNCTURE.

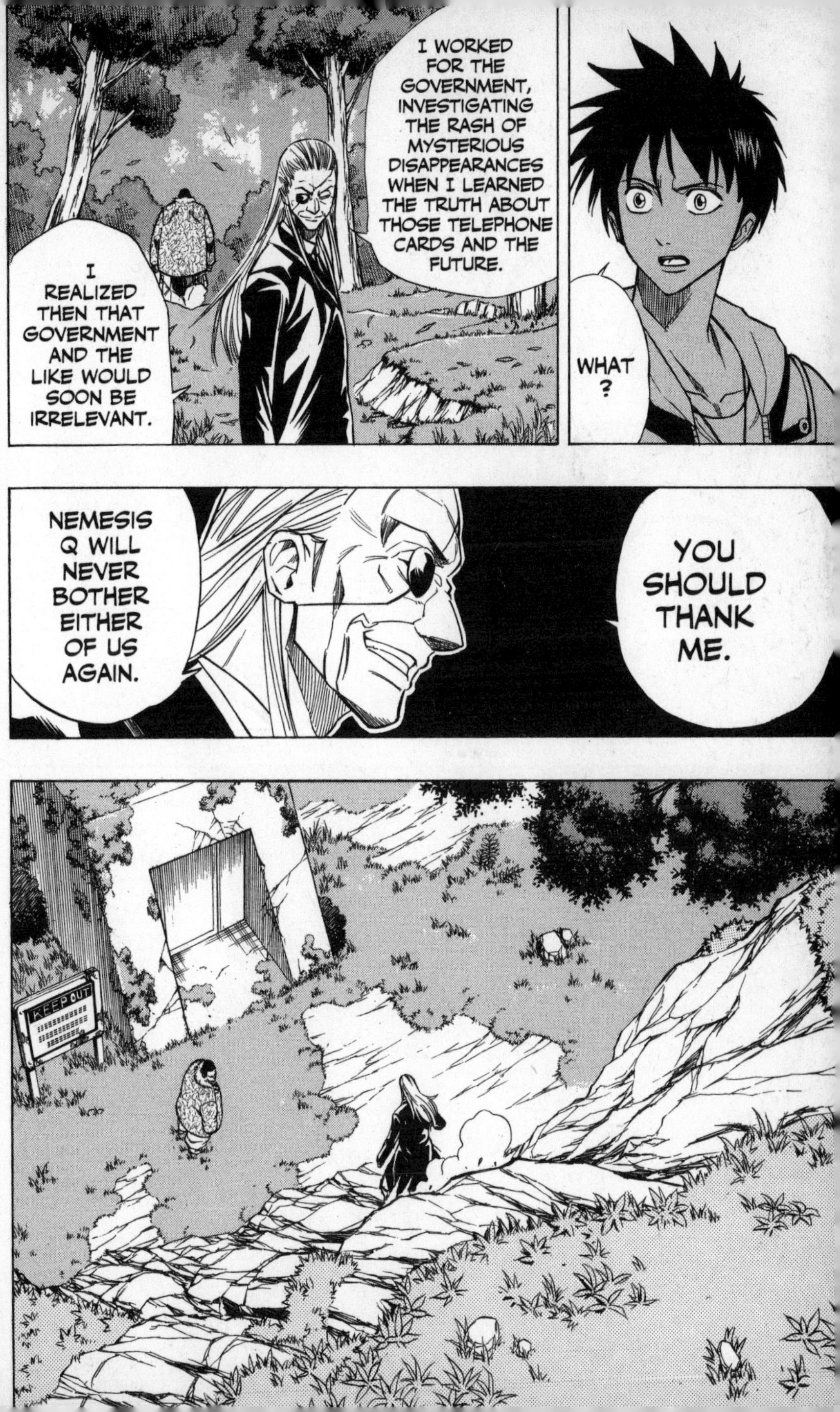
WHAT?
I WORKED FOR THE GOVERNMENT, INVESTIGATING THE RASH OF MYSTERIOUS DISAPPEARANCES WHEN I LEARNED THE TRUTH ABOUT THOSE TELEPHONE CARDS AND THE FUTURE.
I REALIZED THEN THAT GOVERNMENT AND THE LIKE WOULD SOON BE IRRELEVANT.
YOU SHOULD THANK ME.
NEMESIS Q WILL NEVER BOTHER EITHER OF US AGAIN.
KEEP OUT

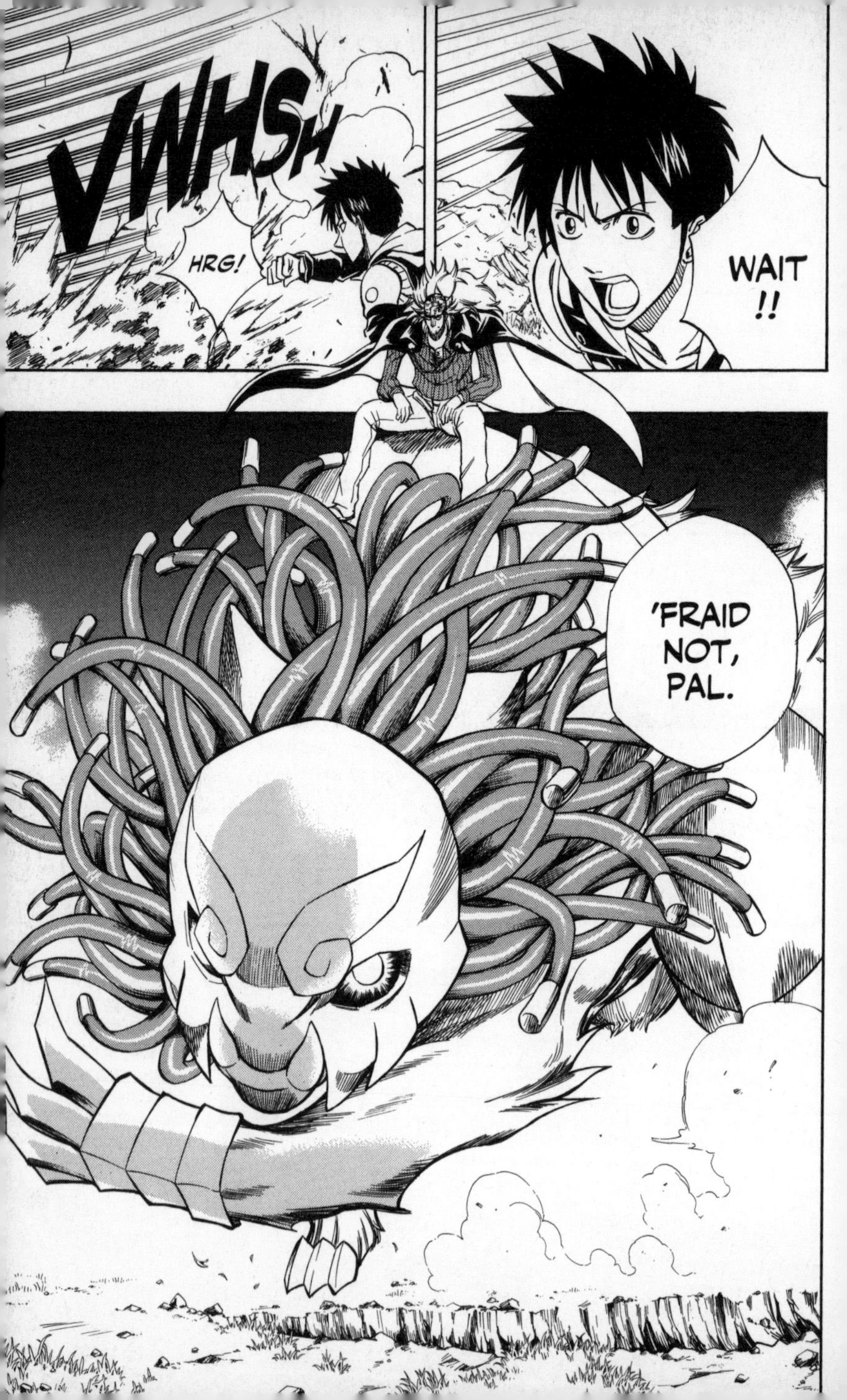
WAIT !!
VWHSH
HRG!
'FRAID NOT, PAL.

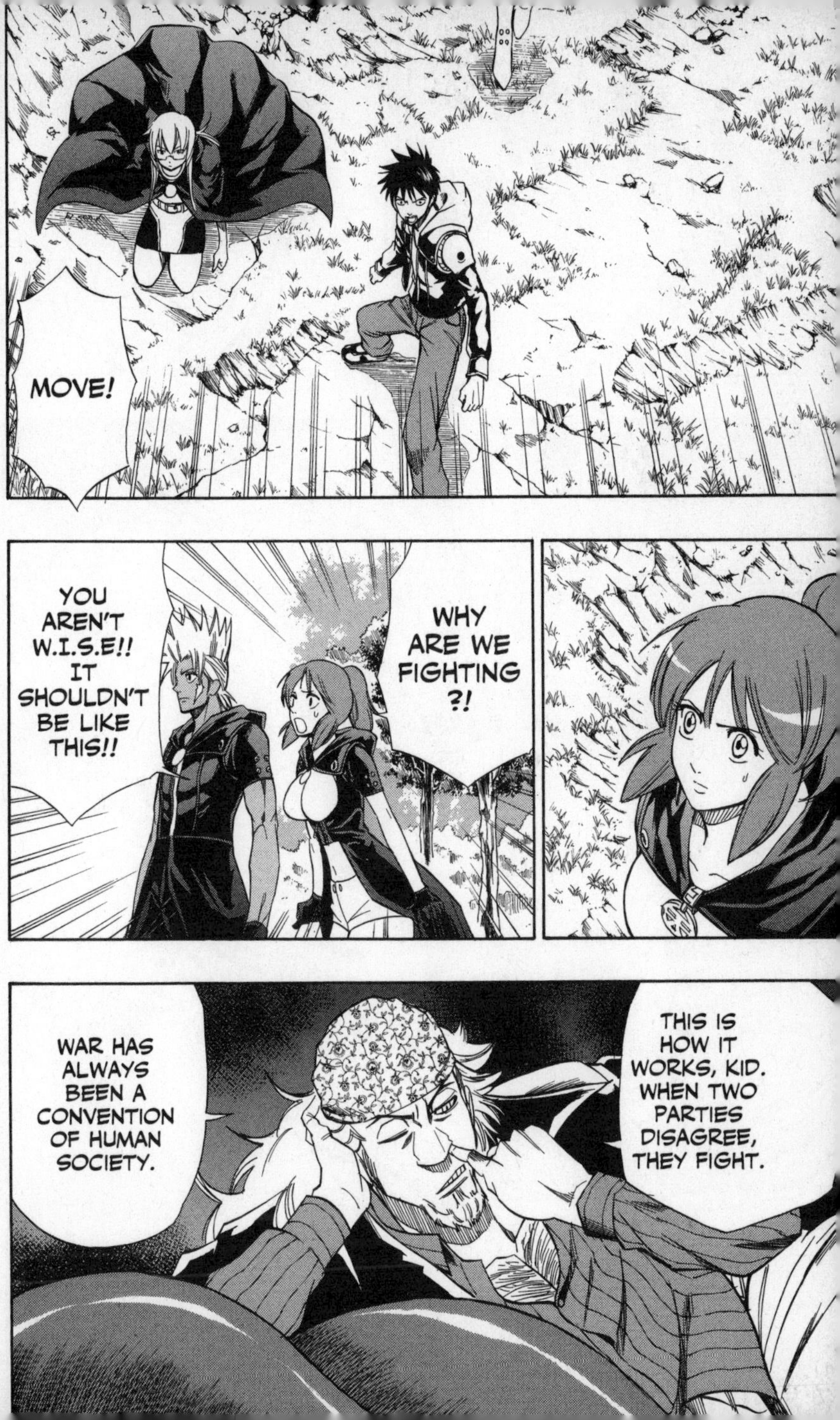
MOVE!
WHY ARE WE FIGHTING?!
YOU AREN'T W.I.S.E!! IT SHOULDN'T BE LIKE THIS!!
THIS IS HOW IT WORKS, KID. WHEN TWO PARTIES DISAGREE, THEY FIGHT.
WAR HAS ALWAYS BEEN A CONVENTION OF HUMAN SOCIETY.

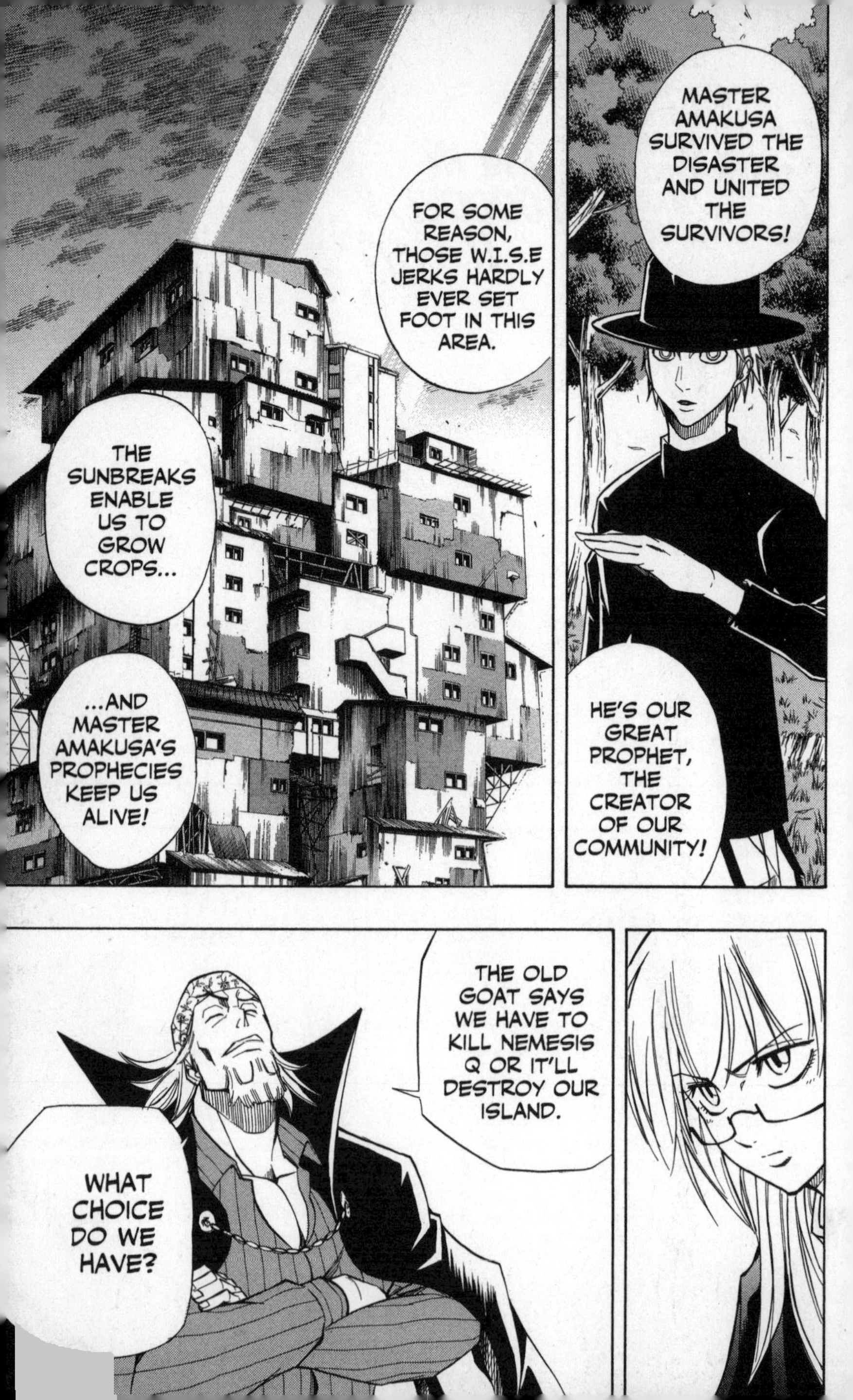
MASTER AMAKUSA SURVIVED THE DISASTER AND UNITED THE SURVIVORS!
HE'S OUR GREAT PROPHET, THE CREATOR OF OUR COMMUNITY!
FOR SOME REASON, THOSE W.I.S.E JERKS HARDLY EVER SET FOOT IN THIS AREA.
THE SUNBREAKS ENABLE US TO GROW CROPS...
...AND MASTER AMAKUSA'S PROPHECIES KEEP US ALIVE!
THE OLD GOAT SAYS WE HAVE TO KILL NEMESIS Q OR IT'LL DESTROY OUR ISLAND.
WHAT CHOICE DO WE HAVE?

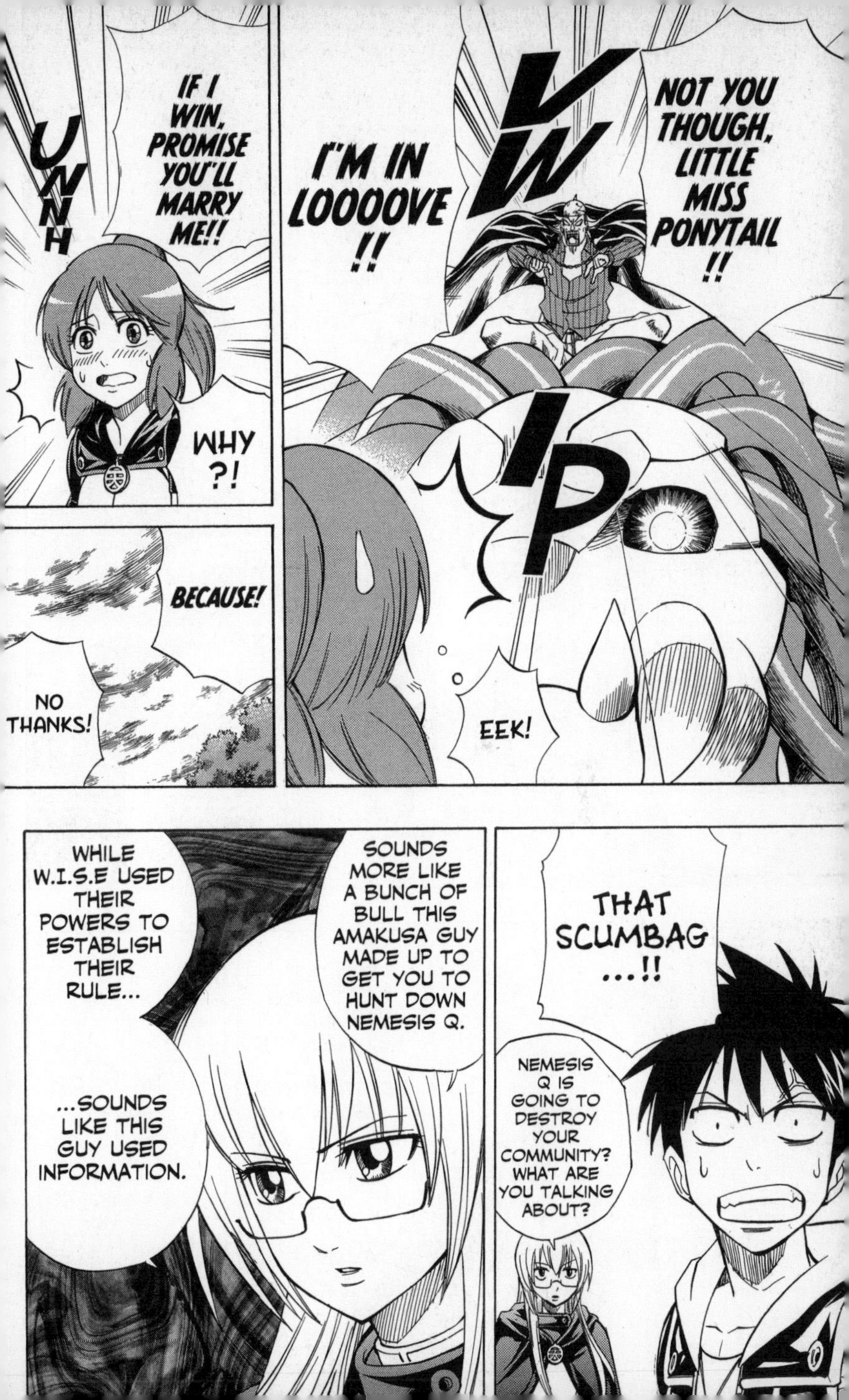
NOT YOU THOUGH, LITTLE MISS PONYTAIL!!
VW
I'M IN LOOOOVE!!
IP
EEK!
IF I WIN, PROMISE YOU'LL MARRY ME!!
UNNH
WHY?!
BECAUSE!
NO THANKS!
THAT SCUMBAG...!!
NEMESIS Q IS GOING TO DESTROY YOUR COMMUNITY? WHAT ARE YOU TALKING ABOUT?
SOUNDS MORE LIKE A BUNCH OF BULL THIS AMAKUSA GUY MADE UP TO GET YOU TO HUNT DOWN NEMESIS Q.
WHILE W.I.S.E USED THEIR POWERS TO ESTABLISH THEIR RULE...
...SOUNDS LIKE THIS GUY USED INFORMATION.

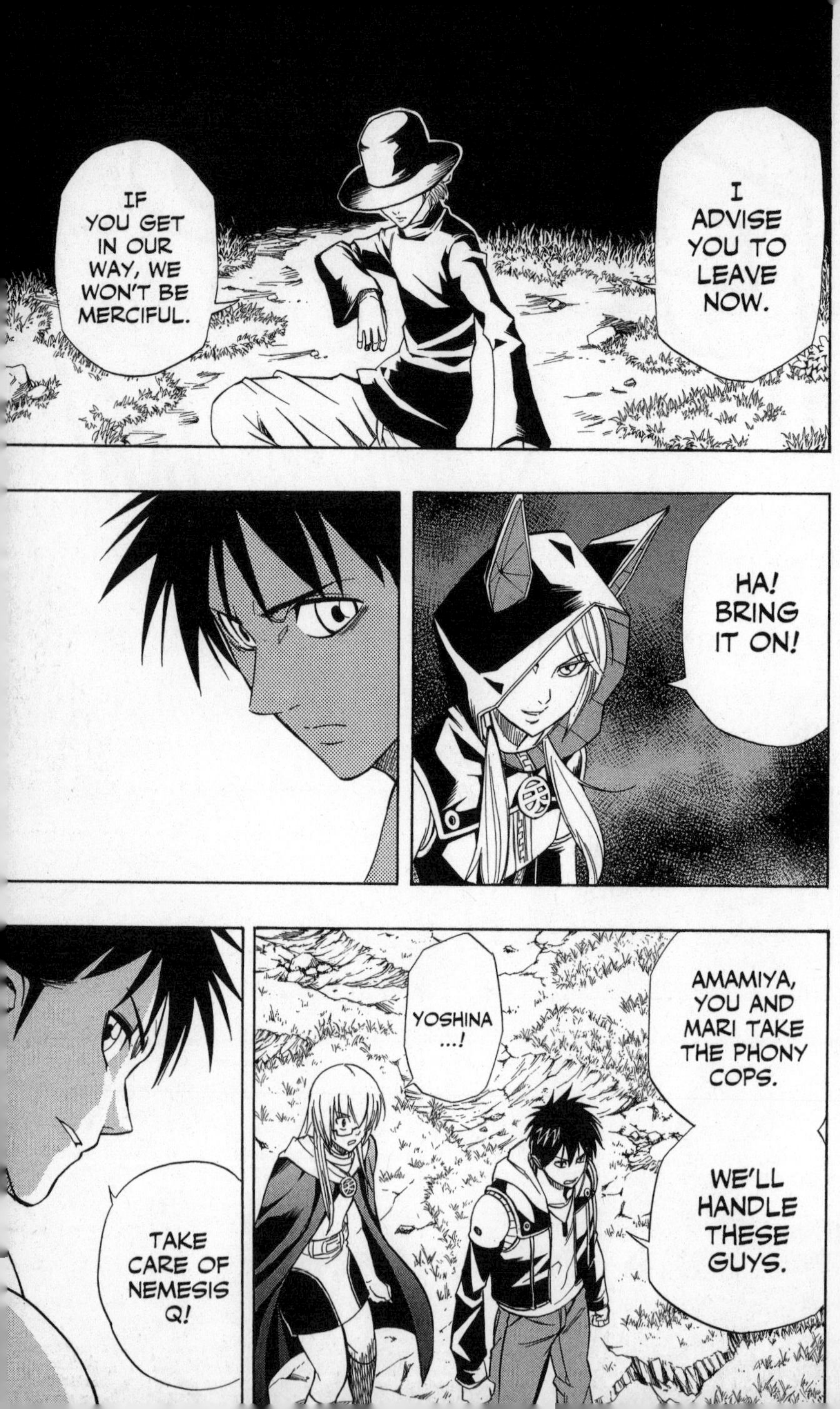
I ADVISE YOU TO LEAVE NOW.
IF YOU GET IN OUR WAY, WE WON'T BE MERCIFUL.
HA! BRING IT ON!
AMAMIYA, YOU AND MARI TAKE THE PHONY COPS.
WE'LL HANDLE THESE GUYS.
YOSHINA ...!
TAKE CARE OF NEMESIS Q!

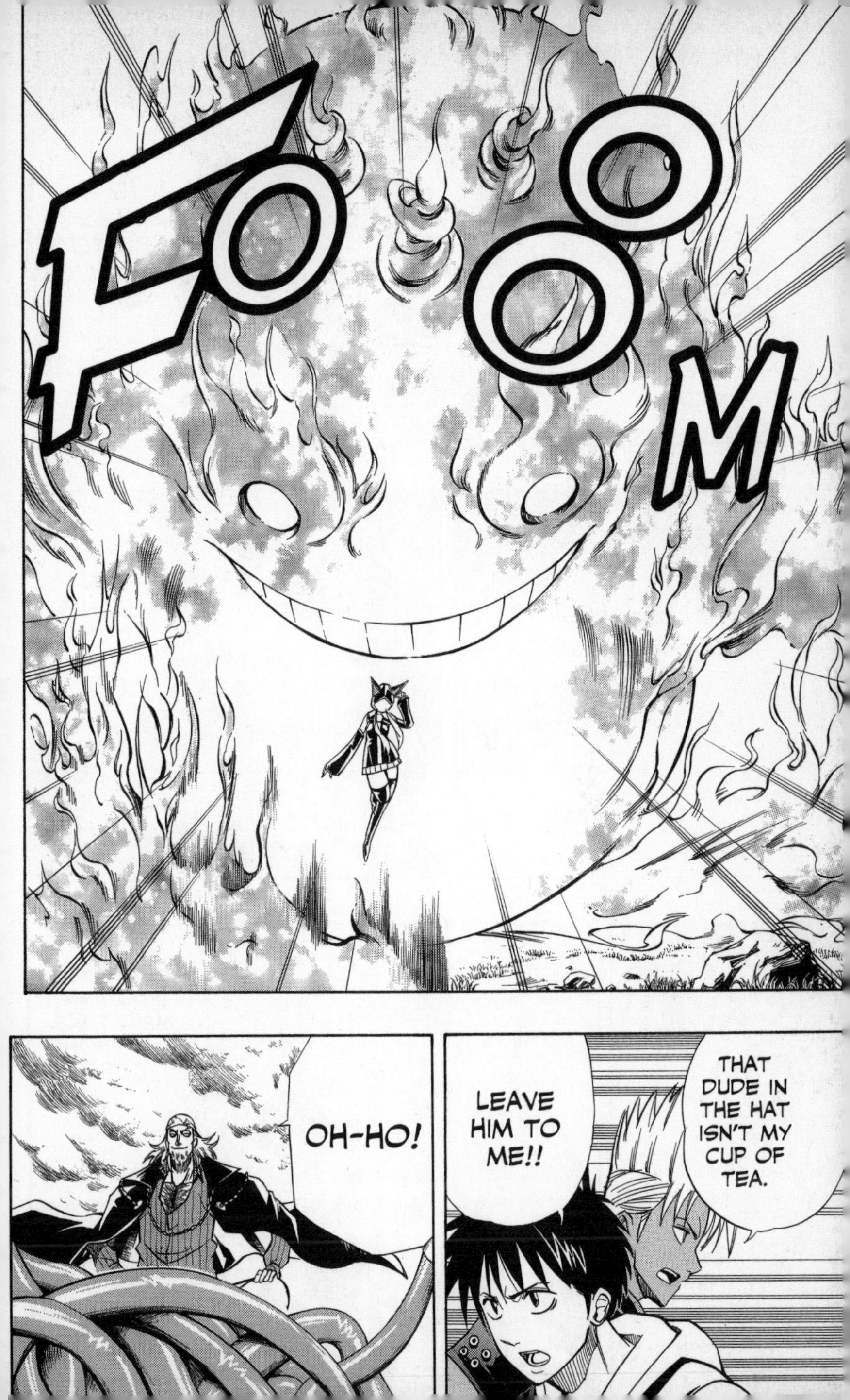
FOOOM
THAT DUDE IN THE HAT ISN'T MY CUP OF TEA.
LEAVE HIM TO ME!!
OH-HO!

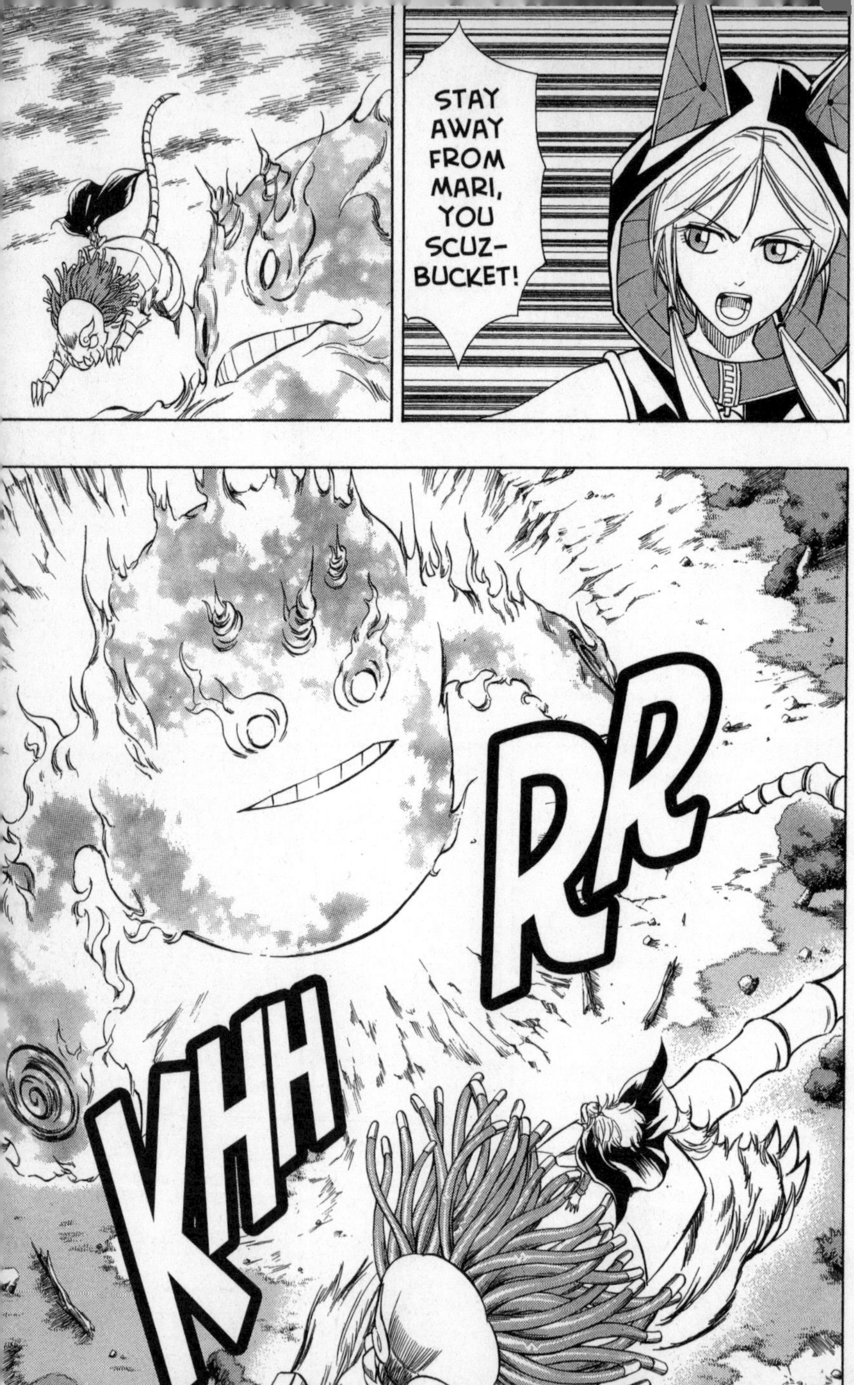
STAY AWAY FROM MARI, YOU SCUZ-BUCKET!
RR
KHH

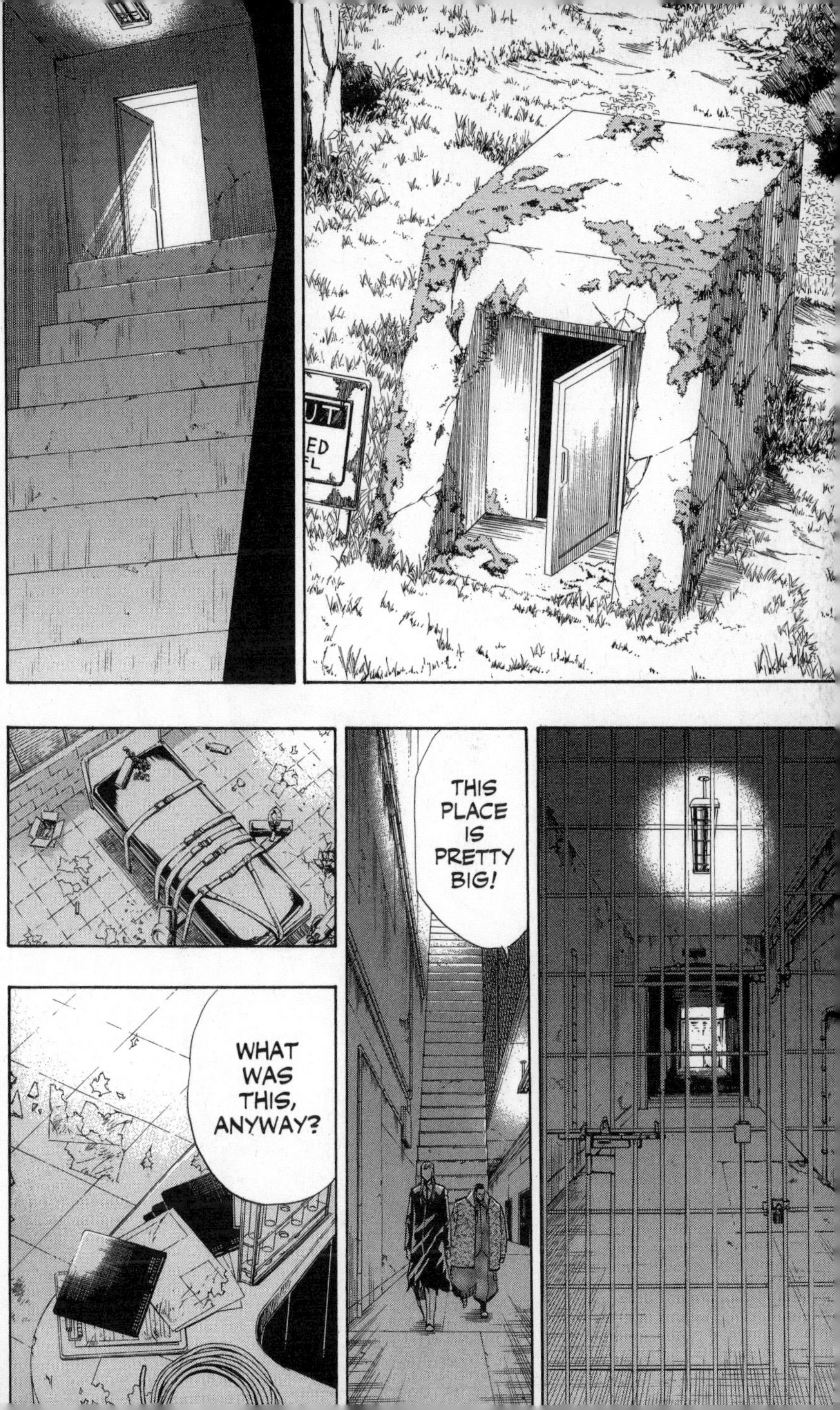
THIS PLACE IS PRETTY BIG!
WHAT WAS THIS, ANYWAY?

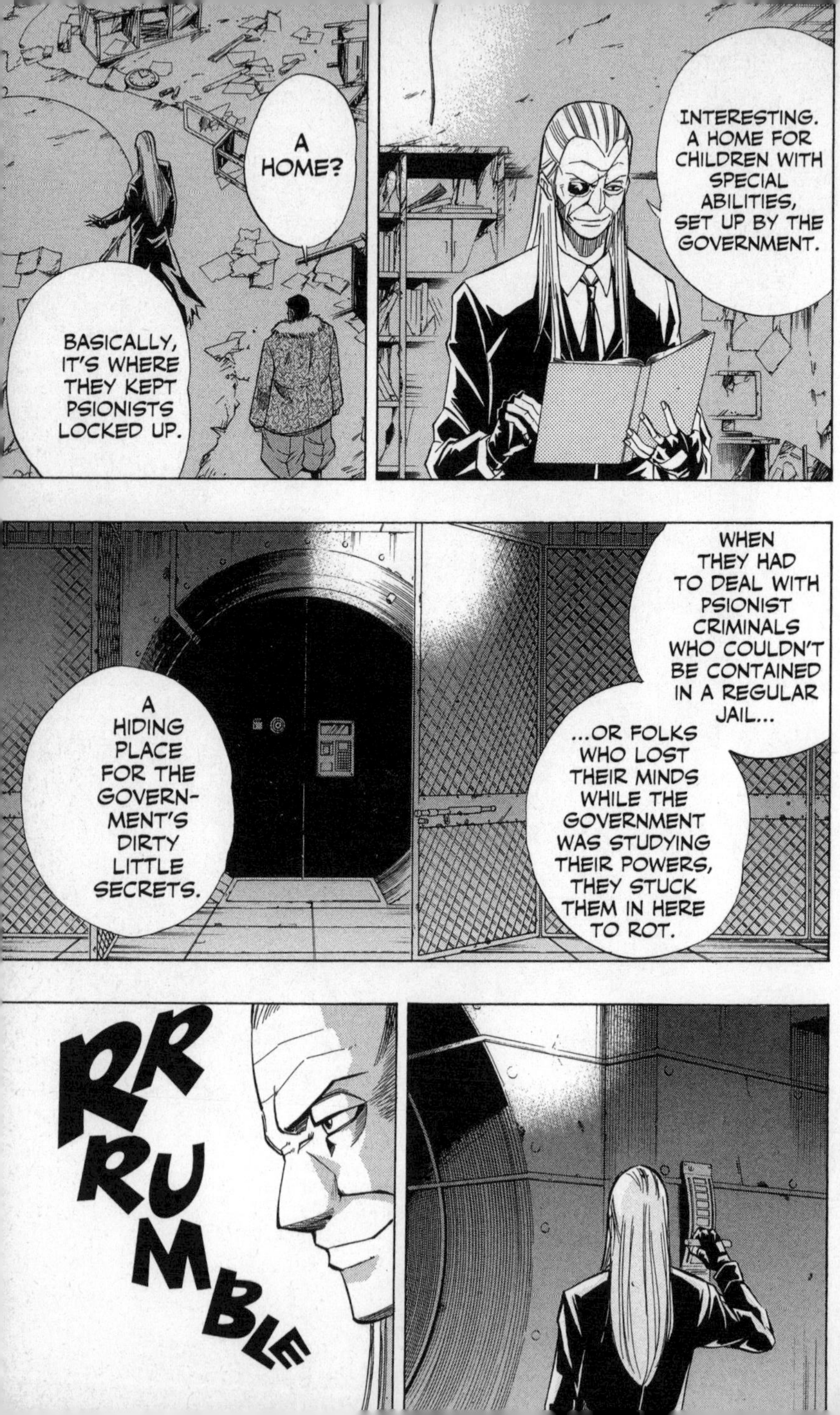
INTERESTING. A HOME FOR CHILDREN WITH SPECIAL ABILITIES, SET UP BY THE GOVERNMENT.
A HOME?
BASICALLY, IT'S WHERE THEY KEPT PSIONISTS LOCKED UP.
WHEN THEY HAD TO DEAL WITH PSIONIST CRIMINALS WHO COULDN'T BE CONTAINED IN A REGULAR JAIL...
...OR FOLKS WHO LOST THEIR MINDS WHILE THE GOVERNMENT WAS STUDYING THEIR POWERS, THEY STUCK THEM IN HERE TO ROT.
A HIDING PLACE FOR THE GOVERN-MENT'S DIRTY LITTLE SECRETS.
RRRUMBLE

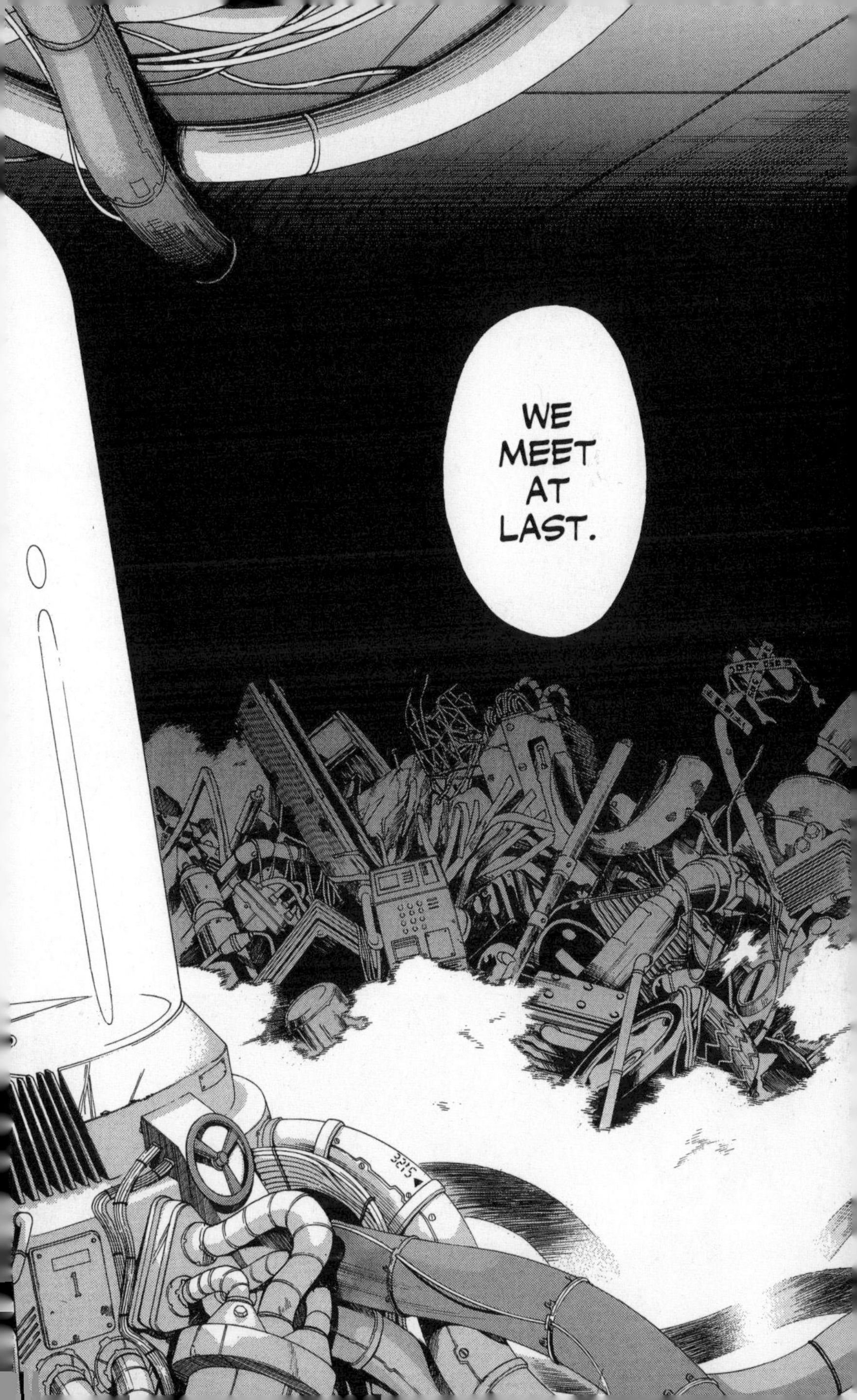
WE MEET AT LAST.

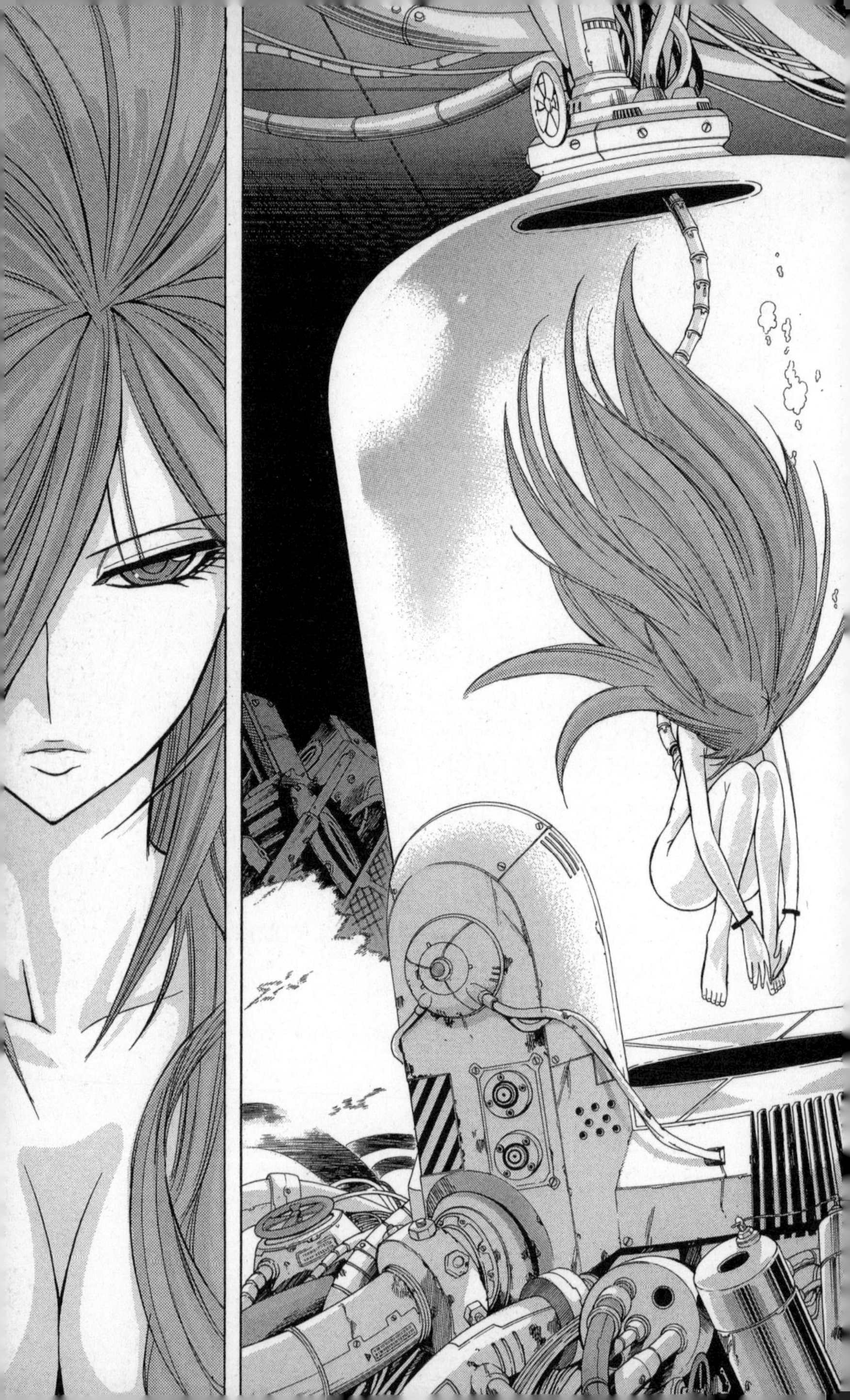

A DAY IN THE LIFE OF VAN

EVENING   DINNER

Oh, honestly!

Ahh!

Ahh!

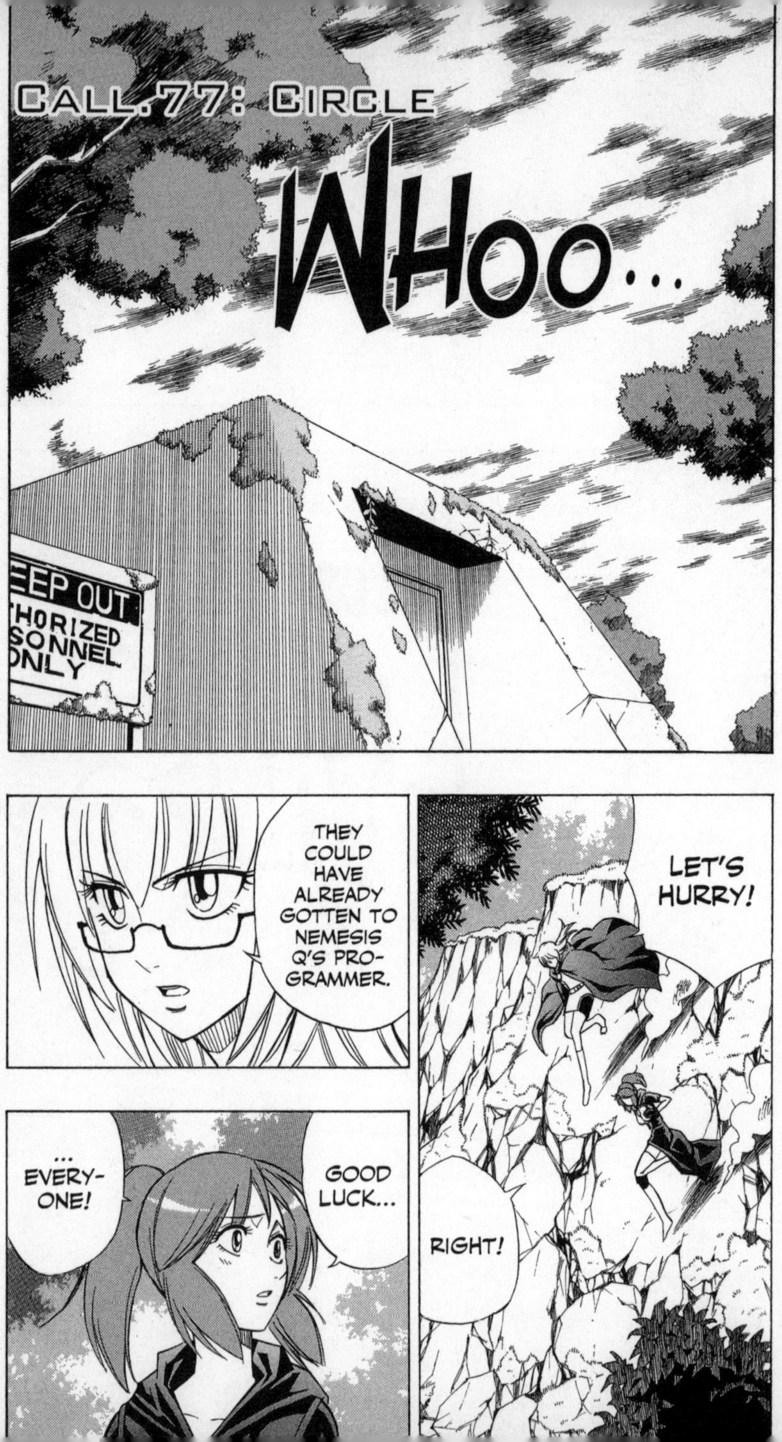
Call.77: Circle
WHOO...
EEP OUT
THORIZED
SONNEL
ONLY
LET'S HURRY!
RIGHT!
THEY COULD HAVE ALREADY GOTTEN TO NEMESIS Q'S PRO-GRAMMER.
GOOD LUCK...
... EVERY-ONE!

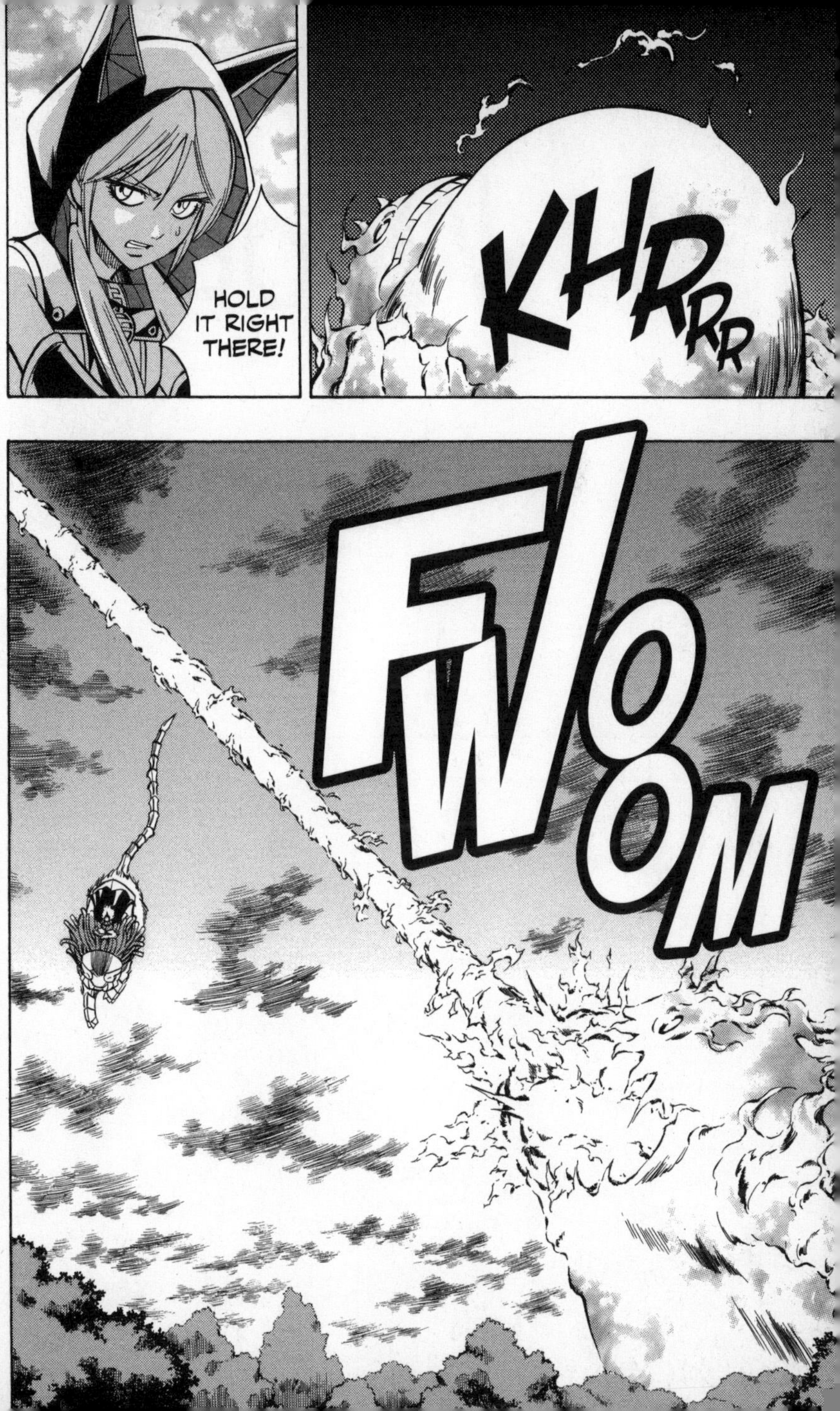
KHRRRR
HOLD IT RIGHT THERE!
FWOOM

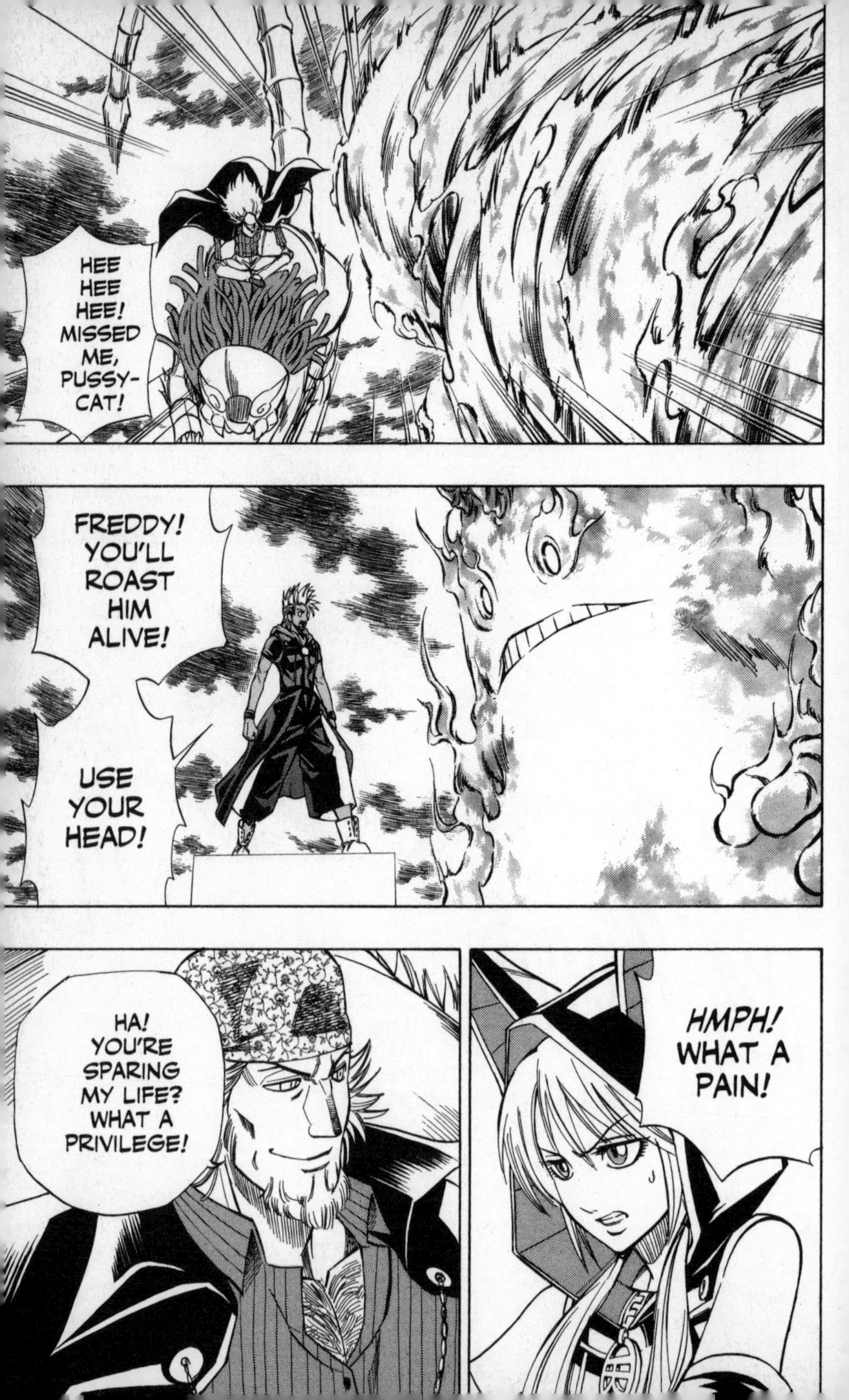
HEE HEE HEE! MISSED ME, PUSSY-CAT!
FREDDY! YOU'LL ROAST HIM ALIVE!
USE YOUR HEAD!
HMPH! WHAT A PAIN!
HA! YOU'RE SPARING MY LIFE? WHAT A PRIVILEGE!

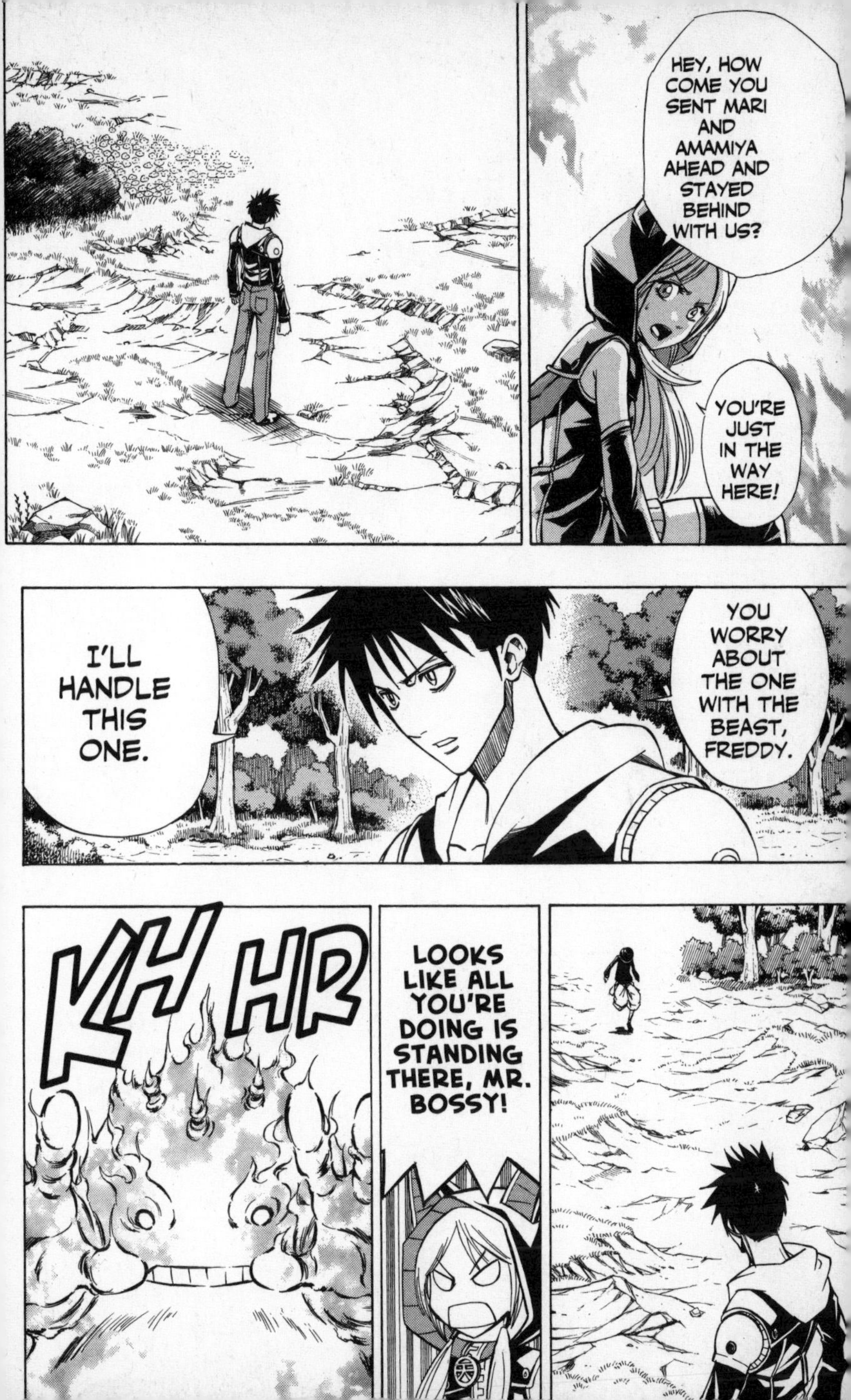
HEY, HOW COME YOU SENT MARI AND AMAMIYA AHEAD AND STAYED BEHIND WITH US?
YOU'RE JUST IN THE WAY HERE!
YOU WORRY ABOUT THE ONE WITH THE BEAST, FREDDY.
I'LL HANDLE THIS ONE.
LOOKS LIKE ALL YOU'RE DOING IS STANDING THERE, MR. BOSSY!
KH HR

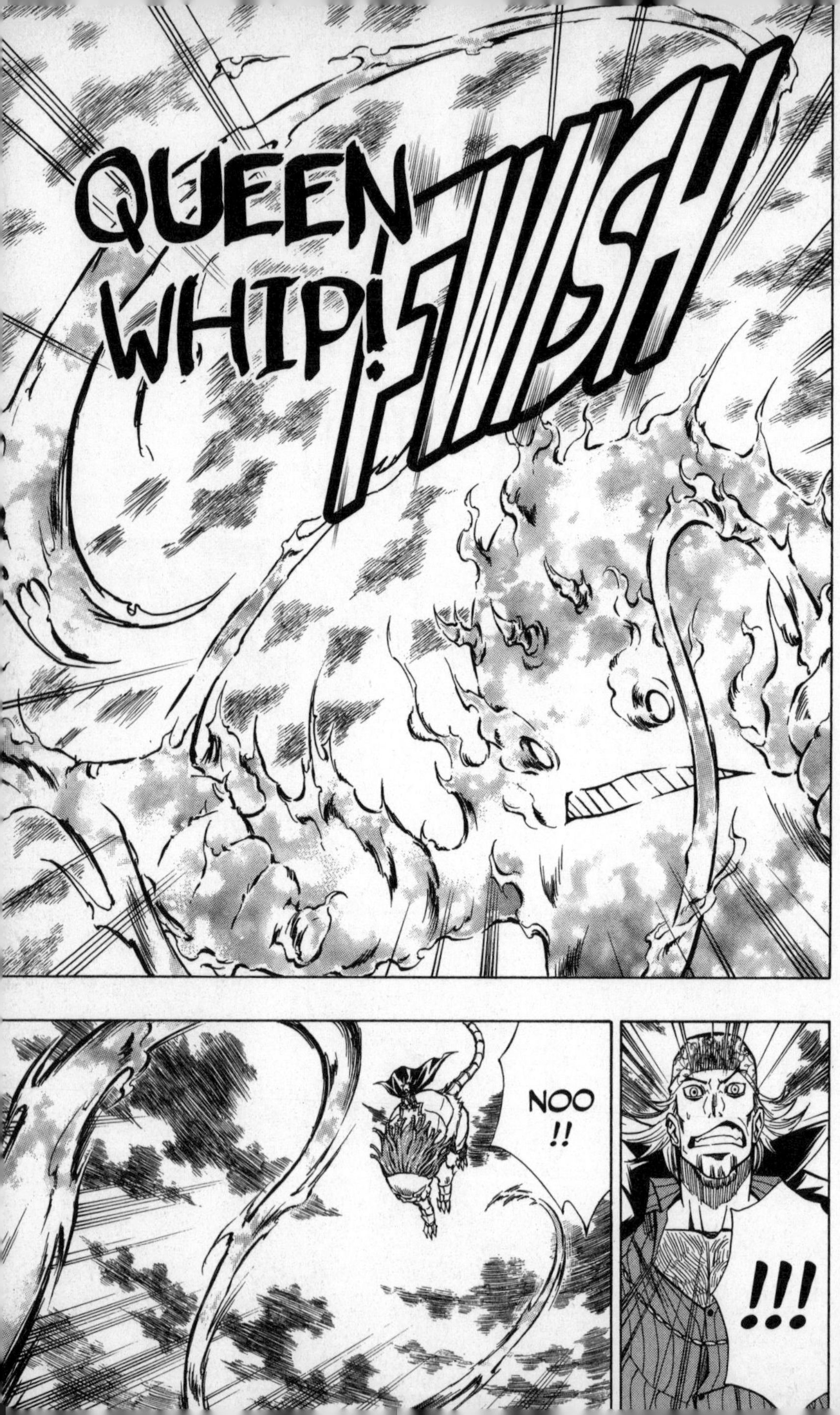
QUEEN WHIP!
FWISH
!!!
NOO !!

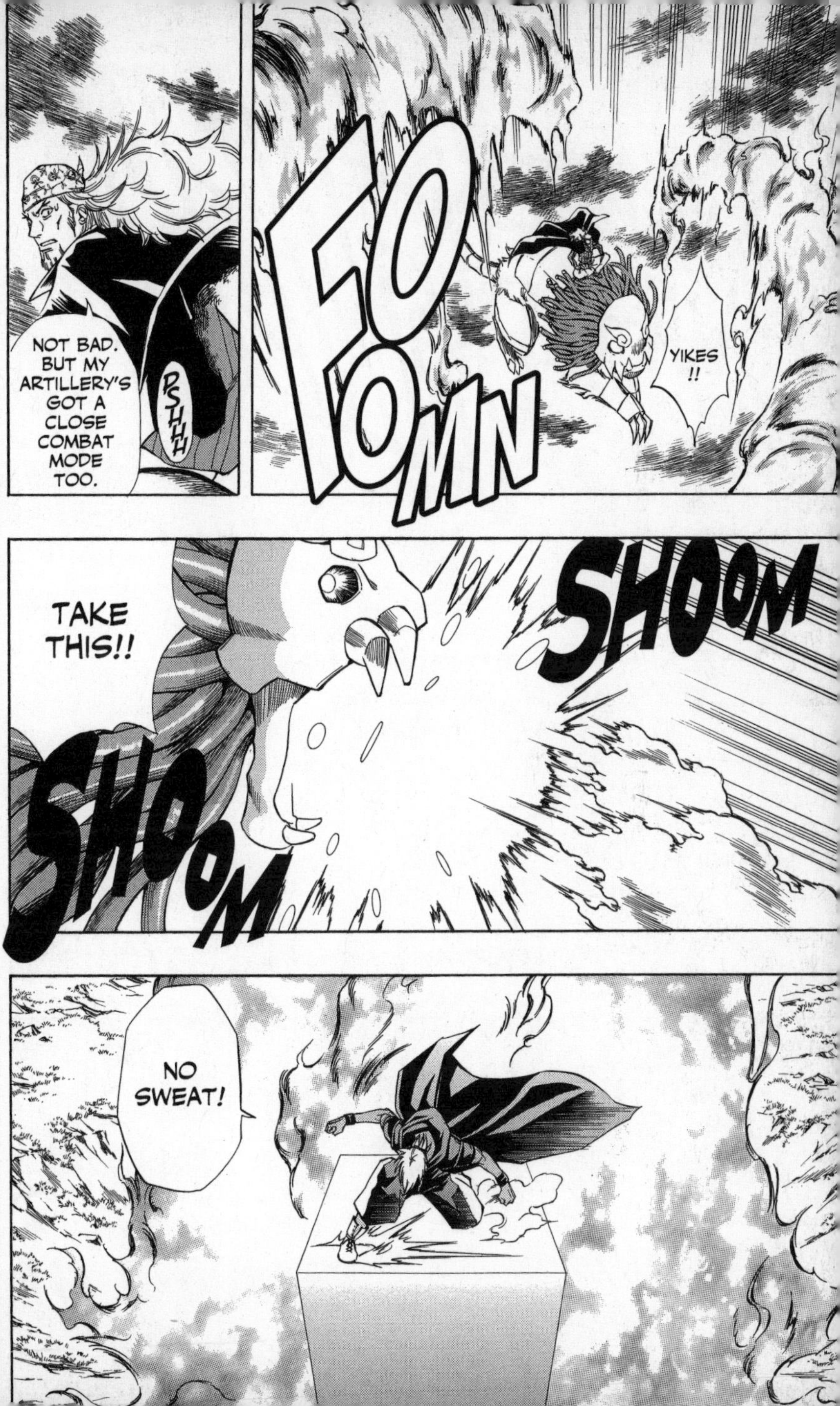
FOOMN
YIKES!!
NOT BAD. BUT MY ARTILLERY'S GOT A CLOSE COMBAT MODE TOO.
PSHHH
SHOOM
TAKE THIS!!
SHOOM
NO SWEAT!

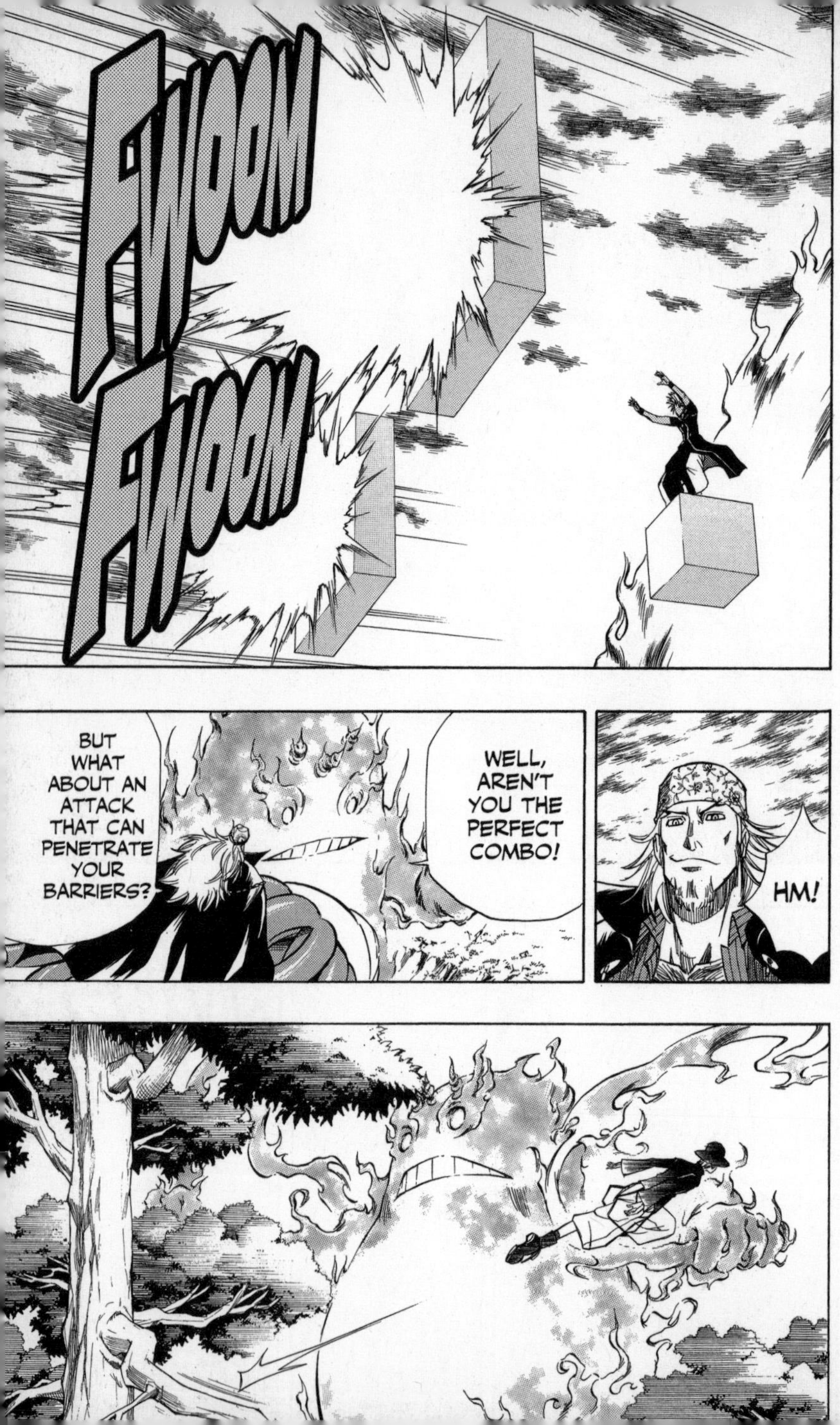
FWOOM
FWOOM
HM!
WELL, AREN'T YOU THE PERFECT COMBO!
BUT WHAT ABOUT AN ATTACK THAT CAN PENETRATE YOUR BARRIERS?

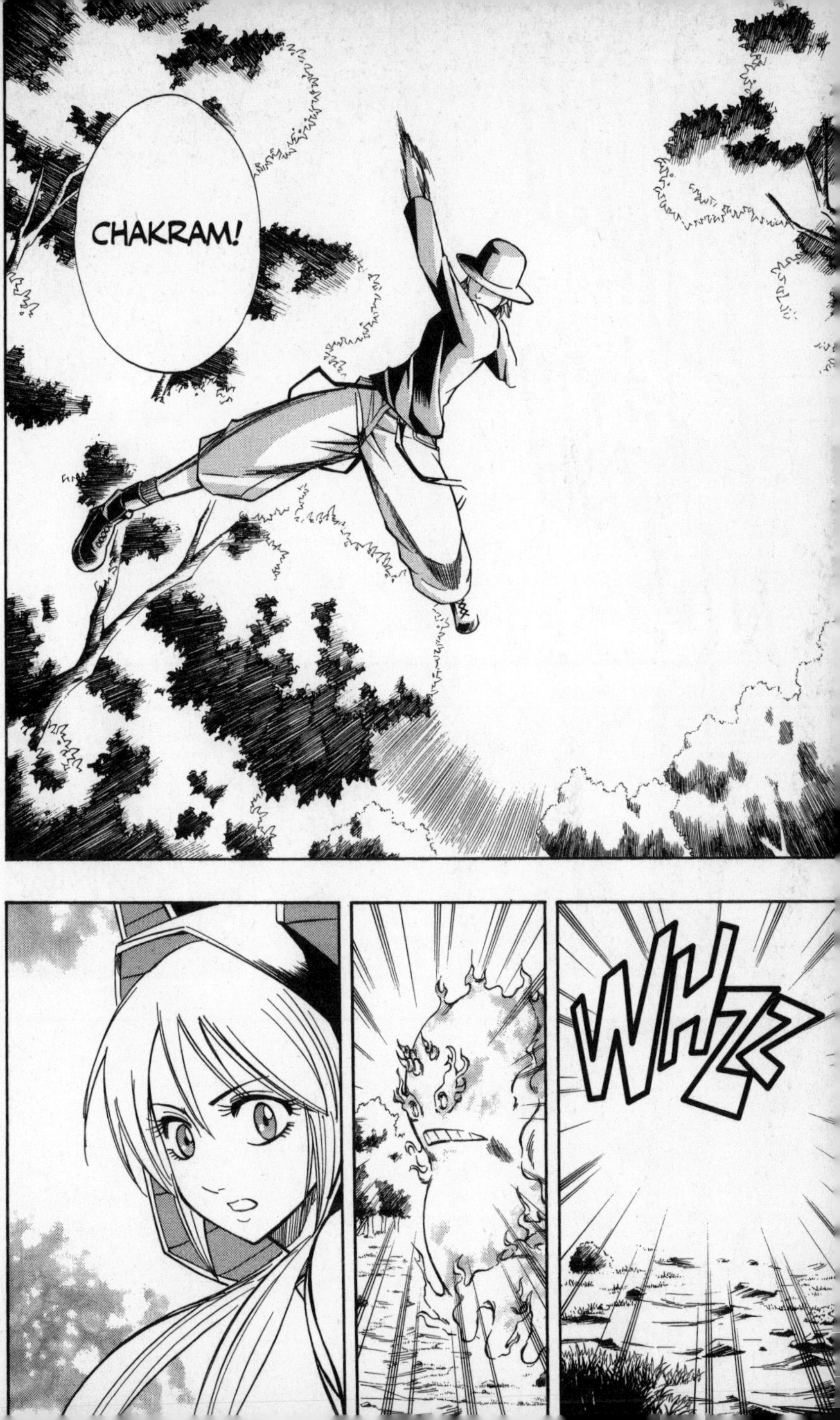
CHAKRAM!
WHIZZ

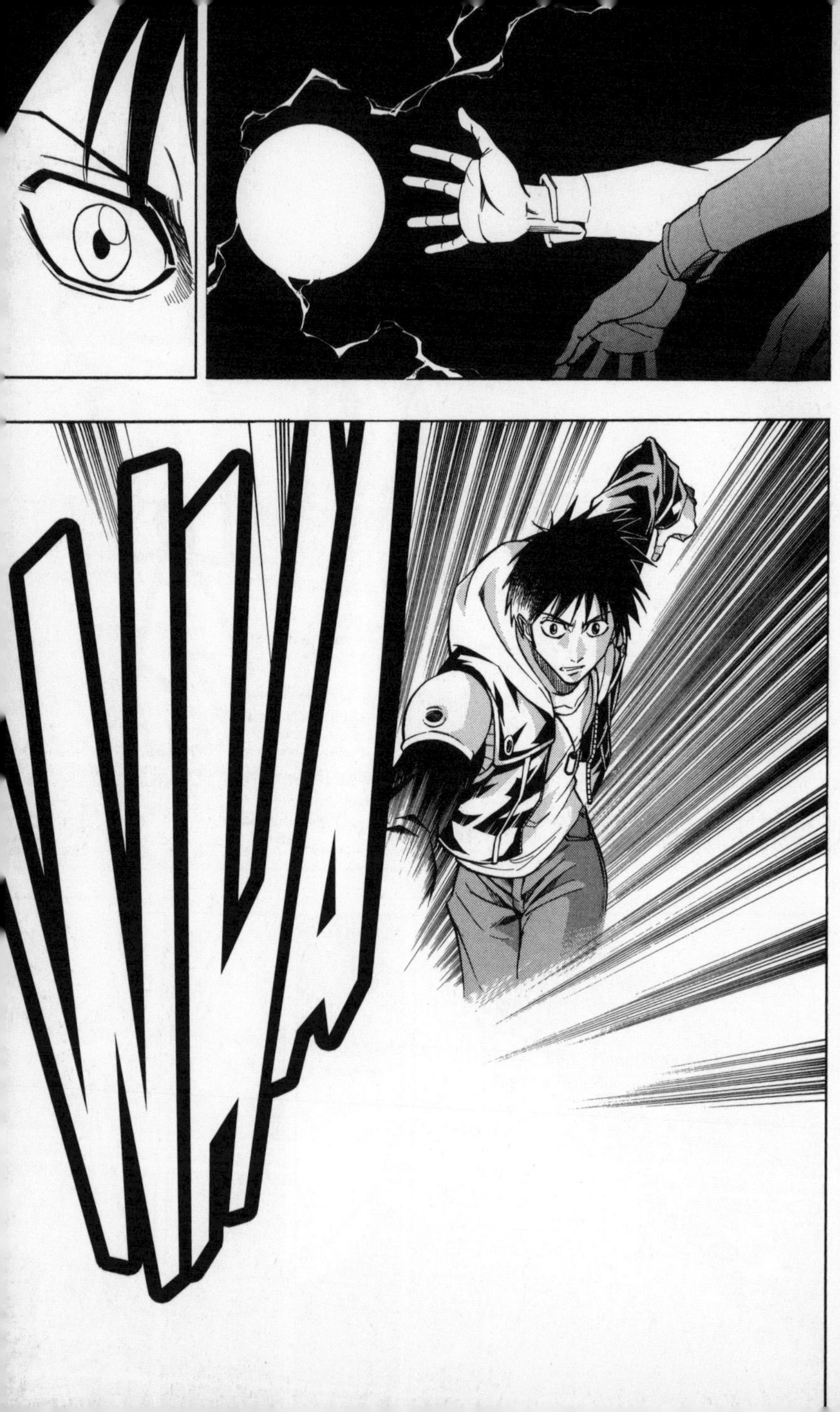

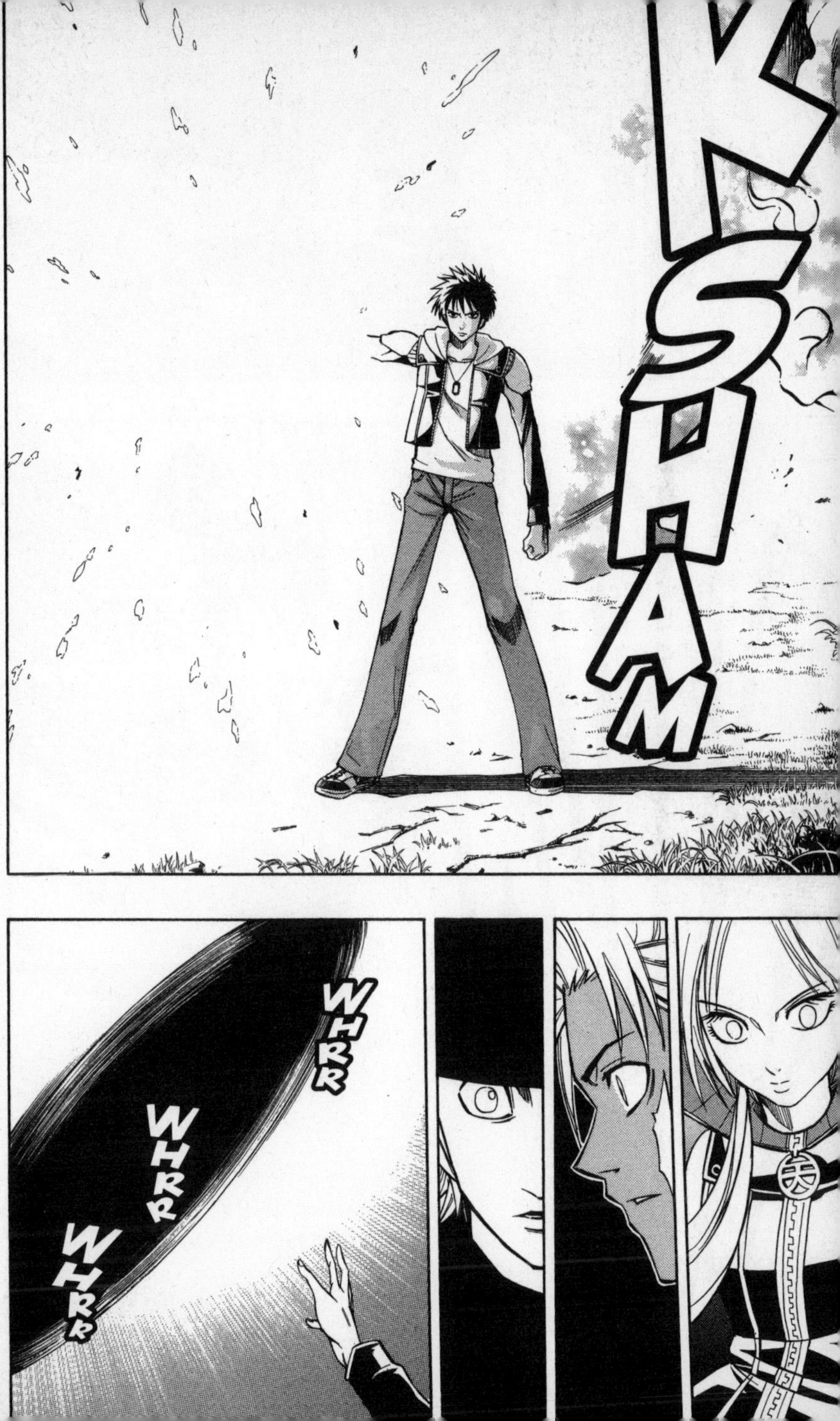
KSHAM
WHRR
WHRR
WHRR

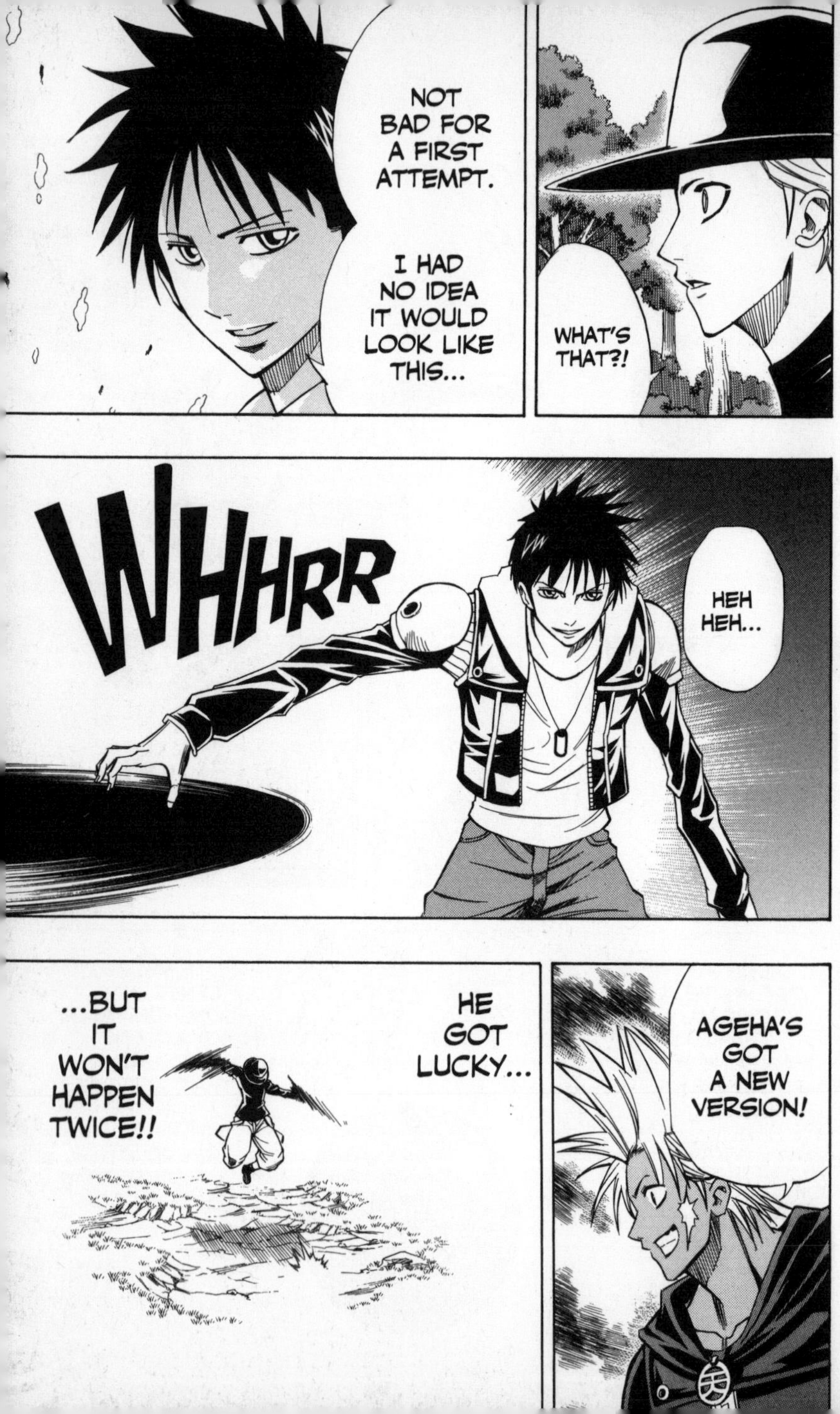

WHAT'S THAT?!
NOT BAD FOR A FIRST ATTEMPT.
I HAD NO IDEA IT WOULD LOOK LIKE THIS...
HEH HEH...
WHHRR
AGEHA'S GOT A NEW VERSION!
HE GOT LUCKY...
...BUT IT WON'T HAPPEN TWICE!!

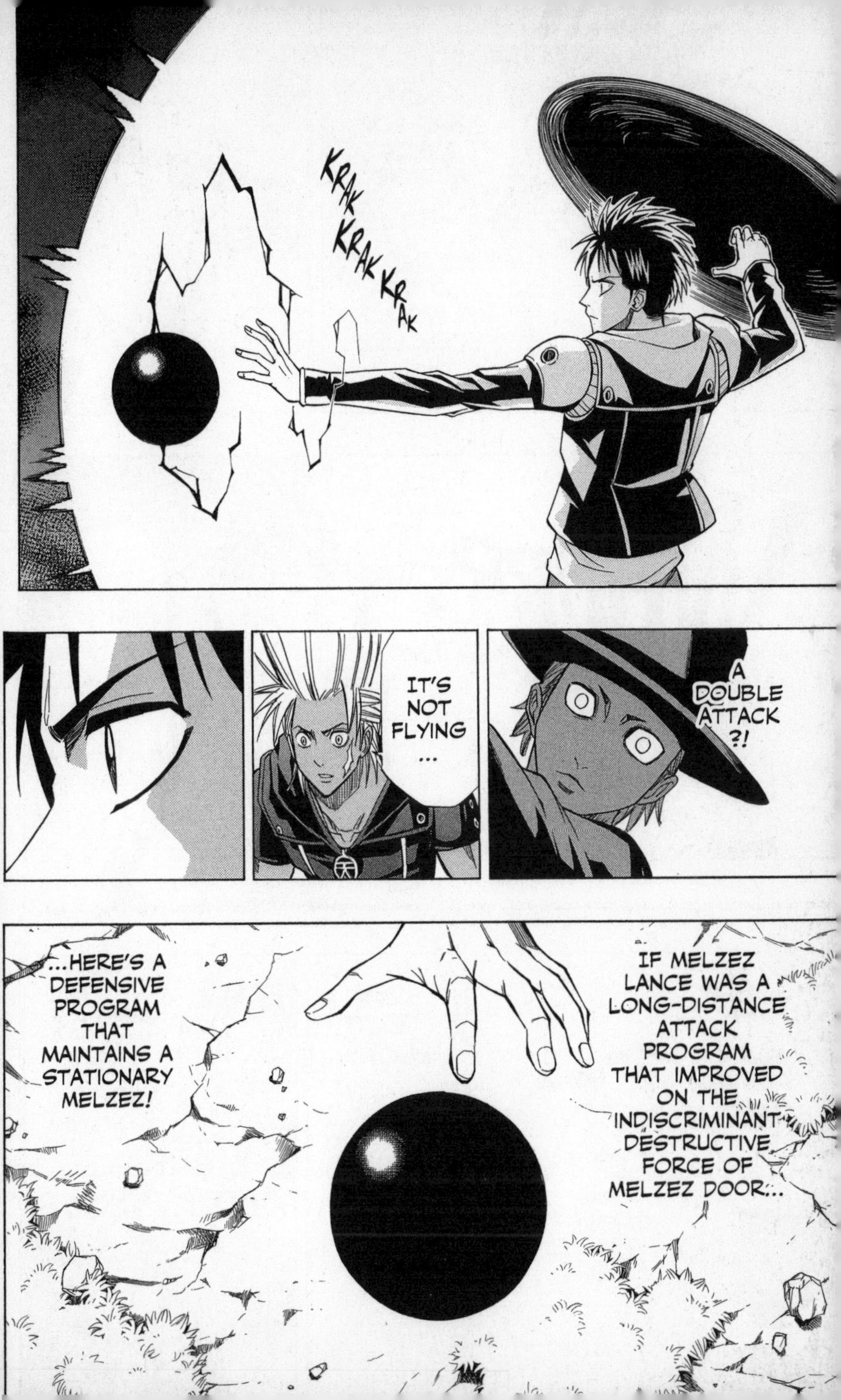
KRAK KRAK KRAK
A DOUBLE ATTACK ?!
IT'S NOT FLYING ...
IF MELZEZ LANCE WAS A LONG-DISTANCE ATTACK PROGRAM THAT IMPROVED ON THE INDISCRIMINANT DESTRUCTIVE FORCE OF MELZEZ DOOR...
...HERE'S A DEFENSIVE PROGRAM THAT MAINTAINS A STATIONARY MELZEZ!

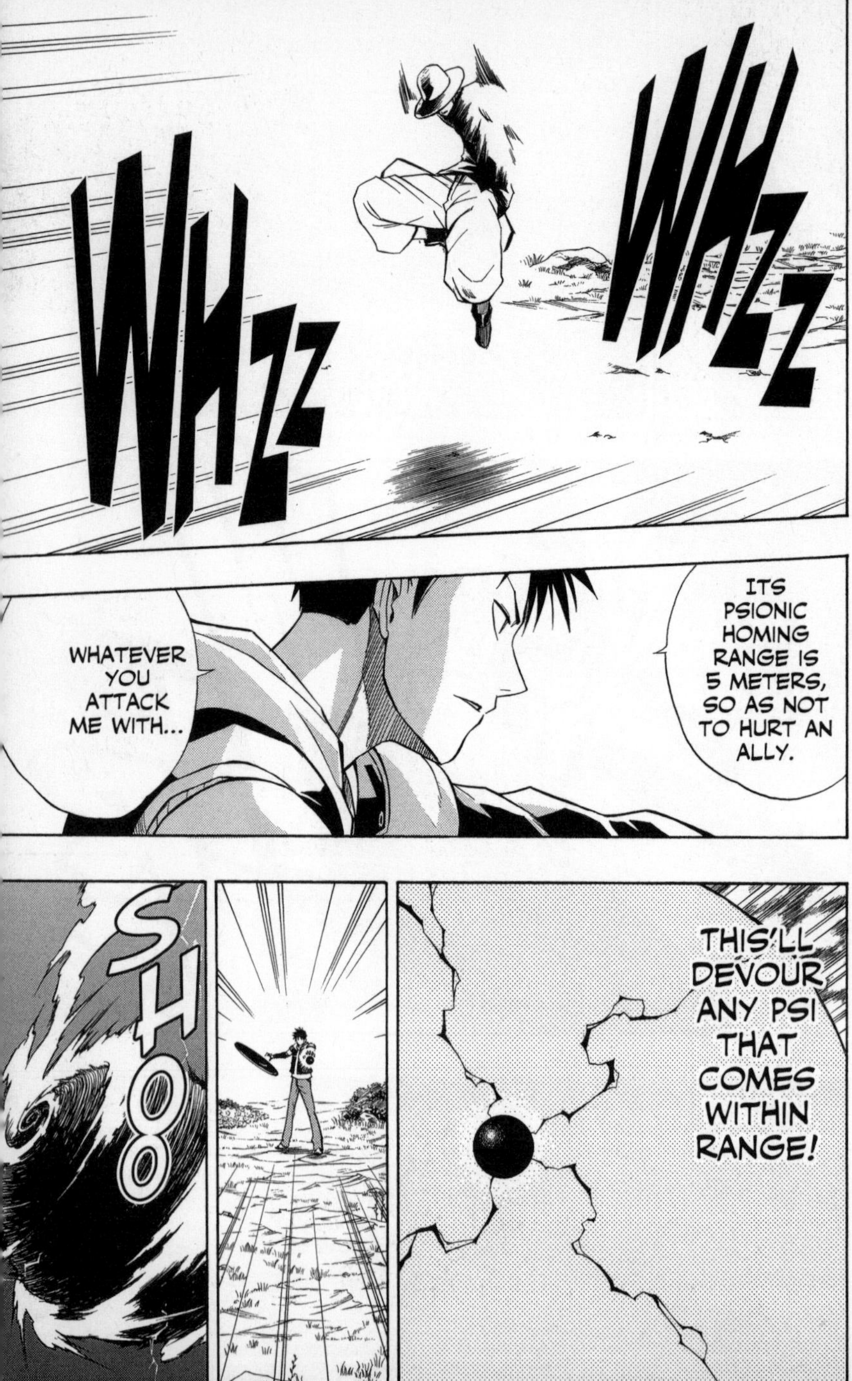
WHZZ
WHZZ
ITS PSIONIC HOMING RANGE IS 5 METERS, SO AS NOT TO HURT AN ALLY.
WHATEVER YOU ATTACK ME WITH...
THIS'LL DEVOUR ANY PSI THAT COMES WITHIN RANGE!
SHOO

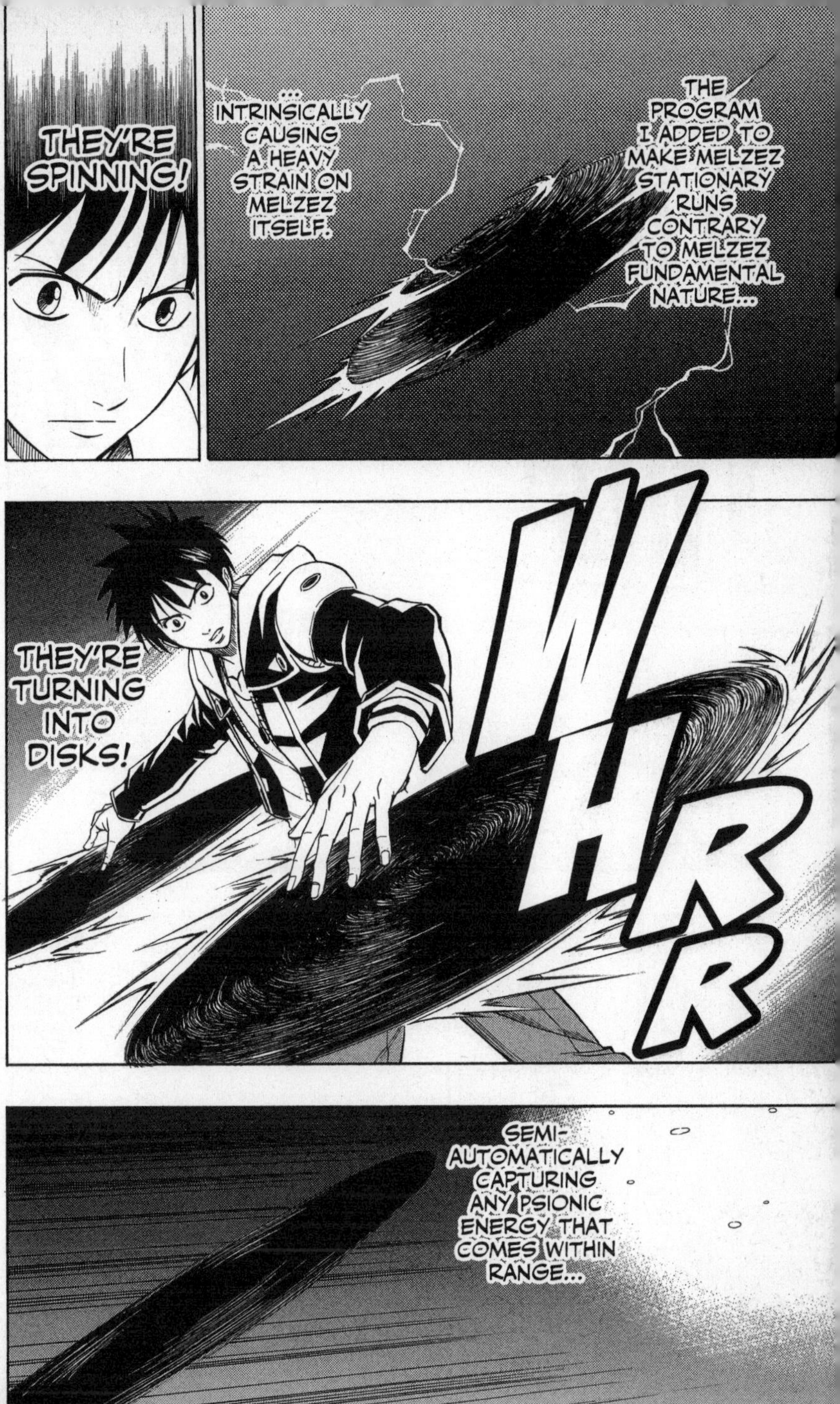
THE PROGRAM I ADDED TO MAKE MELZEZ STATIONARY RUNS CONTRARY TO MELZEZ FUNDAMENTAL NATURE...
...INTRINSICALLY CAUSING A HEAVY STRAIN ON MELZEZ ITSELF.
THEY'RE SPINNING!
WHRR
THEY'RE TURNING INTO DISKS!
SEMI-AUTOMATICALLY CAPTURING ANY PSIONIC ENERGY THAT COMES WITHIN RANGE...

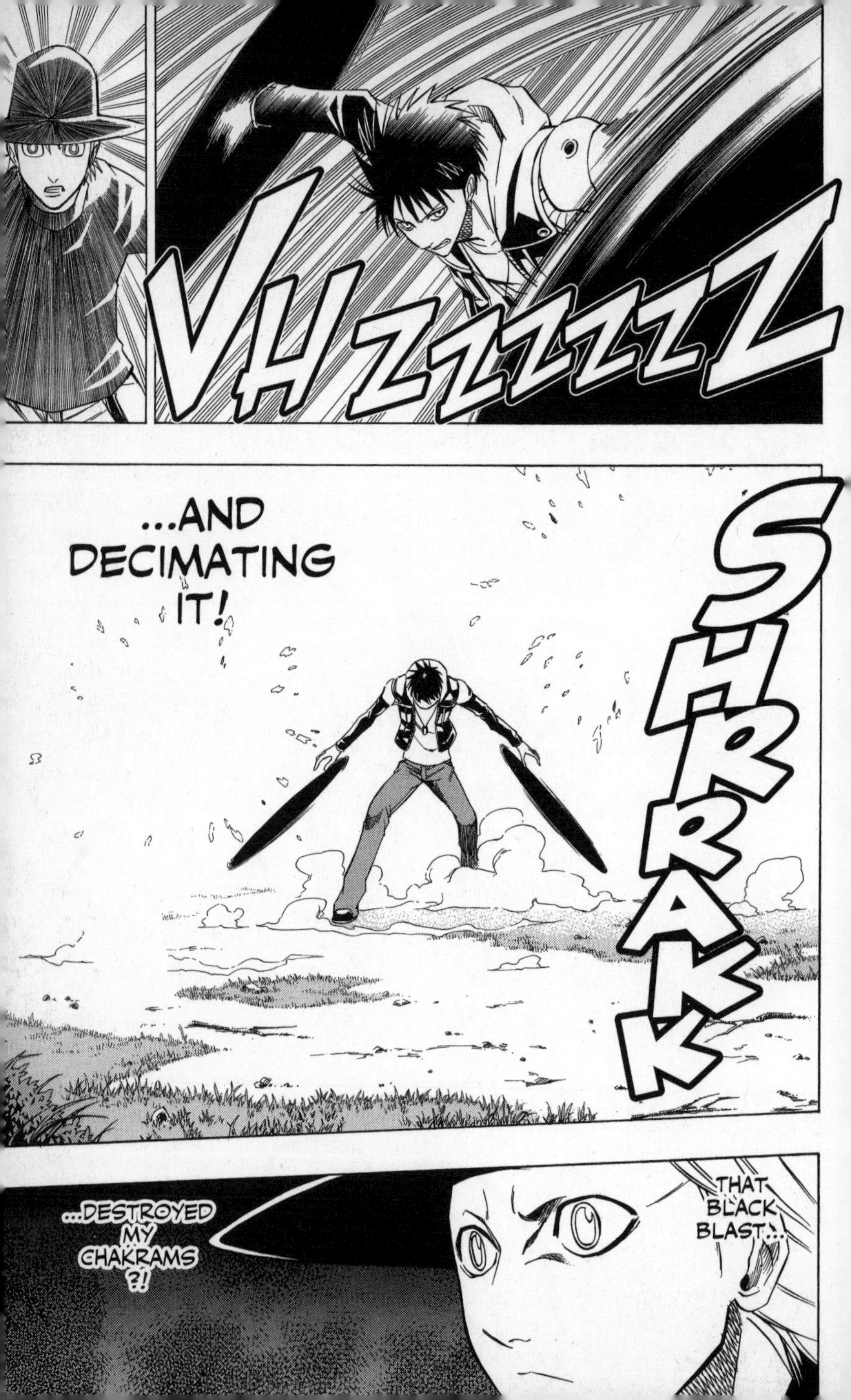
VHZZZZZZ
SHHRRAK
...AND DECIMATING IT!
THAT BLACK BLAST...
...DESTROYED MY CHAKRAMS ?!

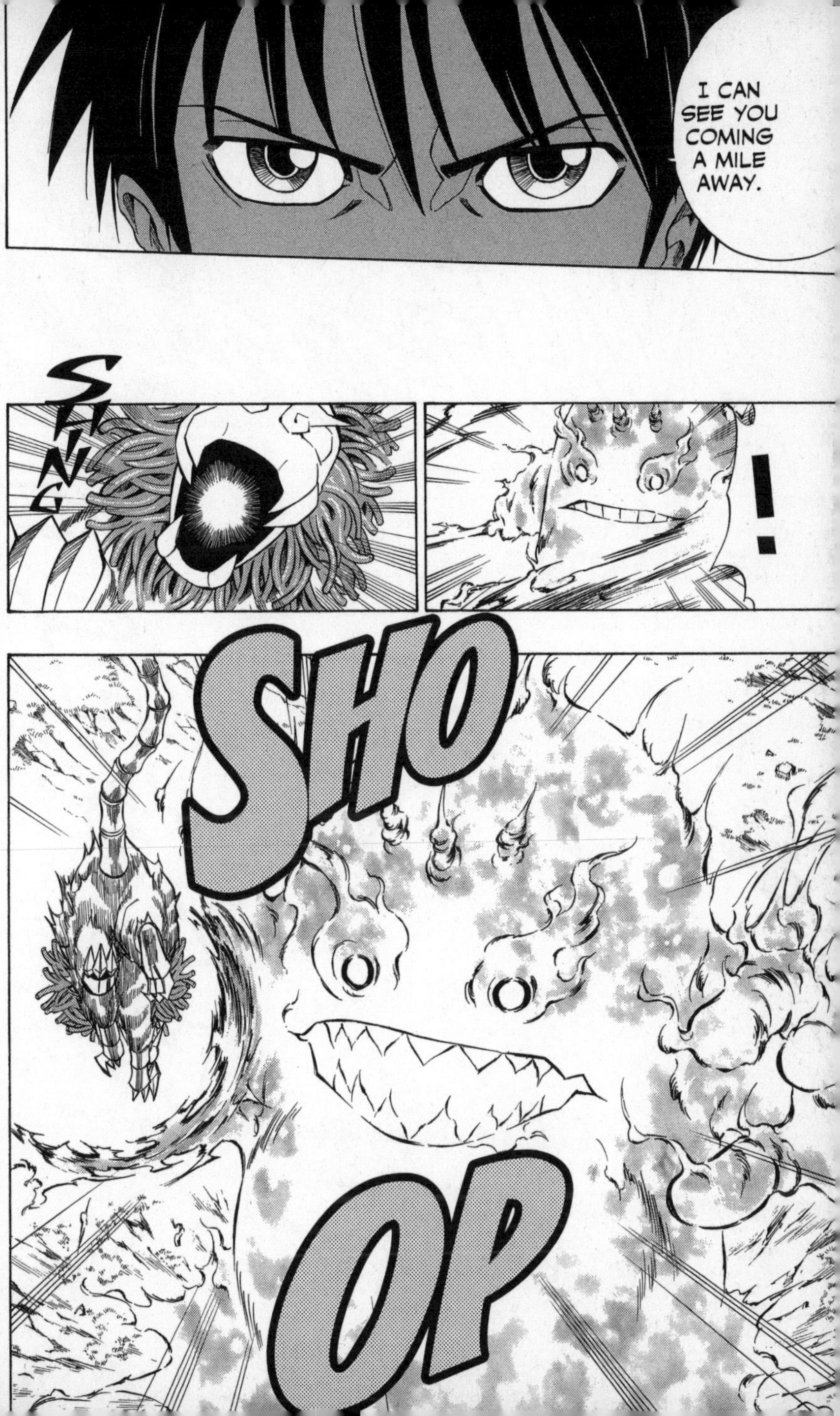
I CAN SEE YOU COMING A MILE AWAY.
SHING
!
SHOOP

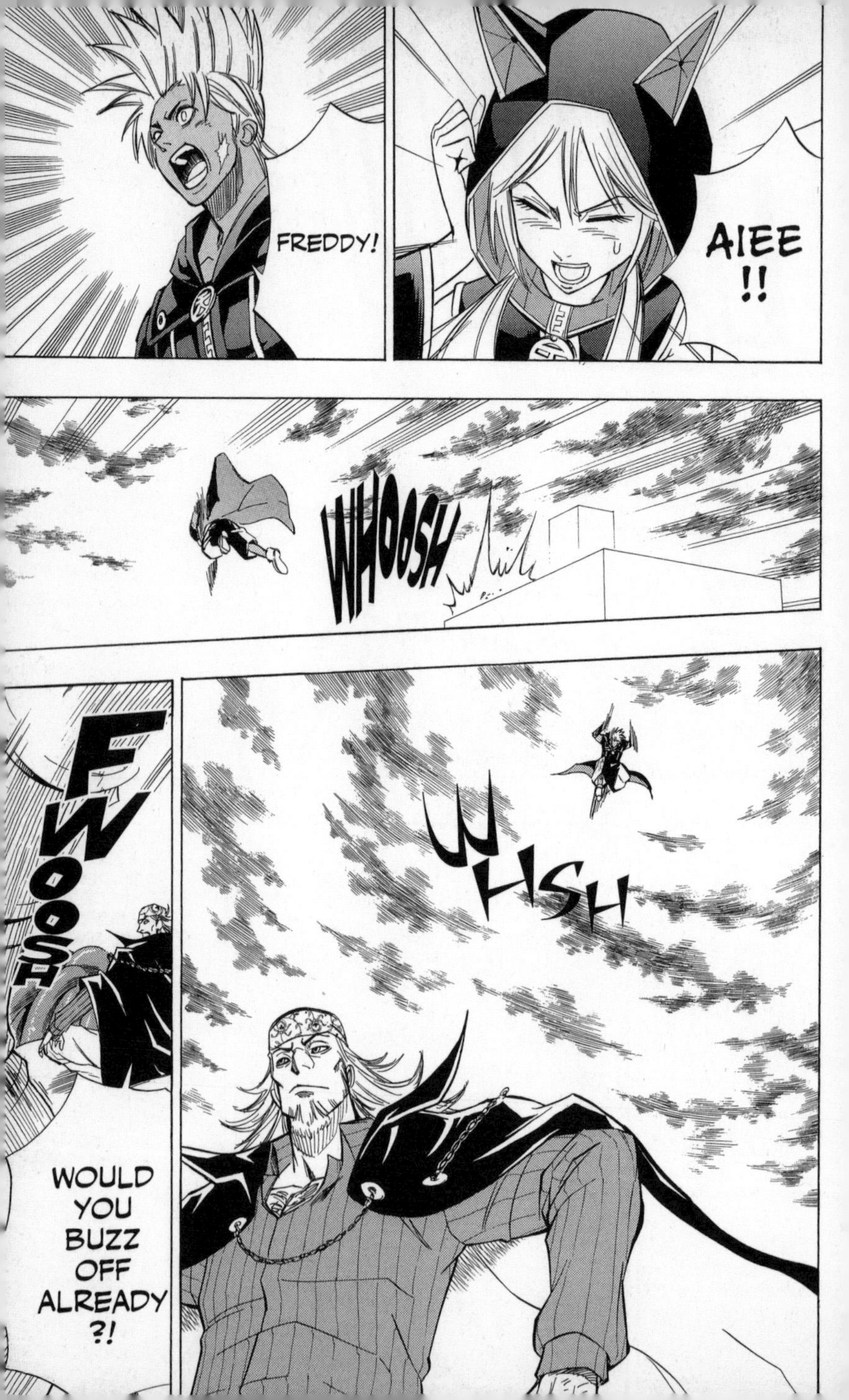
AIEE !!
FREDDY!
WHOOSH
WHSH
FWOOSH
WOULD YOU BUZZ OFF ALREADY ?!

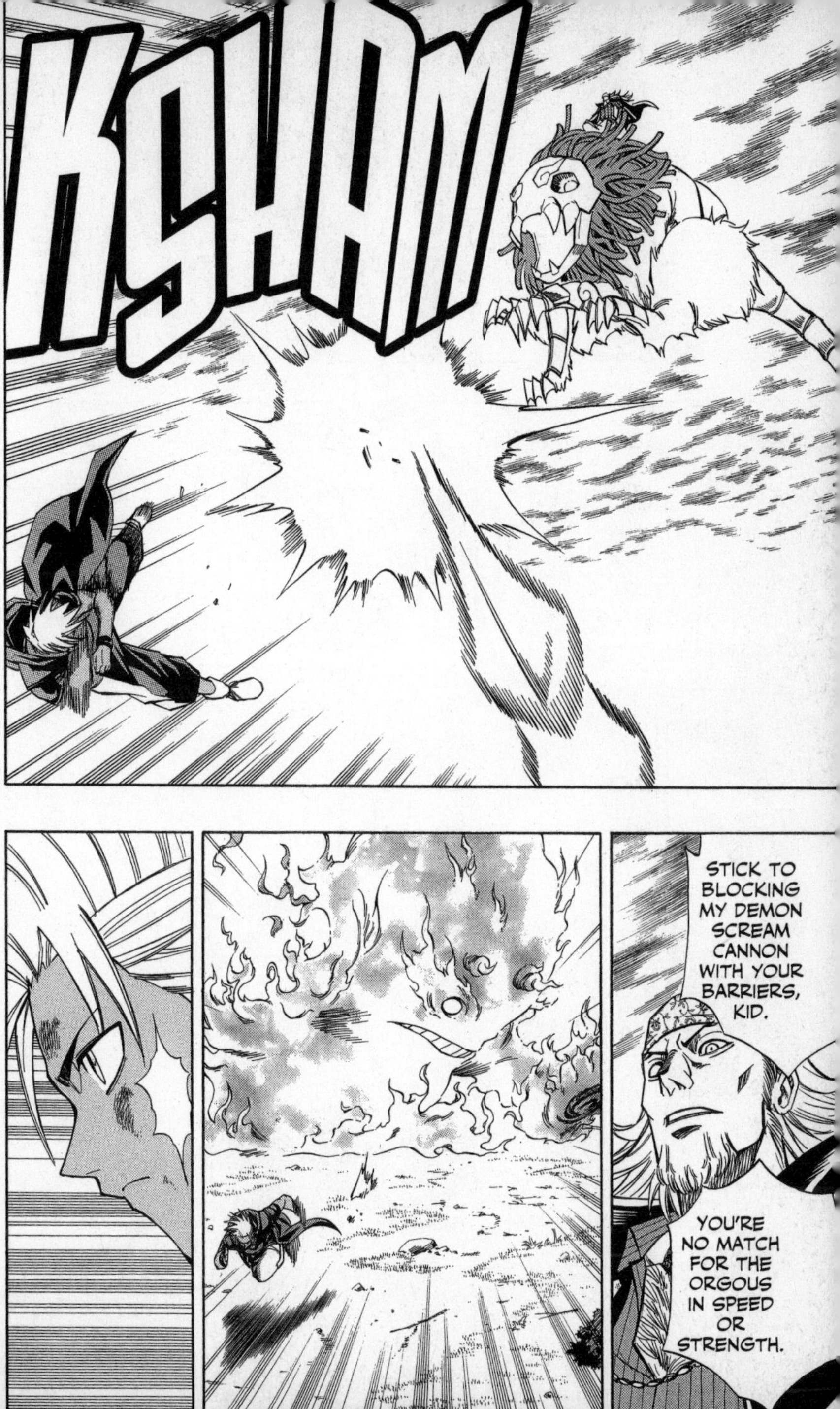
KSHAM
STICK TO BLOCKING MY DEMON SCREAM CANNON WITH YOUR BARRIERS, KID.
YOU'RE NO MATCH FOR THE ORGOUS IN SPEED OR STRENGTH.

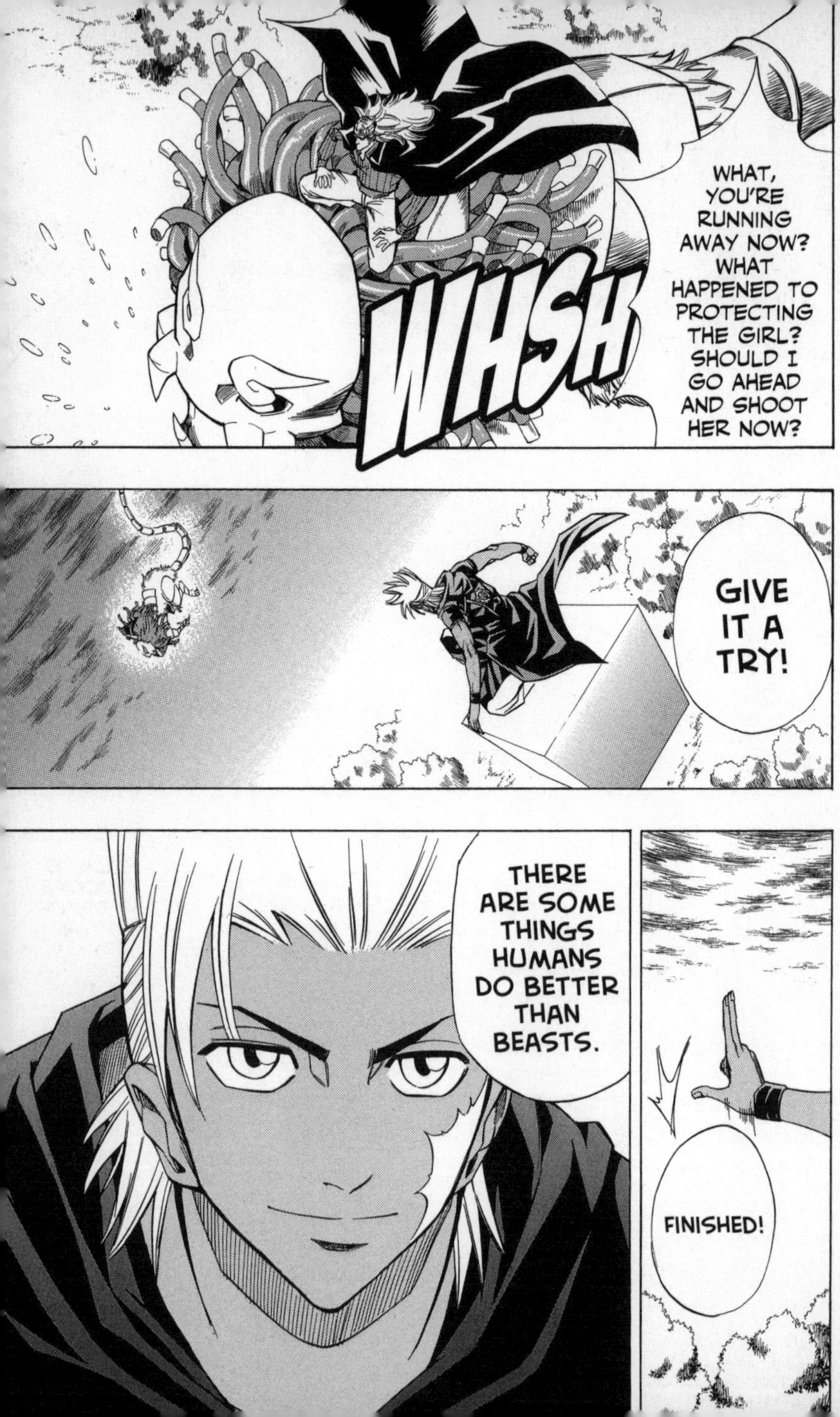
WHAT, YOU'RE RUNNING AWAY NOW? WHAT HAPPENED TO PROTECTING THE GIRL? SHOULD I GO AHEAD AND SHOOT HER NOW?
WHSH
GIVE IT A TRY!
FINISHED!
THERE ARE SOME THINGS HUMANS DO BETTER THAN BEASTS.

Mutters and mumblings...

I LIKE HIKARU IJUUIN'S RADIO SHOW.
 I LIKE TO RECORD THE SHOW AND REPLAY
 IT ON MY IPOD.

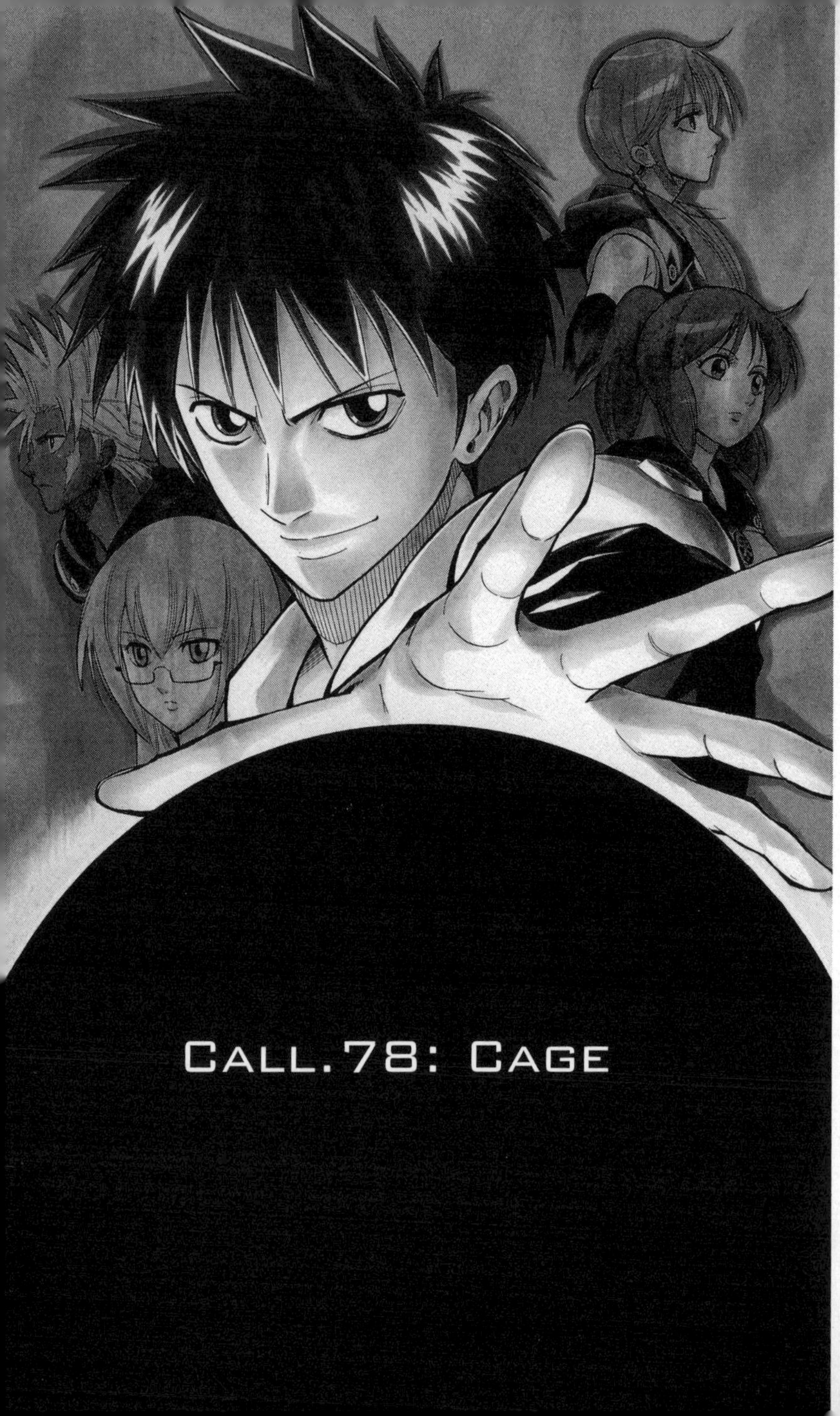

CALL. 78: CAGE

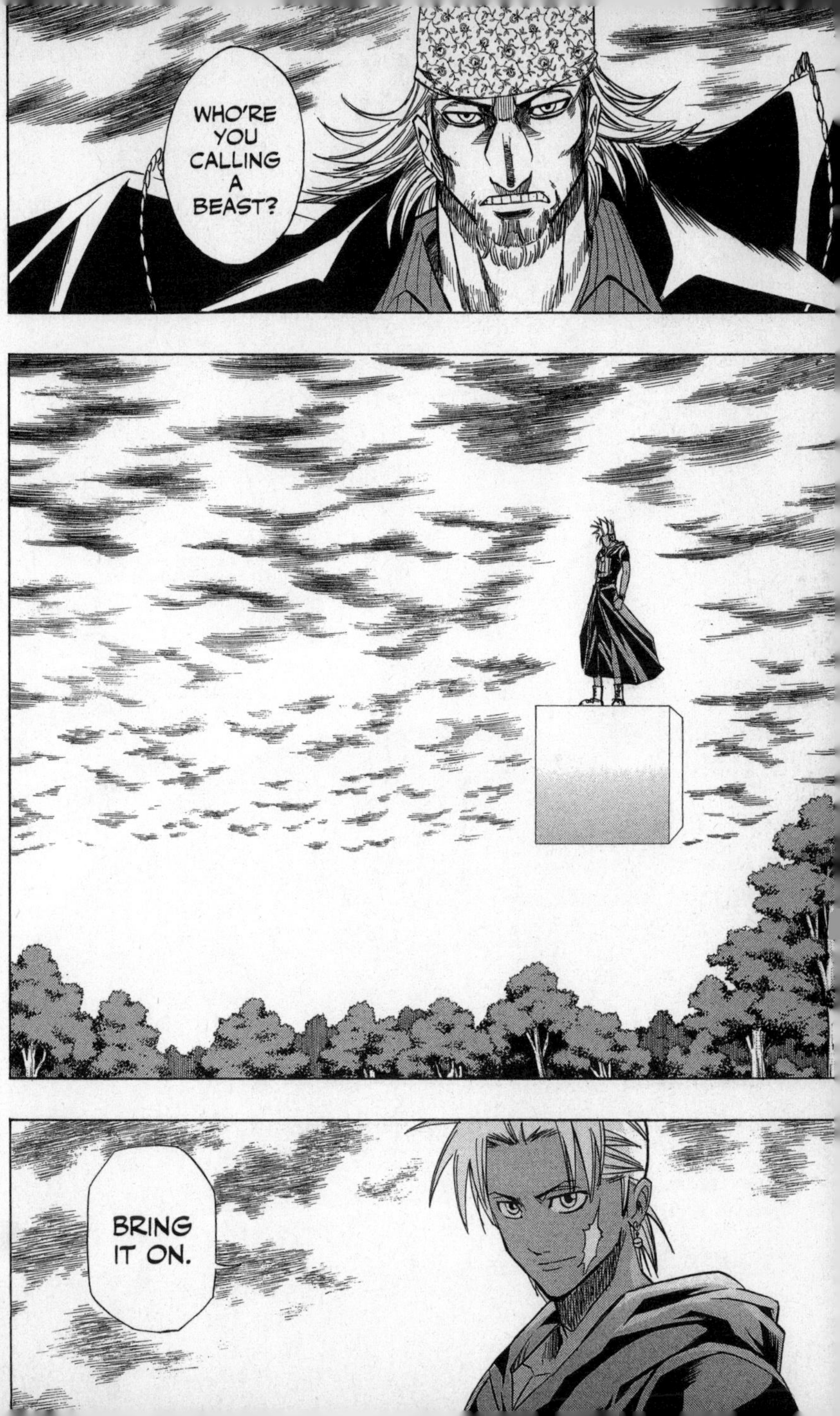
WHO'RE YOU CALLING A BEAST?
BRING IT ON.

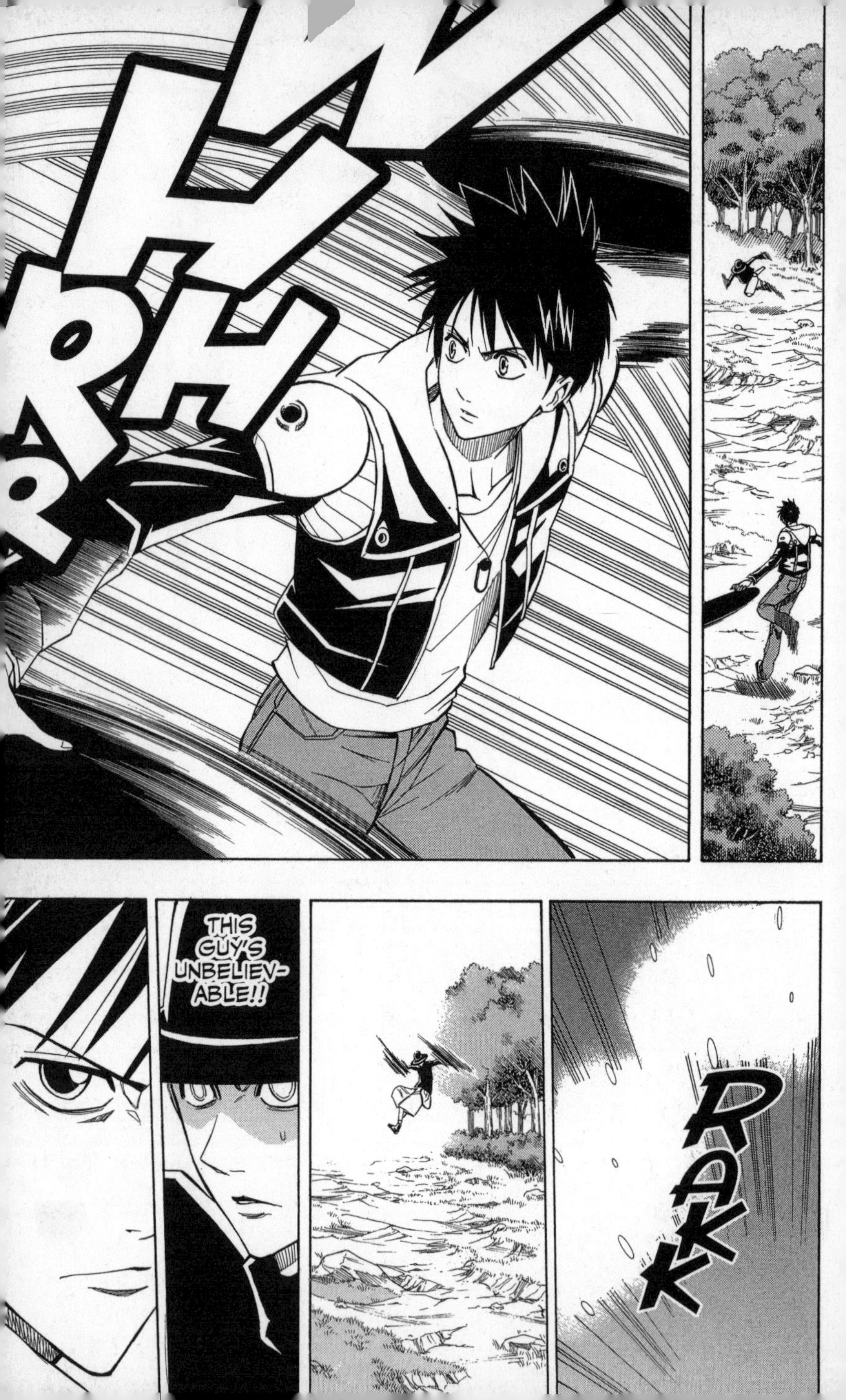
RAKK
THIS GUY'S UNBELIEV-ABLE!!

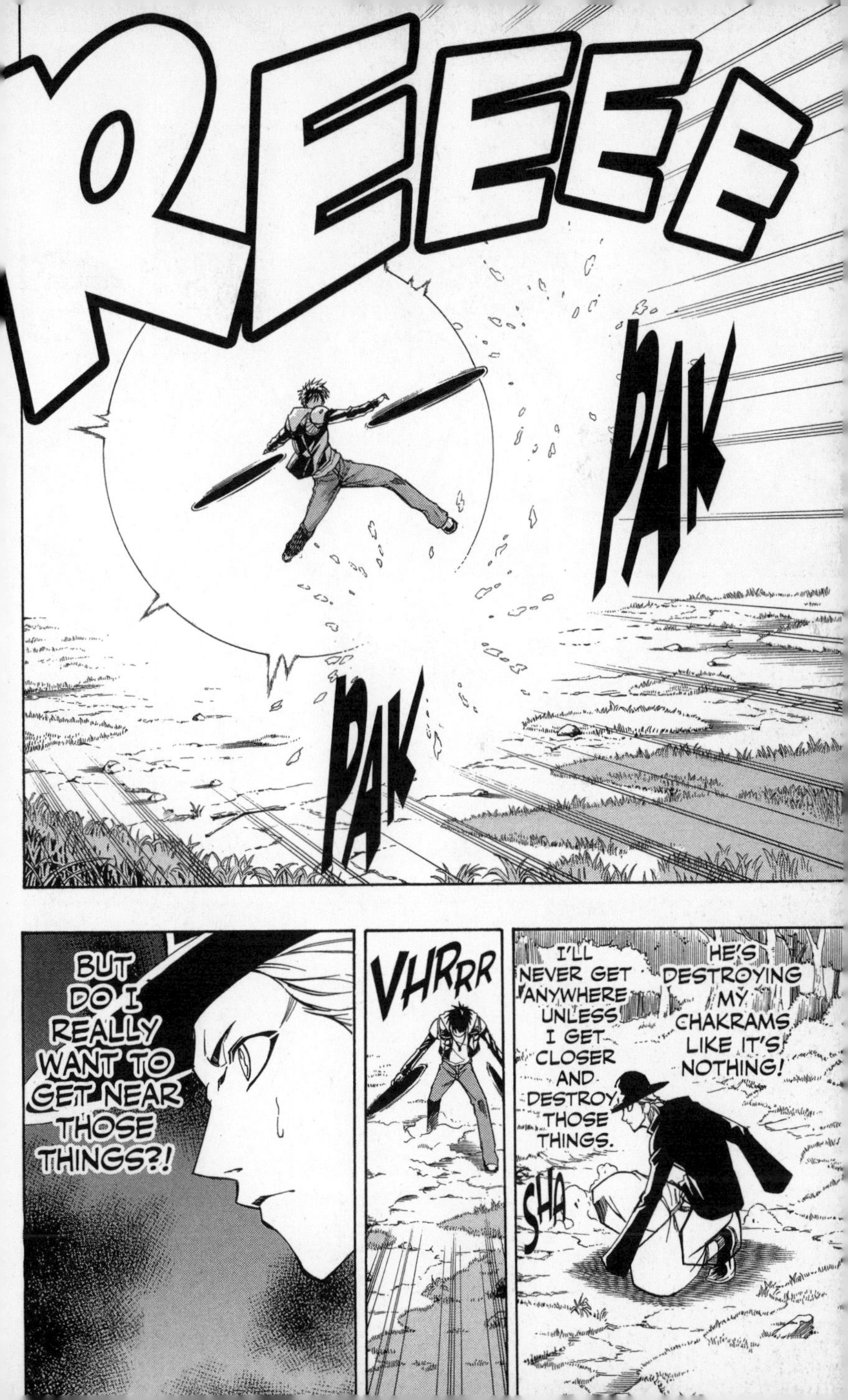
REEEE
PAK
PAK
HE'S DESTROYING MY CHAKRAMS LIKE IT'S NOTHING!
I'LL NEVER GET ANYWHERE UNLESS I GET CLOSER AND DESTROY THOSE THINGS.
SHA
VHRRR
BUT DO I REALLY WANT TO GET NEAR THOSE THINGS?!

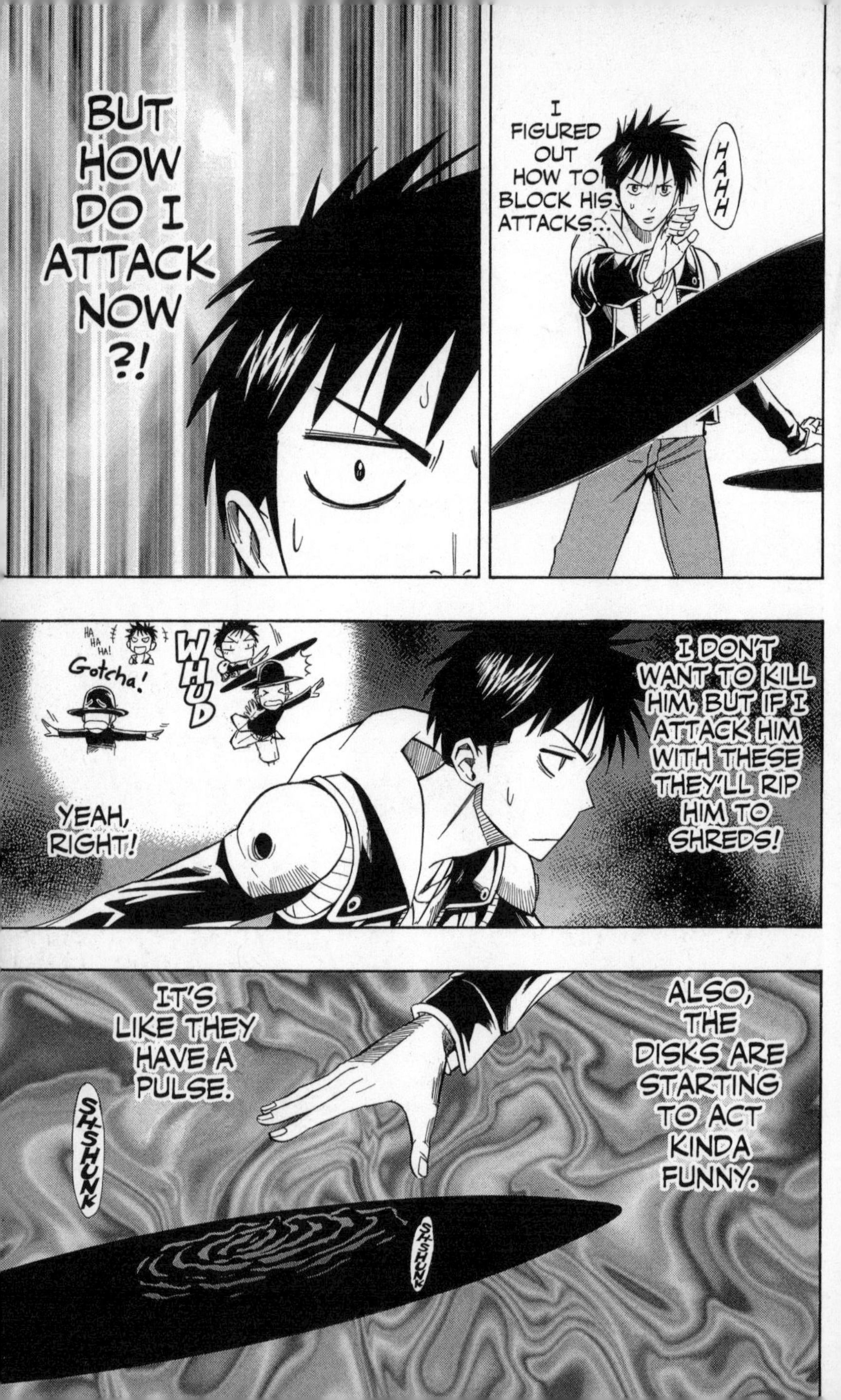
I FIGURED OUT HOW TO BLOCK HIS ATTACKS...
HAHH
BUT HOW DO I ATTACK NOW?!
I DON'T WANT TO KILL HIM, BUT IF I ATTACK HIM WITH THESE THEY'LL RIP HIM TO SHREDS!
WHUD
HA HA HA!
Gotcha!
YEAH, RIGHT!
ALSO, THE DISKS ARE STARTING TO ACT KINDA FUNNY.
SHSHUNK
IT'S LIKE THEY HAVE A PULSE.
SHSHUNK

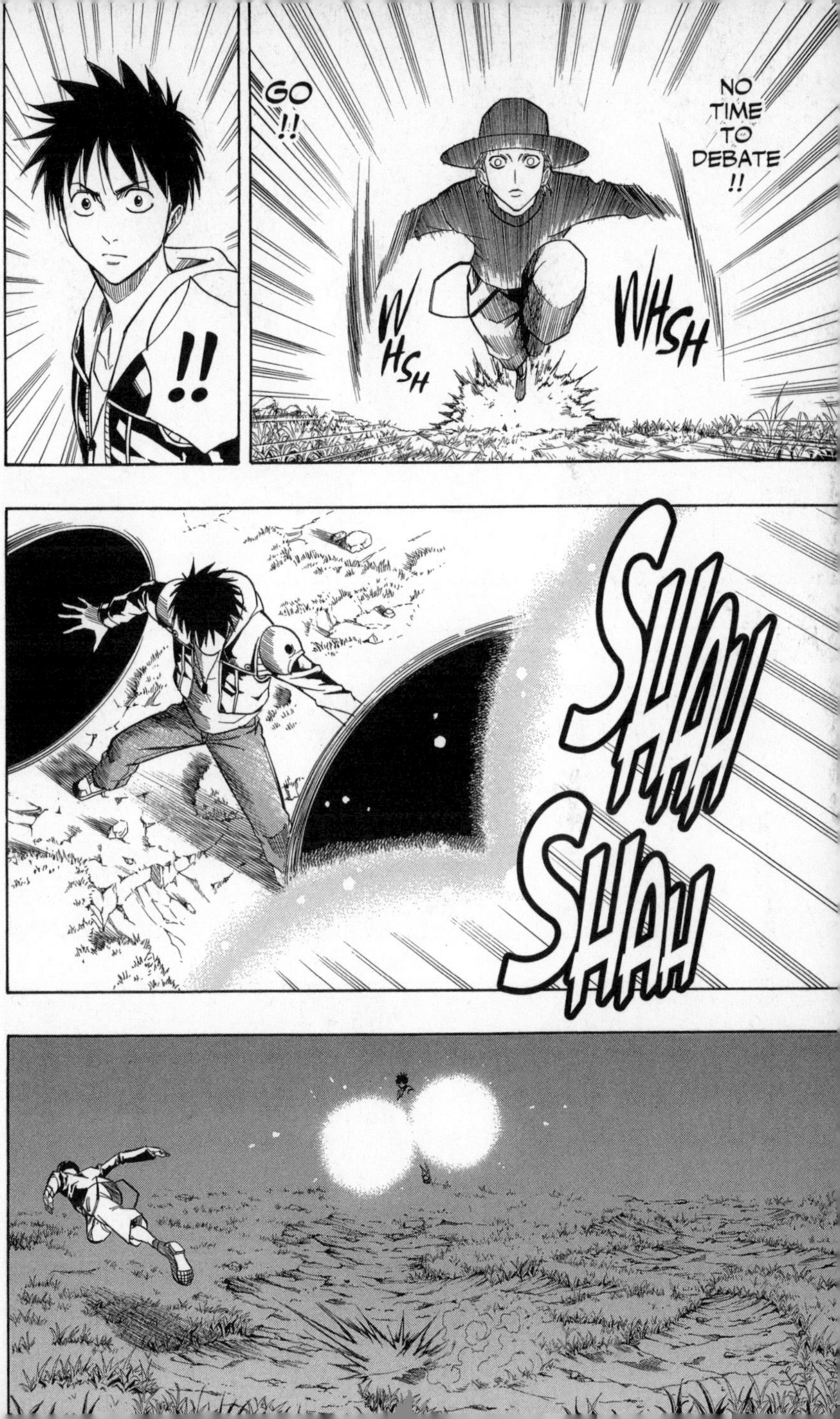
NO TIME TO DEBATE !!
GO !!
WHSH
WHSH
!!
SHAH
SHAH

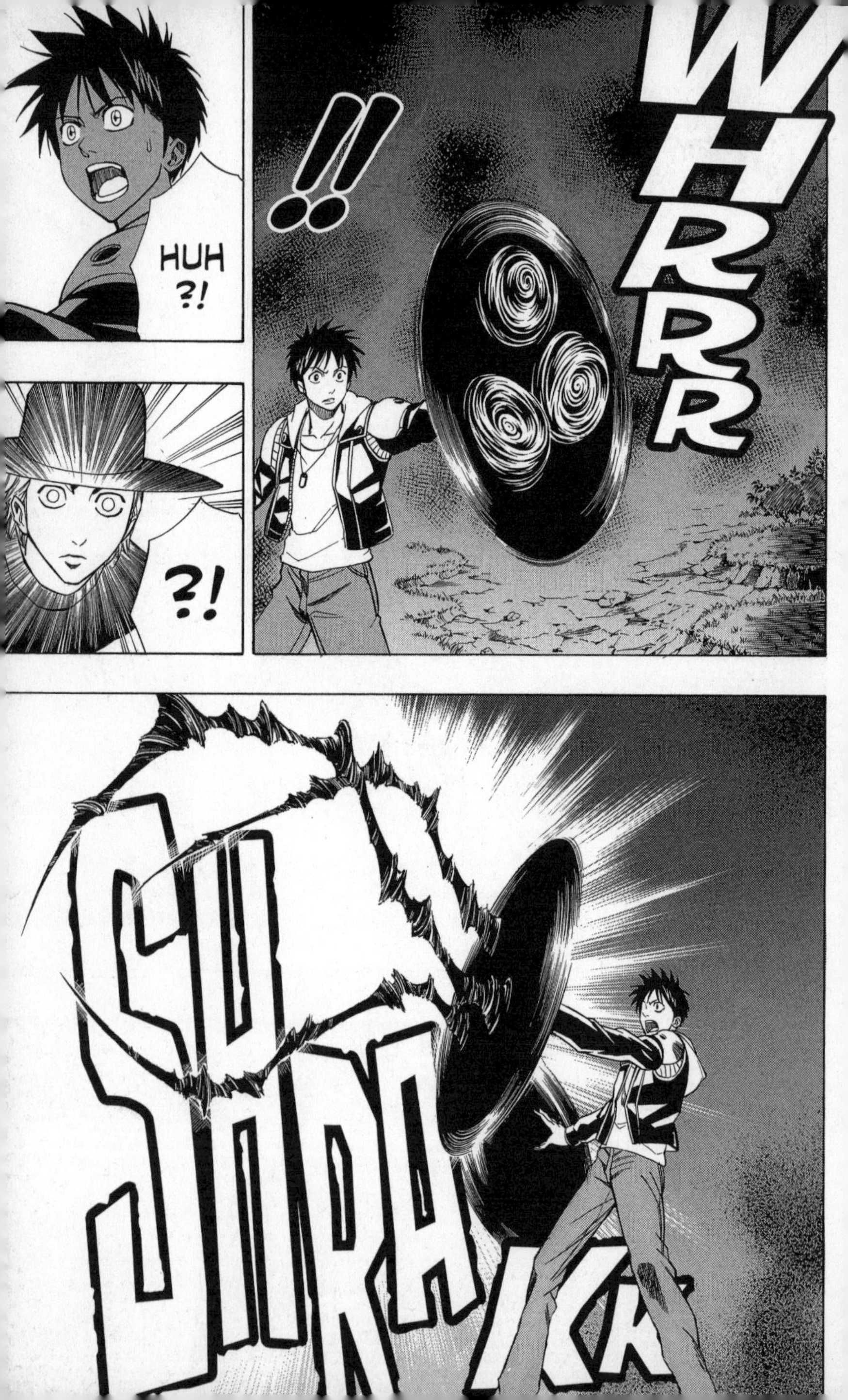
WHRRR
!!
HUH ?!
?!
SHRAKK

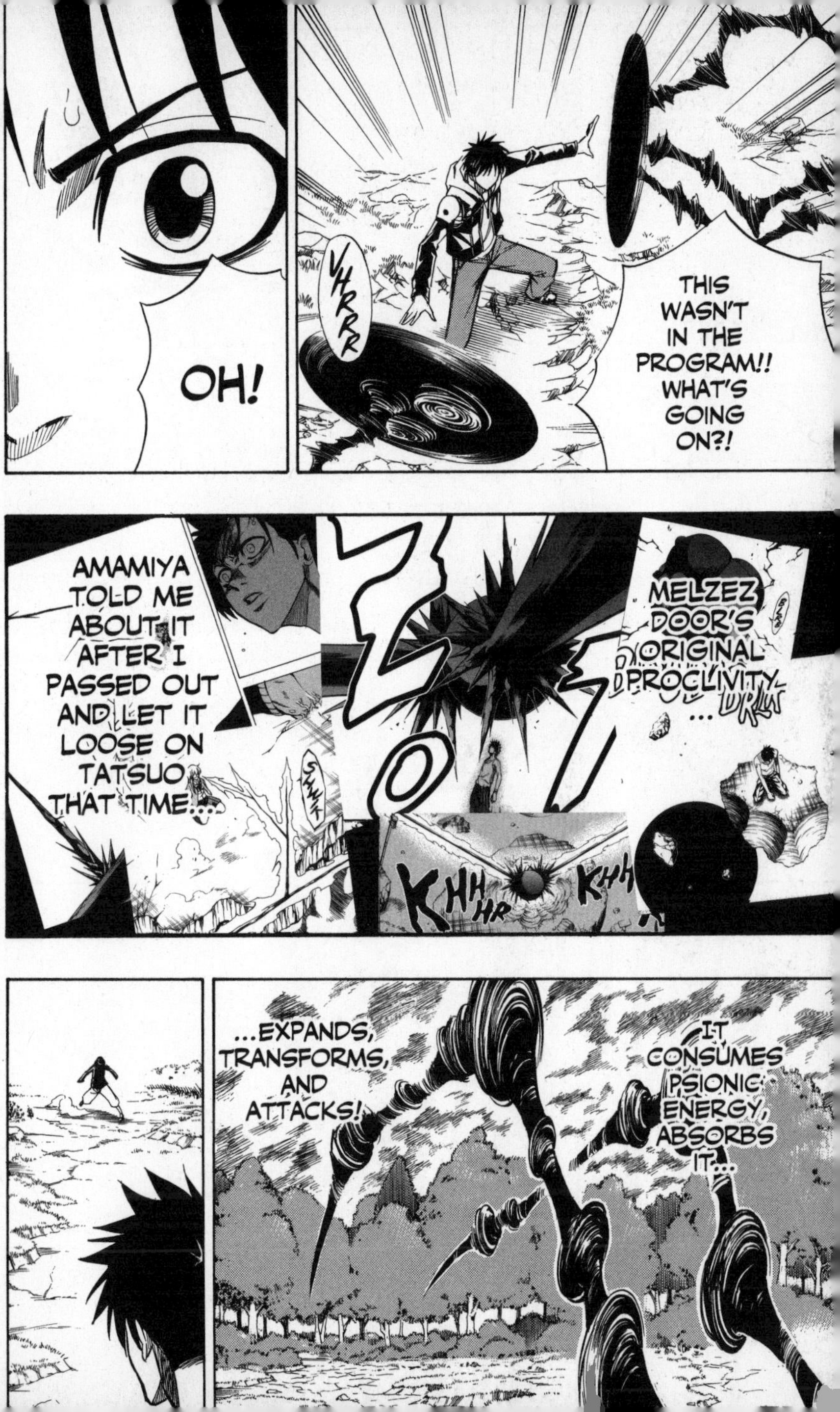
VHRRR
THIS WASN'T IN THE PROGRAM!! WHAT'S GOING ON?!
OH!
MELZEZ DOOR'S ORIGINAL PROCLIVITY...
KHHHR
KHH
AMAMIYA TOLD ME ABOUT IT AFTER I PASSED OUT AND LET IT LOOSE ON TATSUO THAT TIME...
IT CONSUMES PSIONIC ENERGY, ABSORBS IT...
...EXPANDS, TRANSFORMS, AND ATTACKS!

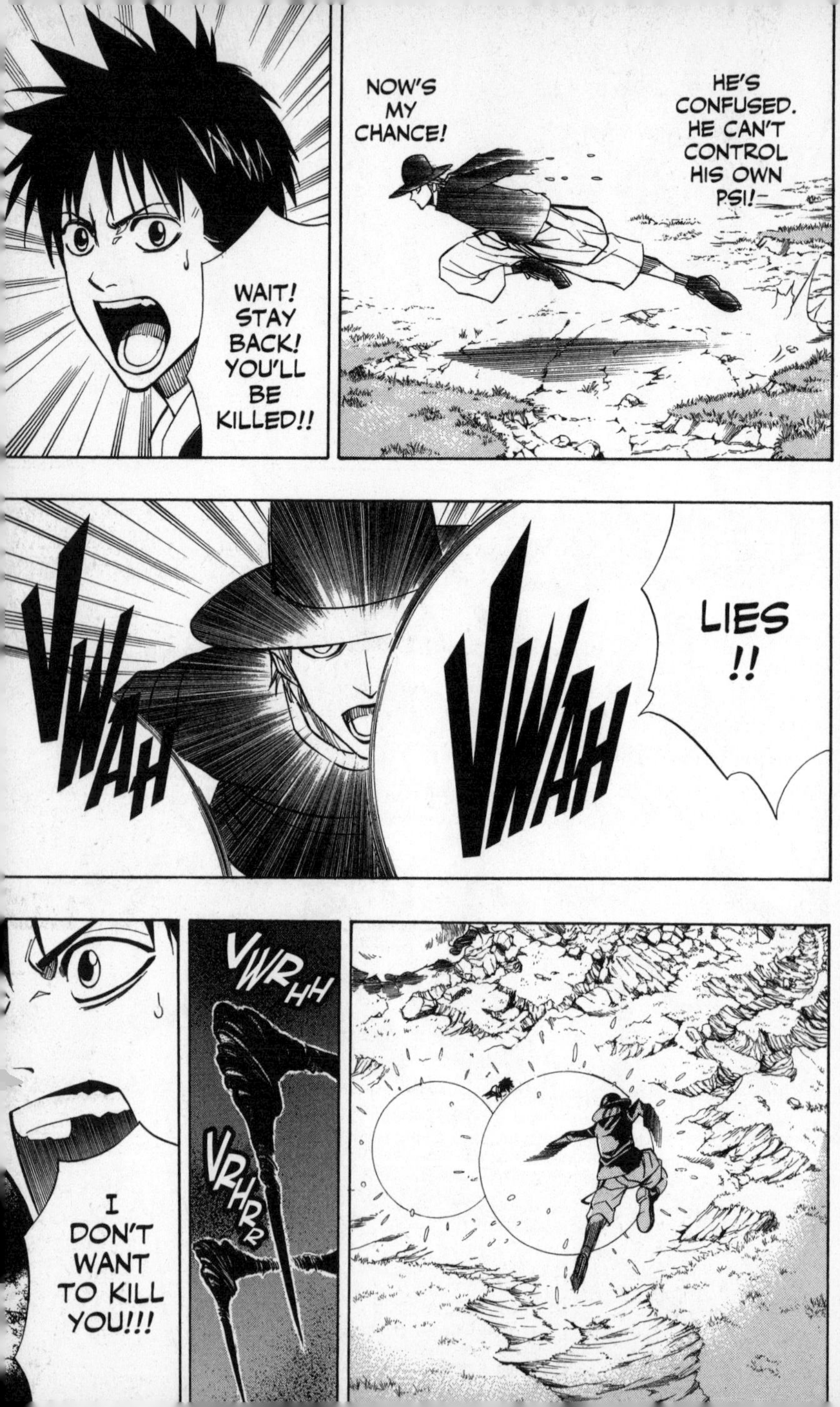
HE'S CONFUSED. HE CAN'T CONTROL HIS OWN PSI!
NOW'S MY CHANCE!
WAIT! STAY BACK! YOU'LL BE KILLED!!
LIES!!
VWAH
VWAH
VWRHH
VRHRR
I DON'T WANT TO KILL YOU!!!

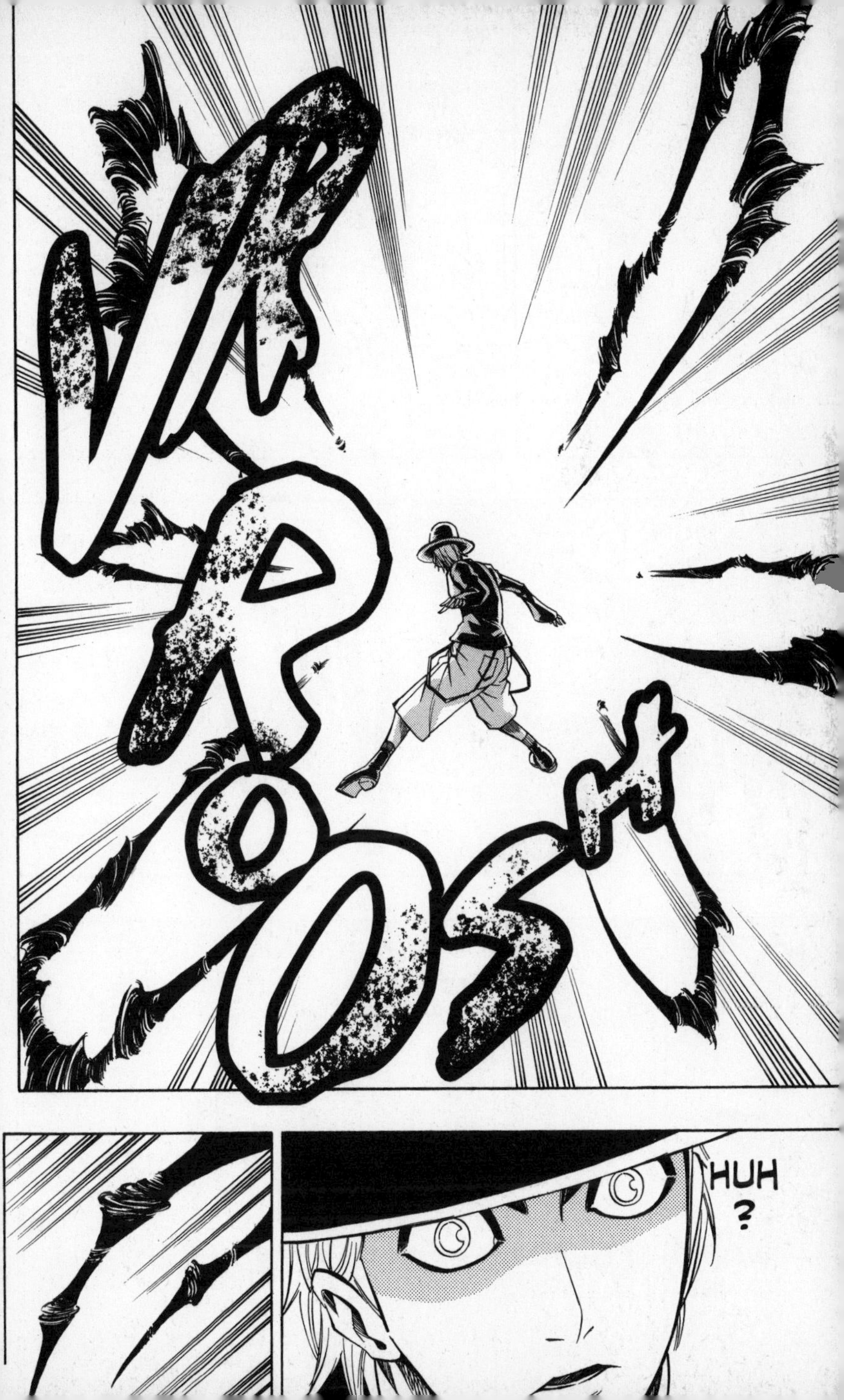
HUH
?

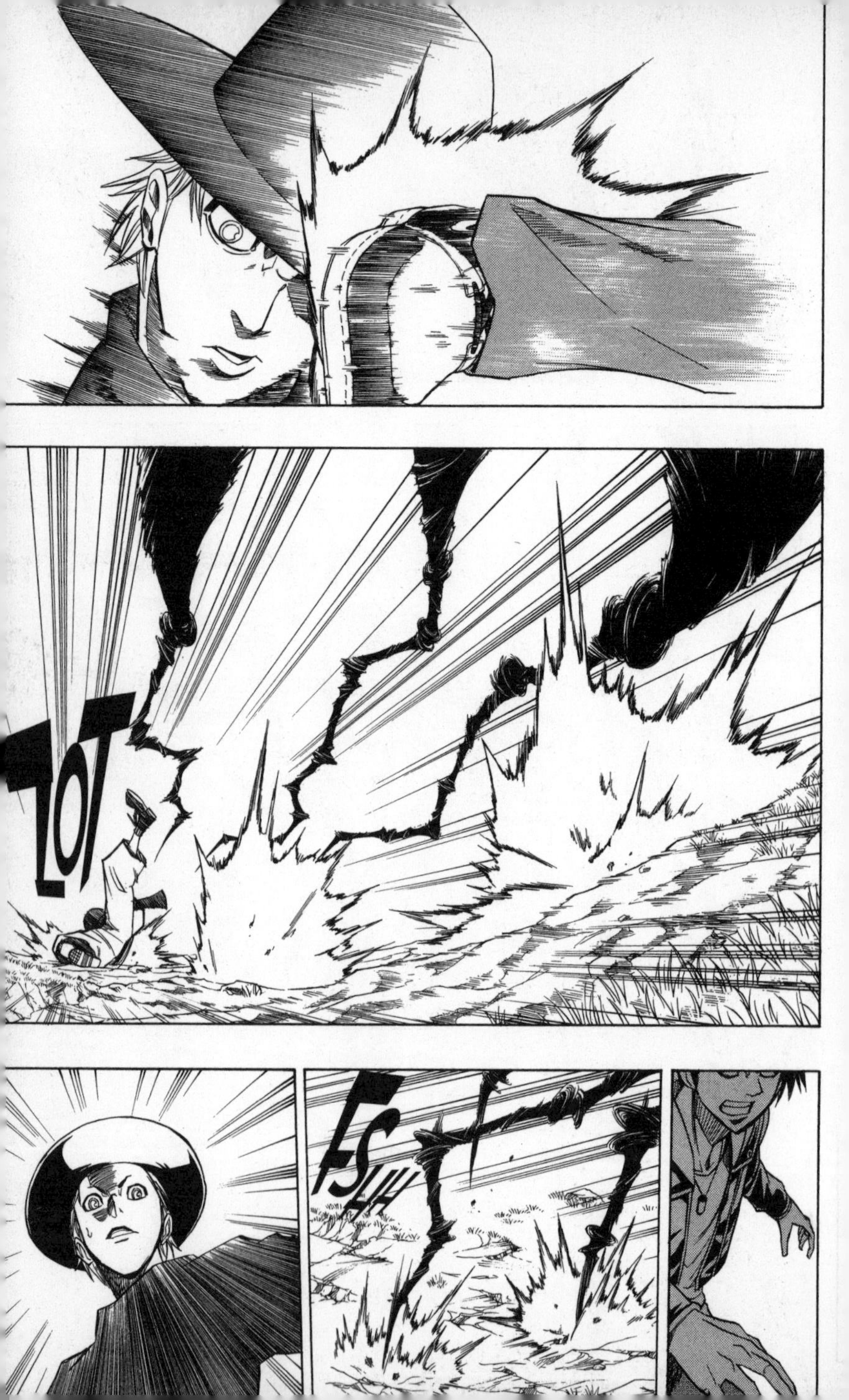
ZOT
FSHH

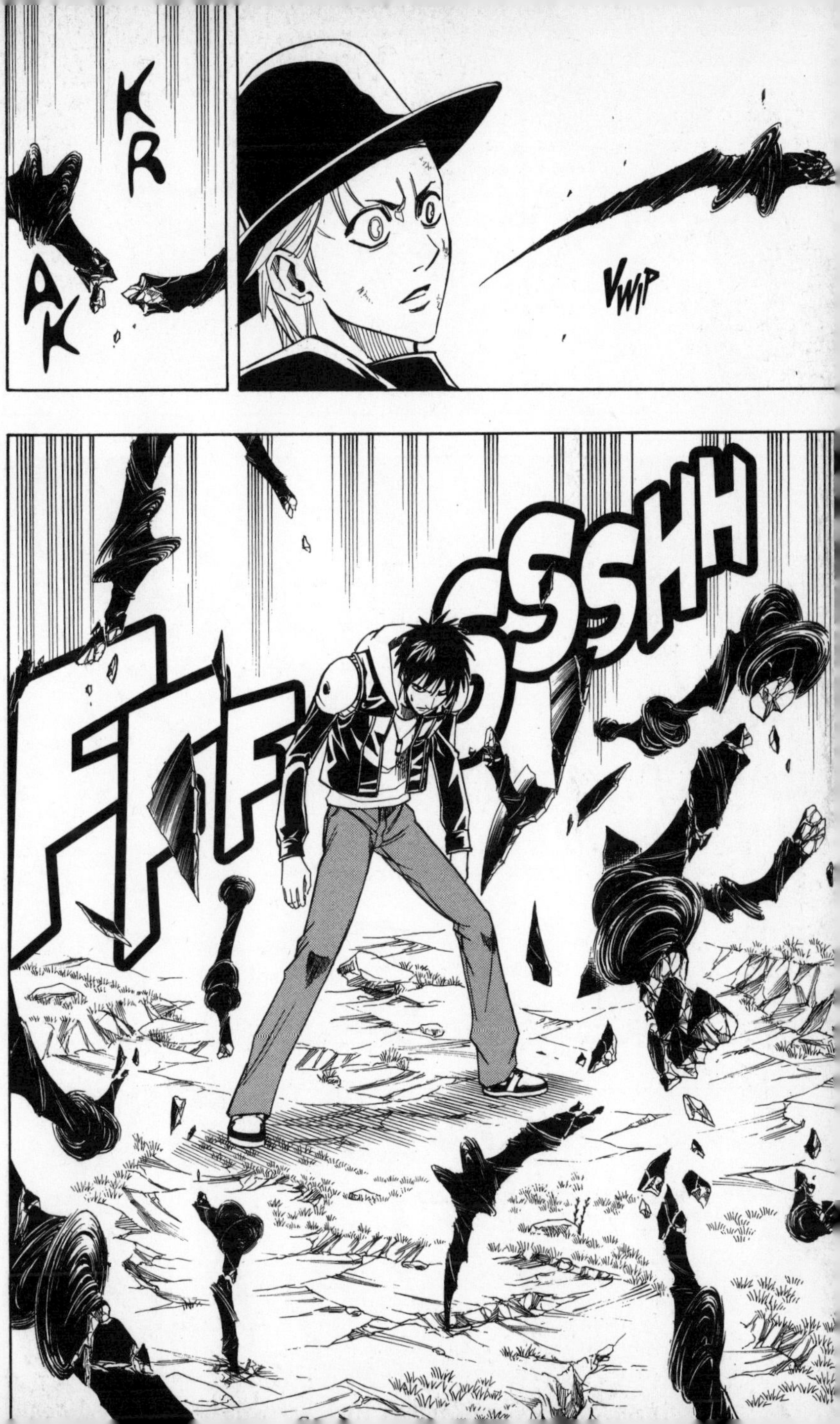
VWIP
KRAK
FFSSSHH

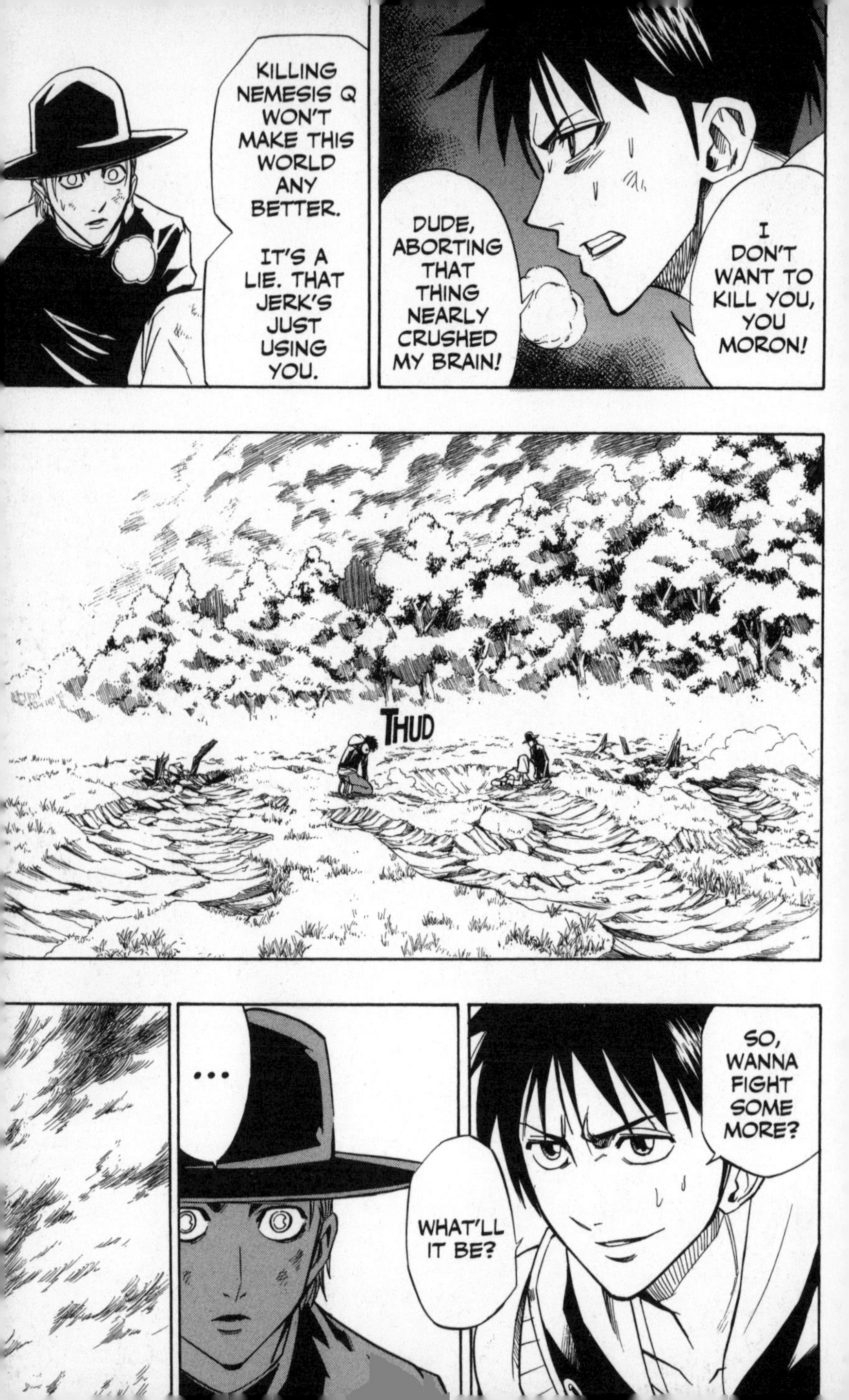
I DON'T WANT TO KILL YOU, YOU MORON!
DUDE, ABORTING THAT THING NEARLY CRUSHED MY BRAIN!
KILLING NEMESIS Q WON'T MAKE THIS WORLD ANY BETTER.
IT'S A LIE. THAT JERK'S JUST USING YOU.
THUD
SO, WANNA FIGHT SOME MORE?
WHAT'LL IT BE?
...

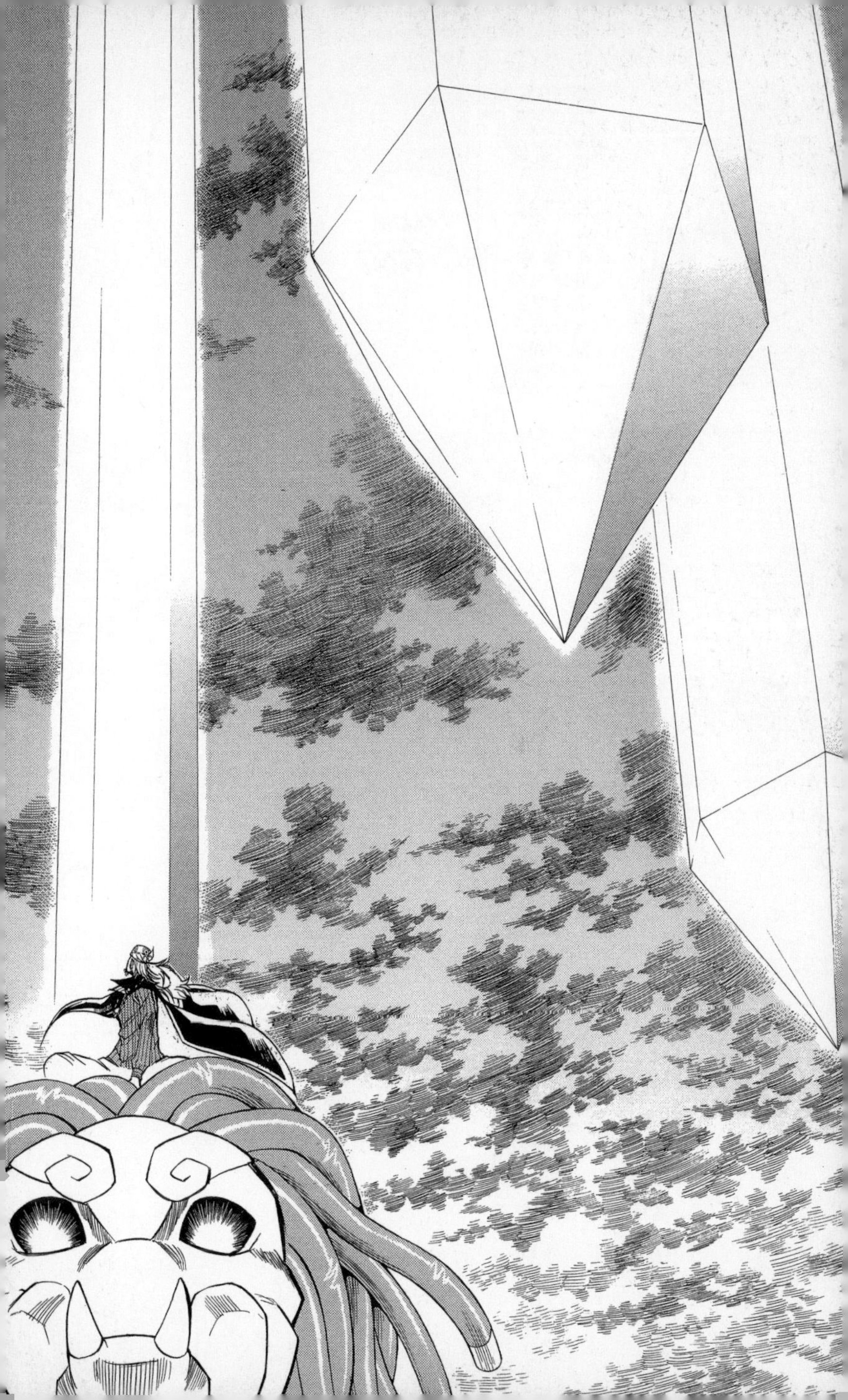

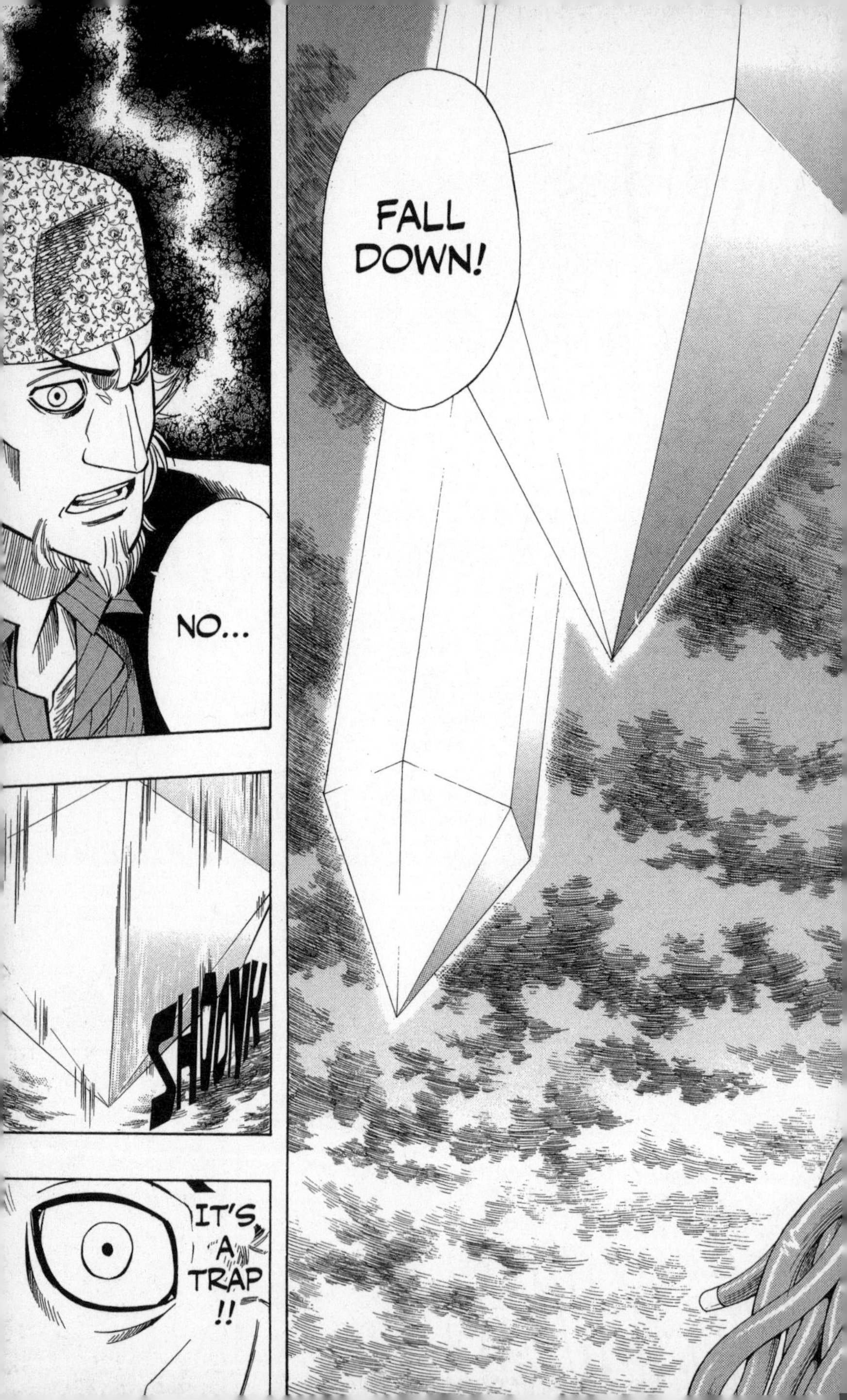
FALL DOWN!
NO...
SHOONK
IT'S A TRAP!!

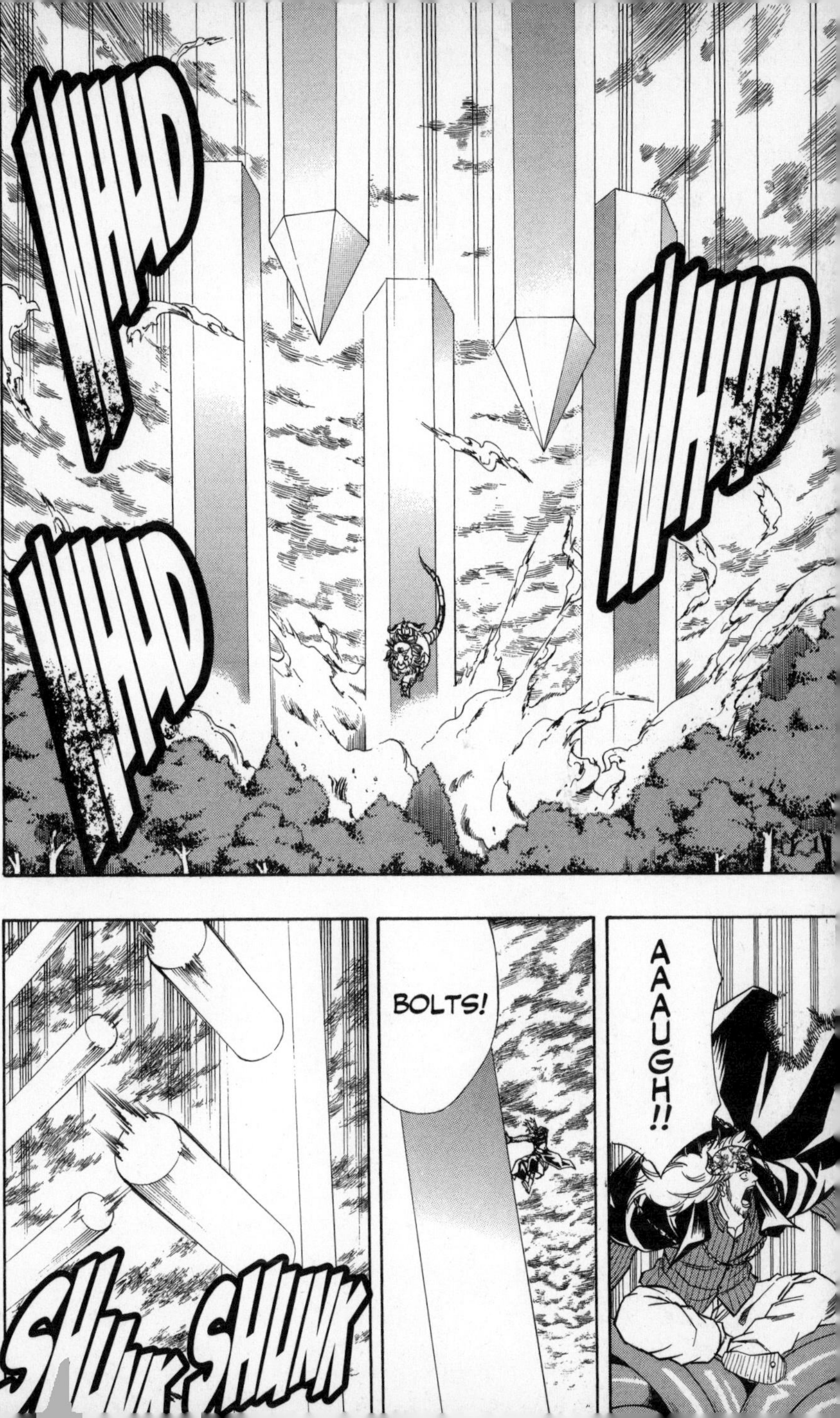
WHUD
WHUD
WHUD
AAAUGH!!
BOLTS!
SHUNK SHUNK

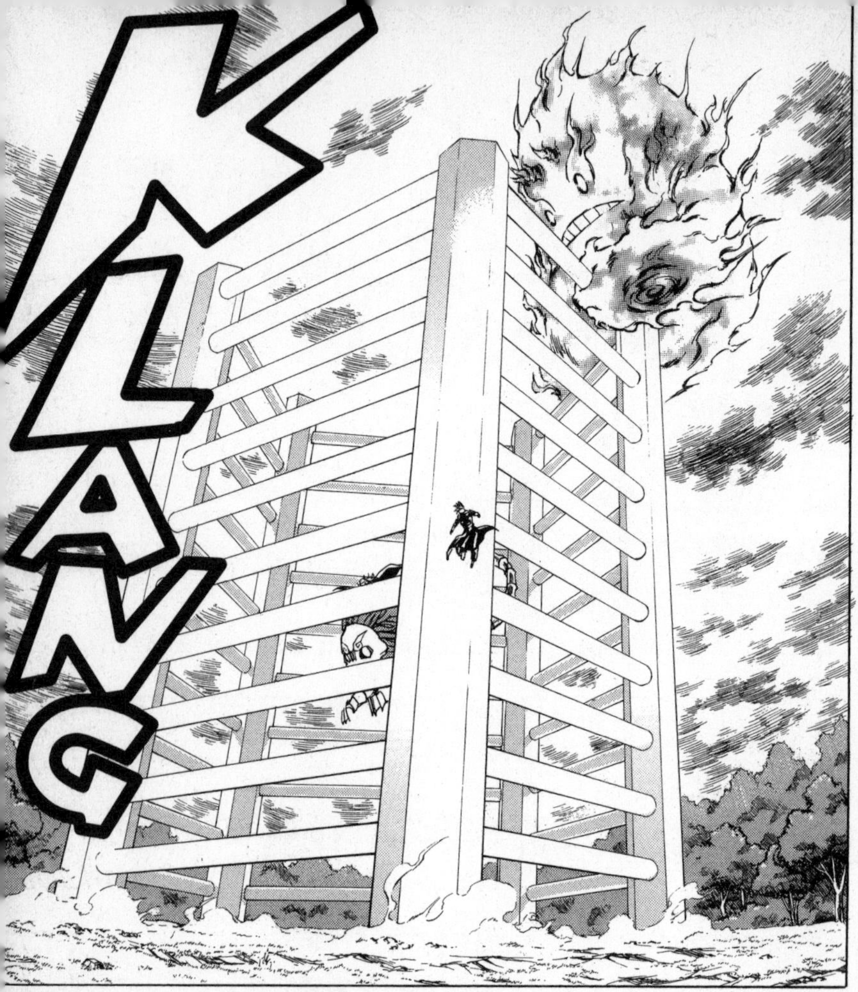
KLANG
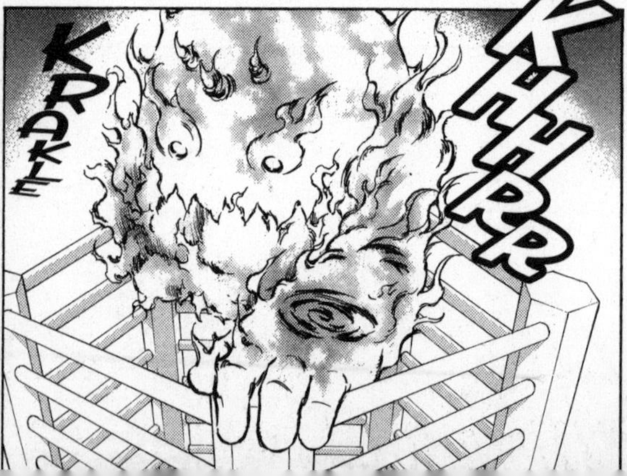
KHHRR
KRAKLE
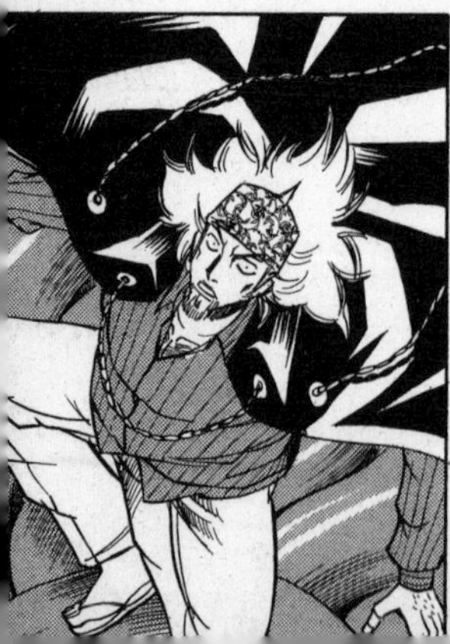

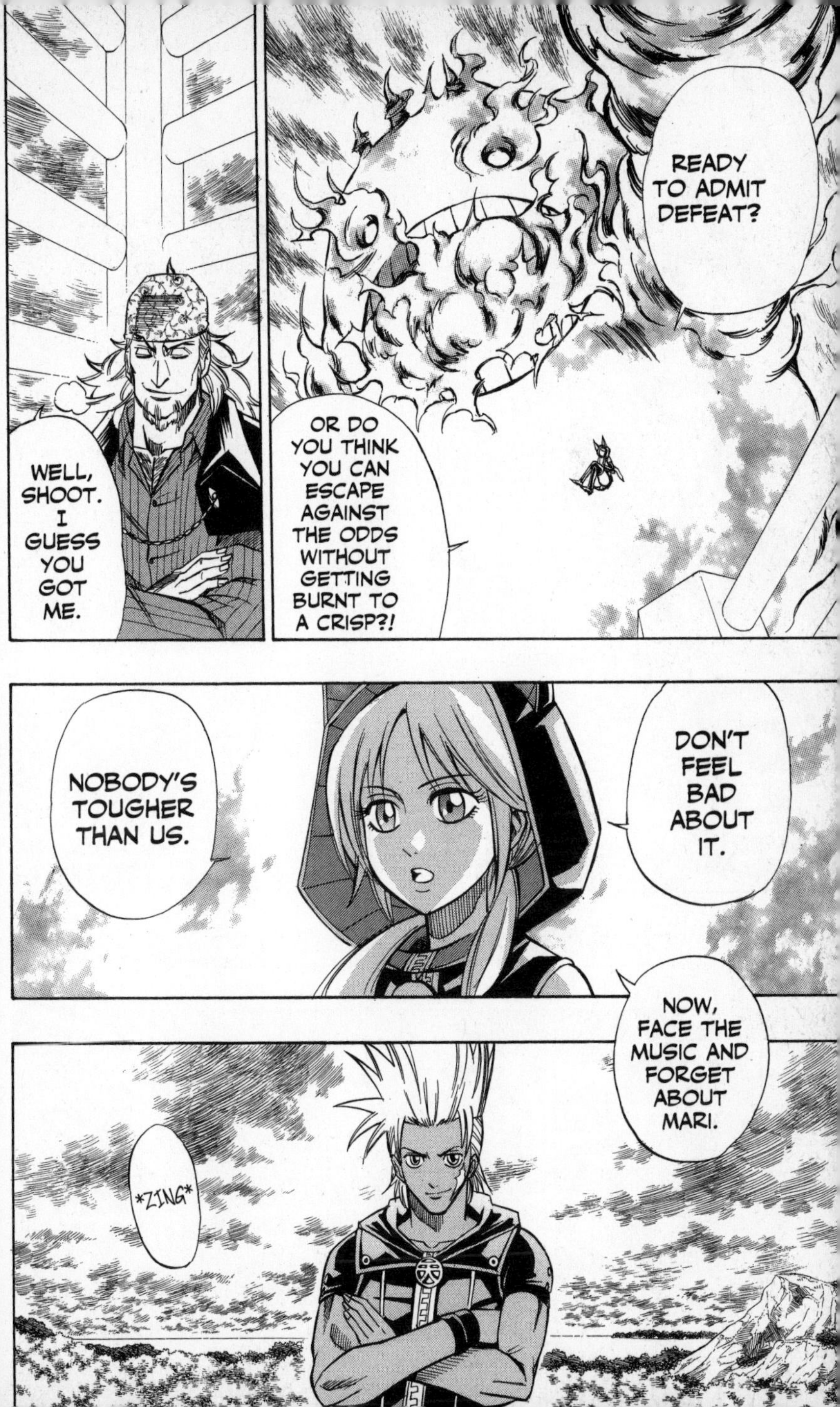
READY TO ADMIT DEFEAT?
OR DO YOU THINK YOU CAN ESCAPE AGAINST THE ODDS WITHOUT GETTING BURNT TO A CRISP?!
WELL, SHOOT. I GUESS YOU GOT ME.
DON'T FEEL BAD ABOUT IT.
NOBODY'S TOUGHER THAN US.
NOW, FACE THE MUSIC AND FORGET ABOUT MARI.
ZING

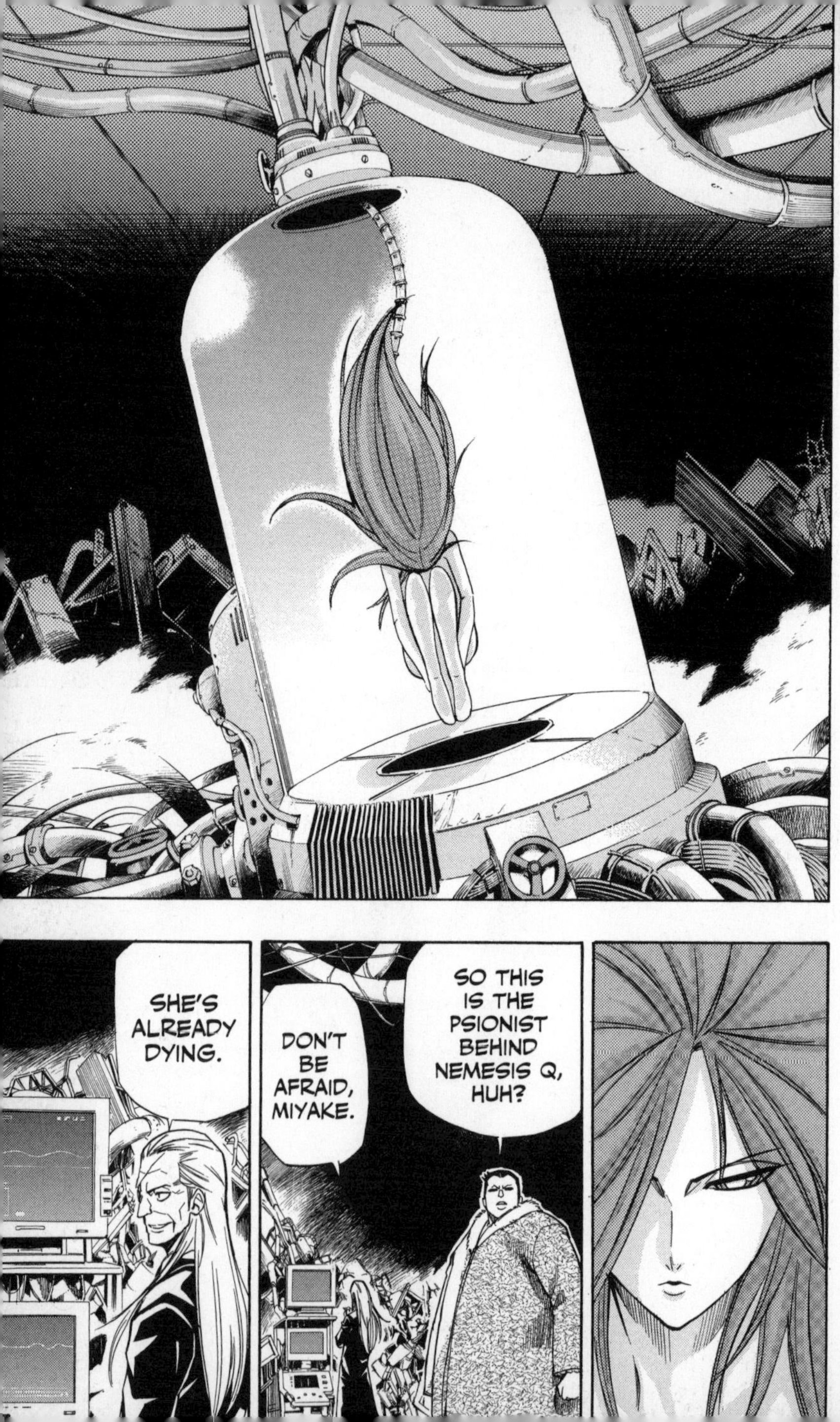
SO THIS IS THE PSIONIST BEHIND NEMESIS Q, HUH?
DON'T BE AFRAID, MIYAKE.
SHE'S ALREADY DYING.

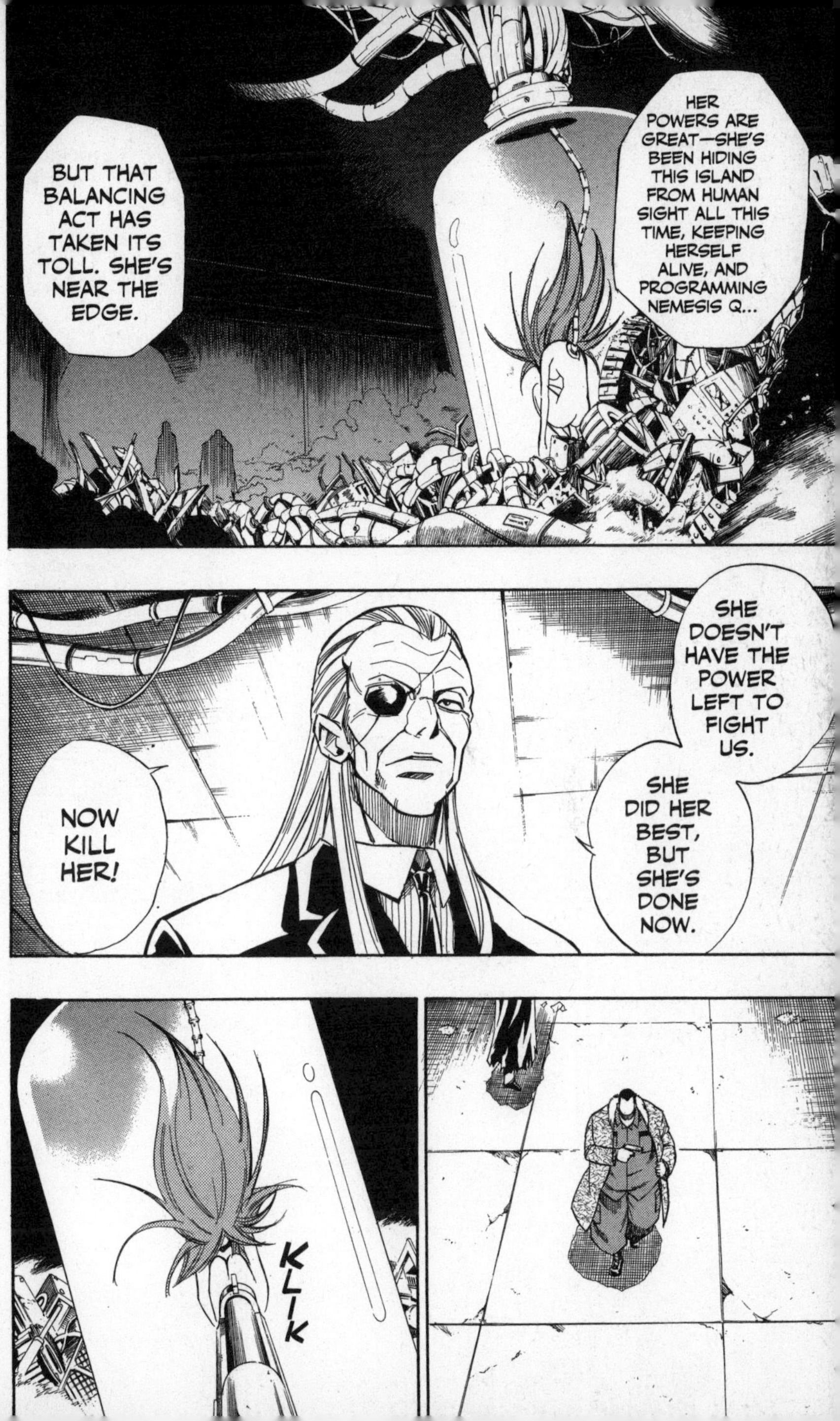
HER POWERS ARE GREAT—SHE'S BEEN HIDING THIS ISLAND FROM HUMAN SIGHT ALL THIS TIME, KEEPING HERSELF ALIVE, AND PROGRAMMING NEMESIS Q...
BUT THAT BALANCING ACT HAS TAKEN ITS TOLL. SHE'S NEAR THE EDGE.
SHE DOESN'T HAVE THE POWER LEFT TO FIGHT US.
SHE DID HER BEST, BUT SHE'S DONE NOW.
NOW KILL HER!
KLIK

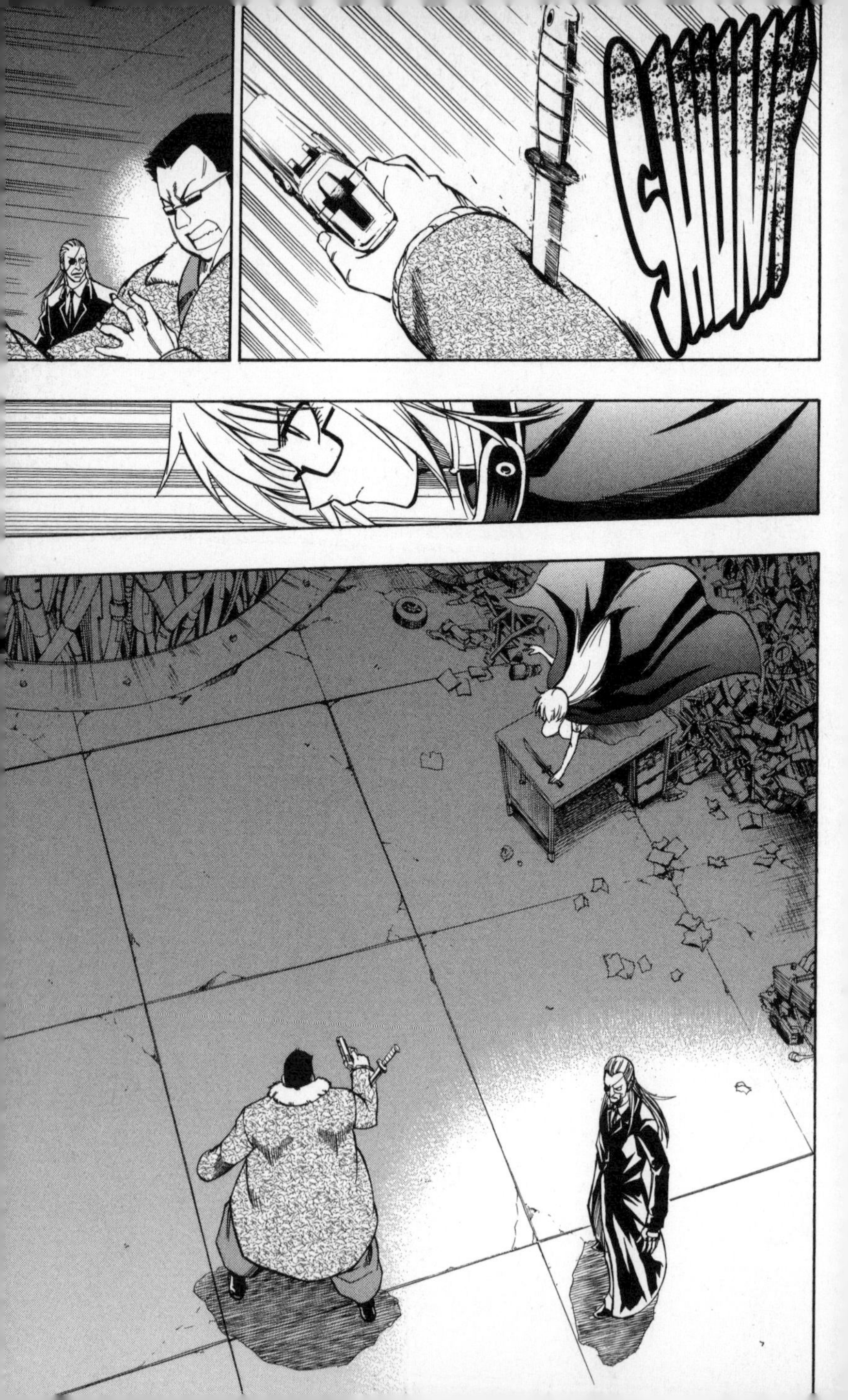
SHUNK

Mutters and mumblings...

MY FAVORITE FAMILYCOM GAMES:
ROCKMAN 1 ¢ 2, HITLER NO FUKKATSU,
SHADOWGATE, HYDLIDE, DRAGON QUEST 2 ¢ 3,
FAMICOM TANTEI CLUB 1¢ 2, FINAL FANTASY 3,
MOTHER

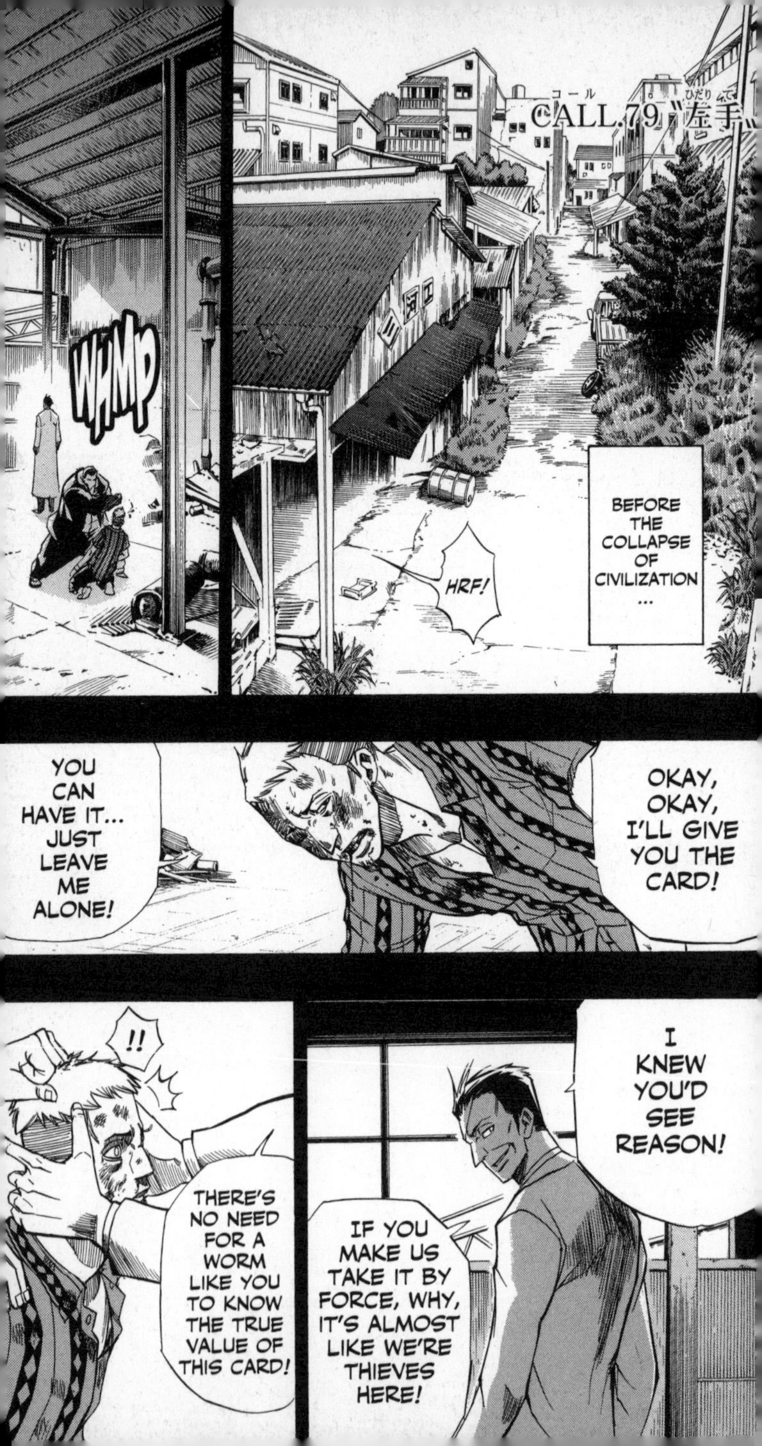
CALL.79 "左手"
BEFORE THE COLLAPSE OF CIVILIZATION...
HRF!
WHMP
OKAY, OKAY, I'LL GIVE YOU THE CARD!
YOU CAN HAVE IT... JUST LEAVE ME ALONE!
I KNEW YOU'D SEE REASON!
IF YOU MAKE US TAKE IT BY FORCE, WHY, IT'S ALMOST LIKE WE'RE THIEVES HERE!
!!
THERE'S NO NEED FOR A WORM LIKE YOU TO KNOW THE TRUE VALUE OF THIS CARD!

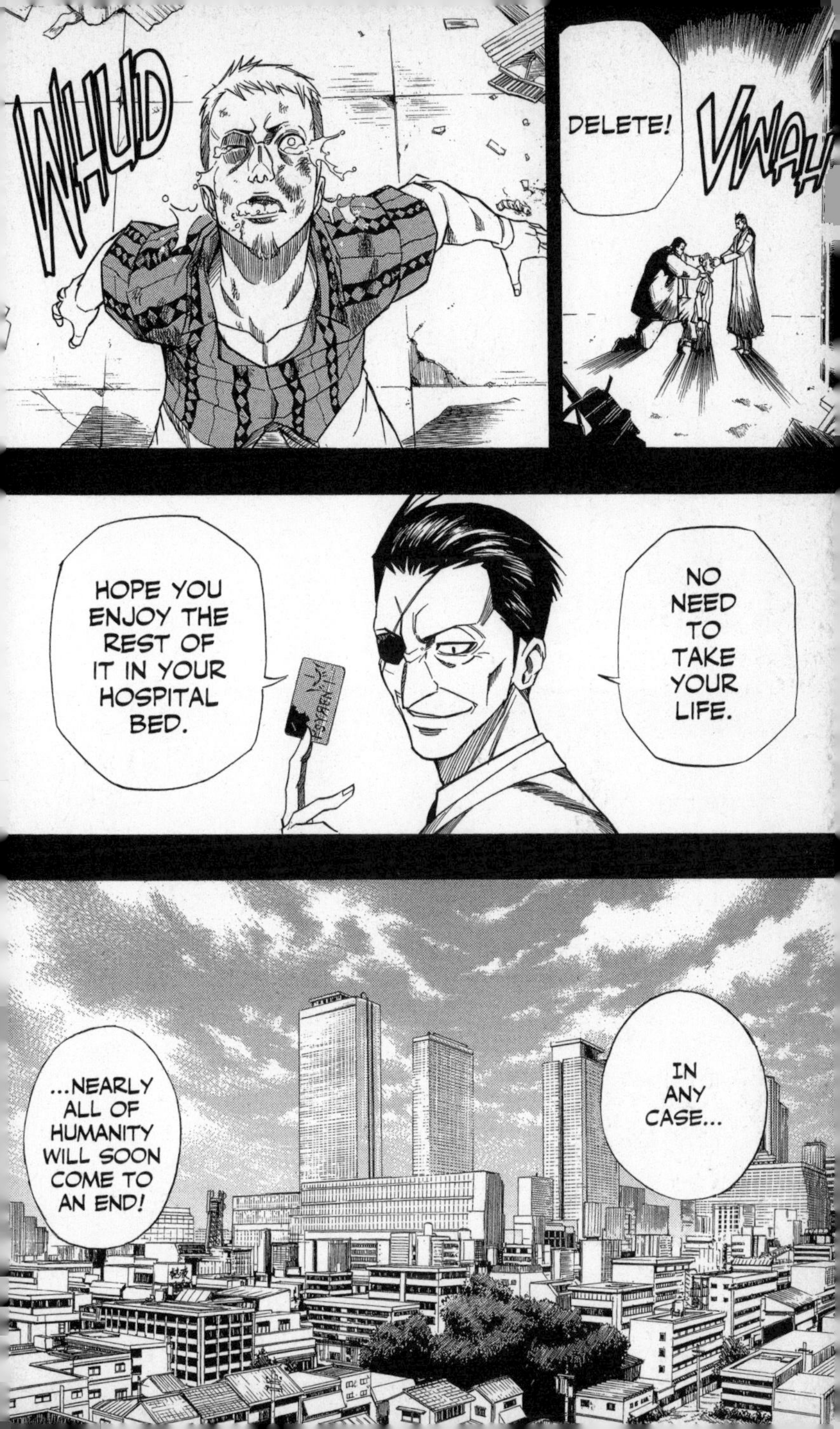
DELETE!
VWAH
WHUD
NO NEED TO TAKE YOUR LIFE.
HOPE YOU ENJOY THE REST OF IT IN YOUR HOSPITAL BED.
IN ANY CASE...
...NEARLY ALL OF HUMANITY WILL SOON COME TO AN END!

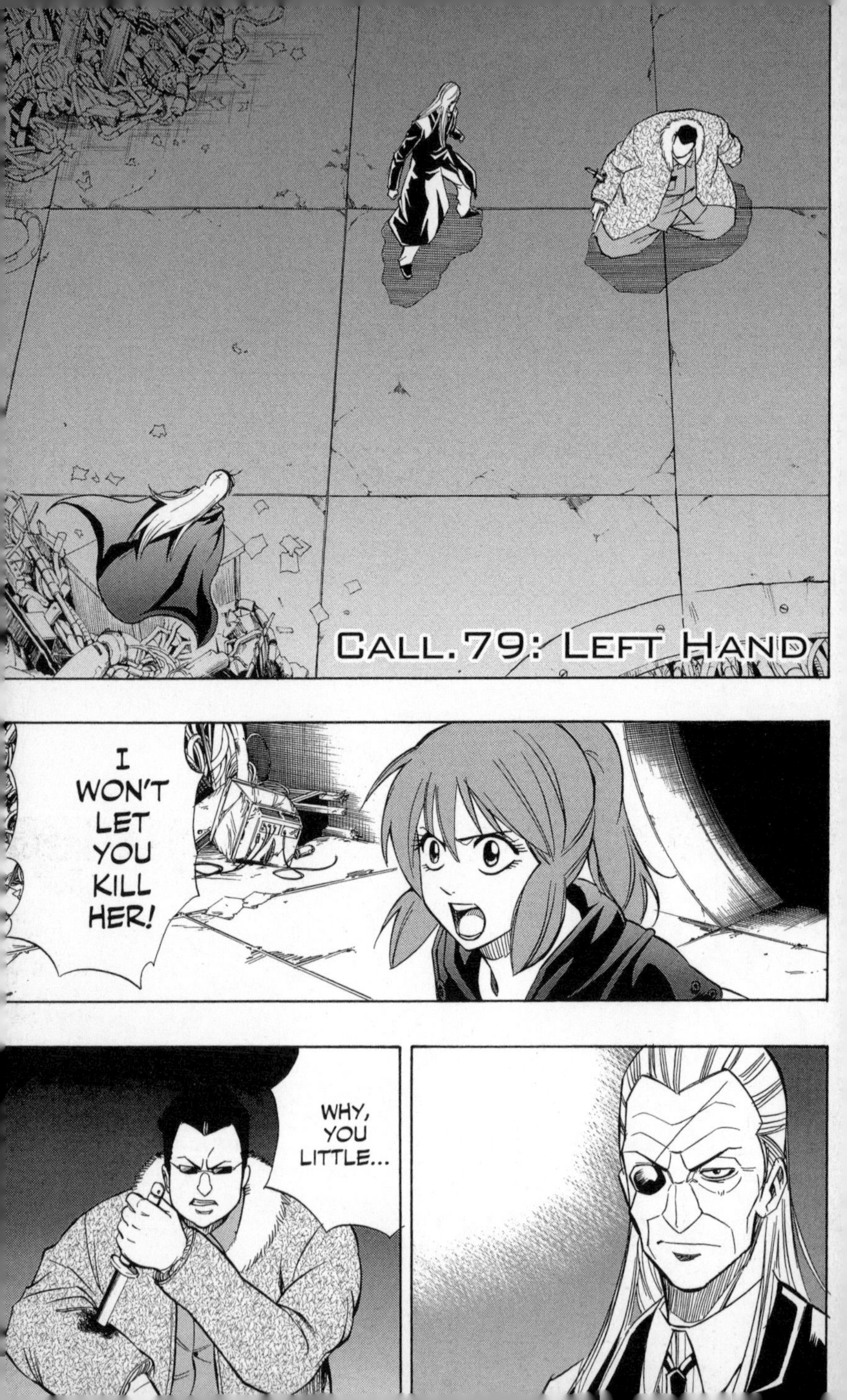
CALL. 79: LEFT HAND
I WON'T LET YOU KILL HER!
WHY, YOU LITTLE...

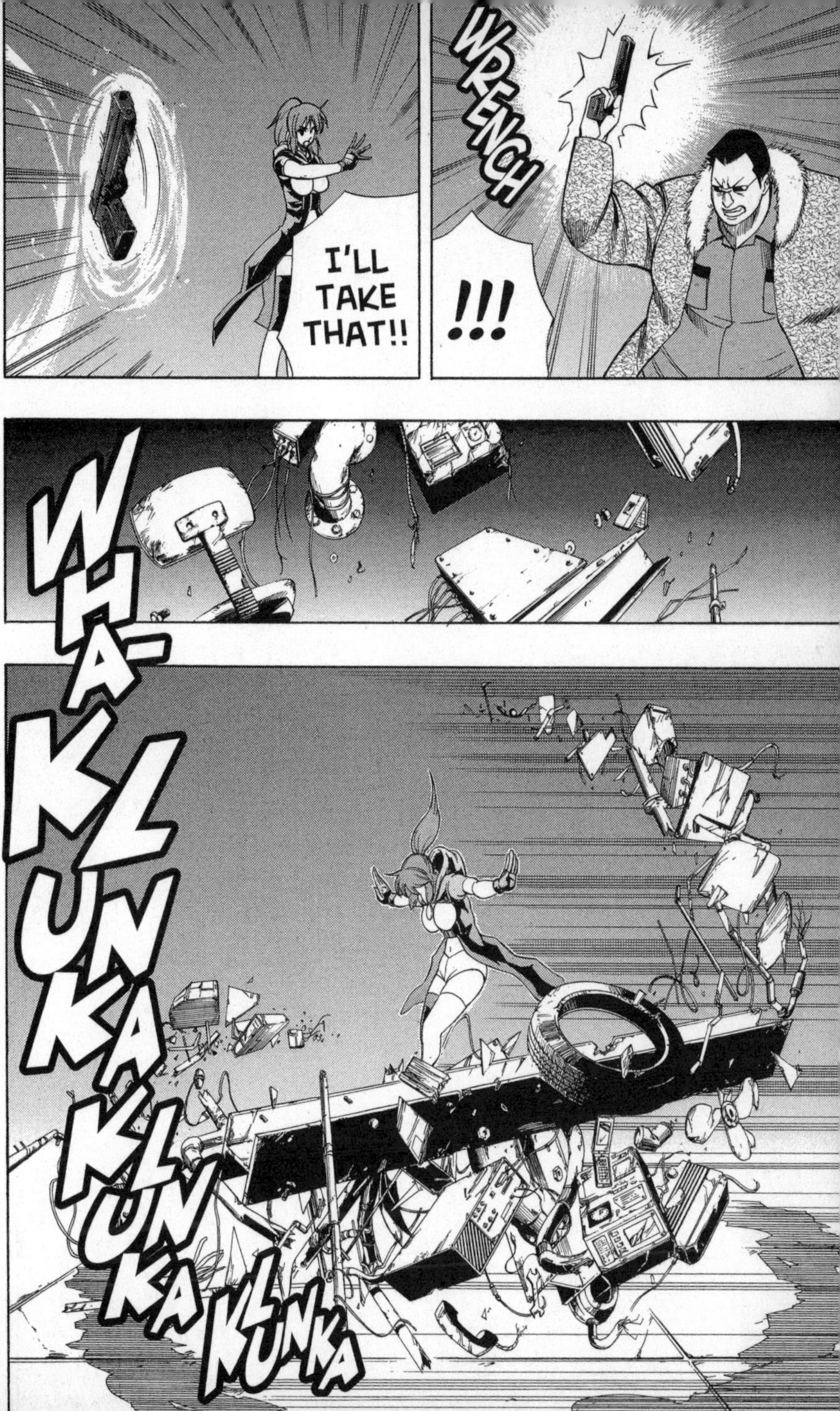
WRENCH
!!!
I'LL TAKE THAT!!
WHA-KLUNKA-KLUNKA KLUNKA

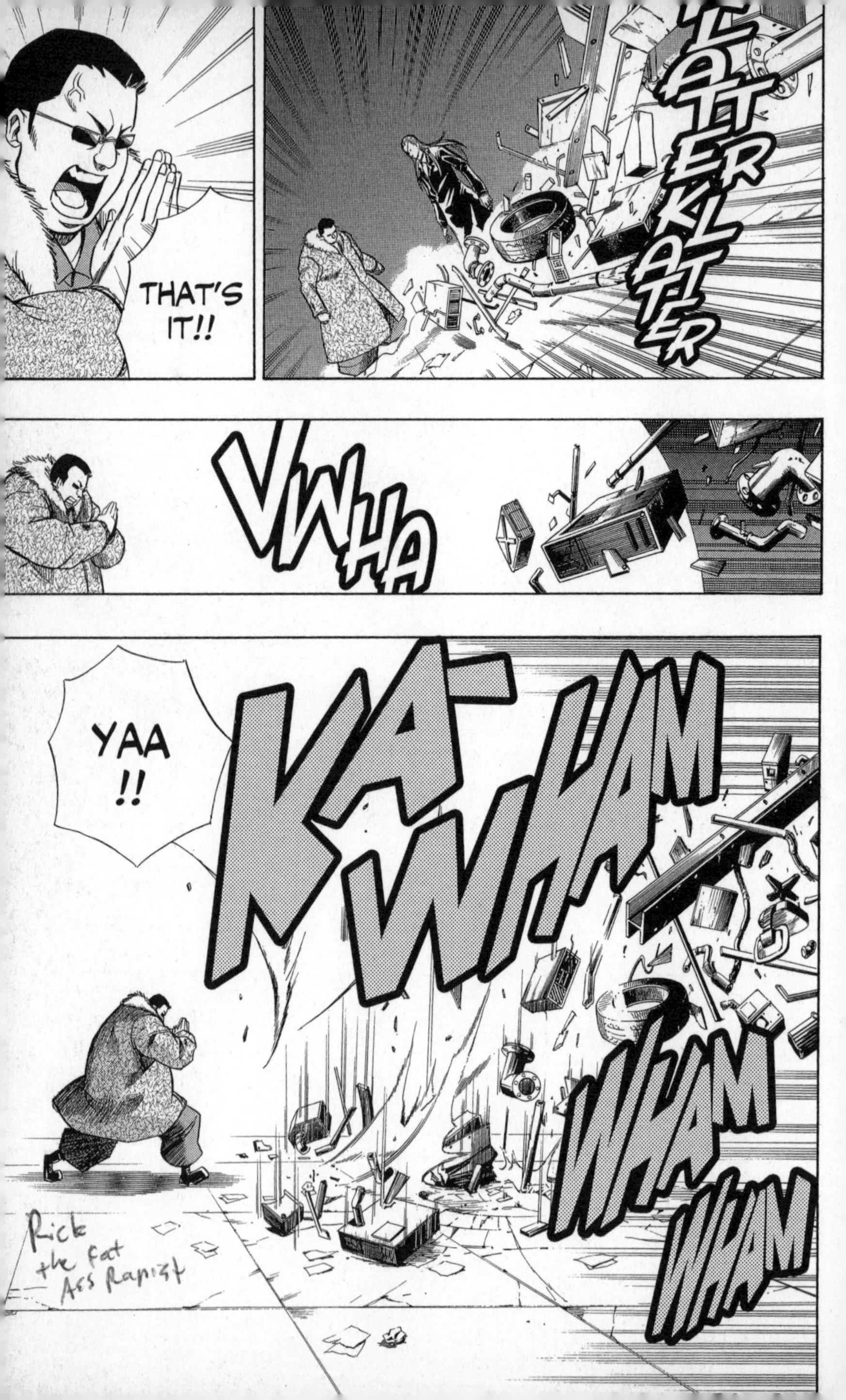
KLATTERKLATTER
THAT'S IT!!
VWHA
YAA !!
KA-WHAM
WHAM
WHAM
Rick the fat Ass Rapist

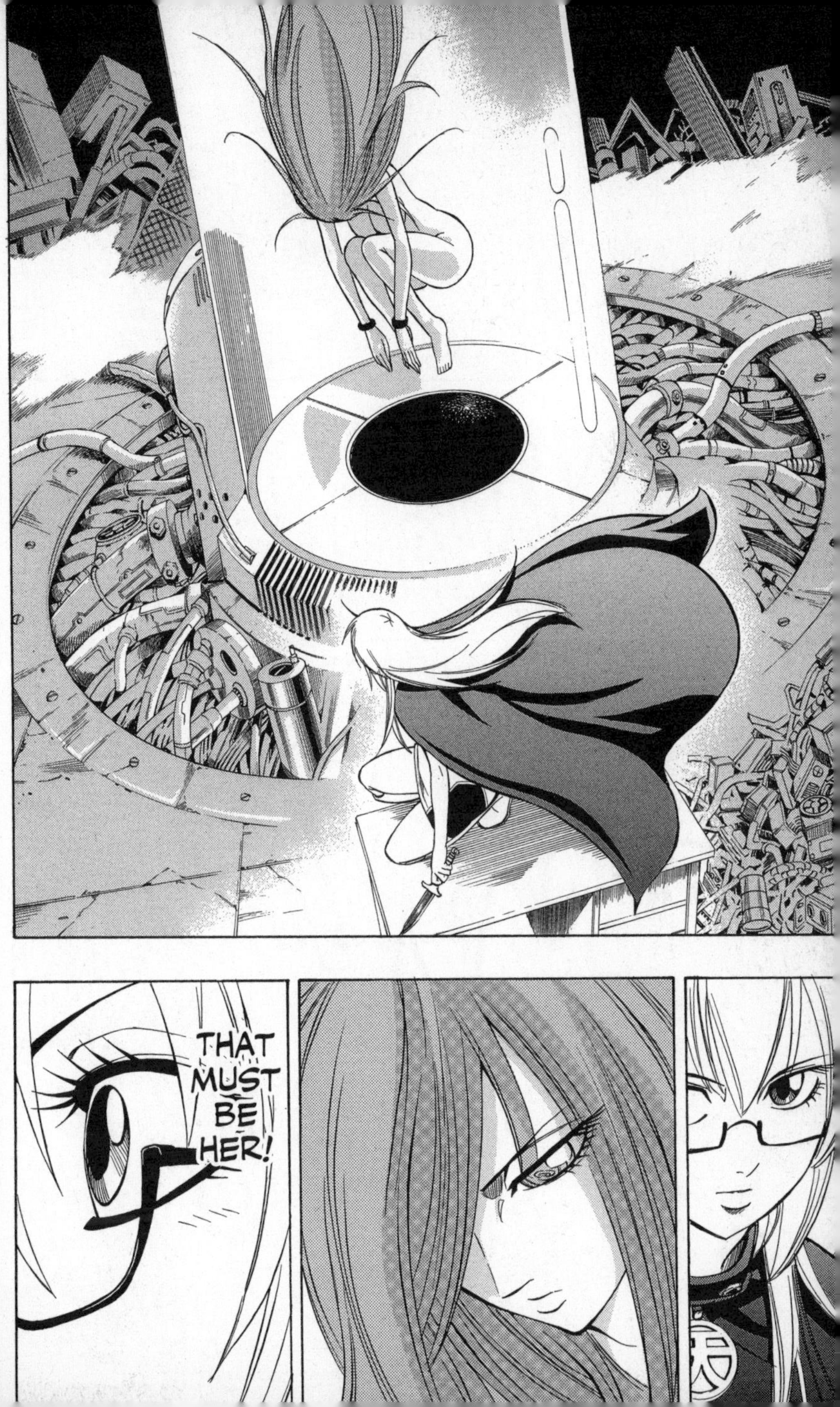
THAT MUST BE HER!

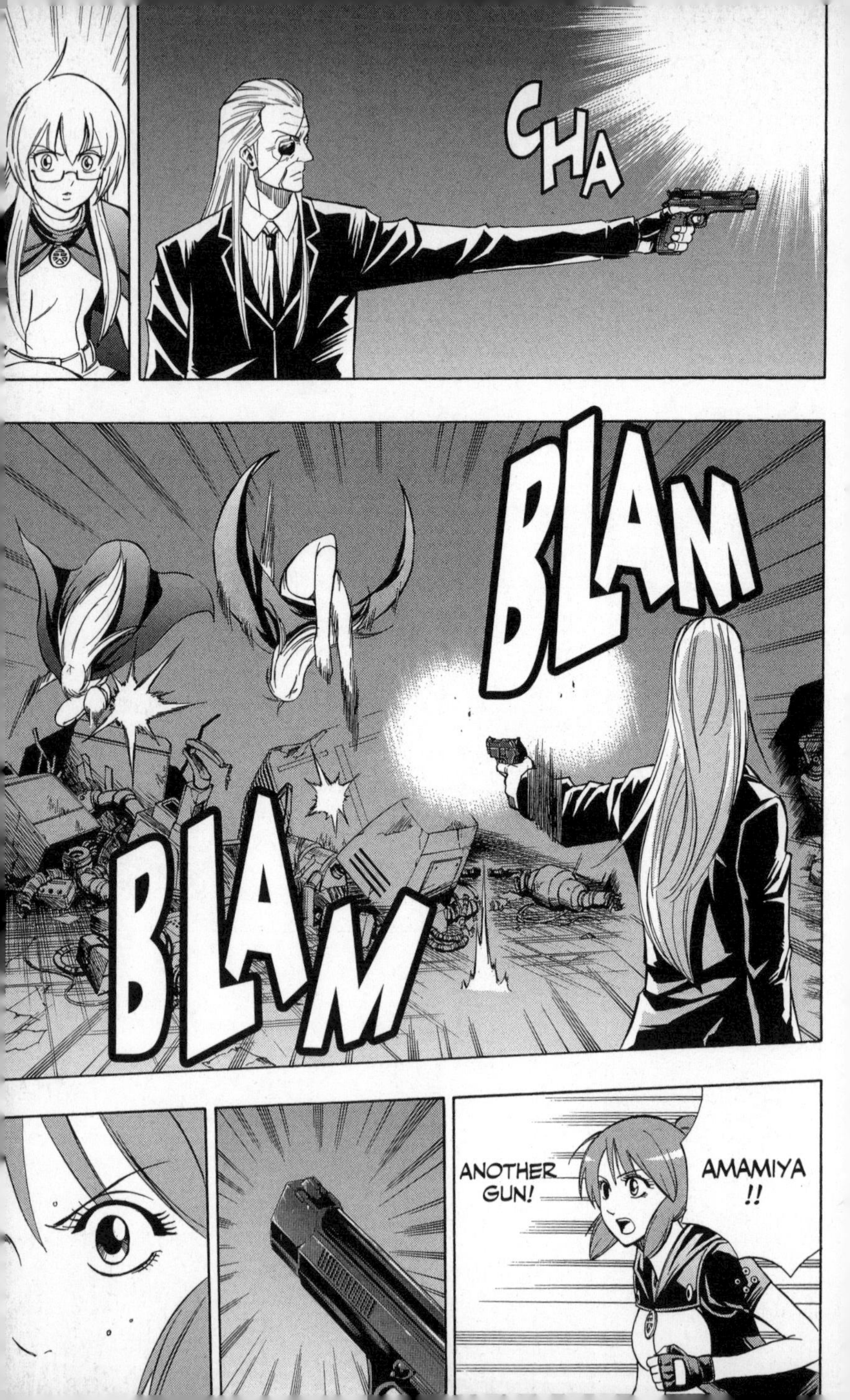
CHA
BLAM
BLAM
AMAMIYA!!
ANOTHER GUN!

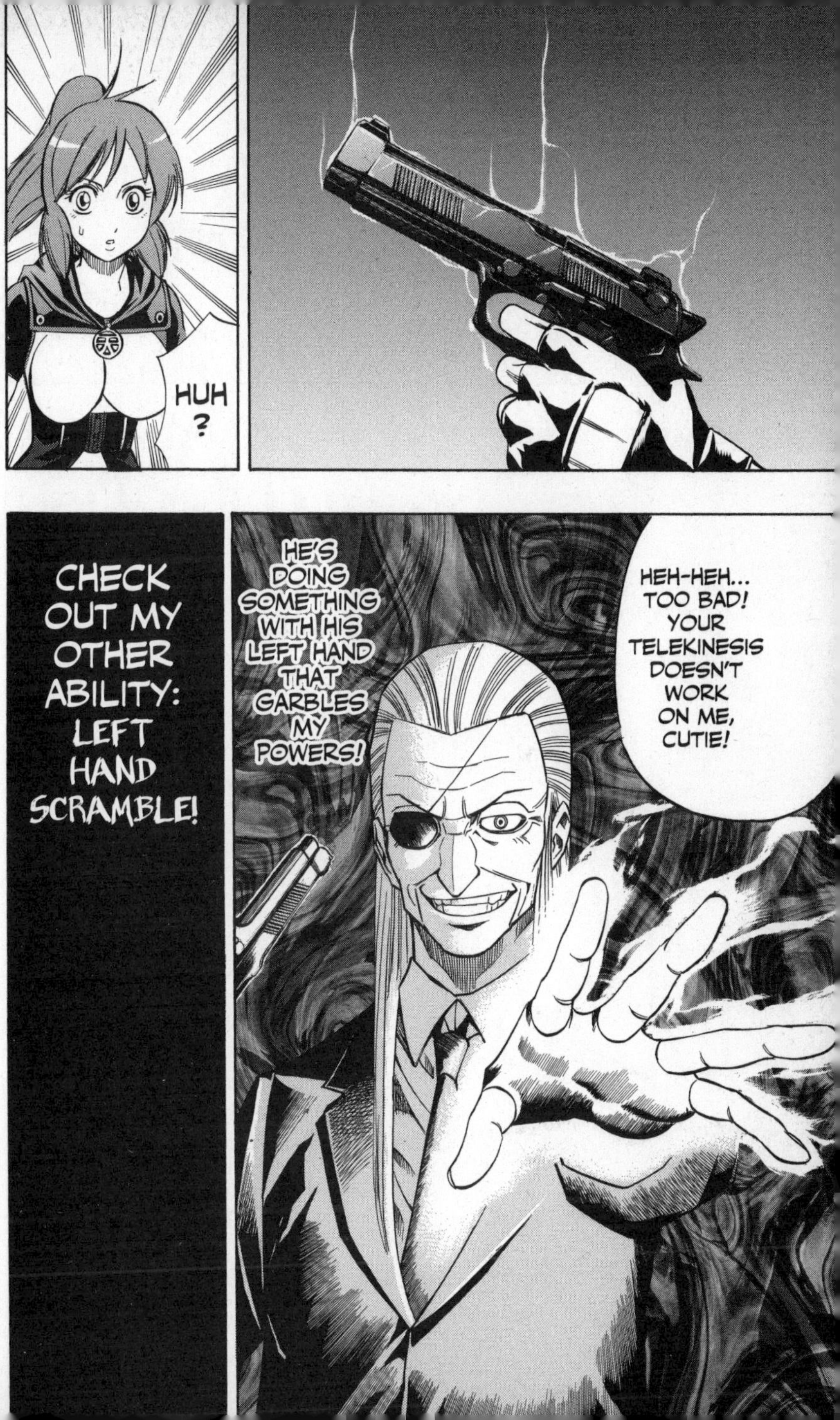
HUH ?
HEH-HEH... TOO BAD! YOUR TELEKINESIS DOESN'T WORK ON ME, CUTIE!
HE'S DOING SOMETHING WITH HIS LEFT HAND THAT GARBLES MY POWERS!
CHECK OUT MY OTHER ABILITY: LEFT HAND SCRAMBLE!

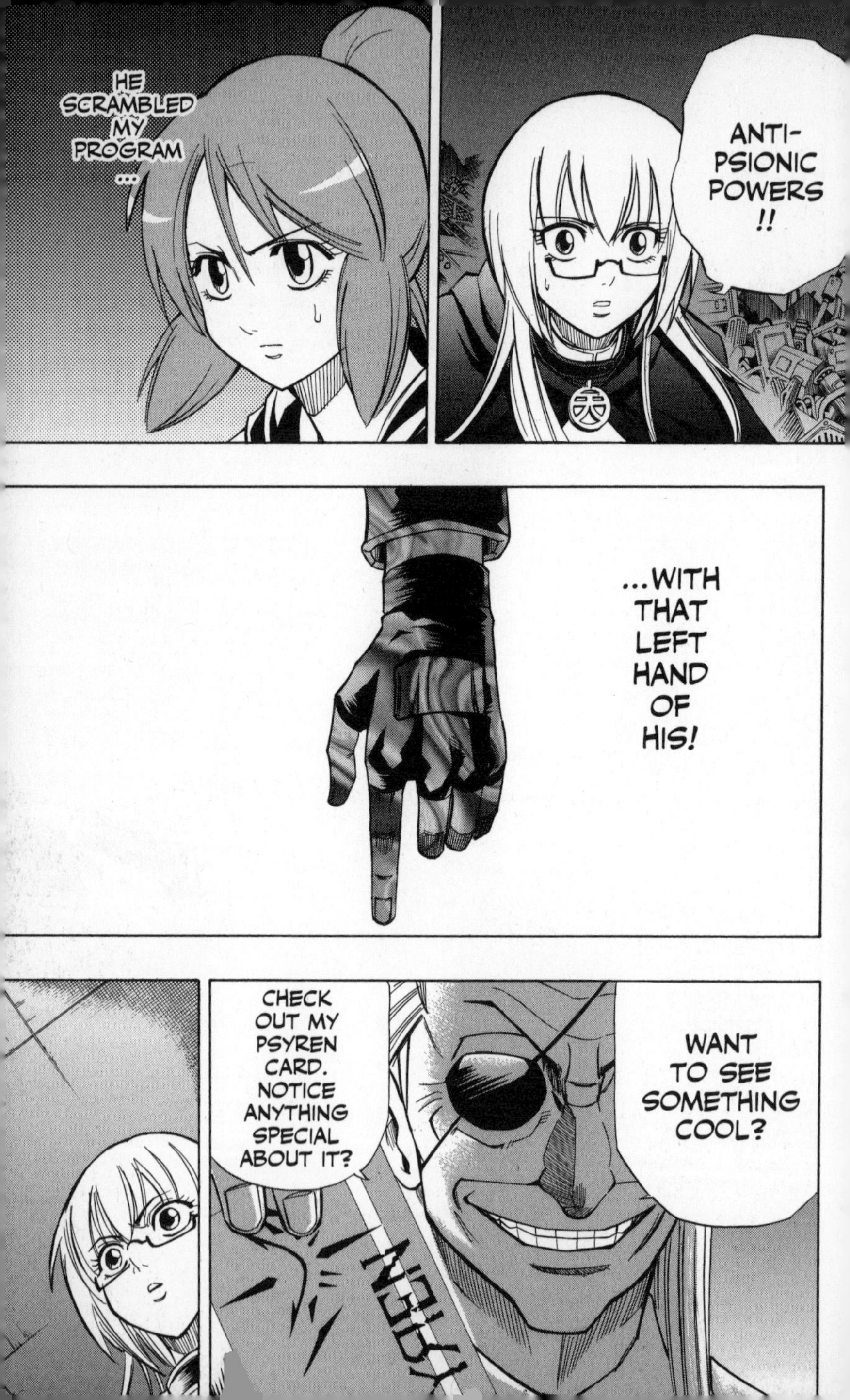
ANTI-PSIONIC POWERS!!
HE SCRAMBLED MY PROGRAM...
...WITH THAT LEFT HAND OF HIS!
WANT TO SEE SOMETHING COOL?
CHECK OUT MY PSYREN CARD. NOTICE ANYTHING SPECIAL ABOUT IT?

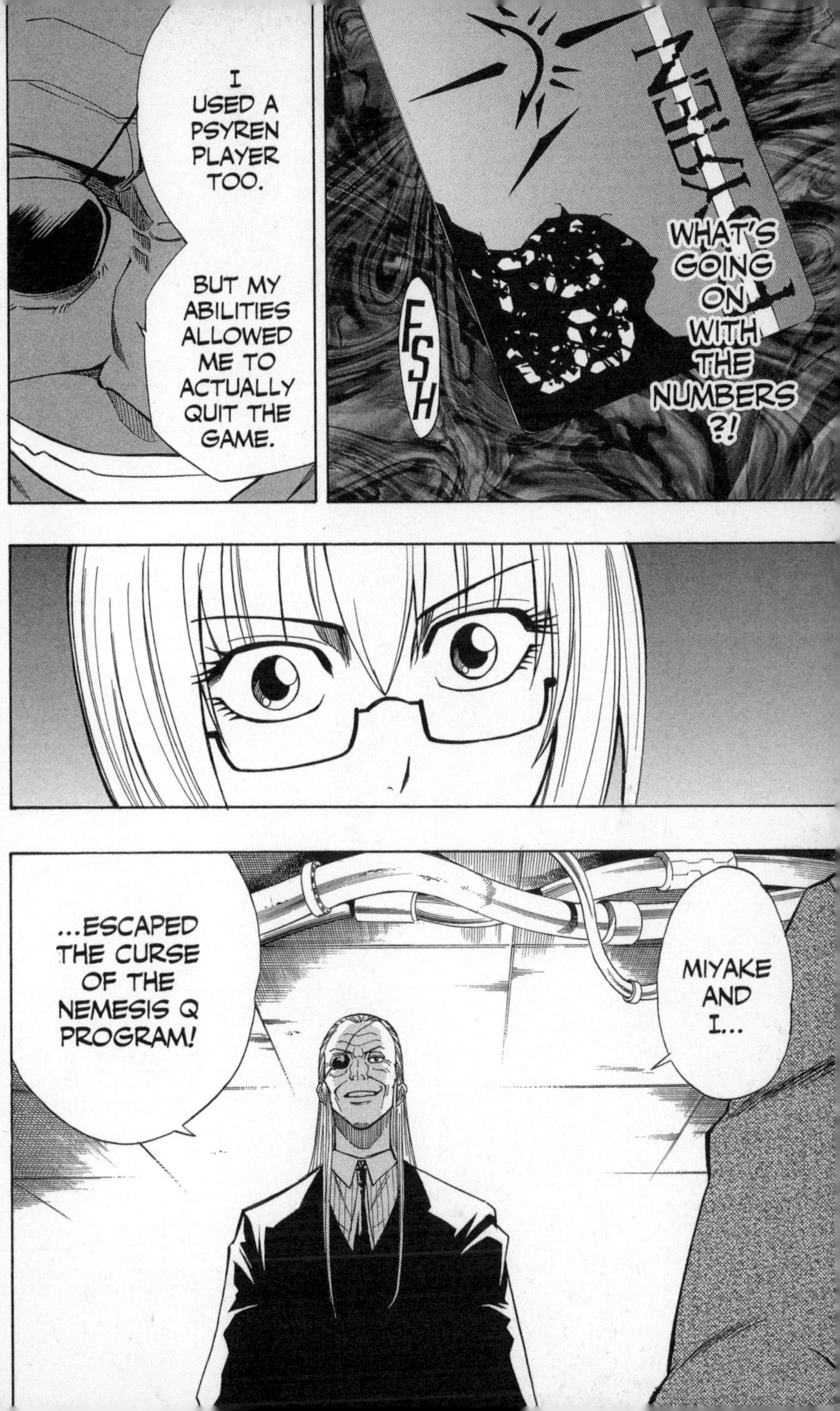
WHAT'S GOING ON WITH THE NUMBERS?!
FSH
I USED A PSYREN PLAYER TOO.
BUT MY ABILITIES ALLOWED ME TO ACTUALLY QUIT THE GAME.
MIYAKE AND I...
...ESCAPED THE CURSE OF THE NEMESIS Q PROGRAM!

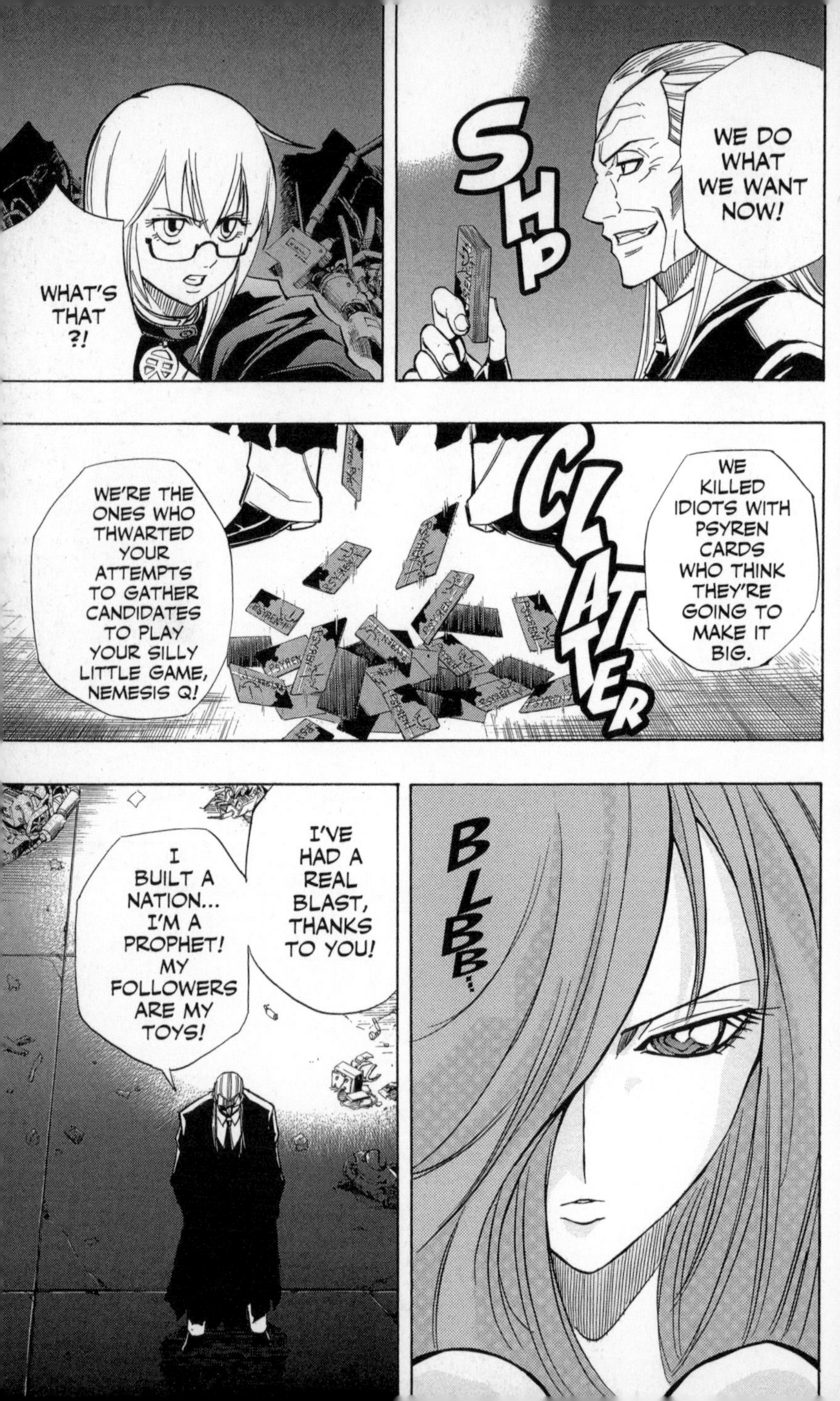
SHP
WE DO WHAT WE WANT NOW!
WHAT'S THAT ?!
WE KILLED IDIOTS WITH PSYREN CARDS WHO THINK THEY'RE GOING TO MAKE IT BIG.
CLATTER
WE'RE THE ONES WHO THWARTED YOUR ATTEMPTS TO GATHER CANDIDATES TO PLAY YOUR SILLY LITTLE GAME, NEMESIS Q!
BLBB...
I'VE HAD A REAL BLAST, THANKS TO YOU!
I BUILT A NATION... I'M A PROPHET! MY FOLLOWERS ARE MY TOYS!

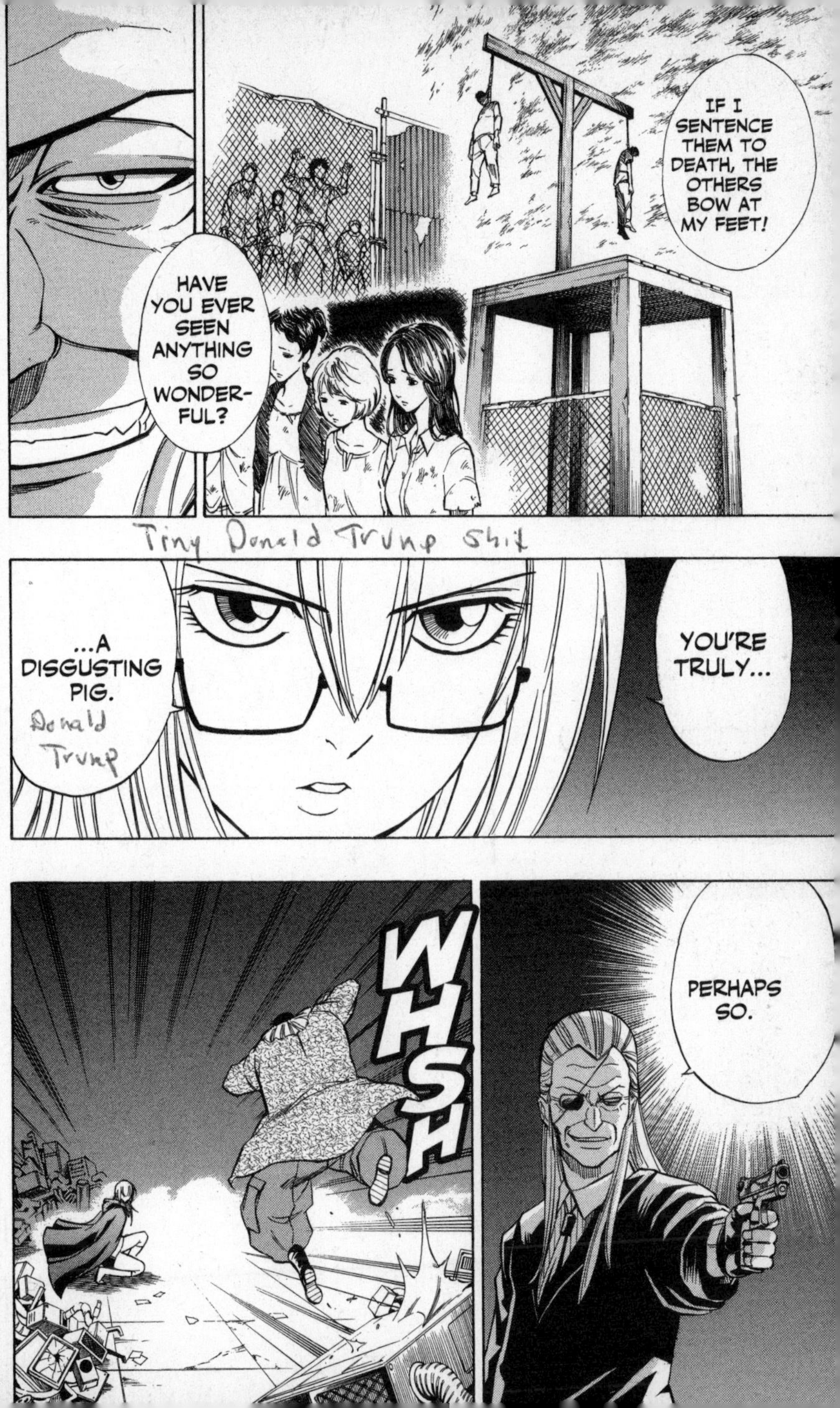
IF I SENTENCE THEM TO DEATH, THE OTHERS BOW AT MY FEET!
HAVE YOU EVER SEEN ANYTHING SO WONDER-FUL?
Tiny Donald Trump shit
YOU'RE TRULY...
...A DISGUSTING PIG.
Donald Trump
PERHAPS SO.
WHSH

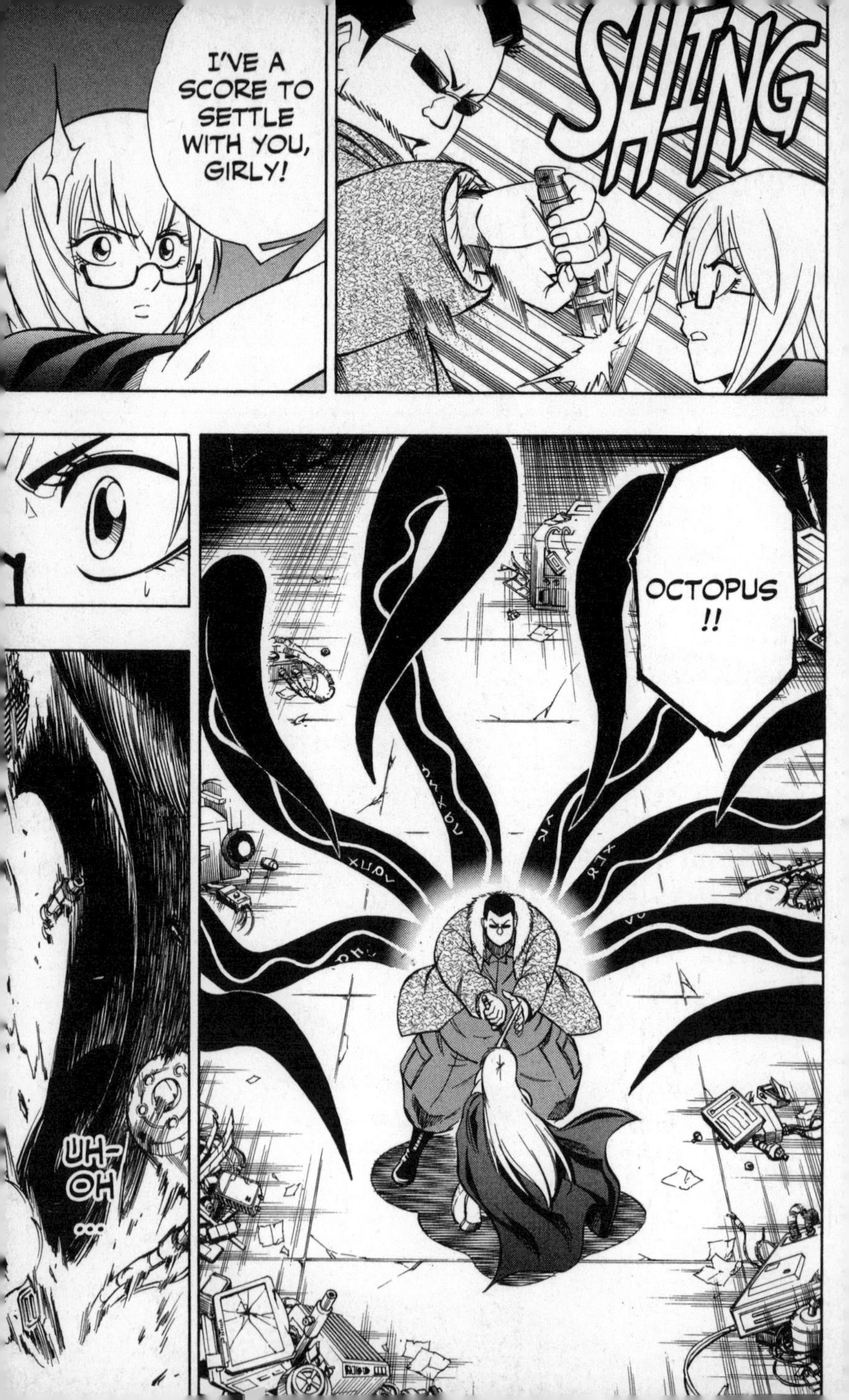
SHING
I'VE A SCORE TO SETTLE WITH YOU, GIRLY!
OCTOPUS !!
UH-OH ...

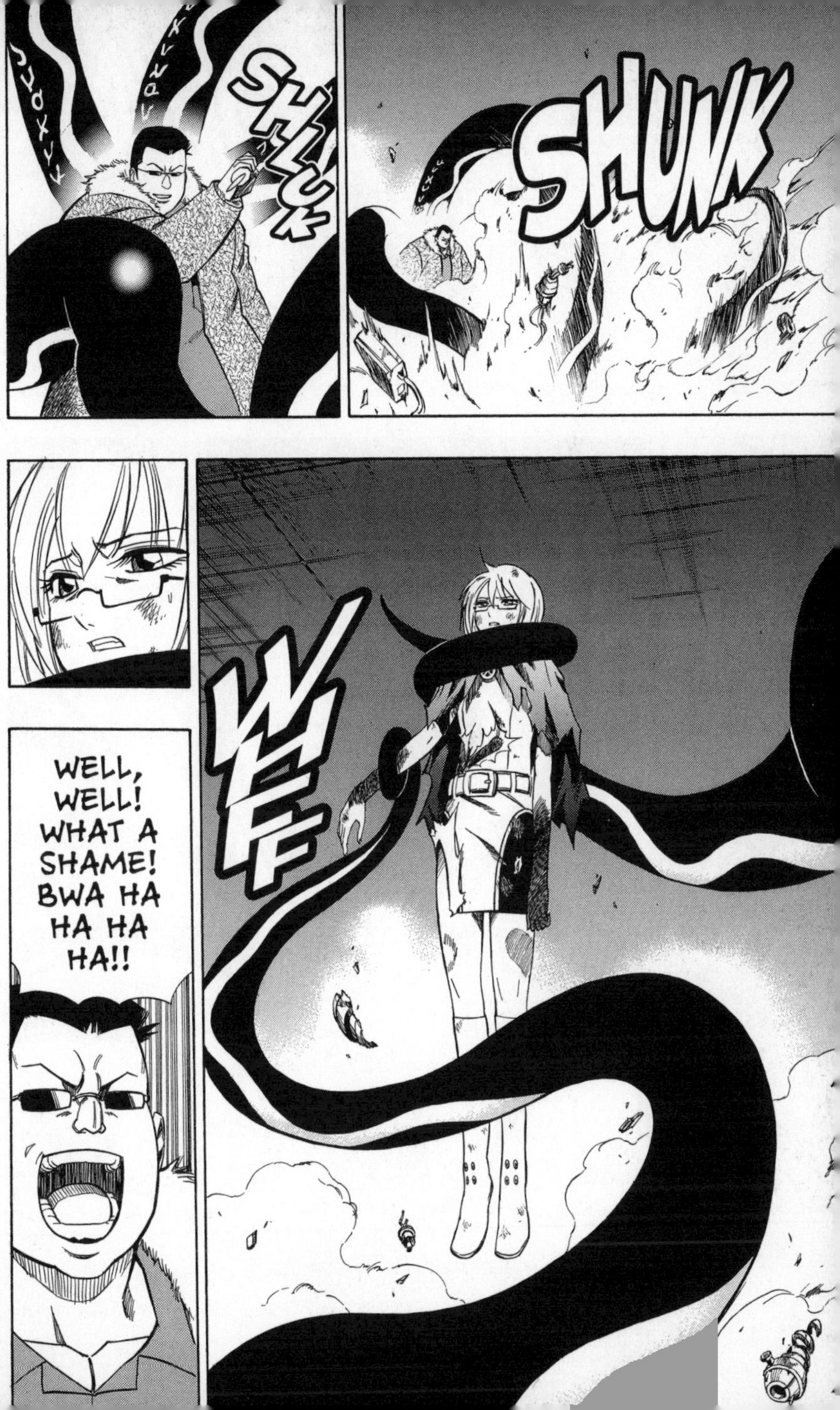
SHUNK
SHLUK
WHIFF
WELL, WELL! WHAT A SHAME! BWA HA HA HA HA HA!!

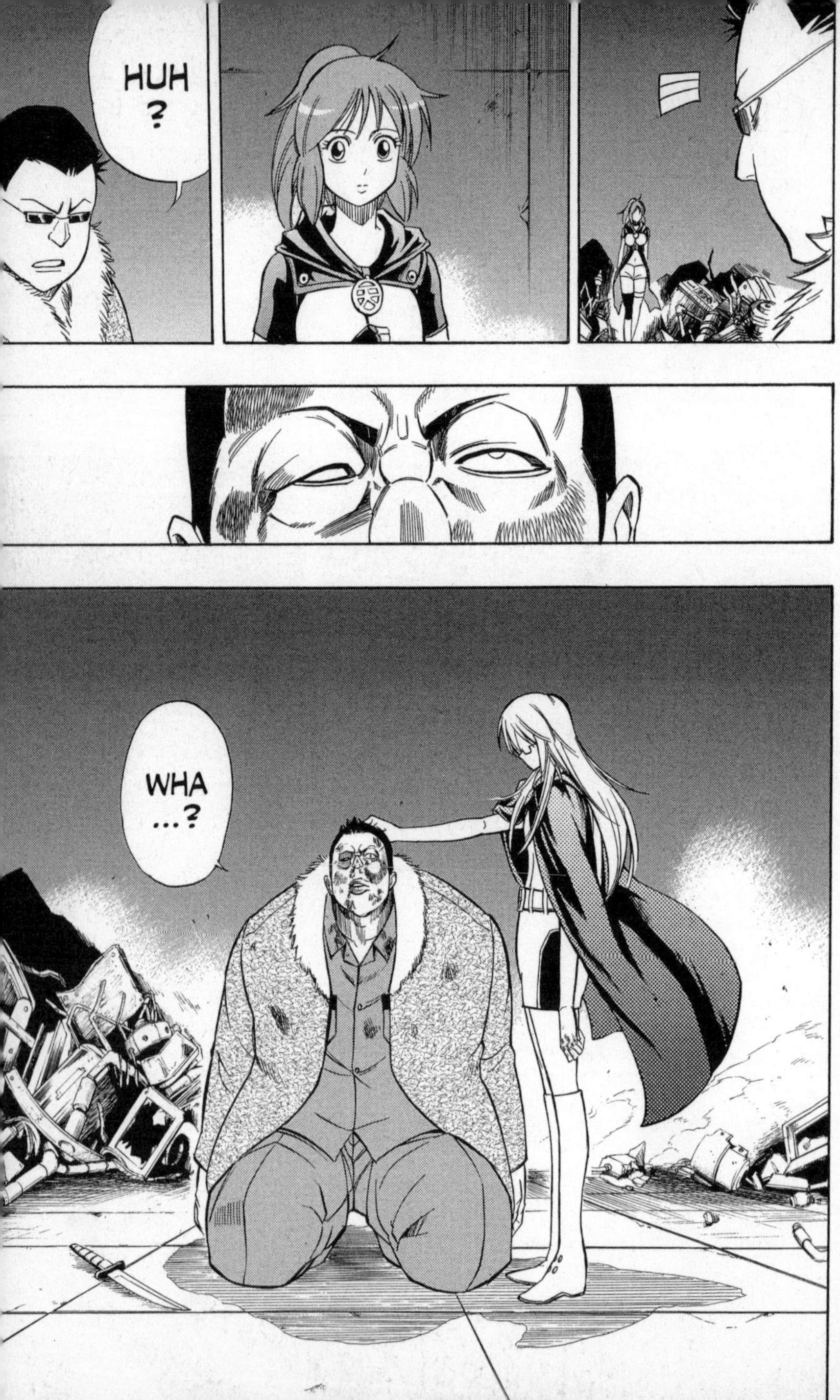
HUH ?
WHA ...?

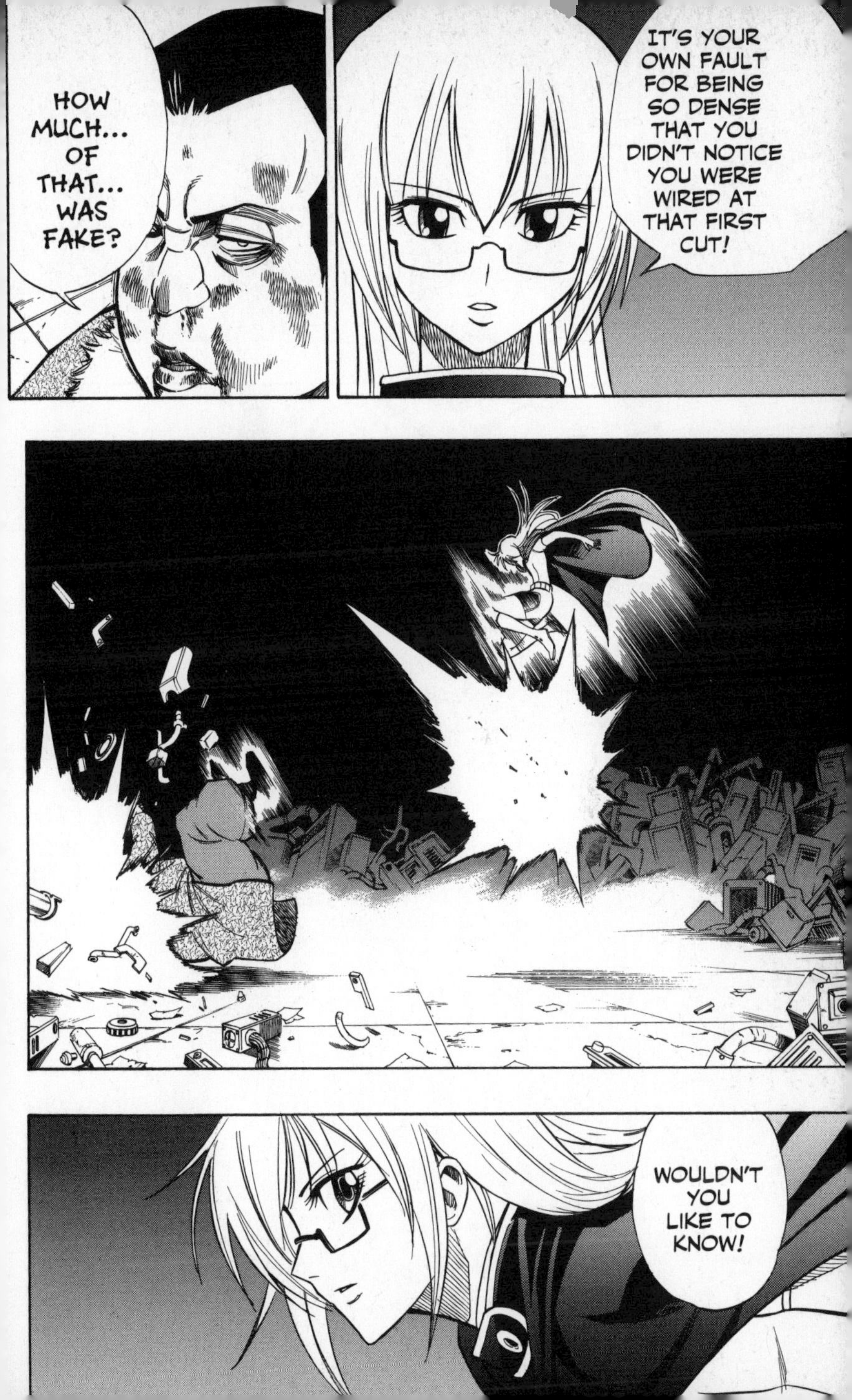
IT'S YOUR OWN FAULT FOR BEING SO DENSE THAT YOU DIDN'T NOTICE YOU WERE WIRED AT THAT FIRST CUT!
HOW MUCH... OF THAT... WAS FAKE?
WOULDN'T YOU LIKE TO KNOW!

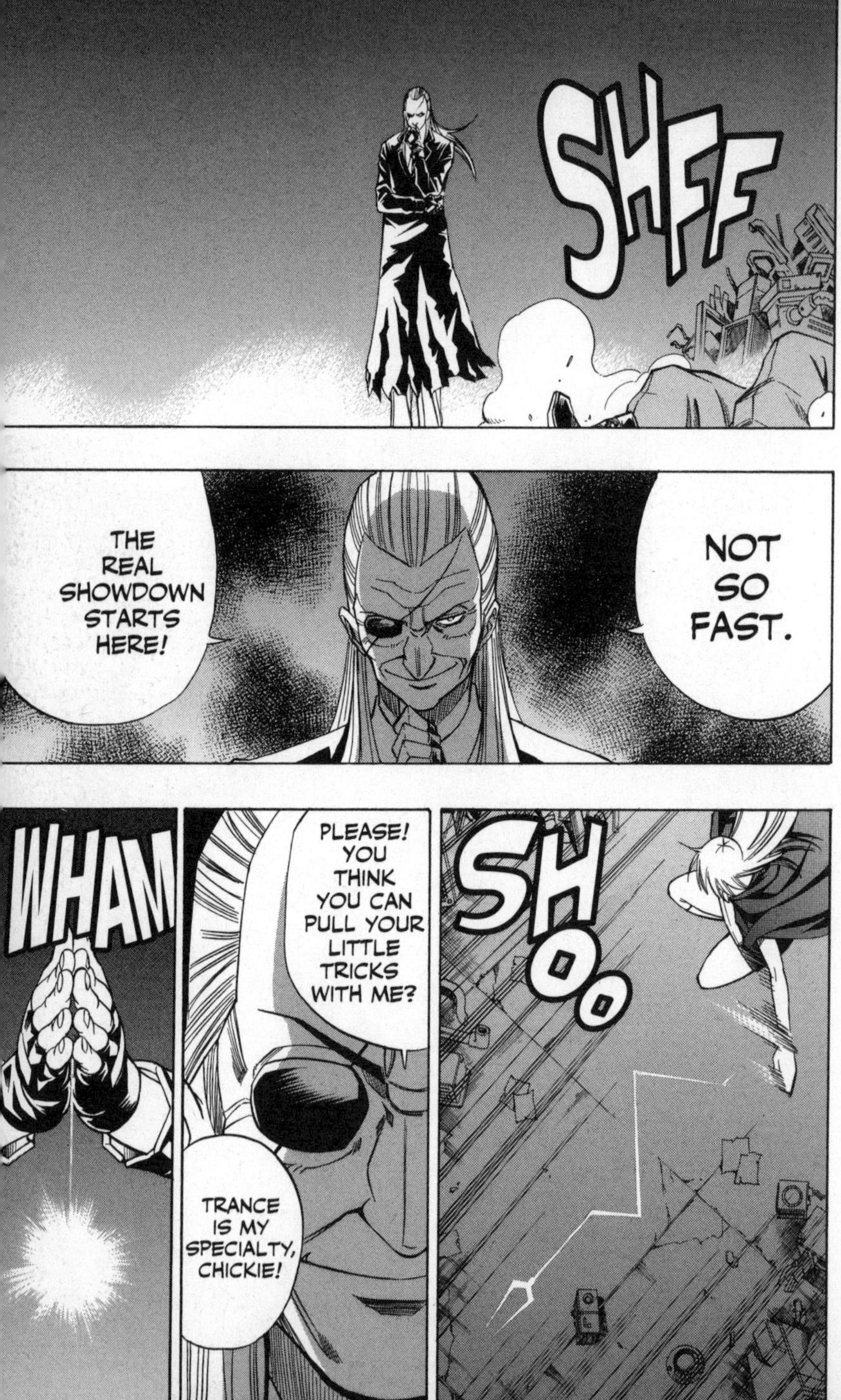
SHFF
NOT SO FAST.
THE REAL SHOWDOWN STARTS HERE!
SHOO
PLEASE! YOU THINK YOU CAN PULL YOUR LITTLE TRICKS WITH ME?
TRANCE IS MY SPECIALTY, CHICKIE!
WHAM

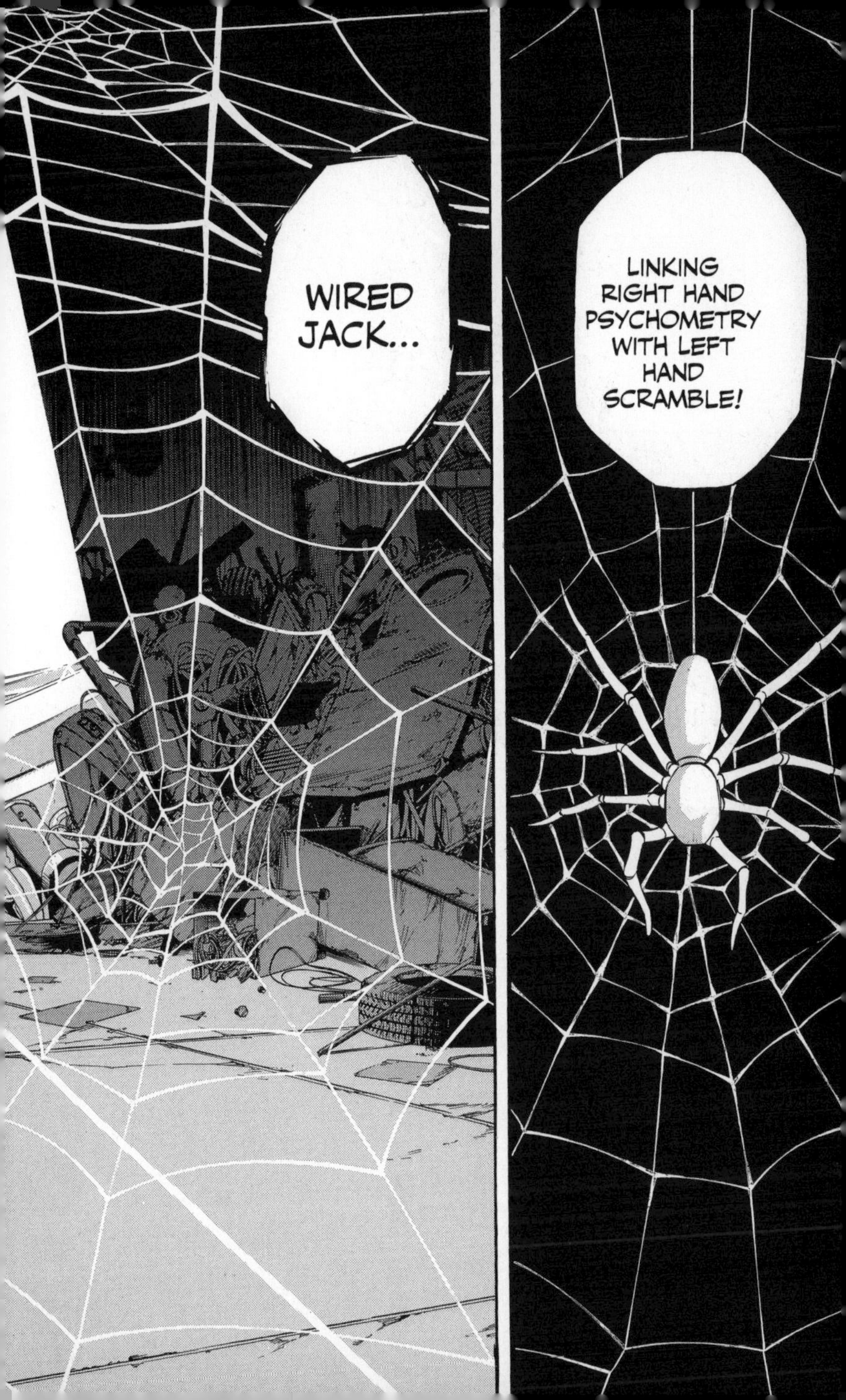
LINKING RIGHT HAND PSYCHOMETRY WITH LEFT HAND SCRAMBLE!
WIRED JACK...

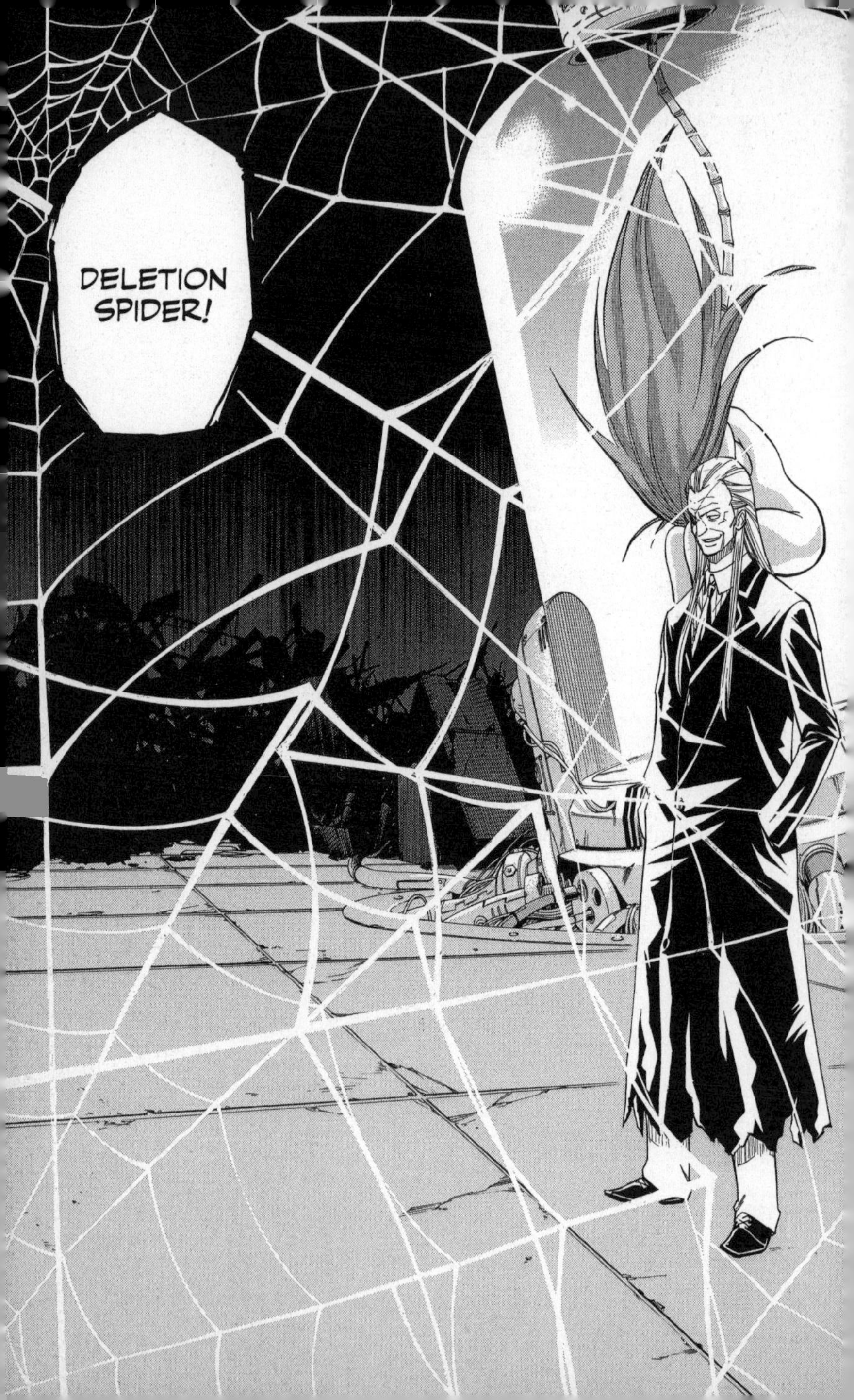
DELETION SPIDER!

Mutters and mumblings

TWITTER'S GETTING PRETTY POPULAR,
SO I CONSIDERED DOING SOME TWEETING.
BUT I GUESS IT'S NOT REALLY SUITED TO
A GUY WHO TAKES HALF AN HOUR TO
COME UP WITH THESE POST-CHAPTER
COMMENTS.

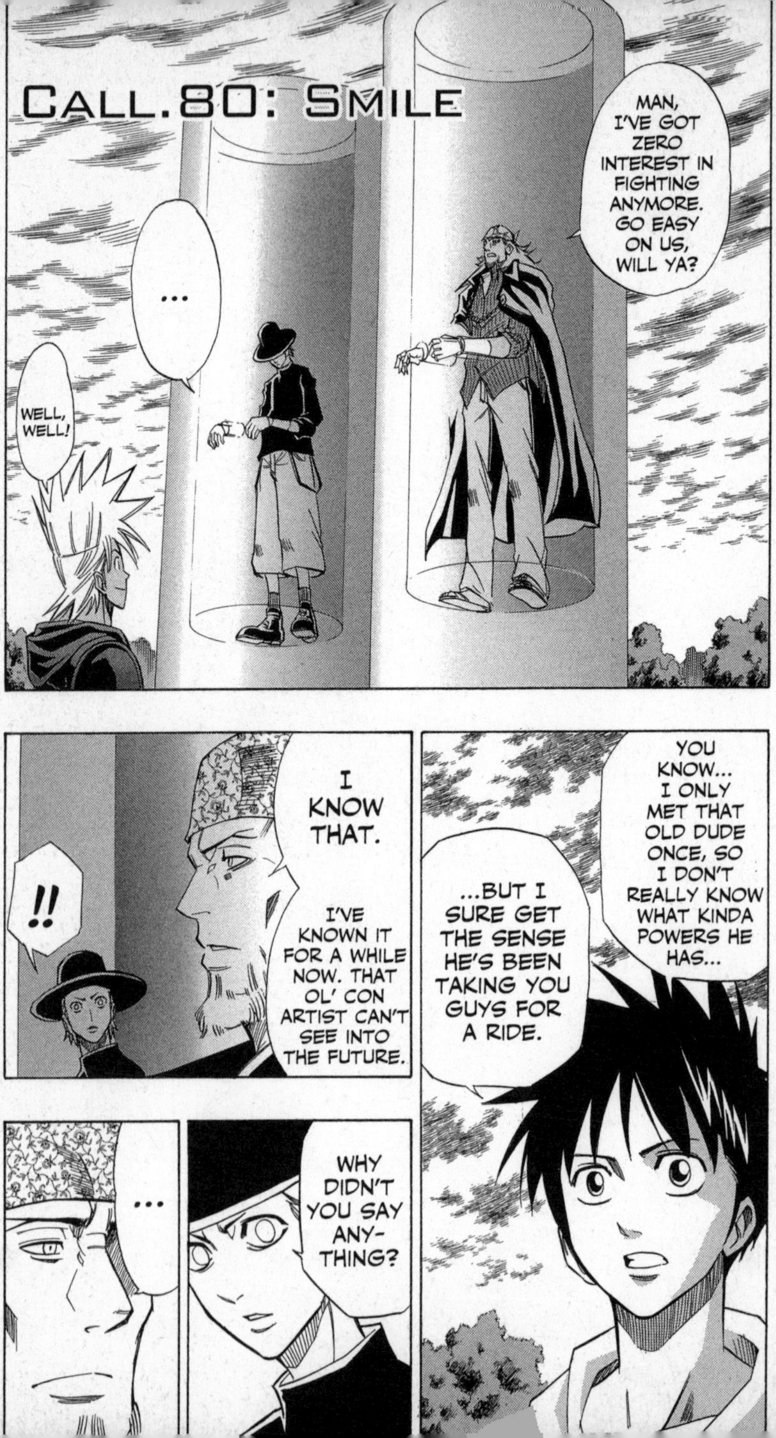
CALL.80: SMILE
MAN, I'VE GOT ZERO INTEREST IN FIGHTING ANYMORE. GO EASY ON US, WILL YA?
...
WELL, WELL!
YOU KNOW... I ONLY MET THAT OLD DUDE ONCE, SO I DON'T REALLY KNOW WHAT KINDA POWERS HE HAS...
...BUT I SURE GET THE SENSE HE'S BEEN TAKING YOU GUYS FOR A RIDE.
I KNOW THAT.
I'VE KNOWN IT FOR A WHILE NOW. THAT OL' CON ARTIST CAN'T SEE INTO THE FUTURE.
!!
WHY DIDN'T YOU SAY ANY-THING?
...

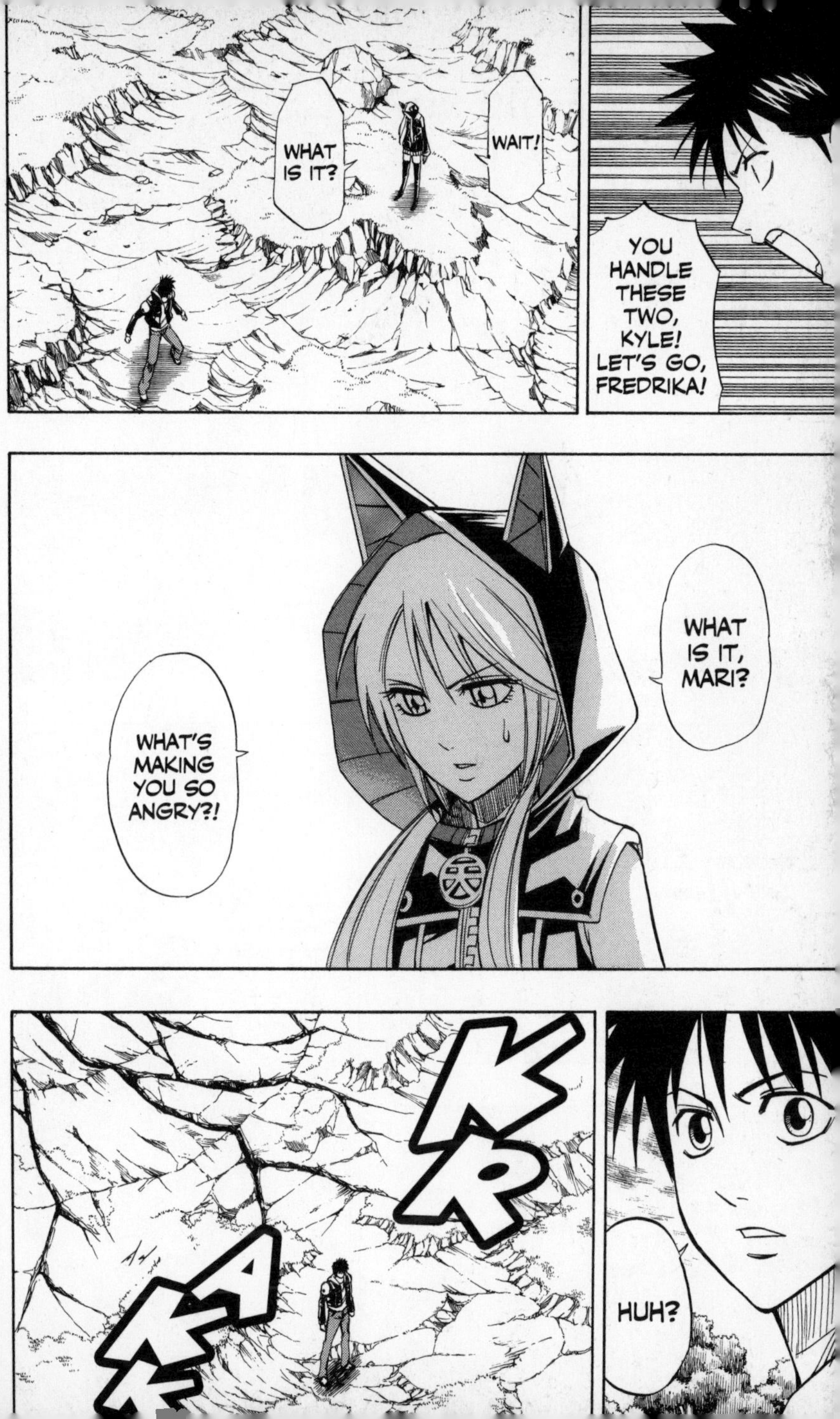
YOU HANDLE THESE TWO, KYLE! LET'S GO, FREDRIKA!
WAIT!
WHAT IS IT?
WHAT IS IT, MARI?
WHAT'S MAKING YOU SO ANGRY?!
HUH?
KRAKK

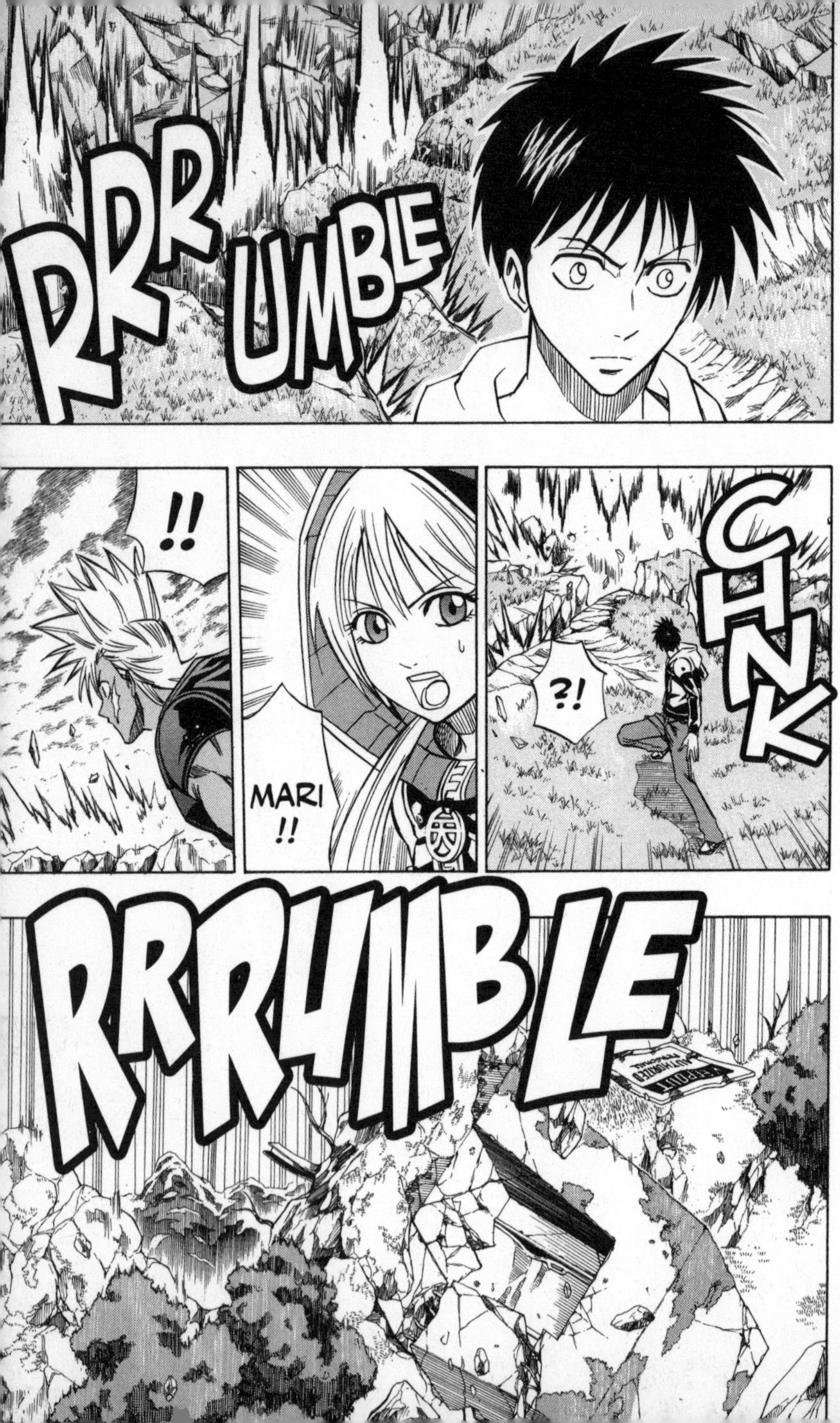
RRRUMBLE
CHNK
?!
MARI !!
!!
RRRUMBLE

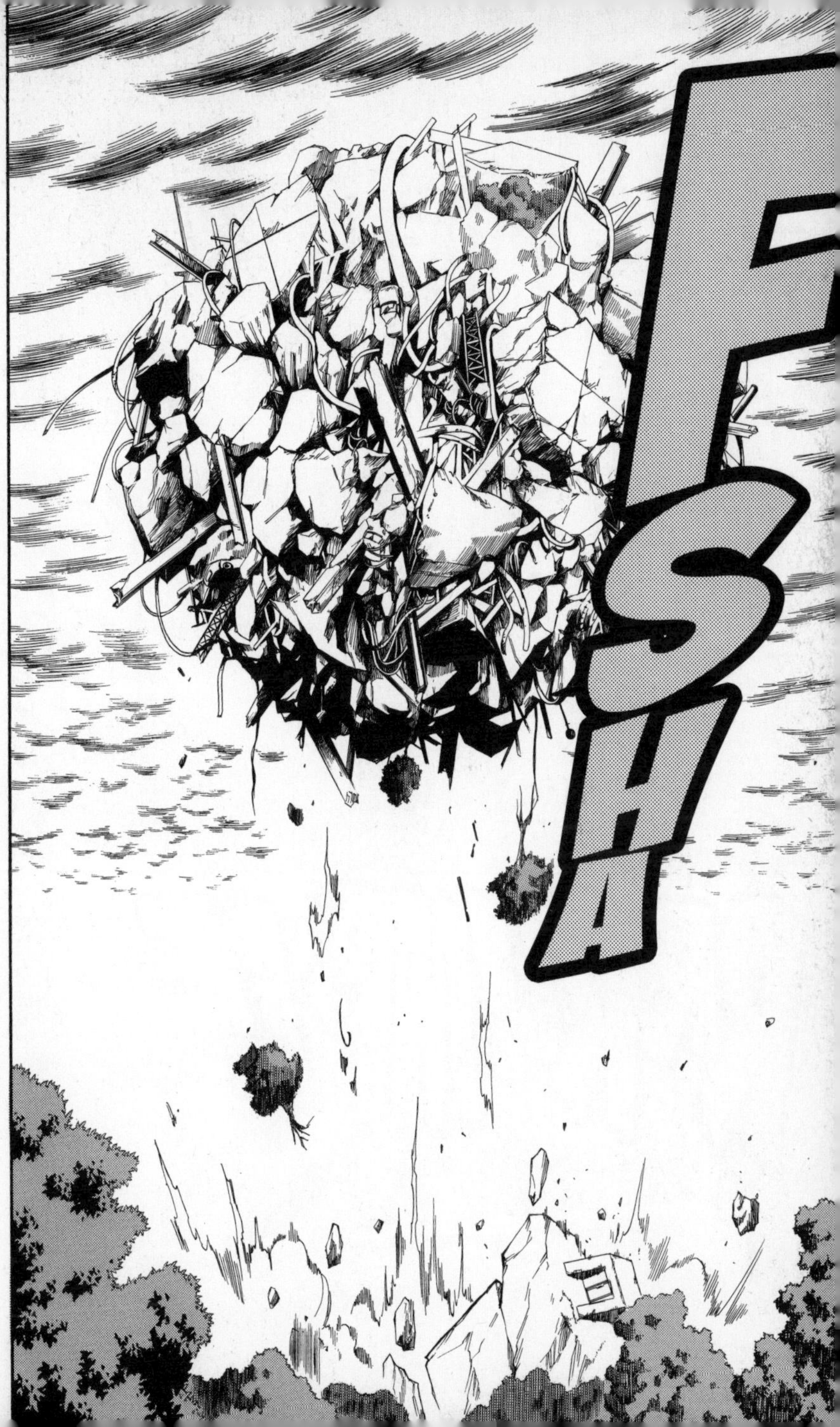
FSHA

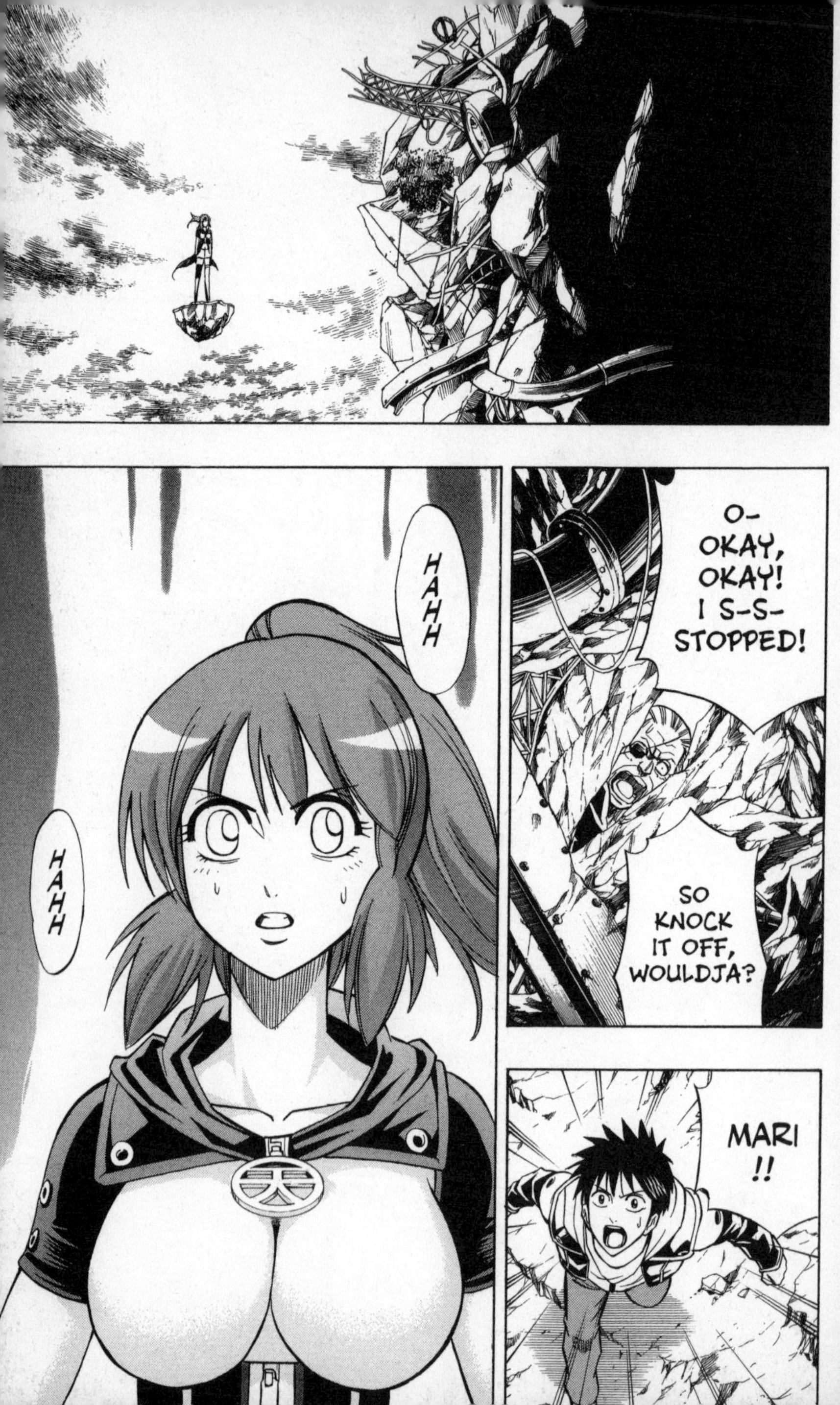
O-OKAY, OKAY! I S-S-STOPPED!
SO KNOCK IT OFF, WOULDJA?
MARI!!
HAHH
HAHH

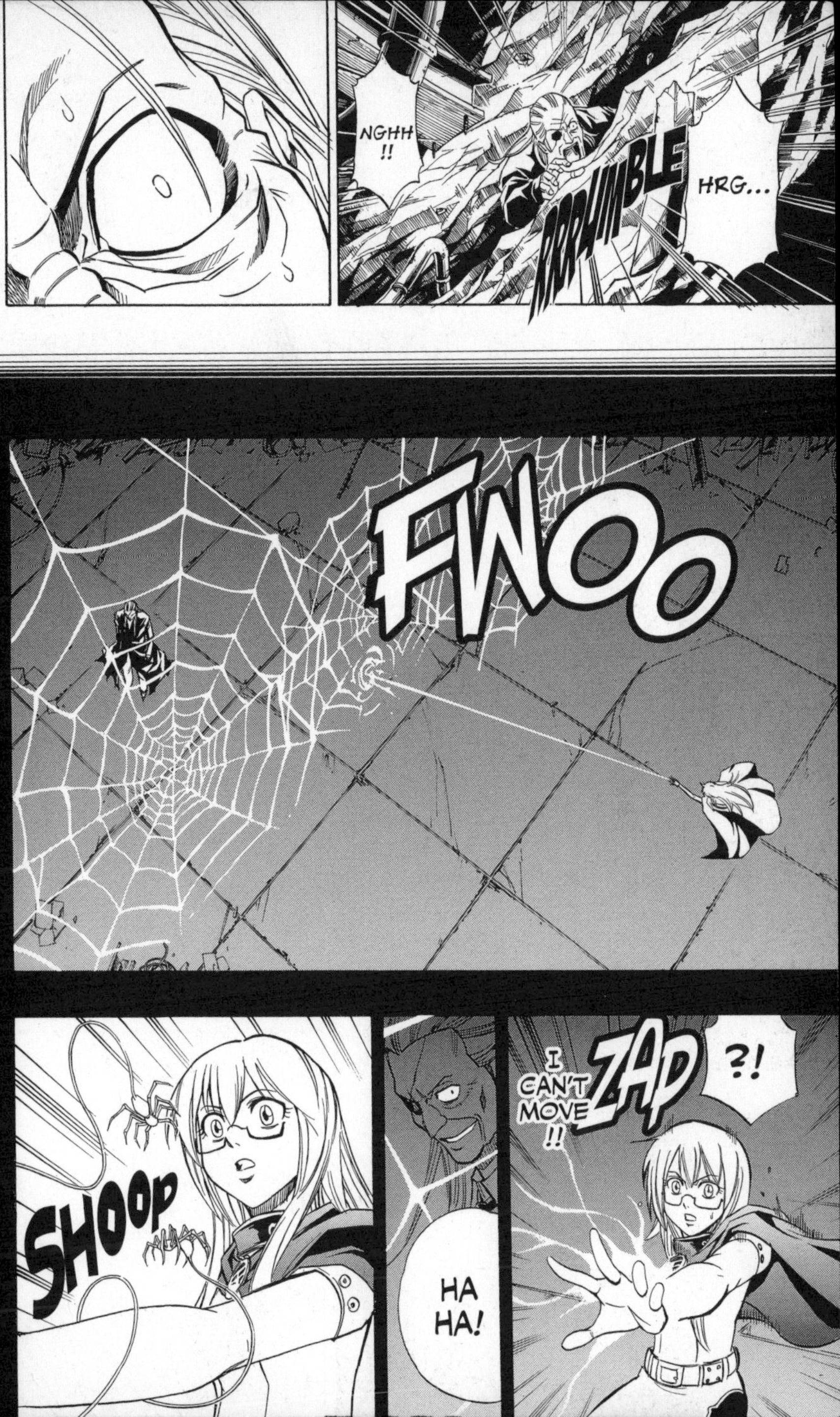
HRG...
RRRUMBLE
NGHH!!
FWOO
?!
ZAP
I CAN'T MOVE!!
HA HA!
SHOOP

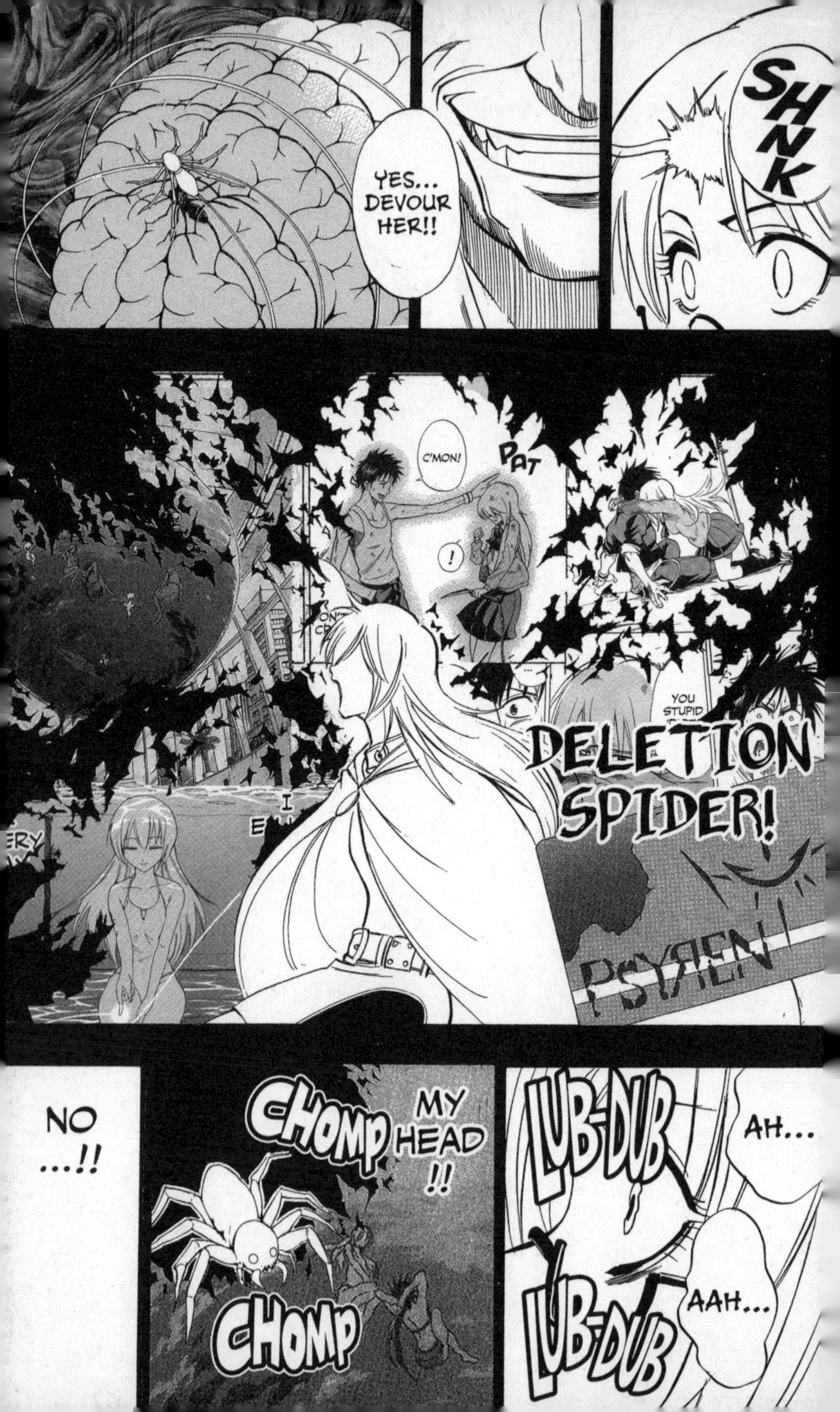
SHNK
YES... DEVOUR HER!!
C'MON!
PAT
!
YOU STUPID
DELETION SPIDER!
PSYREN
LUB-DUB
AH...
LUB-DUB
AAH...
CHOMP
MY HEAD!!
CHOMP
NO ...!!

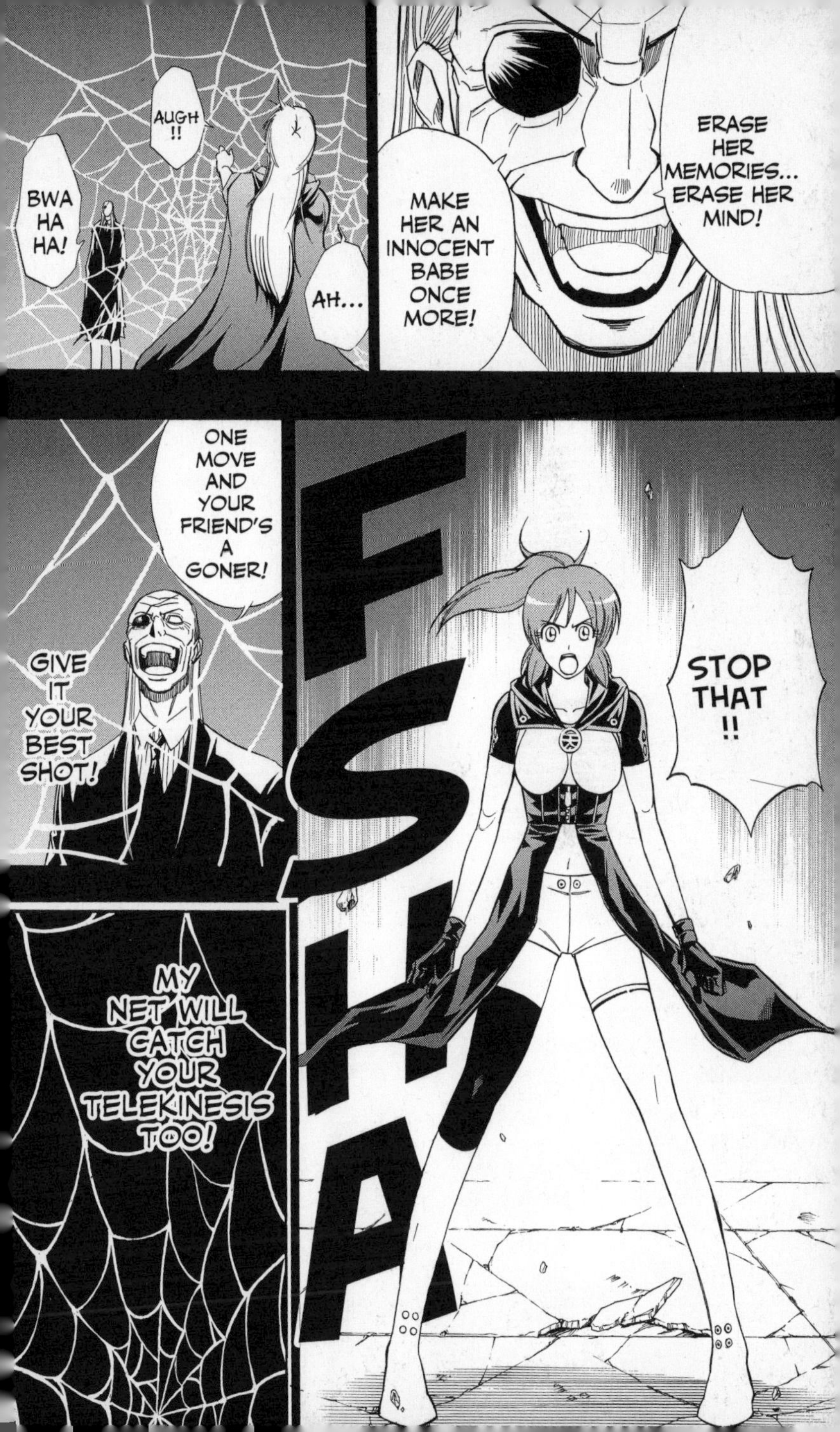

ERASE HER MEMORIES... ERASE HER MIND!
MAKE HER AN INNOCENT BABE ONCE MORE!
AUGH !!
AH...
BWA HA HA!
FSHA
STOP THAT !!
ONE MOVE AND YOUR FRIEND'S A GONER!
GIVE IT YOUR BEST SHOT!
MY NET WILL CATCH YOUR TELEKINESIS TOO!

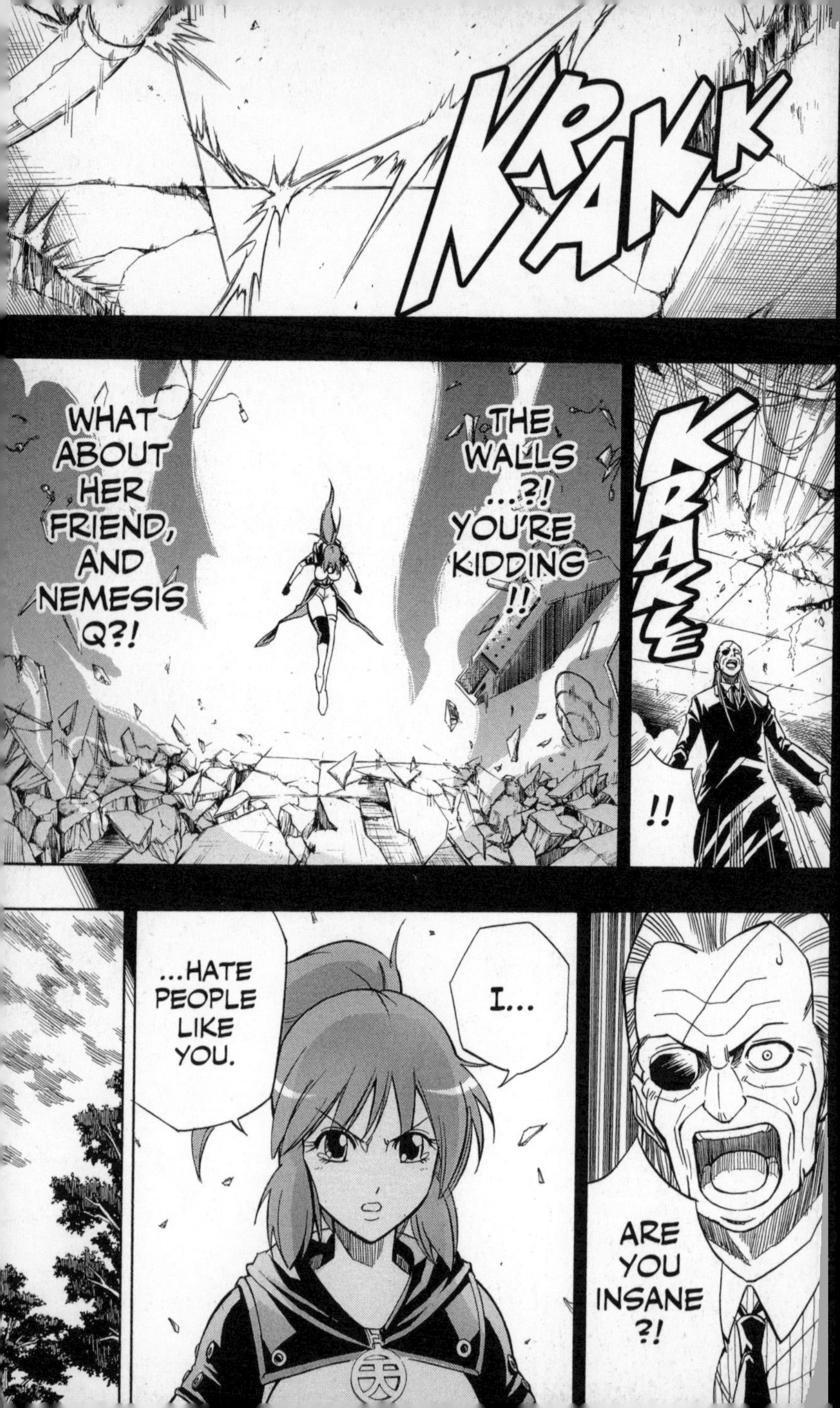
KRAKK
KRAKLE
!!
THE WALLS ...?! YOU'RE KIDDING!!
WHAT ABOUT HER FRIEND, AND NEMESIS Q?!
ARE YOU INSANE?!
I...
...HATE PEOPLE LIKE YOU.

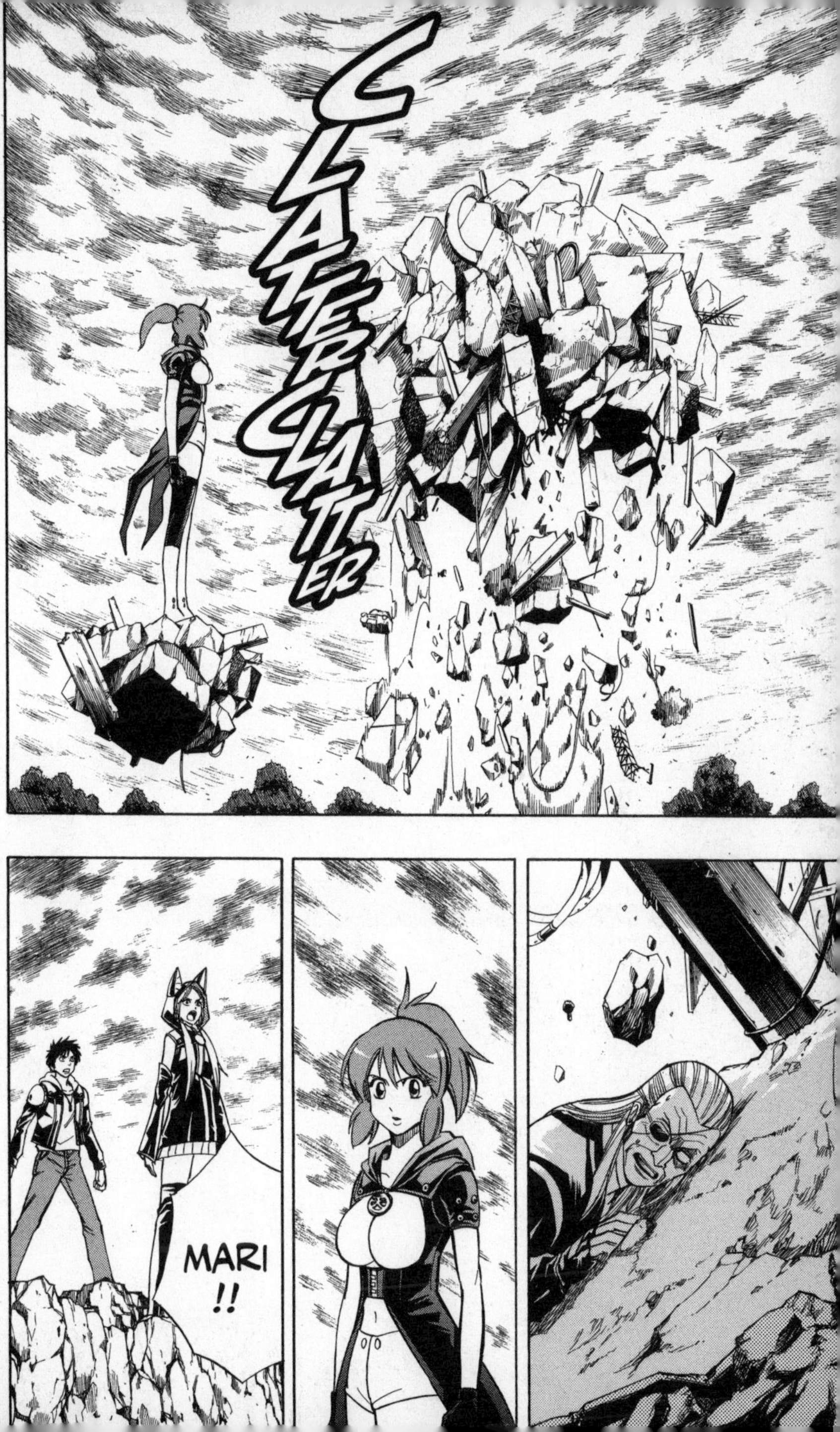
CLATTER CLATTER
MARI !!

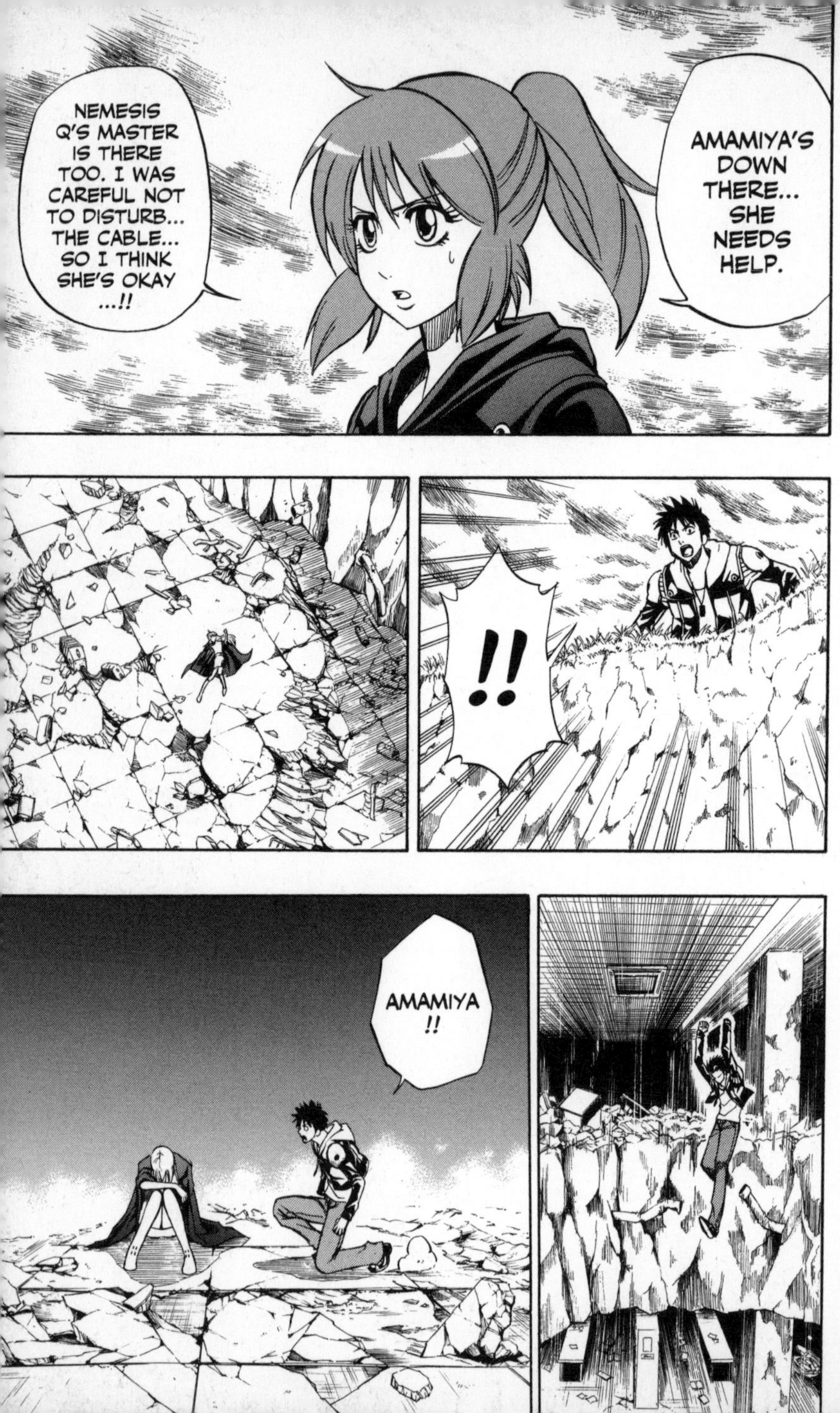
AMAMIYA'S DOWN THERE... SHE NEEDS HELP.
NEMESIS Q'S MASTER IS THERE TOO. I WAS CAREFUL NOT TO DISTURB... THE CABLE... SO I THINK SHE'S OKAY ...!!
!!
AMAMIYA !!

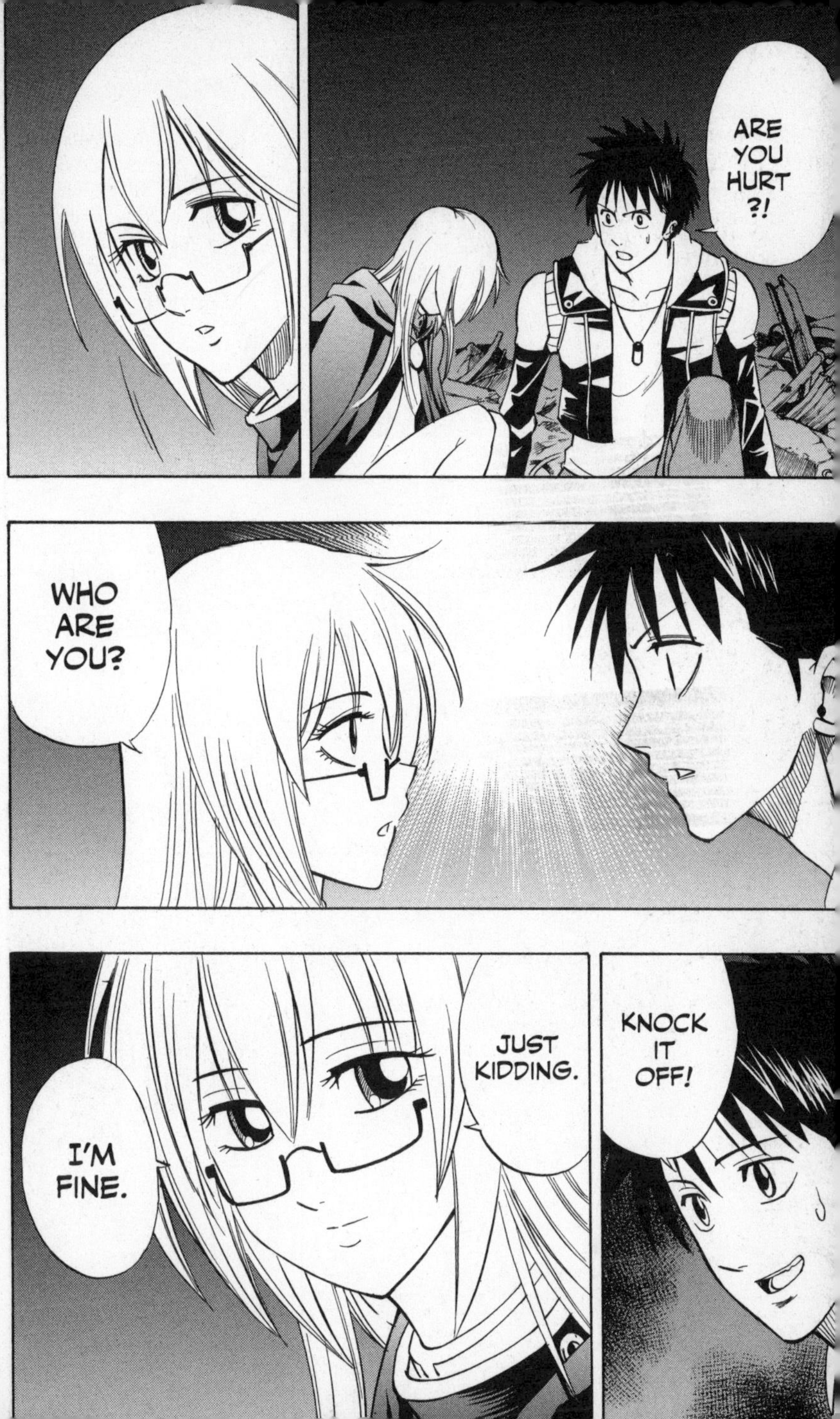
ARE YOU HURT ?!
WHO ARE YOU?
KNOCK IT OFF!
JUST KIDDING.
I'M FINE.

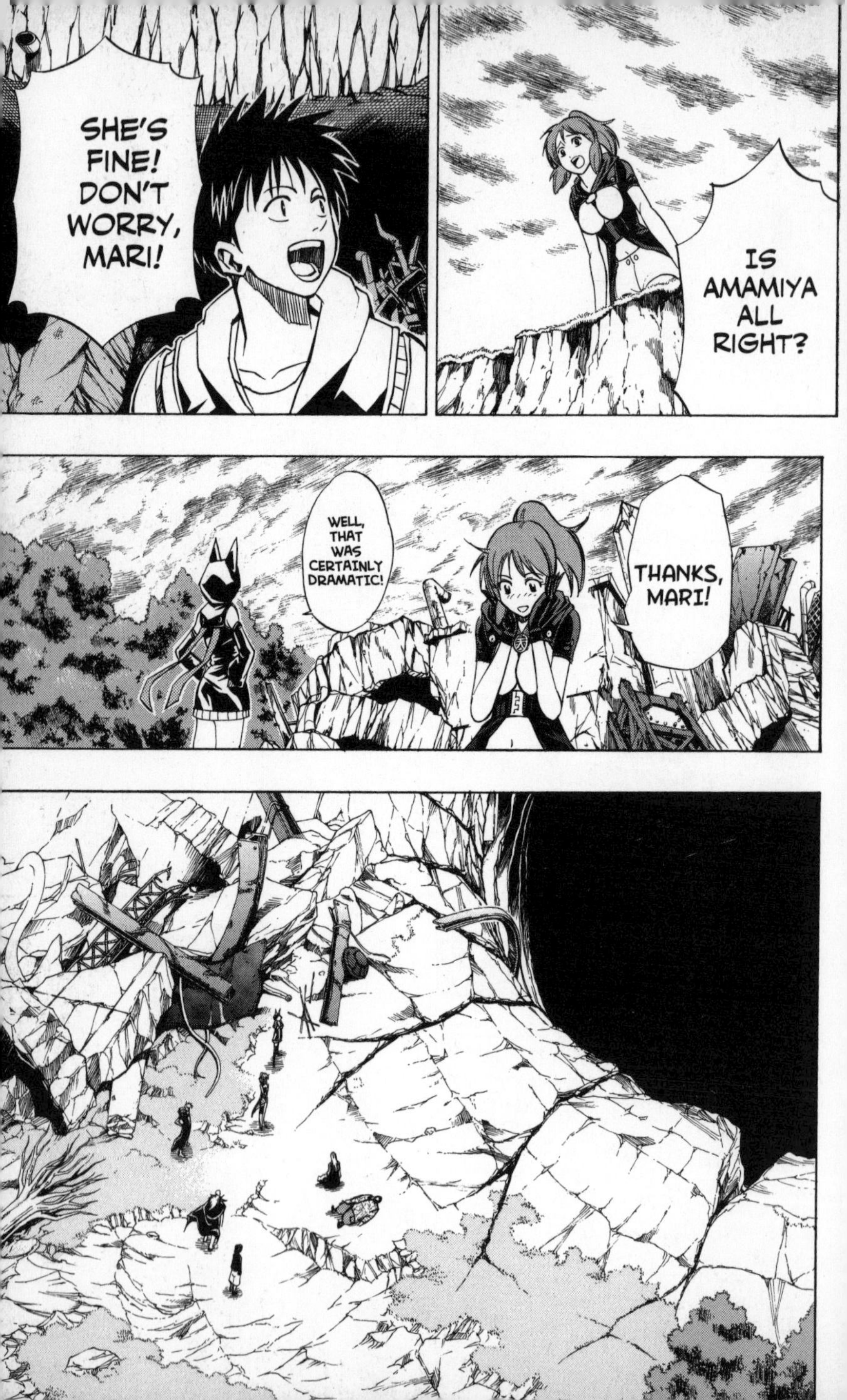
IS AMAMIYA ALL RIGHT?
SHE'S FINE! DON'T WORRY, MARI!
THANKS, MARI!
WELL, THAT WAS CERTAINLY DRAMATIC!

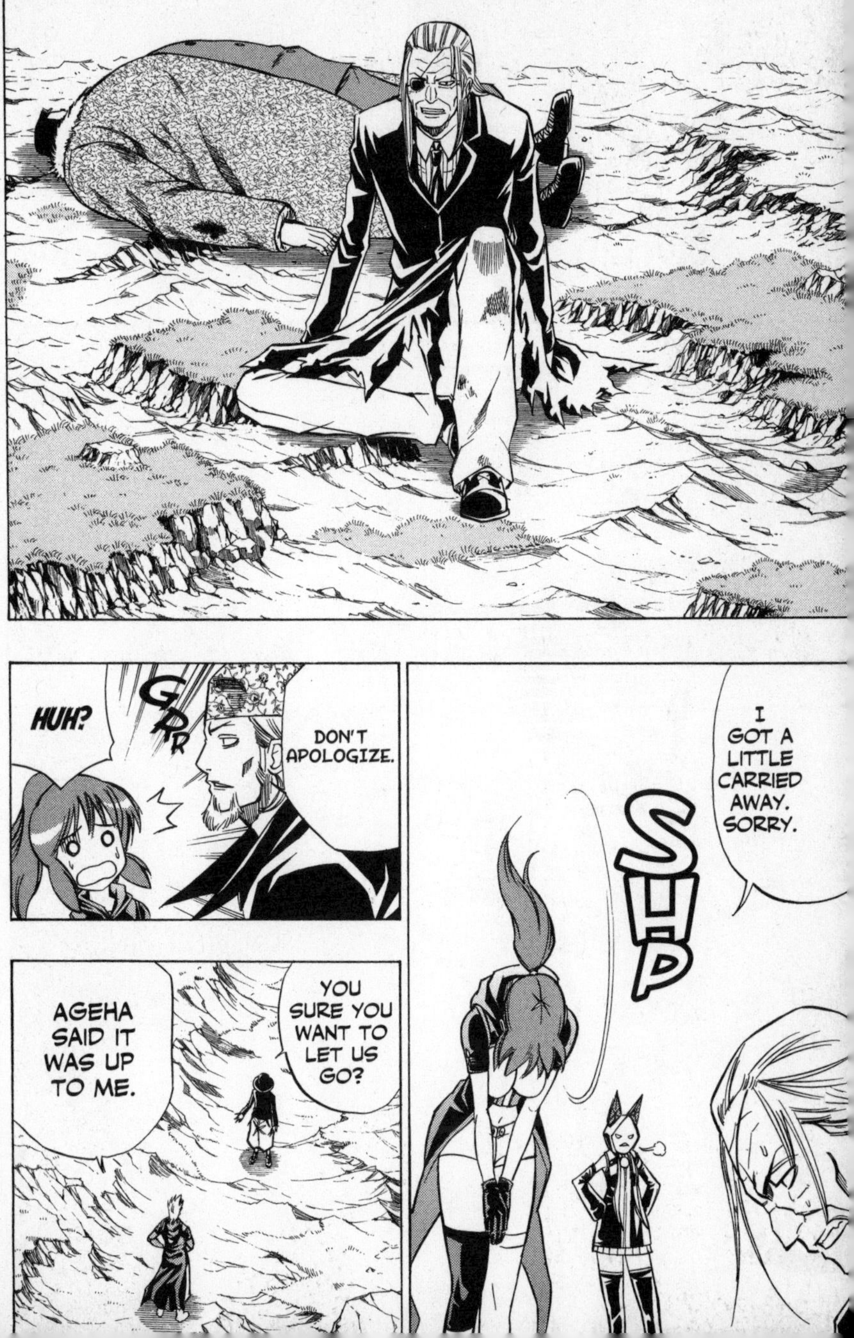
I GOT A LITTLE CARRIED AWAY. SORRY.
SLIP
DON'T APOLOGIZE.
GRR
HUH?
YOU SURE YOU WANT TO LET US GO?
AGEHA SAID IT WAS UP TO ME.

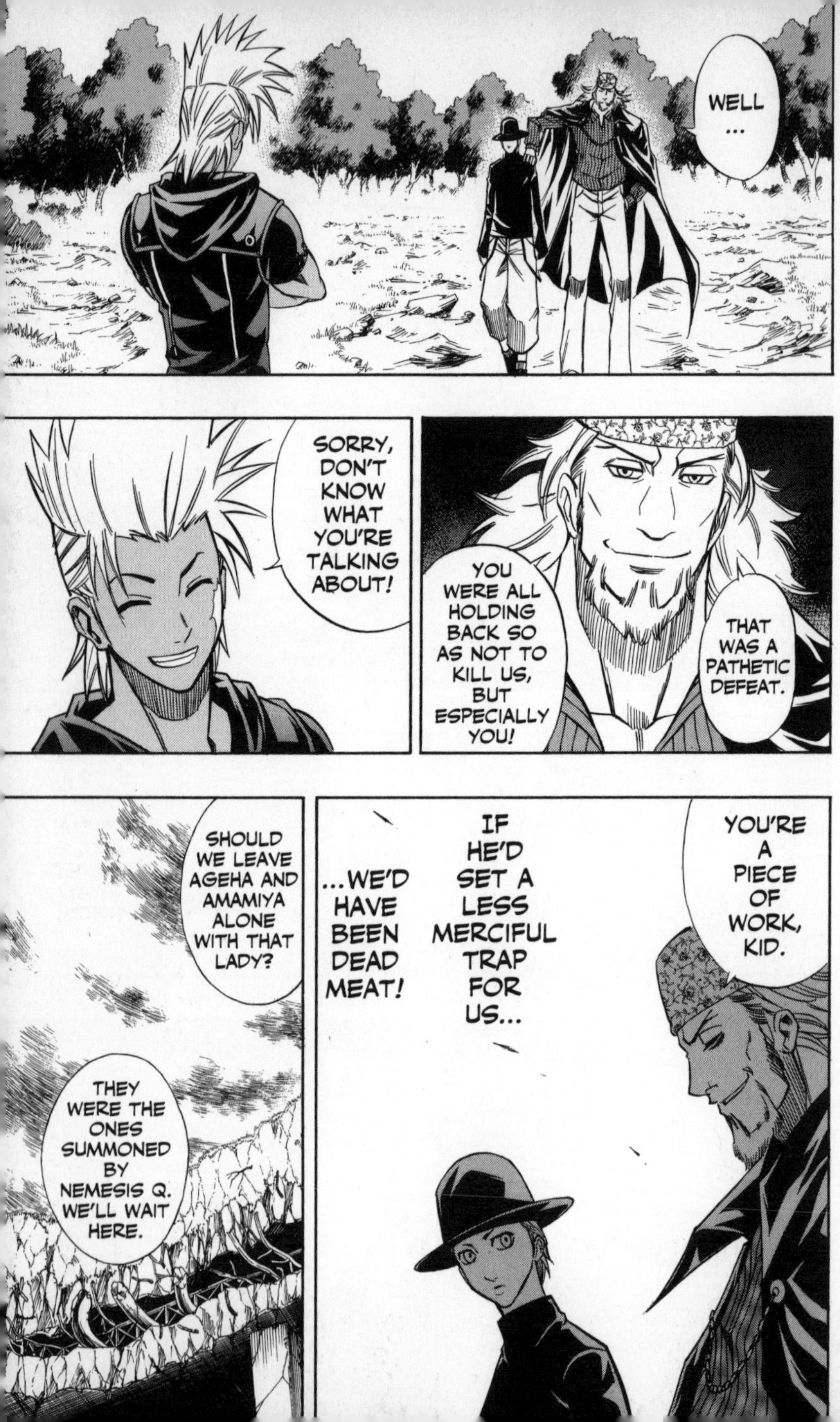
WELL ...
THAT WAS A PATHETIC DEFEAT.
YOU WERE ALL HOLDING BACK SO AS NOT TO KILL US, BUT ESPECIALLY YOU!
SORRY, DON'T KNOW WHAT YOU'RE TALKING ABOUT!
YOU'RE A PIECE OF WORK, KID.
IF HE'D SET A LESS MERCIFUL TRAP FOR US...
...WE'D HAVE BEEN DEAD MEAT!
SHOULD WE LEAVE AGEHA AND AMAMIYA ALONE WITH THAT LADY?
THEY WERE THE ONES SUMMONED BY NEMESIS Q. WE'LL WAIT HERE.

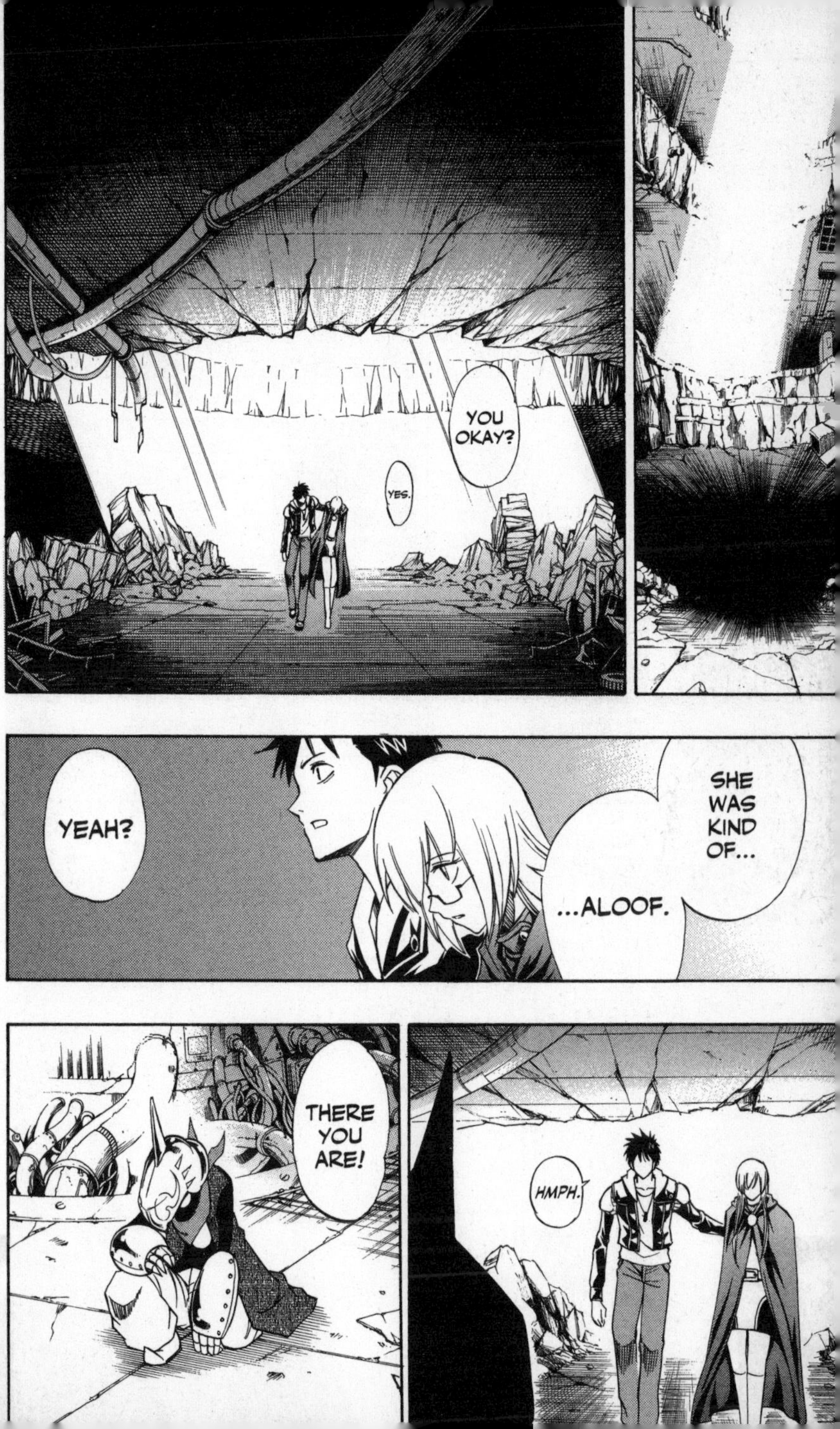
YOU OKAY?
YES.
SHE WAS KIND OF...
...ALOOF.
YEAH?
HMPH.
THERE YOU ARE!

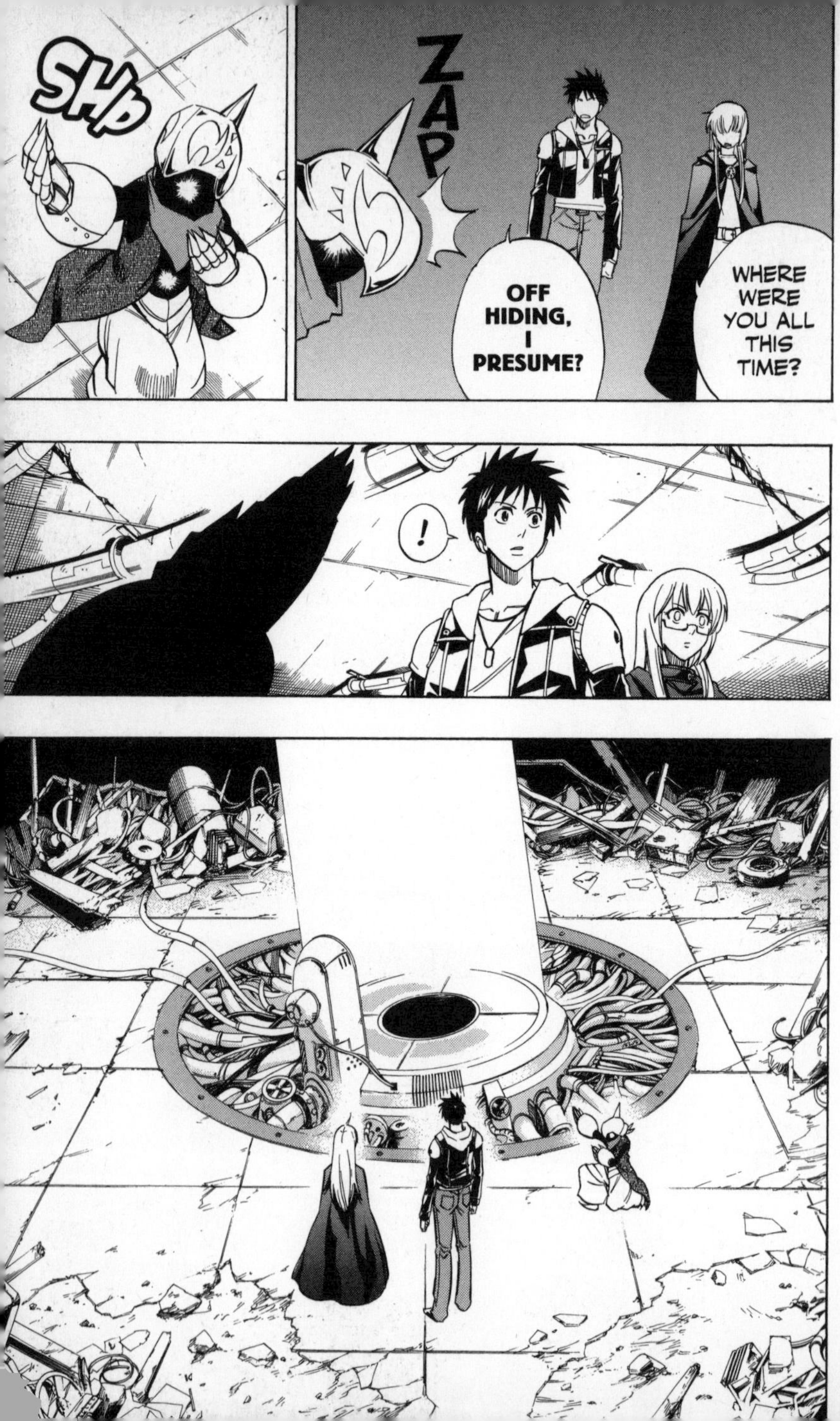
ZAP
WHERE WERE YOU ALL THIS TIME?
OFF HIDING, I PRESUME?
SHP
!

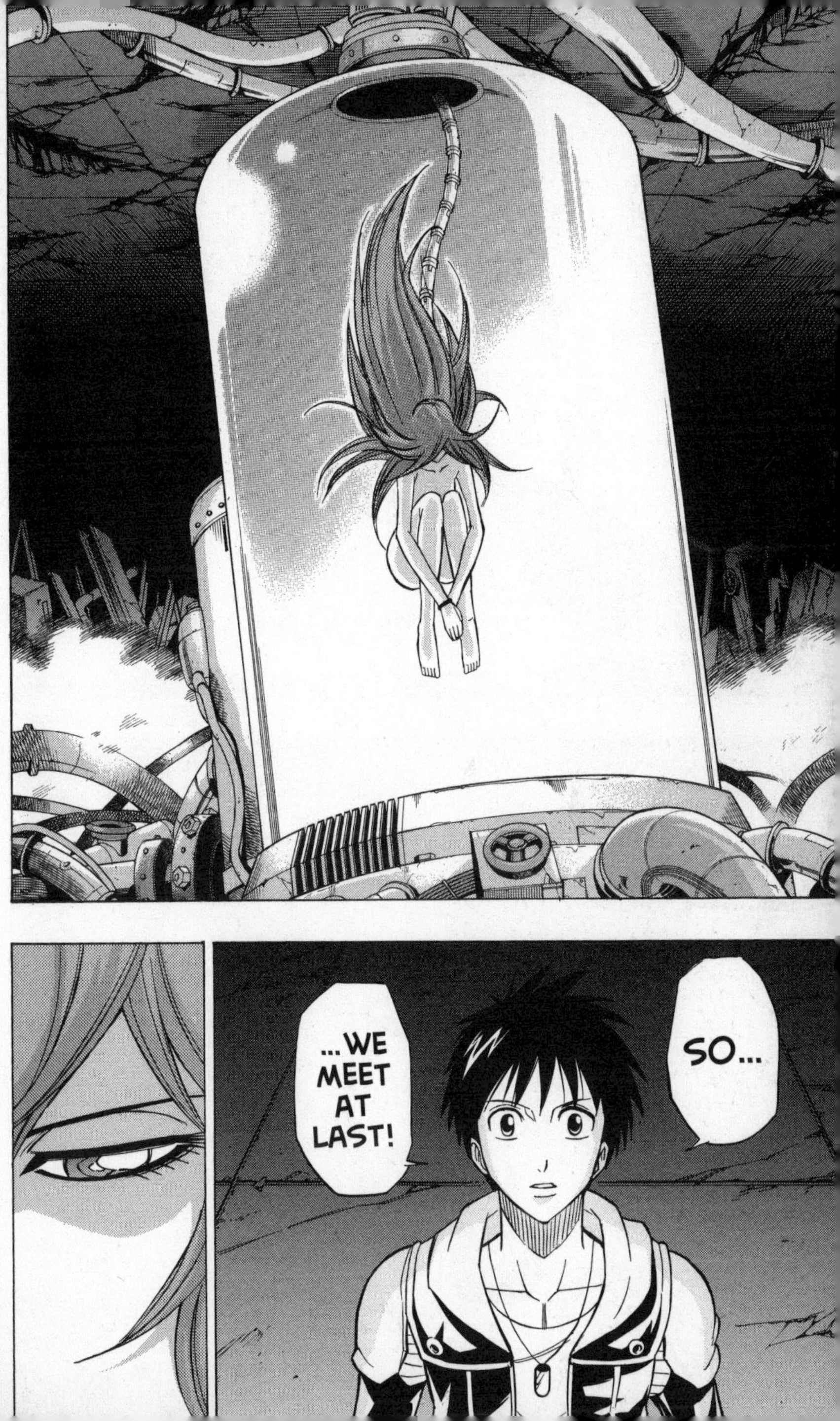
SO...
...WE MEET AT LAST!

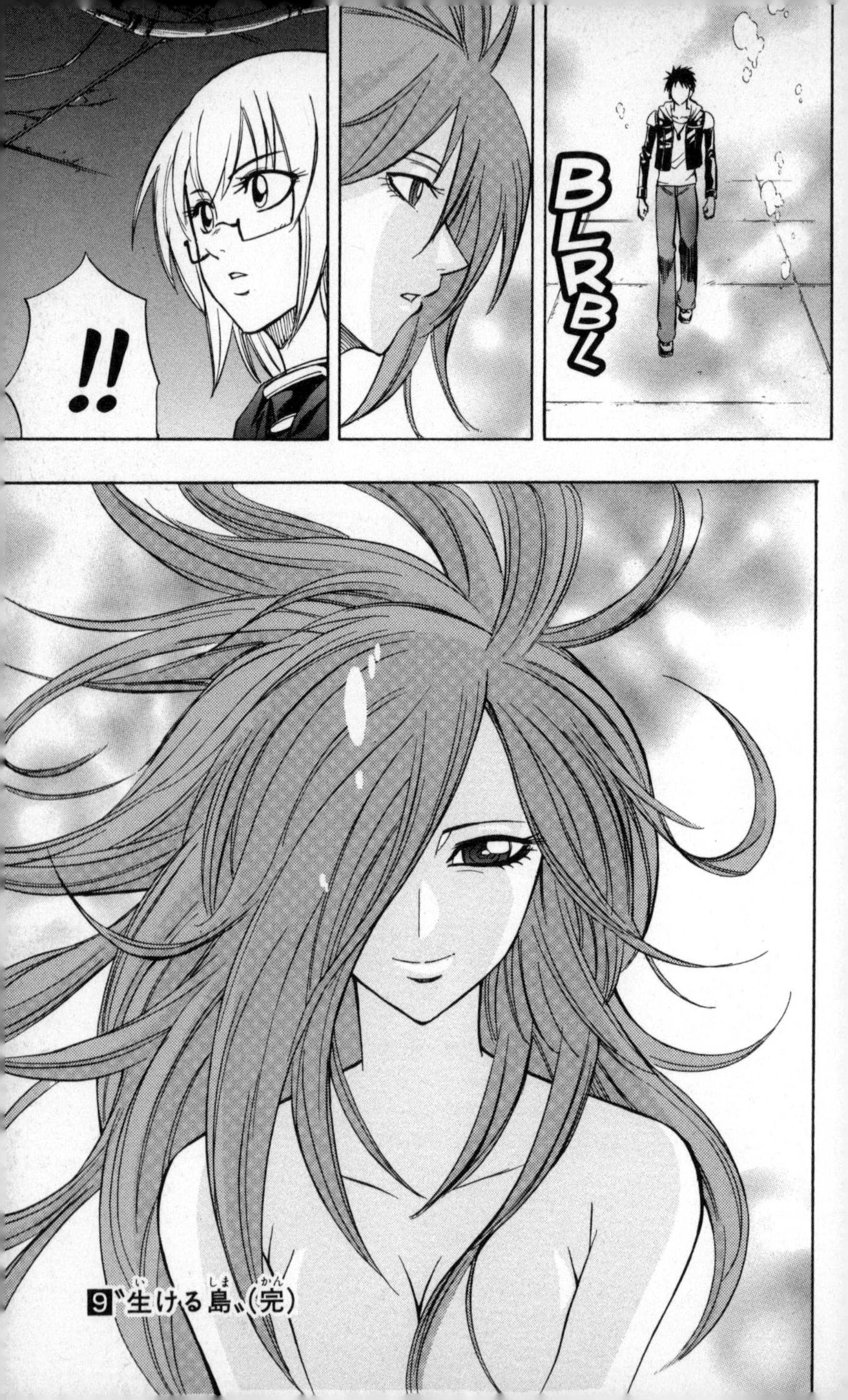
BLRBL
!!
9 "生ける島"(完)

PSYREN

9

Afterword

THANK YOU FOR READING
VOLUME 9.

MAN, THE END OF THE YEAR HAS
BEEN REALLY BUSY FOR ME THIS
YEAR! I'VE BARELY GIVEN A THOUGHT
TO CHRISTMAS.

I'M JUST TRYING TO TAKE THINGS
ONE THING AT A TIME, AND HOPEFULLY
I'LL AT LEAST GET TO TAKE A DAY
OFF FOR NEW YEAR'S.

THEN, I'M READY TO WORK HARD
AGAIN IN 2010! THANK YOU FOR
YOUR CONTINUED SUPPORT!

TOSHIAKI IWASHIRO,
DECEMBER 2009

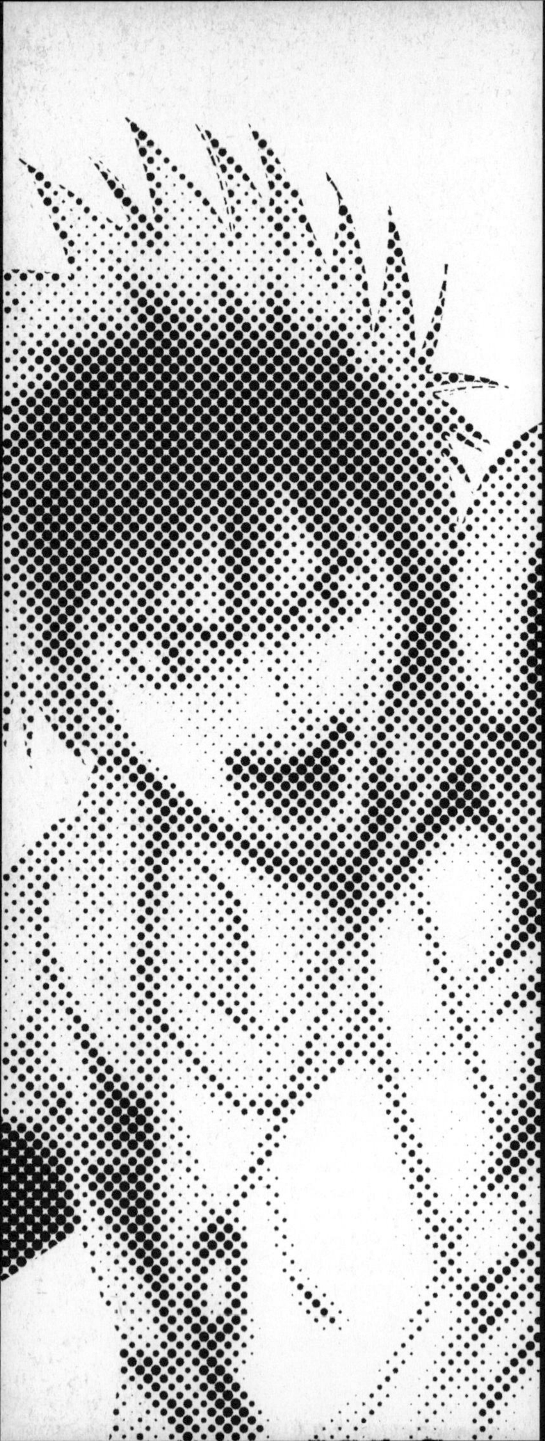

IN THE NEXT VOLUME...

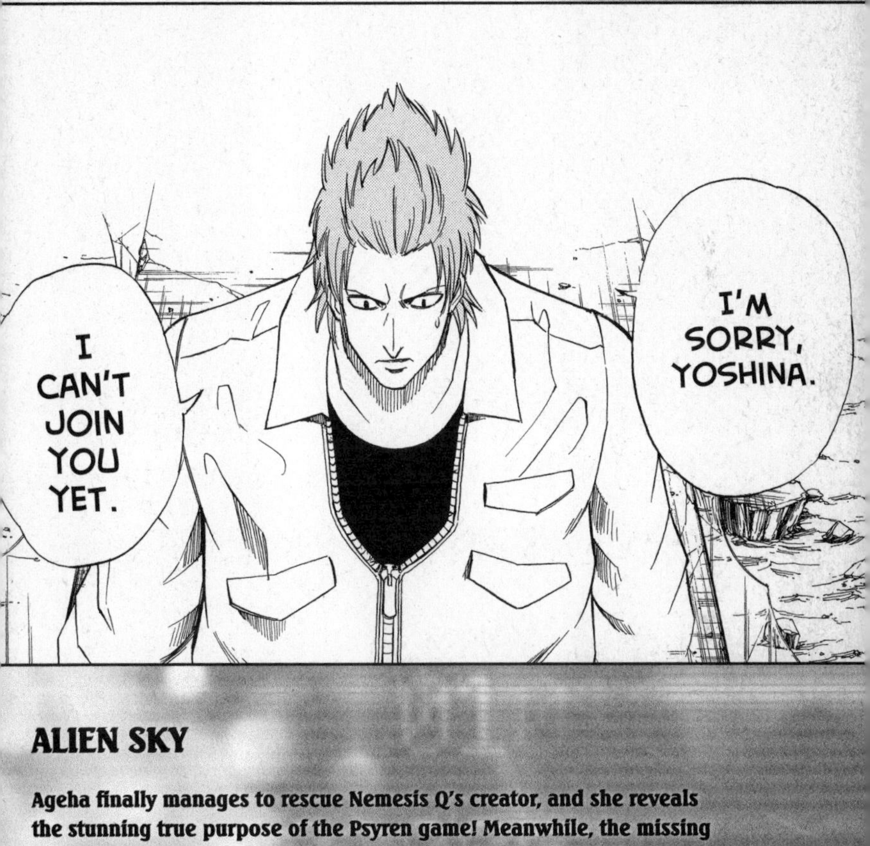
I'M SORRY, YOSHINA.
I CAN'T JOIN YOU YET.

ALIEN SKY

Ageha finally manages to rescue Nemesis Q's creator, and she reveals the stunning true purpose of the Psyren game! Meanwhile, the missing Hiryu and Oboro have survived but are left behind while Ageha, Amamiya, and Kabuto return home without them...

Available MAY 2013!

You're Reading in the Wrong Direction!!

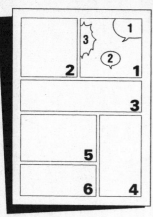

Whoops! Guess what? You're starting at the wrong end of the comic!

...It's true! In keeping with the original Japanese format, **Psyren** is meant to be read from right to left, starting in the upper-right corner.

Unlike English, which is read from left to right, Japanese is read from right to left, meaning that action, sound effects and word-balloon order are completely reversed—something which can make readers unfamiliar with Japanese feel pretty backwards themselves. For this reason, manga or Japanese comics published in the U.S. in English have sometimes been published "flopped"—that is, printed in exact reverse order, as though seen from the other side of a mirror.

By flopping pages, U.S. publishers can avoid confusing readers, but the compromise is not without its downside. For one thing, a character in a flopped manga series who once wore in the original Japanese version a T-shirt emblazoned with "M A Y" (as in "the merry month of") now wears one which reads "Y A M"! Additionally, many manga creators in Japan are themselves unhappy with the process, as some feel the mirror-imaging of their art changes their original intentions.

We are proud to bring you Toshiaki Iwashiro's **Psyren** in the original unflopped format. For now, though, turn to the other side of the book and let the fun begin...!

—Editor